LAND OF THE LUSTROUS

8

HARUKO ICHIKAWA

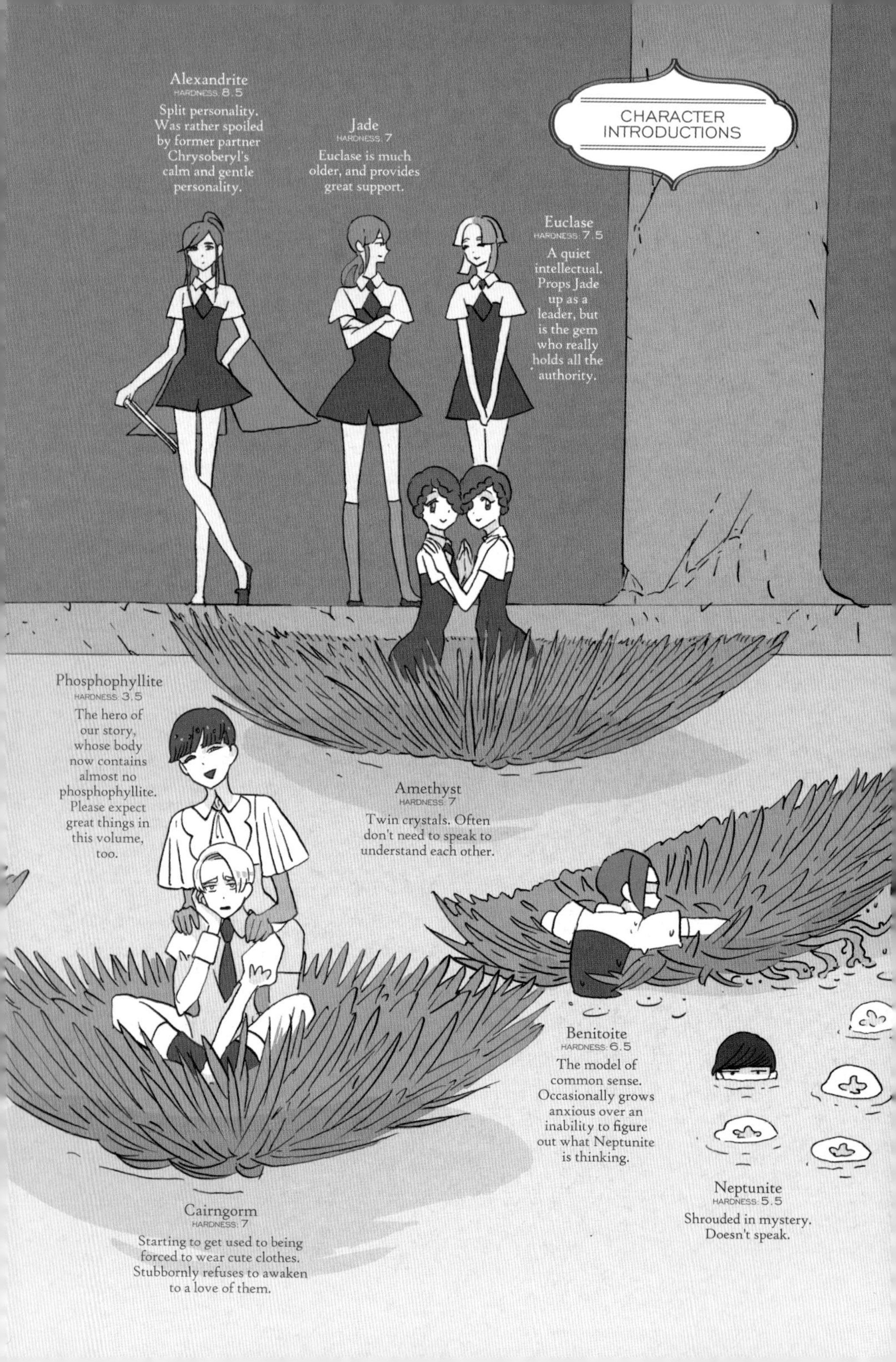
CHARACTER INTRODUCTIONS
Alexandrite
HARDNESS: 8.5
Split personality. Was rather spoiled by former partner Chrysoberyl's calm and gentle personality.
Jade
HARDNESS: 7
Euclase is much older, and provides great support.
Euclase
HARDNESS: 7.5
A quiet intellectual. Props Jade up as a leader, but is the gem who really holds all the authority.
Phosphophyllite
HARDNESS: 3.5
The hero of our story, whose body now contains almost no phosphophyllite. Please expect great things in this volume, too.
Amethyst
HARDNESS: 7
Twin crystals. Often don't need to speak to understand each other.
Benitoite
HARDNESS: 6.5
The model of common sense. Occasionally grows anxious over an inability to figure out what Neptunite is thinking.
Neptunite
HARDNESS: 5.5
Shrouded in mystery. Doesn't speak.
Cairngorm
HARDNESS: 7
Starting to get used to being forced to wear cute clothes. Stubbornly refuses to awaken to a love of them.

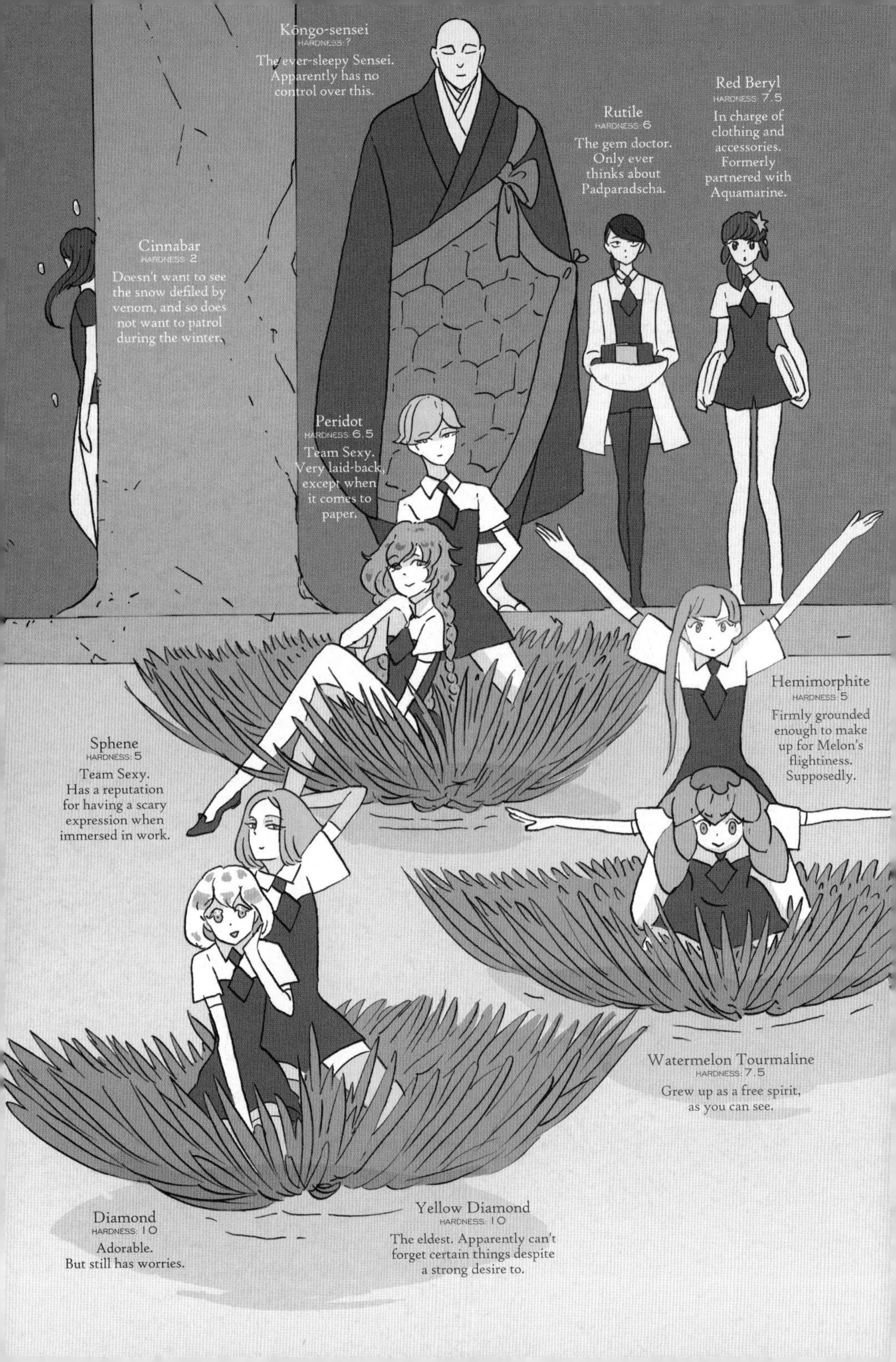
Kōngo-sensei
HARDNESS: ?
The ever-sleepy Sensei. Apparently has no control over this.
Red Beryl
HARDNESS: 7.5
In charge of clothing and accessories. Formerly partnered with Aquamarine.
Rutile
HARDNESS: 6
The gem doctor. Only ever thinks about Padparadscha.
Cinnabar
HARDNESS: 2
Doesn't want to see the snow defiled by venom, and so does not want to patrol during the winter.
Peridot
HARDNESS: 6.5
Team Sexy. Very laid-back, except when it comes to paper.
Hemimorphite
HARDNESS: 5
Firmly grounded enough to make up for Melon's flightiness. Supposedly.
Sphene
HARDNESS: 5
Team Sexy. Has a reputation for having a scary expression when immersed in work.
Watermelon Tourmaline
HARDNESS: 7.5
Grew up as a free spirit, as you can see.
Yellow Diamond
HARDNESS: 10
The eldest. Apparently can't forget certain things despite a strong desire to.
Diamond
HARDNESS: 10
Adorable. But still has worries.

CONTENTS

CHAPTER 53:

Moon World

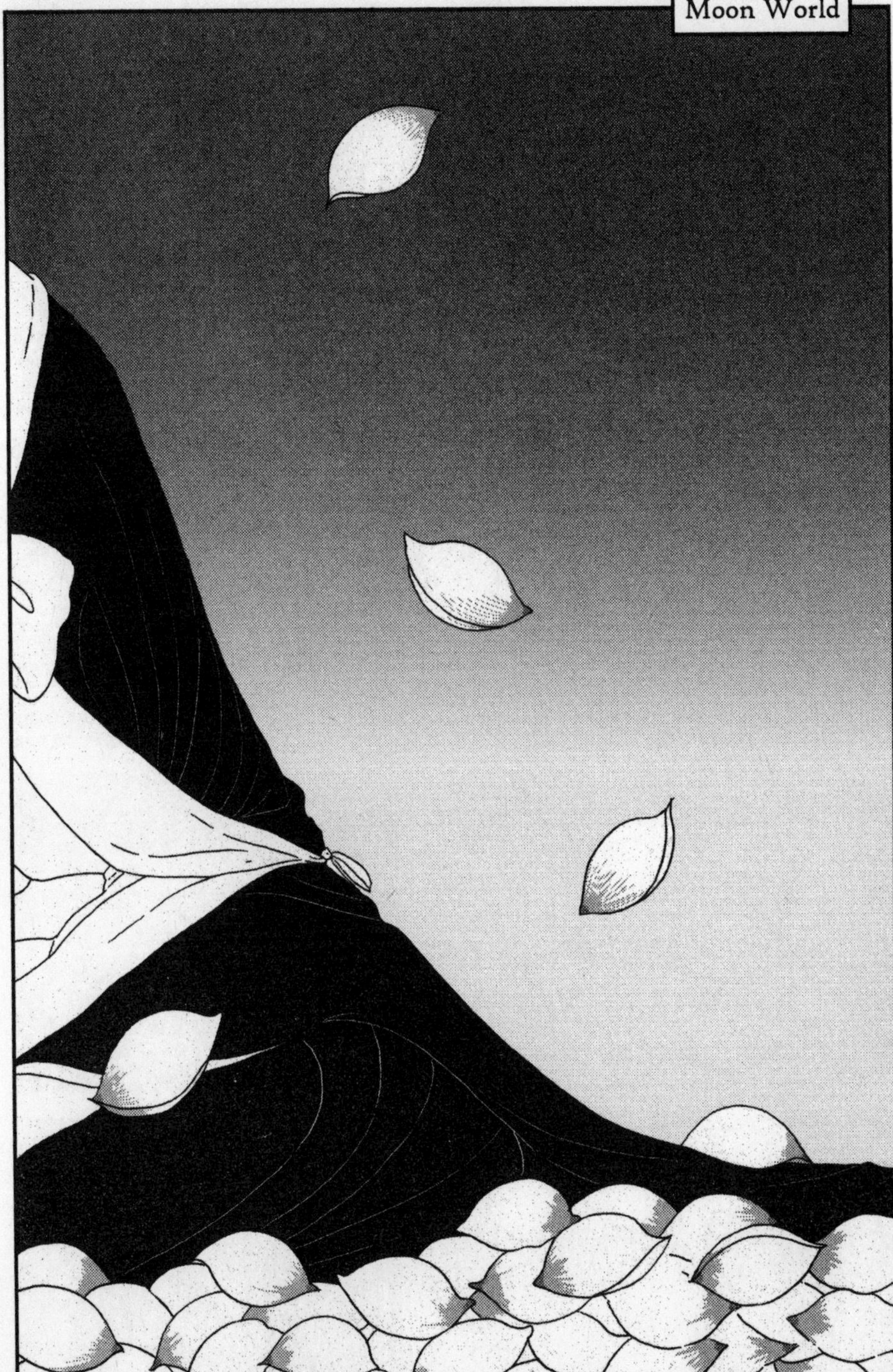

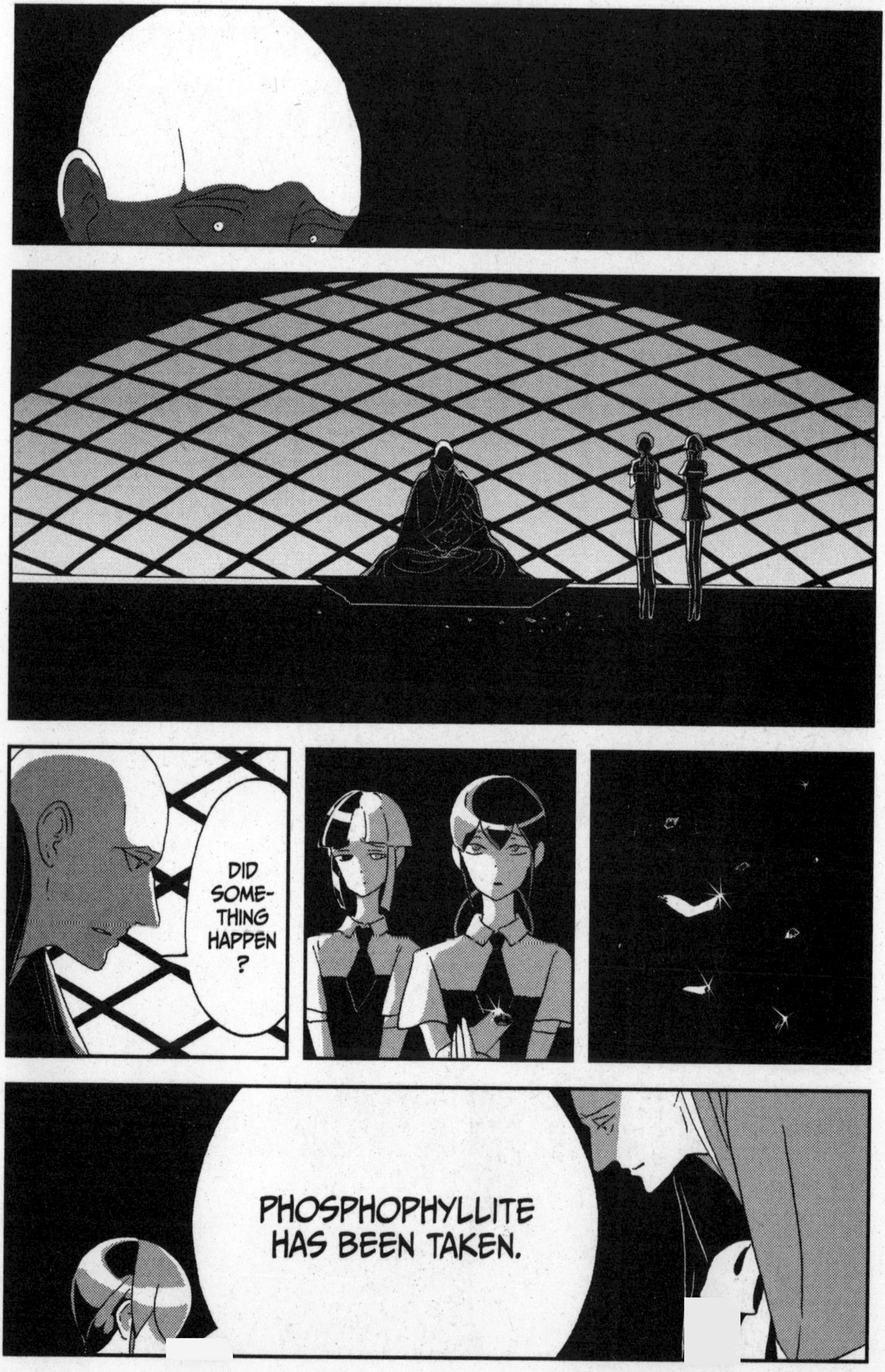
DID SOME-THING HAPPEN ?
PHOSPHOPHYLLITE HAS BEEN TAKEN.

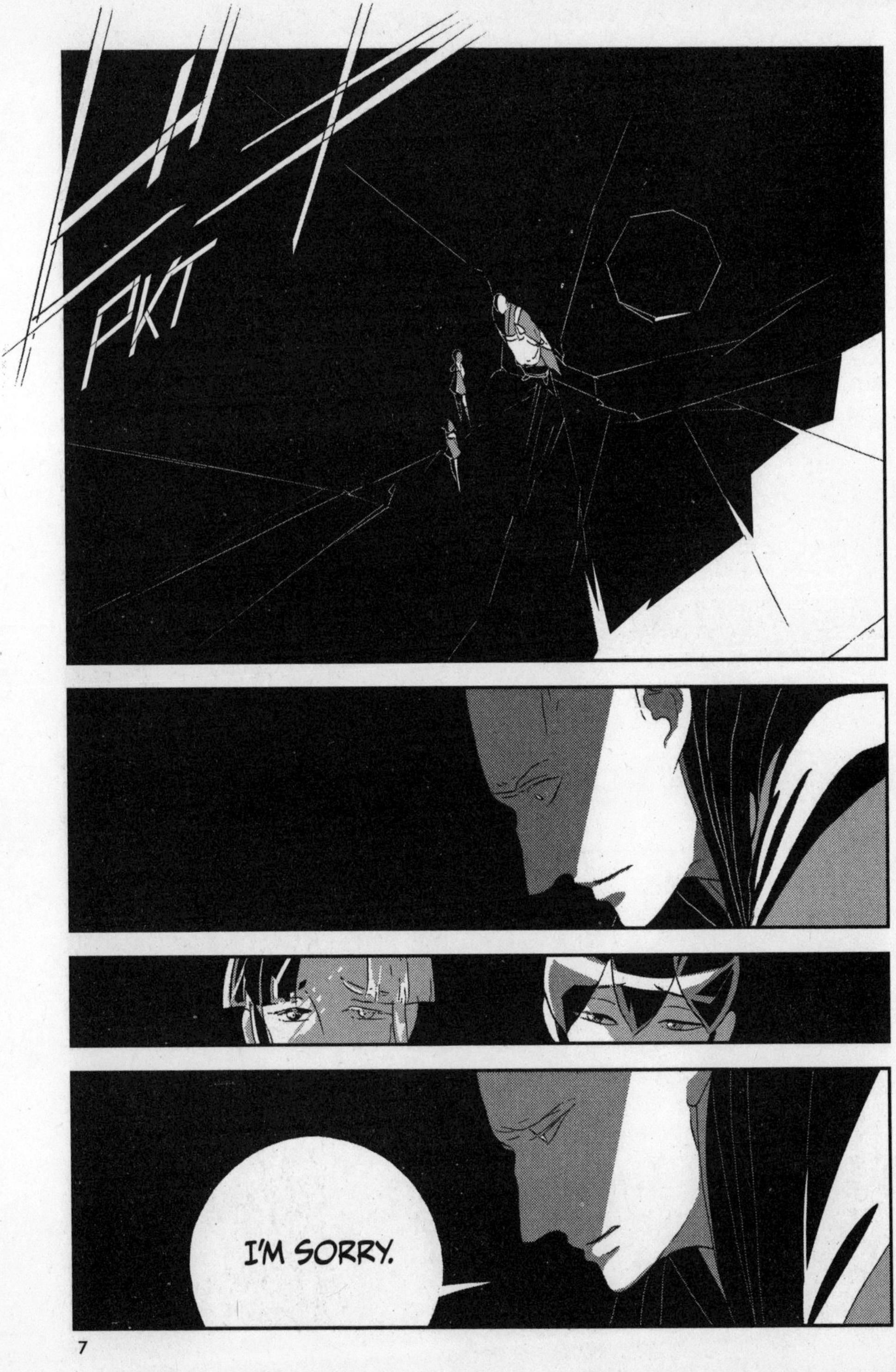
PKT
I'M SORRY.

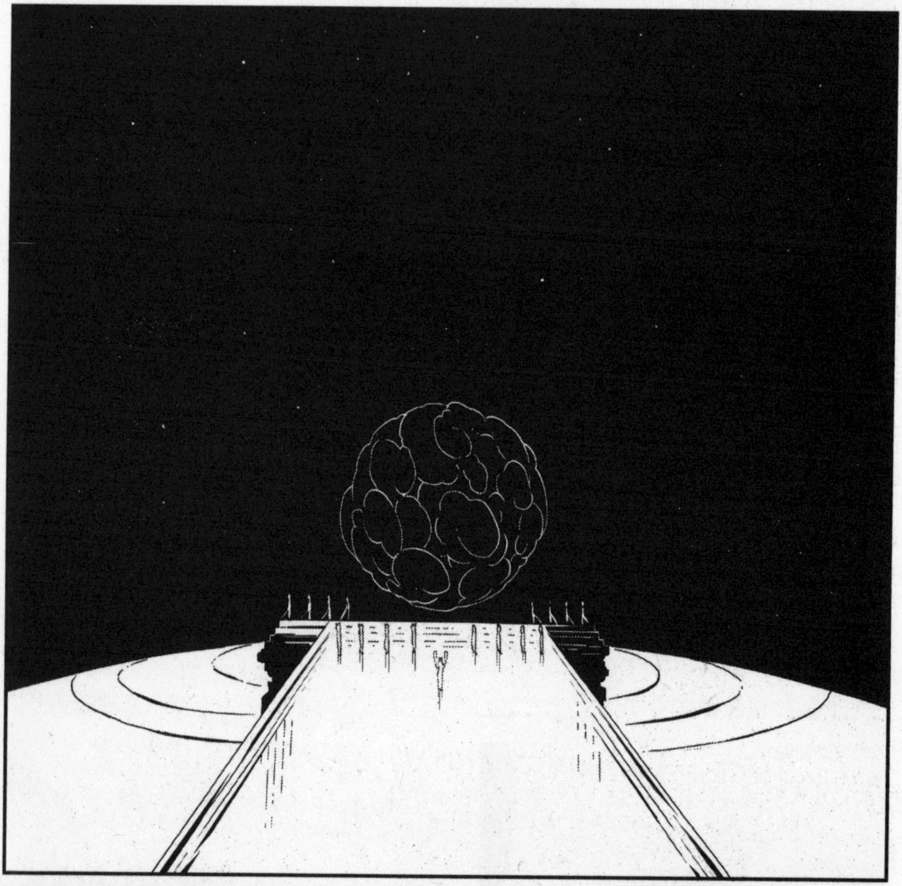
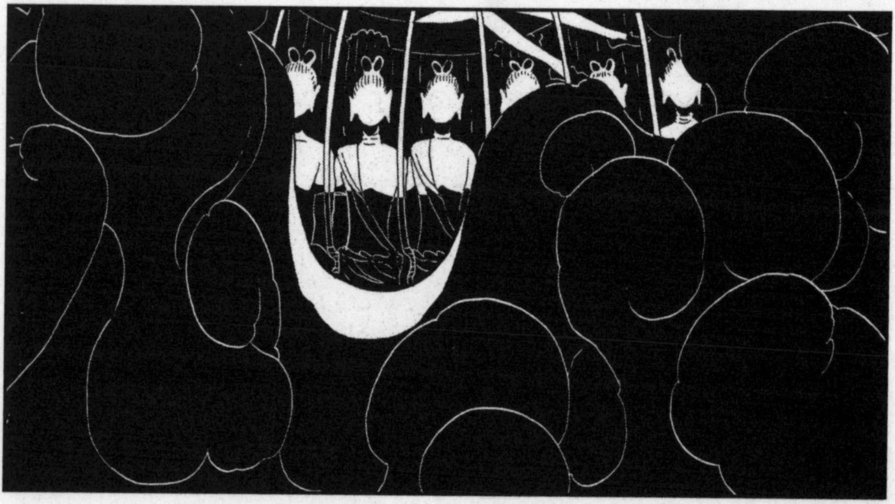

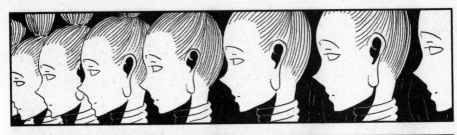

WHEW!

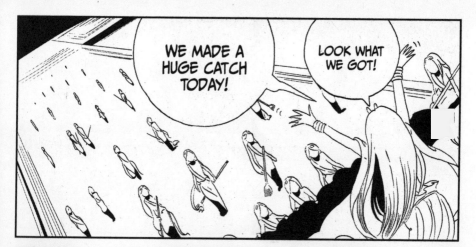

LOOK WHAT WE GOT!
WE MADE A HUGE CATCH TODAY!
HERE'S A HINT!
WHOA!
WAIT, IS THIS...
PHOSPHO-PHYLLITE?
YUP!
YOU MEAN THE VARIANT?
THAT'S RIGHT!
AND! WE GOT IT IN ONE PIECE!
THAT'S AMAZING!
I KNOW, RIGHT?

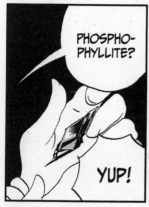

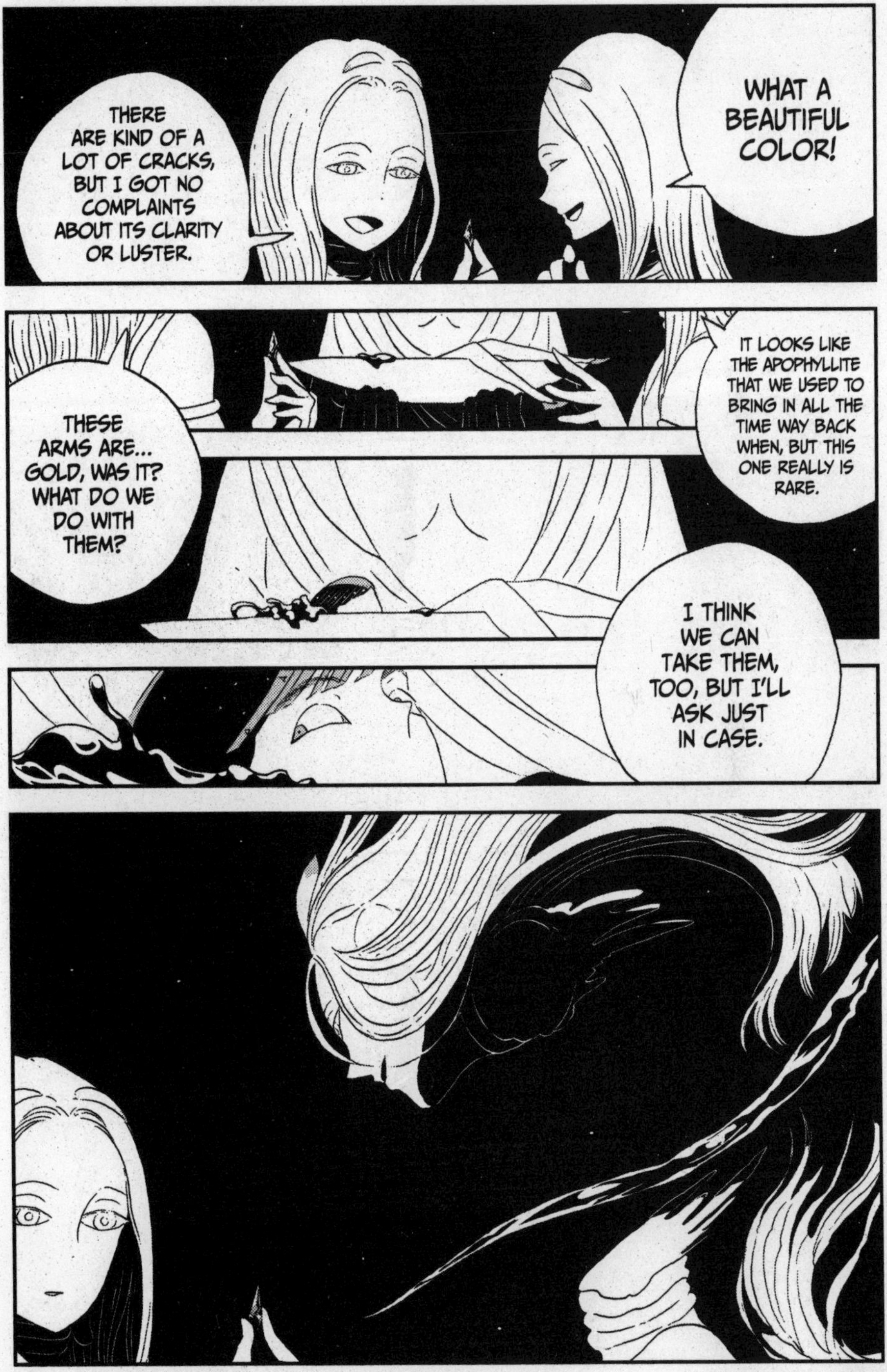
WHAT A BEAUTIFUL COLOR!
THERE ARE KIND OF A LOT OF CRACKS, BUT I GOT NO COMPLAINTS ABOUT ITS CLARITY OR LUSTER.
IT LOOKS LIKE THE APOPHYLLITE THAT WE USED TO BRING IN ALL THE TIME WAY BACK WHEN, BUT THIS ONE REALLY IS RARE.
THESE ARMS ARE... GOLD, WAS IT? WHAT DO WE DO WITH THEM?
I THINK WE CAN TAKE THEM, TOO, BUT I'LL ASK JUST IN CASE.

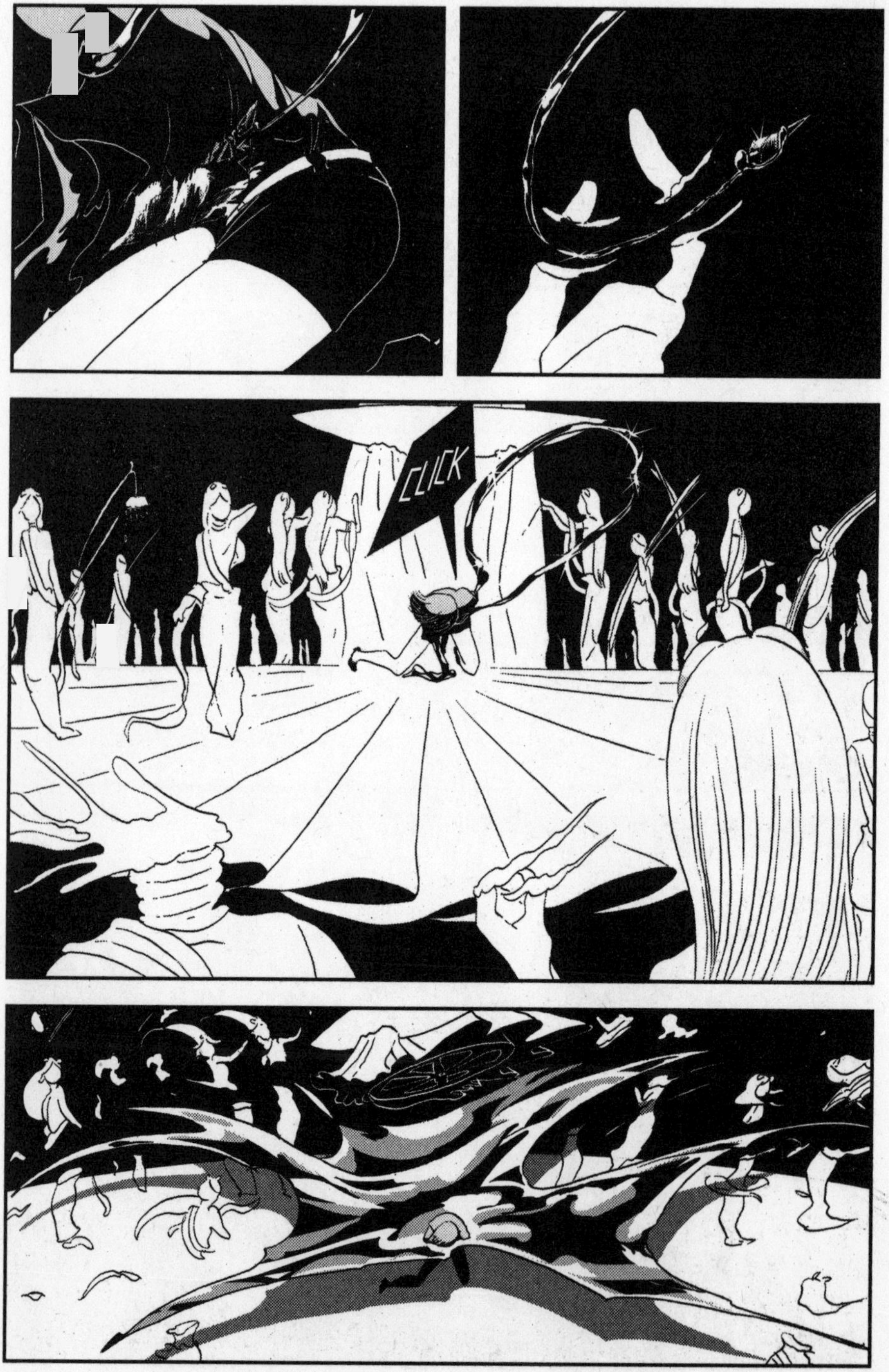
CLICK

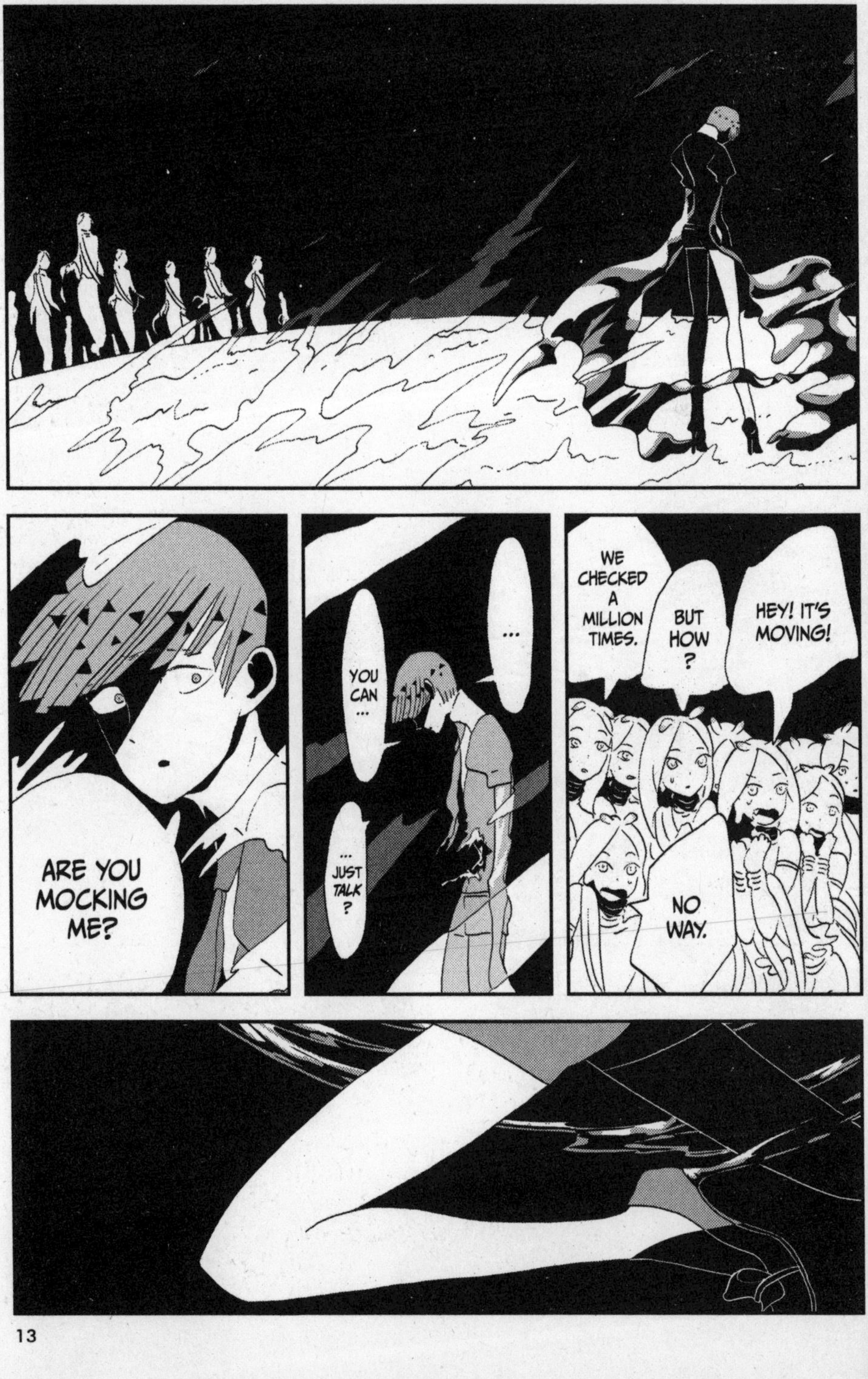
HEY! IT'S MOVING!
BUT HOW ?
WE CHECKED A MILLION TIMES.
NO WAY.
...
YOU CAN ...
... JUST TALK ?
ARE YOU MOCKING ME?

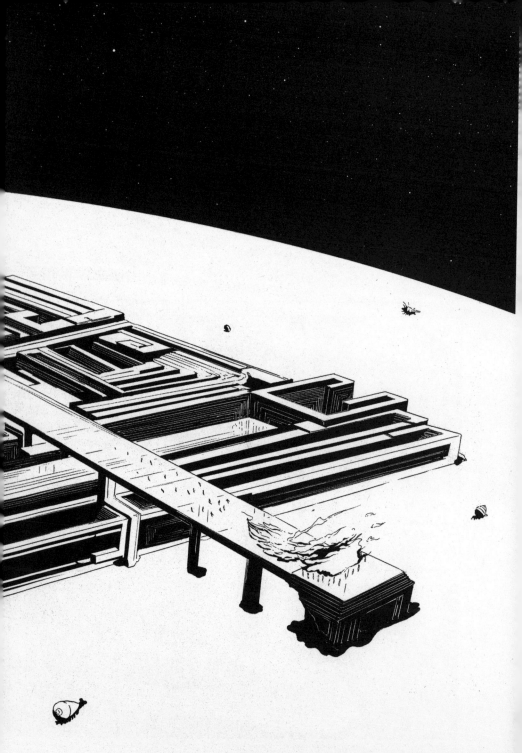

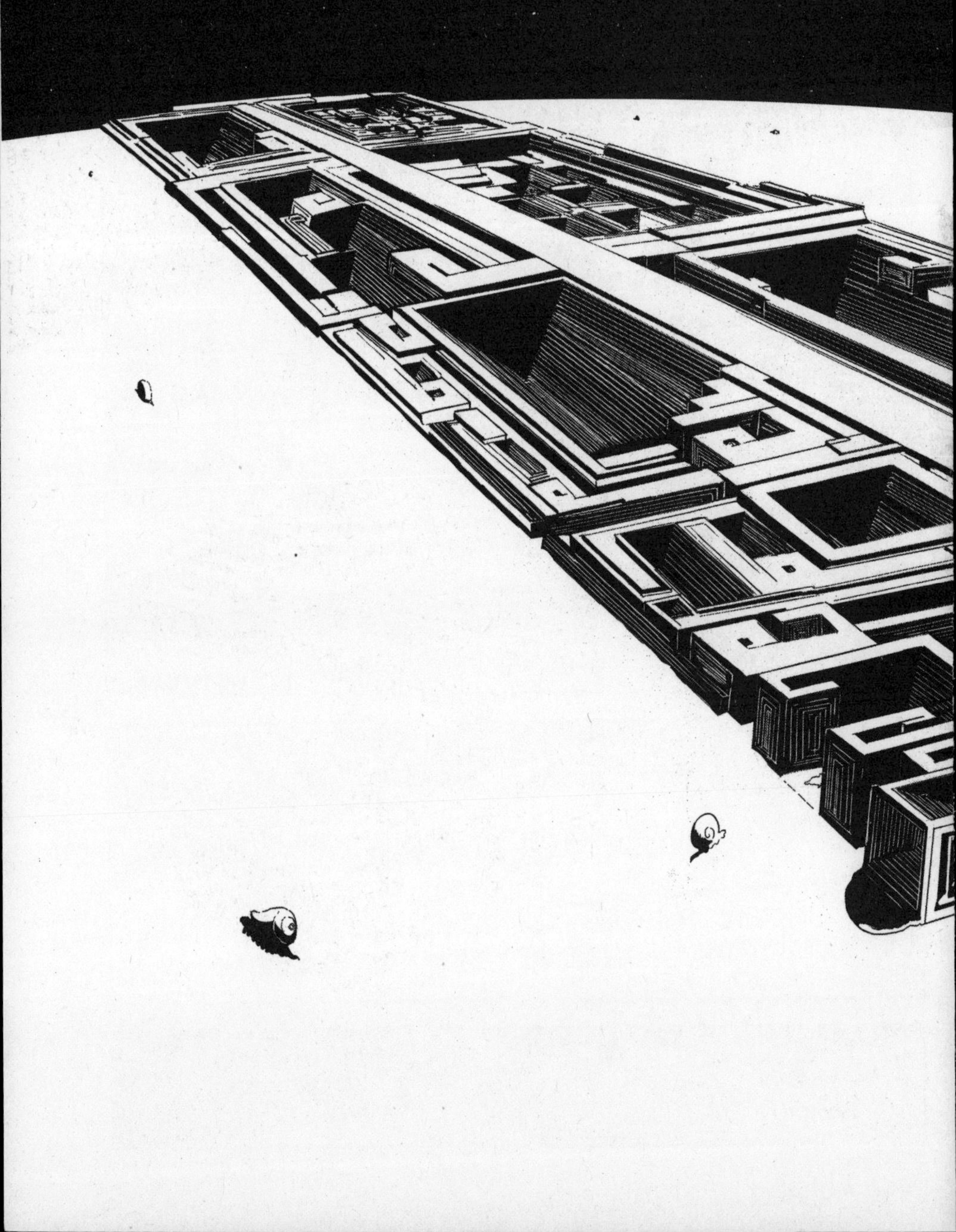

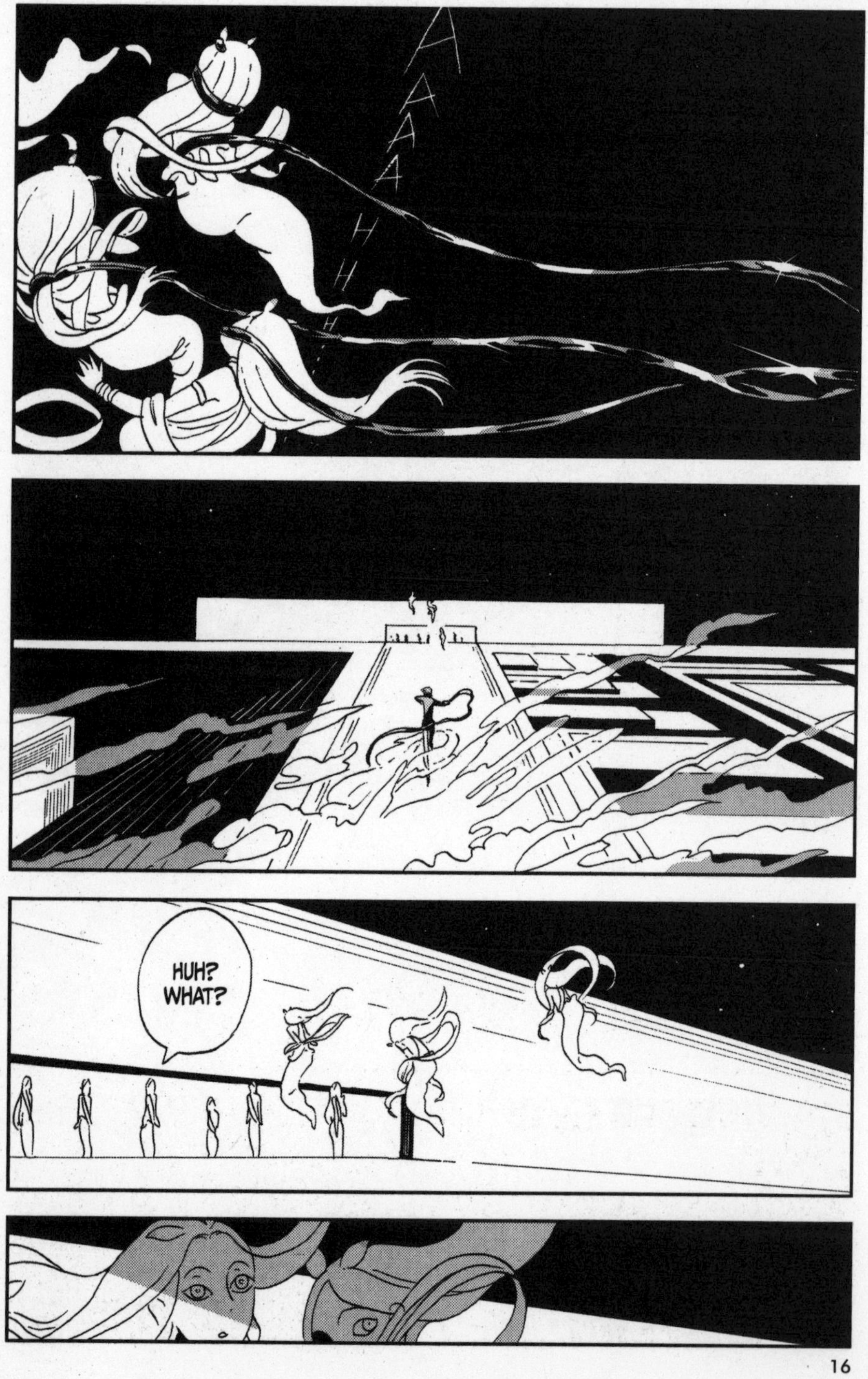
AAAAHHH...
HUH? WHAT?

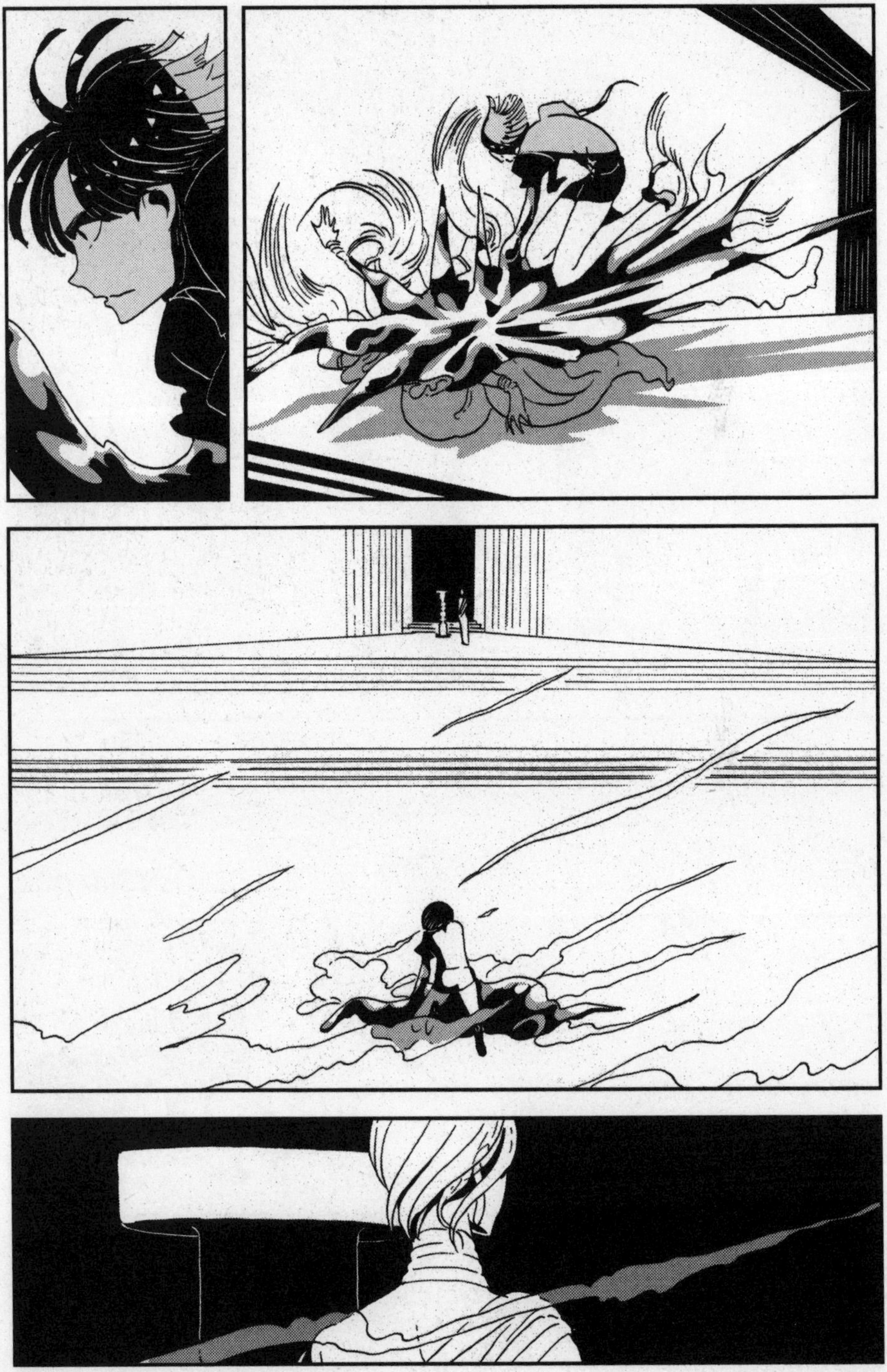

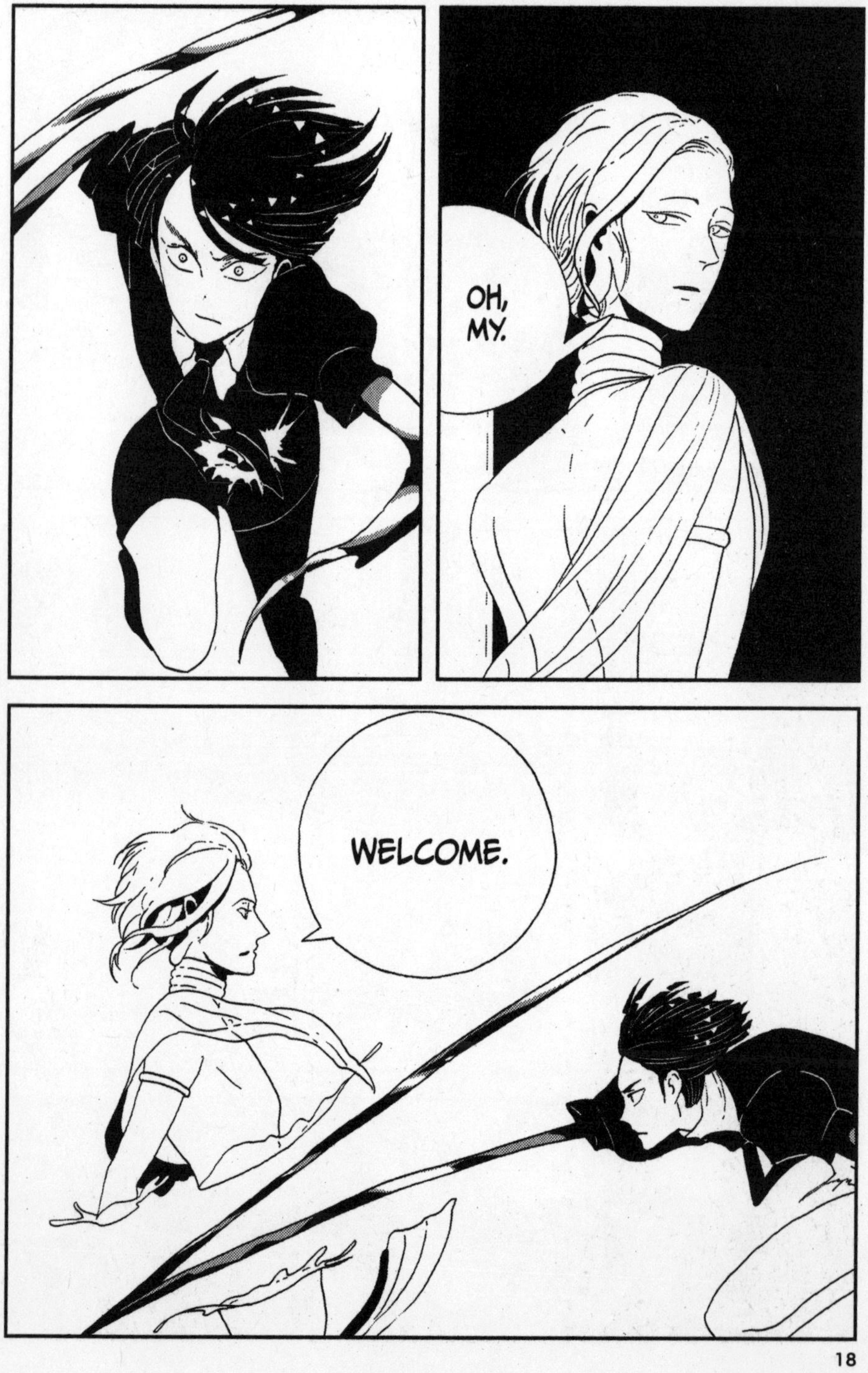
OH, MY.
WELCOME.

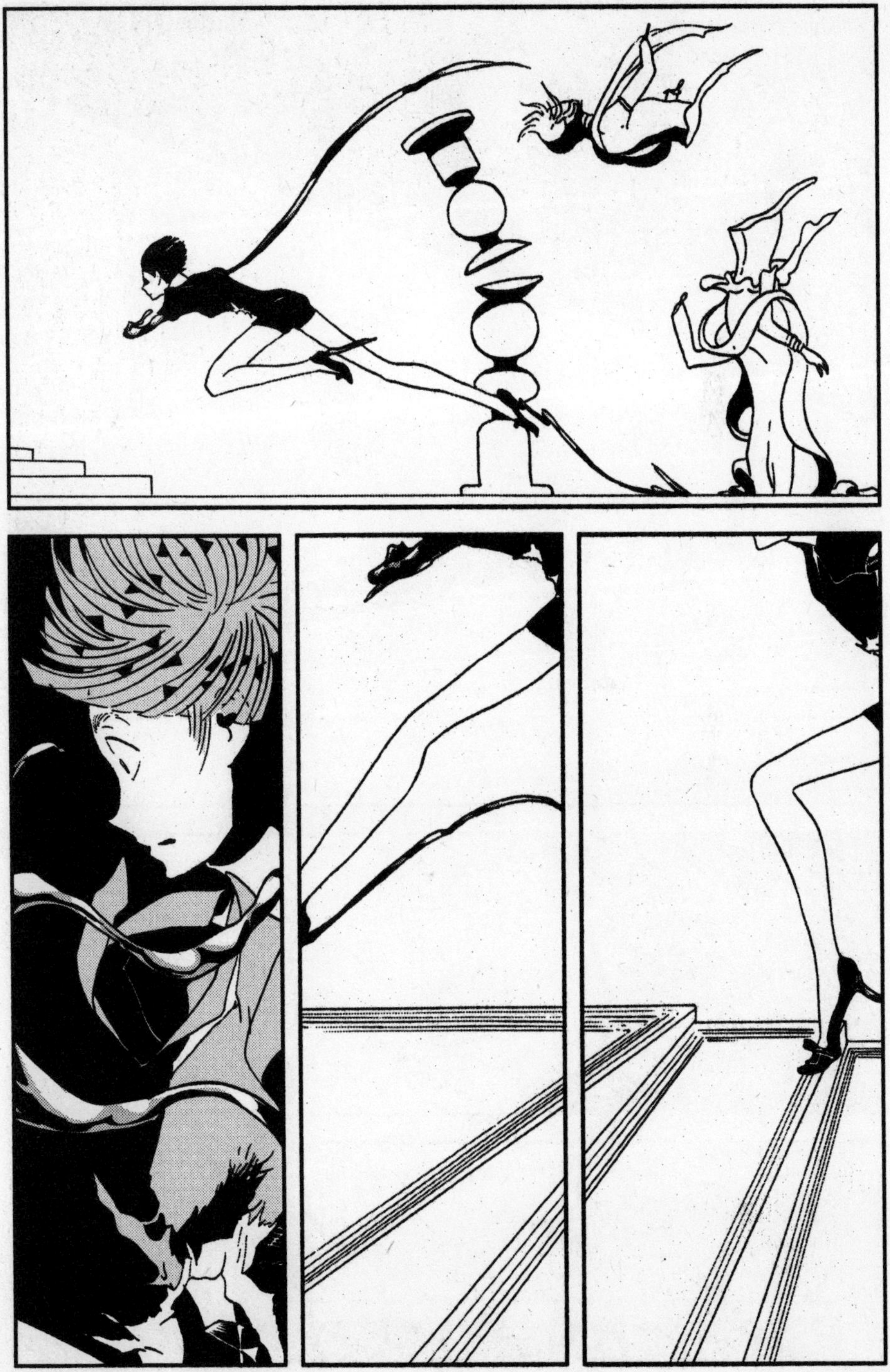

TO THE MOON WORLD.

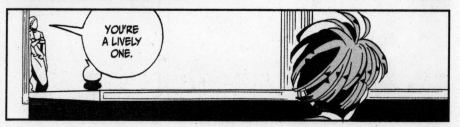

YOU'RE A LIVELY ONE.

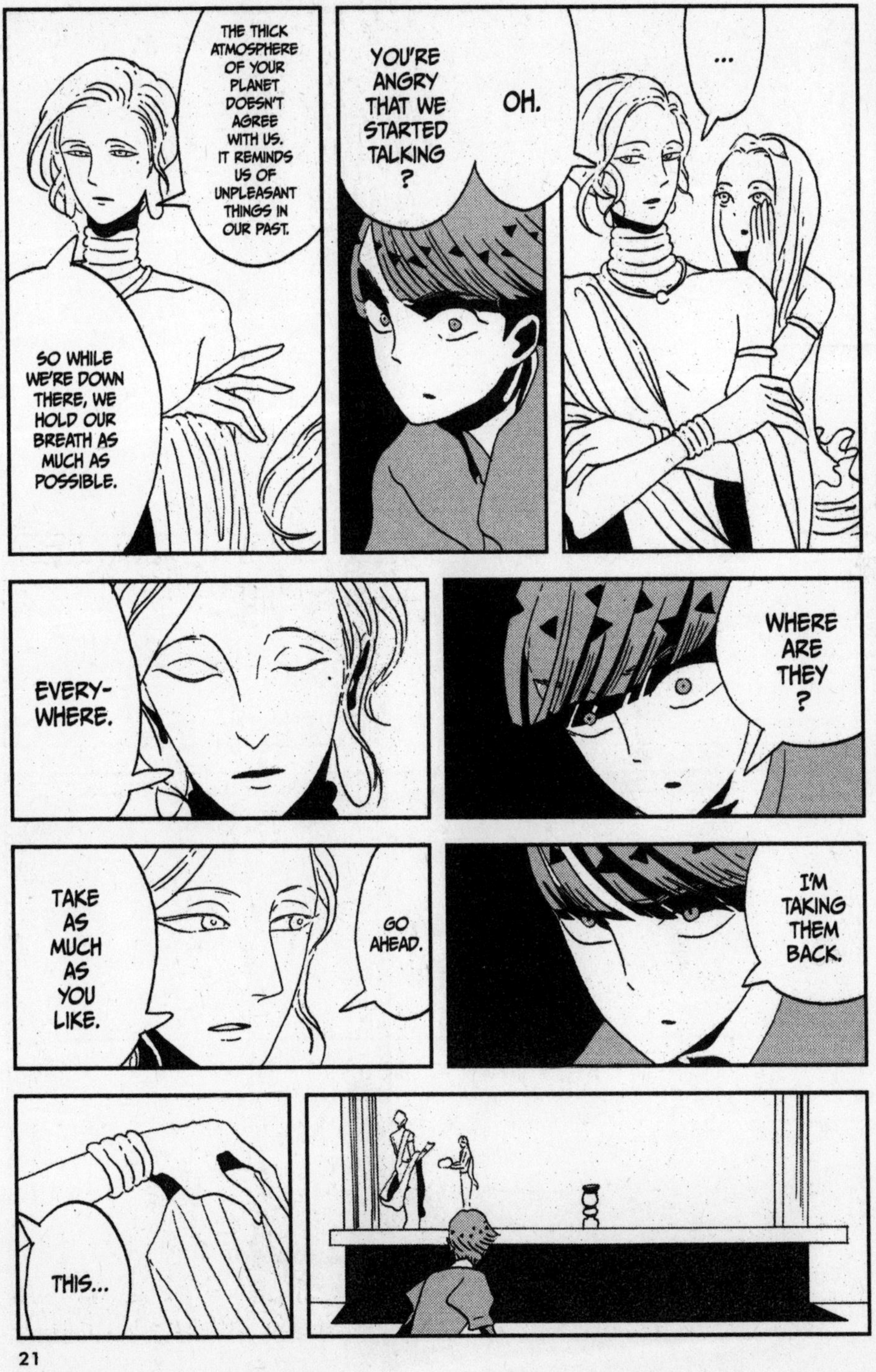
...
OH.
YOU'RE ANGRY THAT WE STARTED TALKING?
THE THICK ATMOSPHERE OF YOUR PLANET DOESN'T AGREE WITH US. IT REMINDS US OF UNPLEASANT THINGS IN OUR PAST.
SO WHILE WE'RE DOWN THERE, WE HOLD OUR BREATH AS MUCH AS POSSIBLE.
WHERE ARE THEY?
EVERY-WHERE.
I'M TAKING THEM BACK.
GO AHEAD.
TAKE AS MUCH AS YOU LIKE.
THIS...

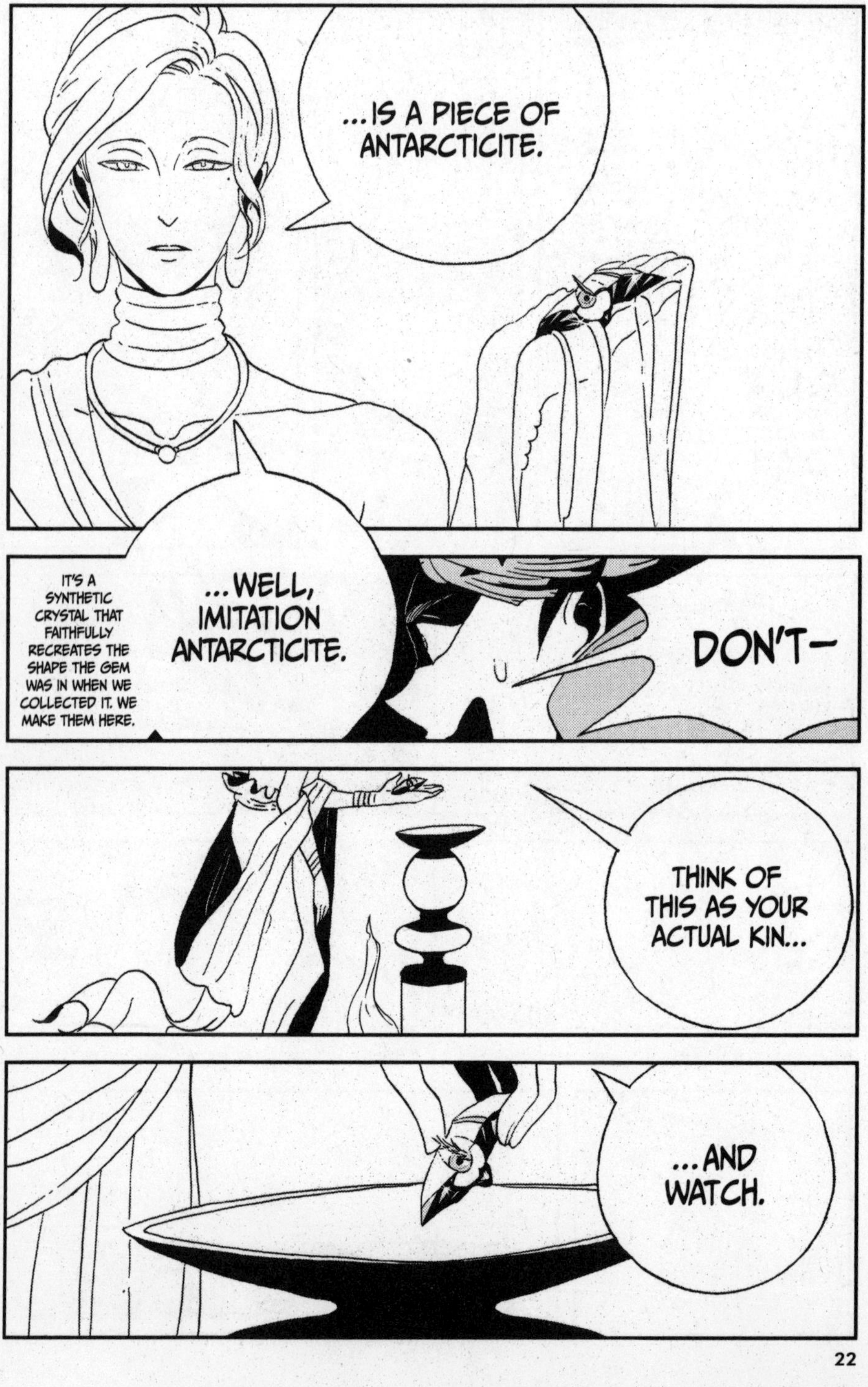
...IS A PIECE OF ANTARCTICITE.
DON'T—
...WELL, IMITATION ANTARCTICITE.
IT'S A SYNTHETIC CRYSTAL THAT FAITHFULLY RECREATES THE SHAPE THE GEM WAS IN WHEN WE COLLECTED IT. WE MAKE THEM HERE.
THINK OF THIS AS YOUR ACTUAL KIN...
...AND WATCH.

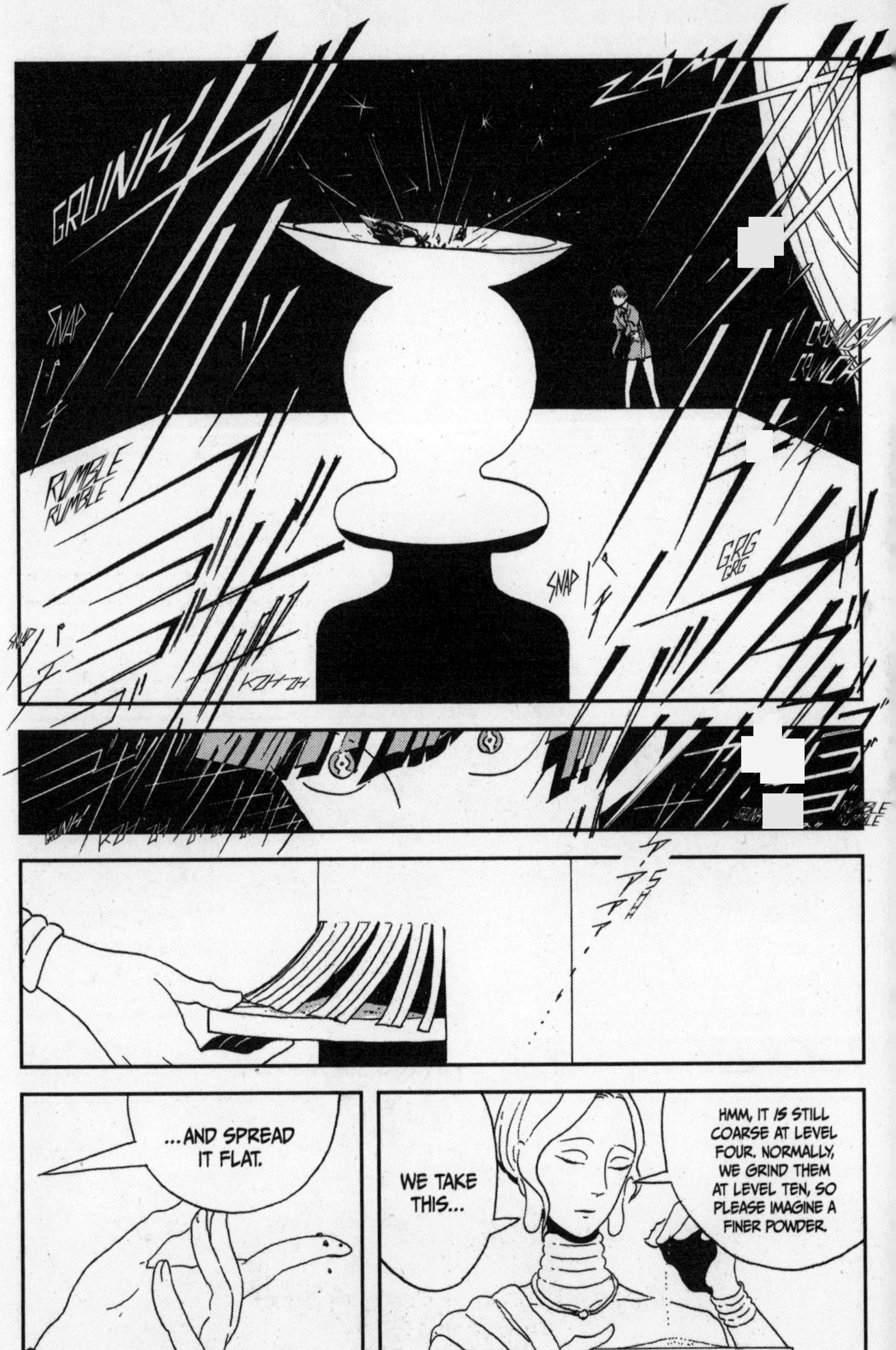
ZAM
CRUNCH CRUNCH
GRUNK
SNAP
RUMBLE RUMBLE
GRG GRG
SNAP
SNAP
RUMBLE RUMBLE
GRUNK
HMM, IT IS STILL COARSE AT LEVEL FOUR. NORMALLY, WE GRIND THEM AT LEVEL TEN, SO PLEASE IMAGINE A FINER POWDER.
WE TAKE THIS...
...AND SPREAD IT FLAT.

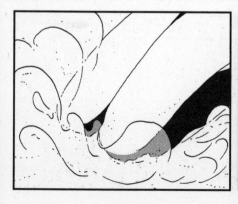

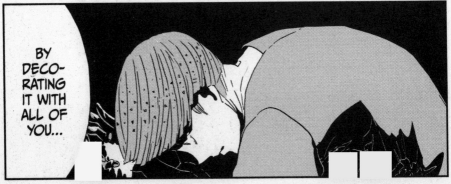

BY DECO-RATING IT WITH ALL OF YOU...

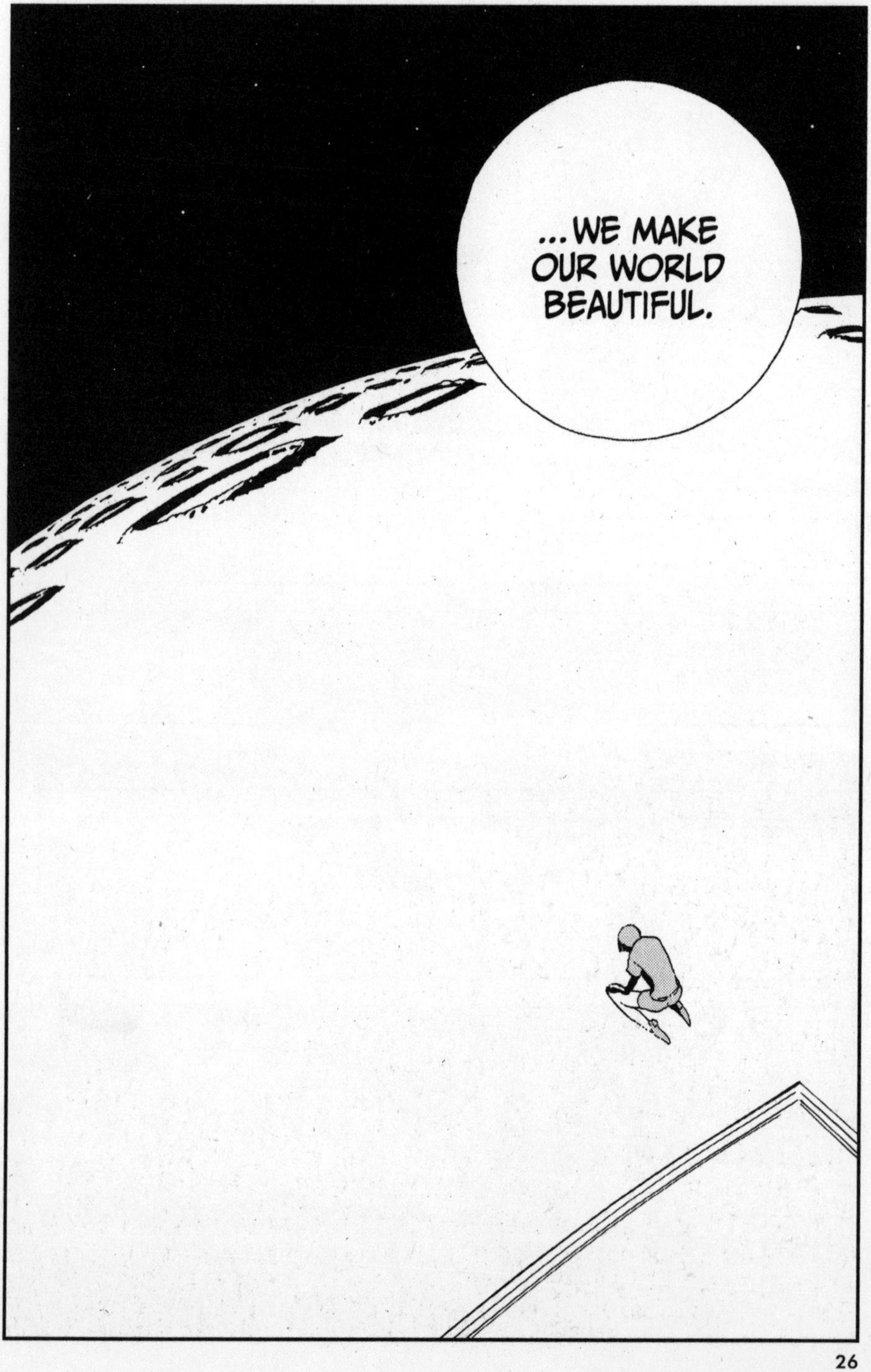
...WE MAKE OUR WORLD BEAUTIFUL.

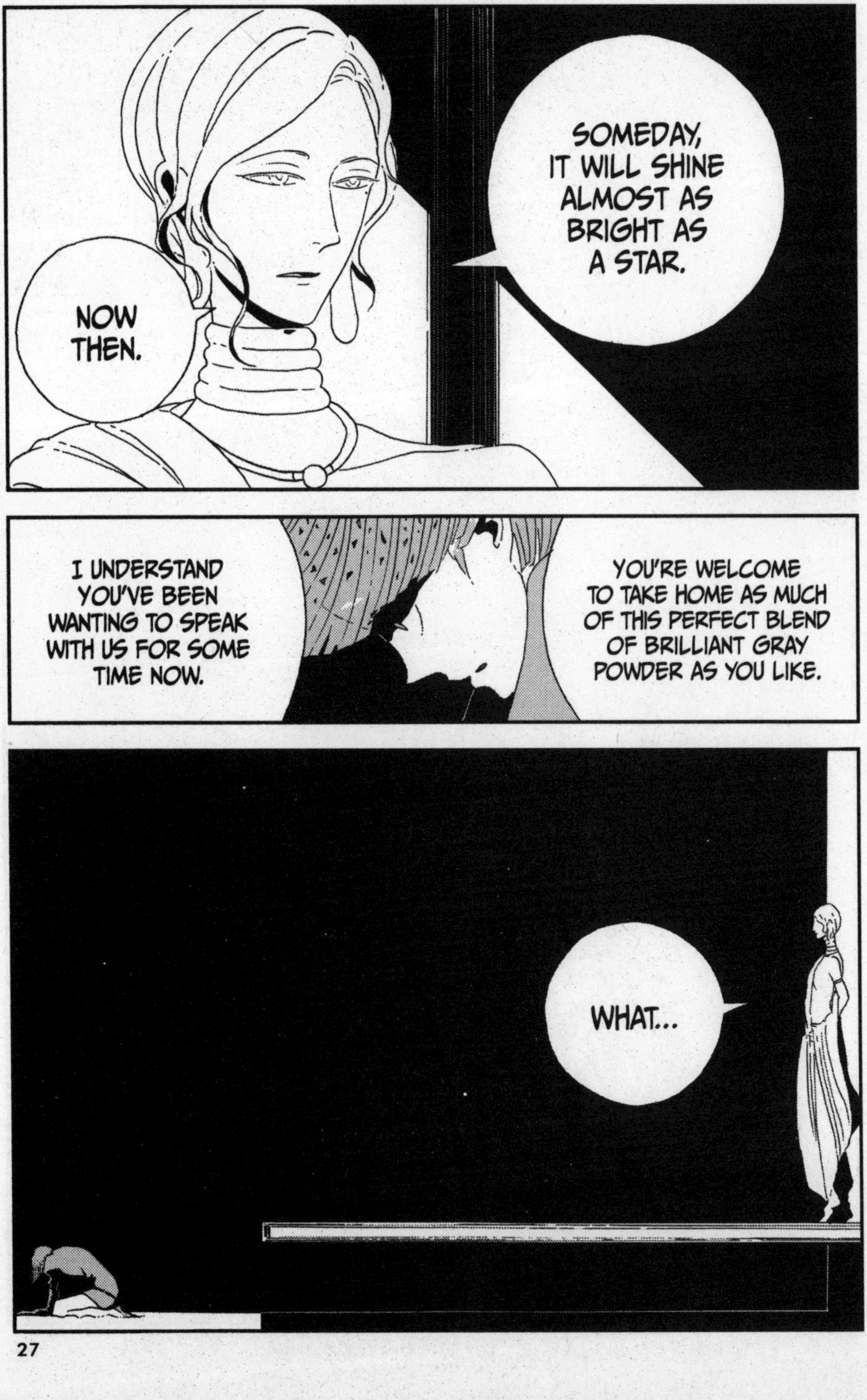
SOMEDAY, IT WILL SHINE ALMOST AS BRIGHT AS A STAR.
NOW THEN.
YOU'RE WELCOME TO TAKE HOME AS MUCH OF THIS PERFECT BLEND OF BRILLIANT GRAY POWDER AS YOU LIKE.
I UNDERSTAND YOU'VE BEEN WANTING TO SPEAK WITH US FOR SOME TIME NOW.
WHAT...

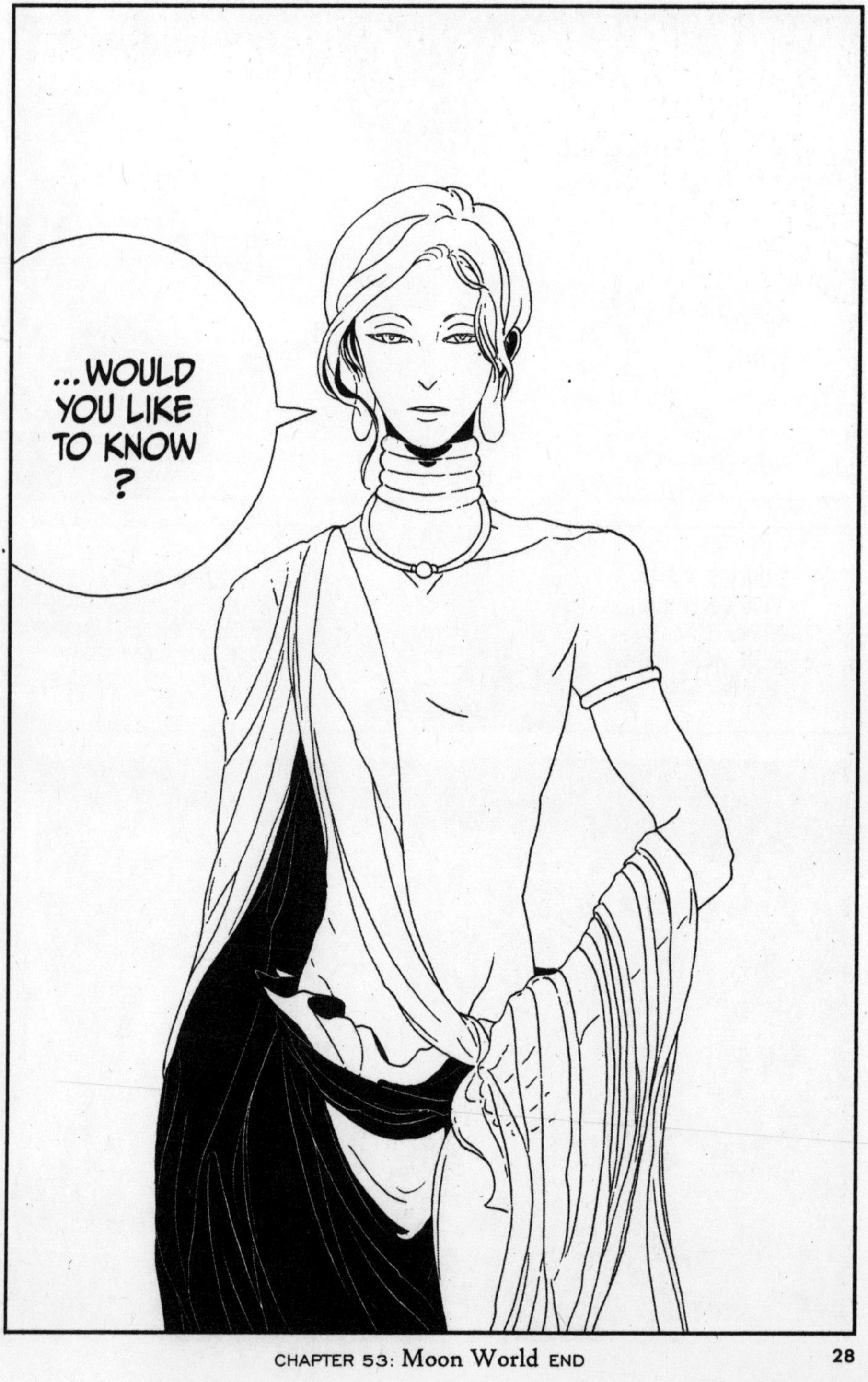
...WOULD YOU LIKE TO KNOW ?

CHAPTER 53: Moon World END

CHAPTER 54:

A Machine For Prayer

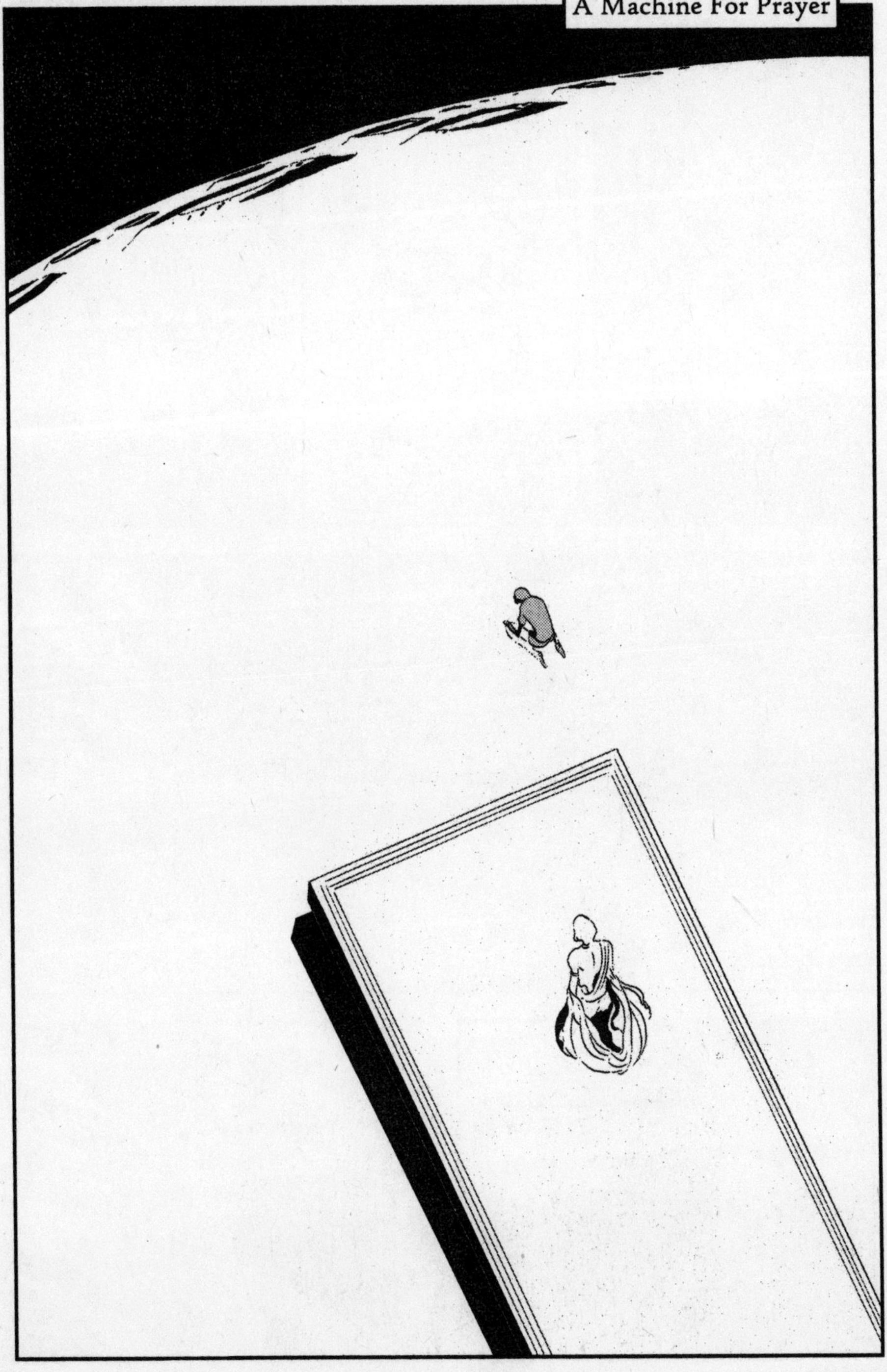

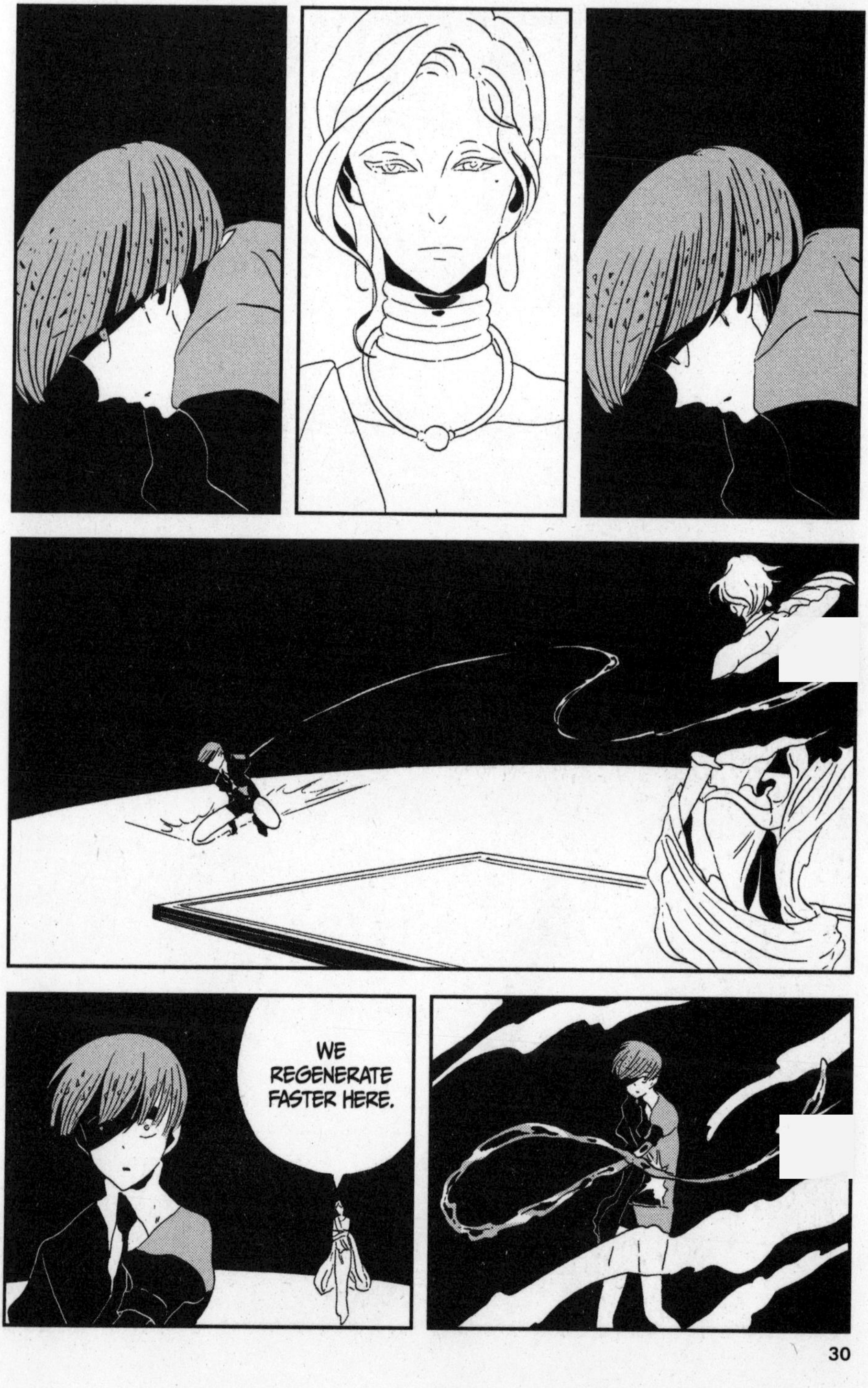
WE REGENERATE FASTER HERE.

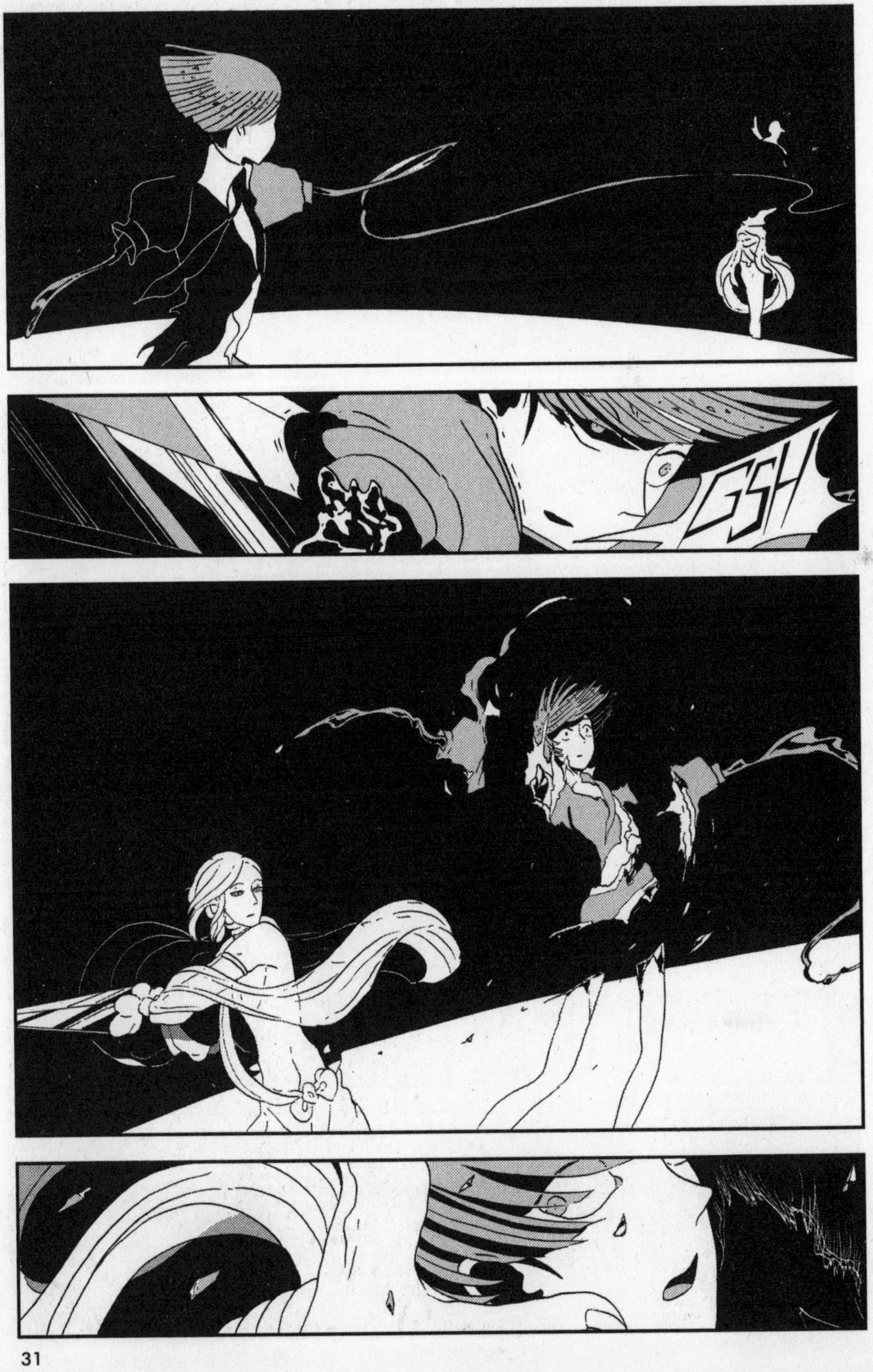
GSH

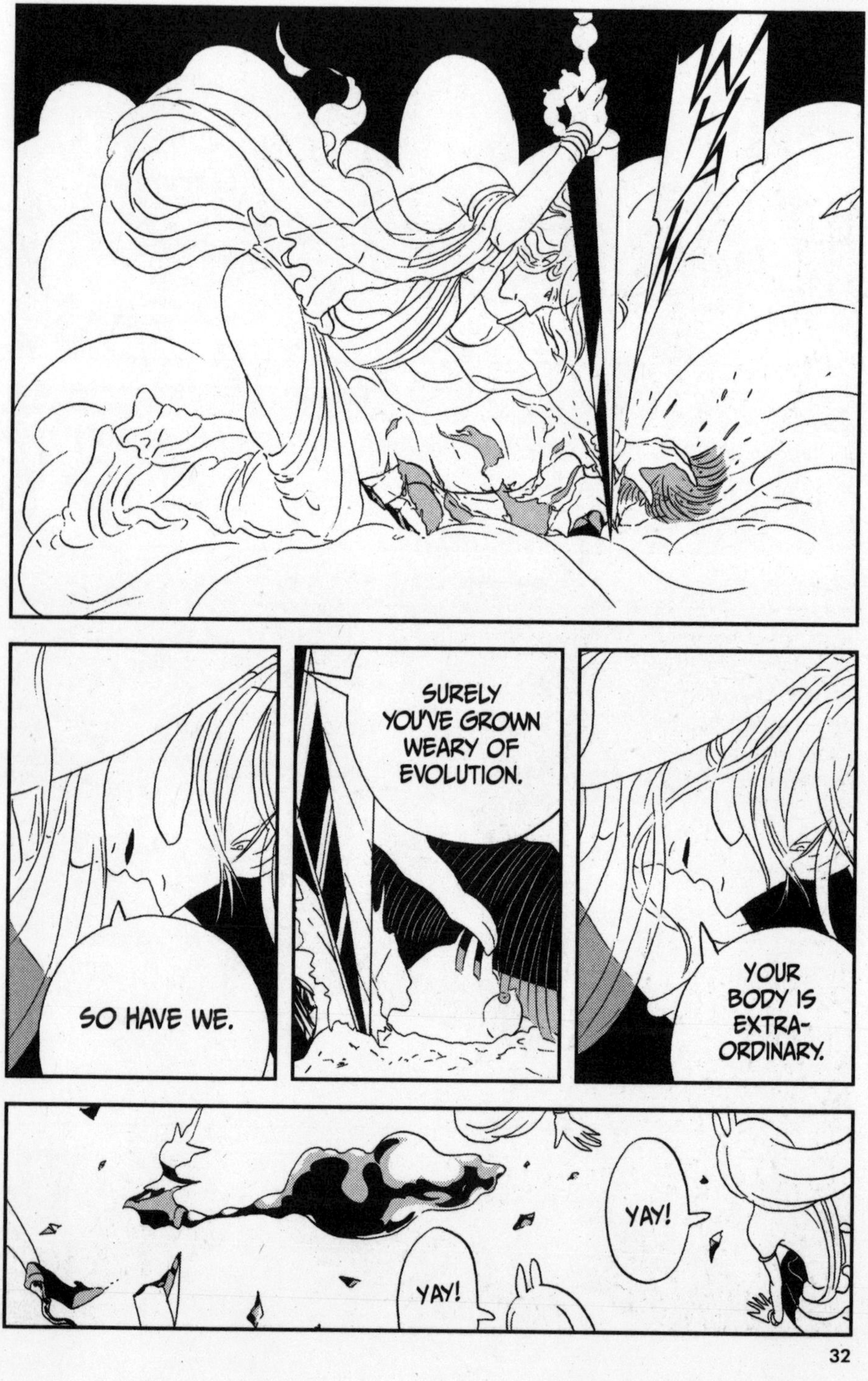
YOUR BODY IS EXTRA-ORDINARY.
SURELY YOU'VE GROWN WEARY OF EVOLUTION.
SO HAVE WE.
YAY!
YAY!

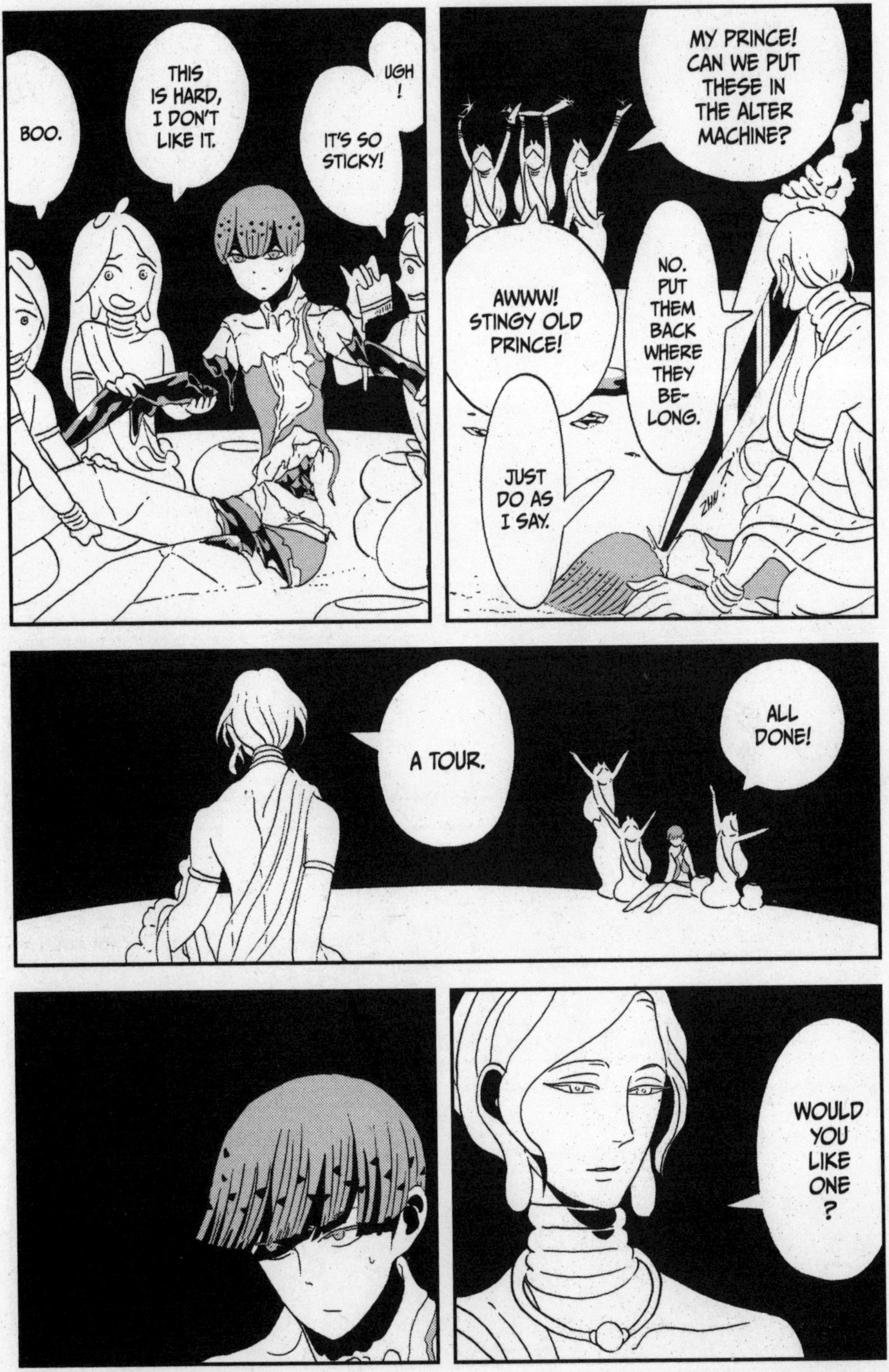
MY PRINCE! CAN WE PUT THESE IN THE ALTER MACHINE?
NO. PUT THEM BACK WHERE THEY BE-LONG.
AWWW! STINGY OLD PRINCE!
JUST DO AS I SAY.
UGH!
IT'S SO STICKY!
THIS IS HARD, I DON'T LIKE IT.
BOO.
ALL DONE!
A TOUR.
WOULD YOU LIKE ONE?

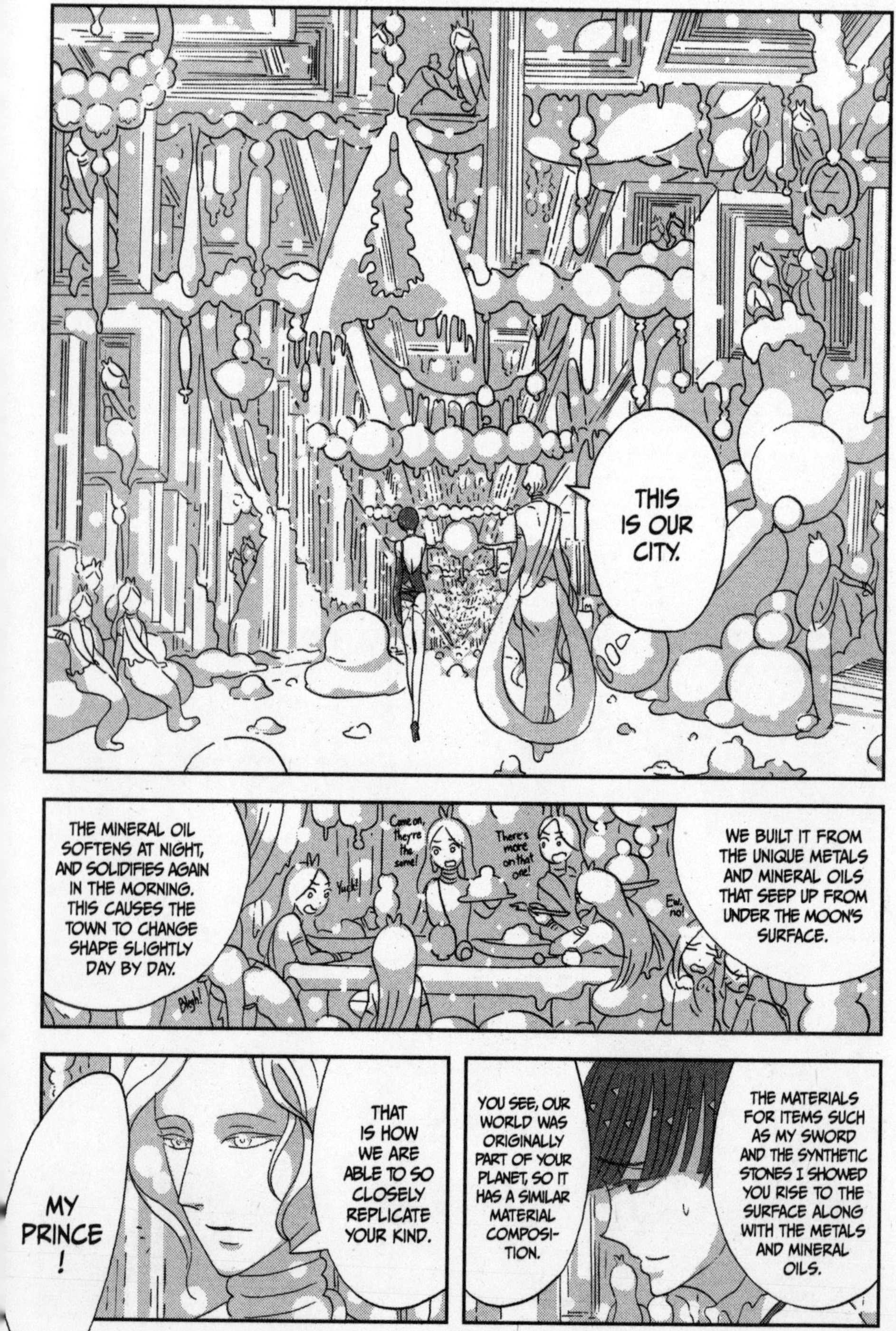

THIS IS OUR CITY.
WE BUILT IT FROM THE UNIQUE METALS AND MINERAL OILS THAT SEEP UP FROM UNDER THE MOON'S SURFACE.
Ew, no!
There's more on that one!
Come on, they're the same!
Yuck!
THE MINERAL OIL SOFTENS AT NIGHT, AND SOLIDIFIES AGAIN IN THE MORNING. THIS CAUSES THE TOWN TO CHANGE SHAPE SLIGHTLY DAY BY DAY.
Blegh!
THE MATERIALS FOR ITEMS SUCH AS MY SWORD AND THE SYNTHETIC STONES I SHOWED YOU RISE TO THE SURFACE ALONG WITH THE METALS AND MINERAL OILS.
YOU SEE, OUR WORLD WAS ORIGINALLY PART OF YOUR PLANET, SO IT HAS A SIMILAR MATERIAL COMPOSITION.
THAT IS HOW WE ARE ABLE TO SO CLOSELY REPLICATE YOUR KIND.
MY PRINCE!

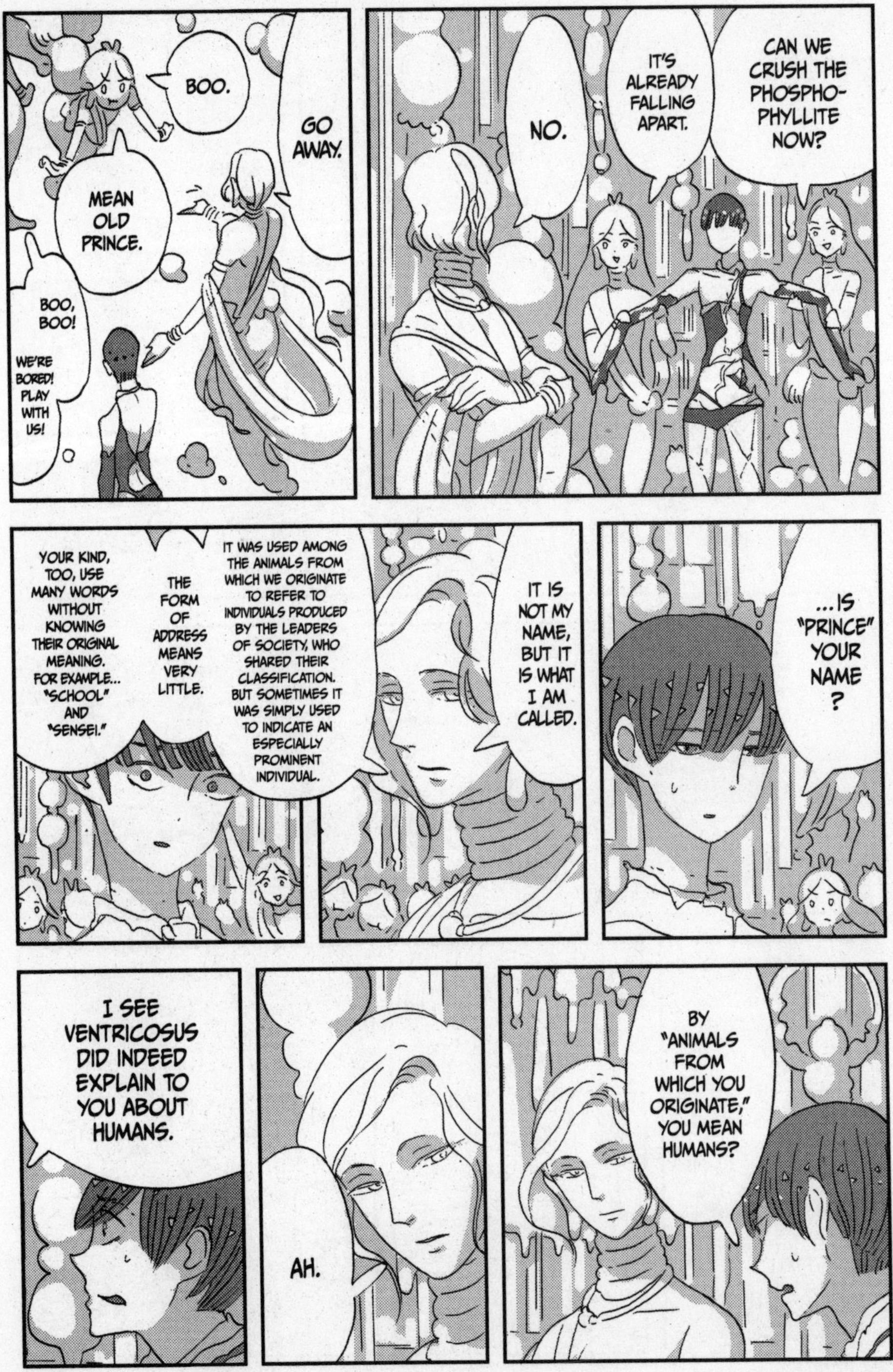
CAN WE CRUSH THE PHOSPHO-PHYLLITE NOW?
IT'S ALREADY FALLING APART.
NO.
BOO.
GO AWAY.
MEAN OLD PRINCE.
BOO, BOO!
WE'RE BORED! PLAY WITH US!
...IS "PRINCE" YOUR NAME?
IT IS NOT MY NAME, BUT IT IS WHAT I AM CALLED.
IT WAS USED AMONG THE ANIMALS FROM WHICH WE ORIGINATE TO REFER TO INDIVIDUALS PRODUCED BY THE LEADERS OF SOCIETY, WHO SHARED THEIR CLASSIFICATION. BUT SOMETIMES IT WAS SIMPLY USED TO INDICATE AN ESPECIALLY PROMINENT INDIVIDUAL.
THE FORM OF ADDRESS MEANS VERY LITTLE.
YOUR KIND, TOO, USE MANY WORDS WITHOUT KNOWING THEIR ORIGINAL MEANING. FOR EXAMPLE... "SCHOOL" AND "SENSEI."
BY "ANIMALS FROM WHICH YOU ORIGINATE," YOU MEAN HUMANS?
AH.
I SEE VENTRICOSUS DID INDEED EXPLAIN TO YOU ABOUT HUMANS.

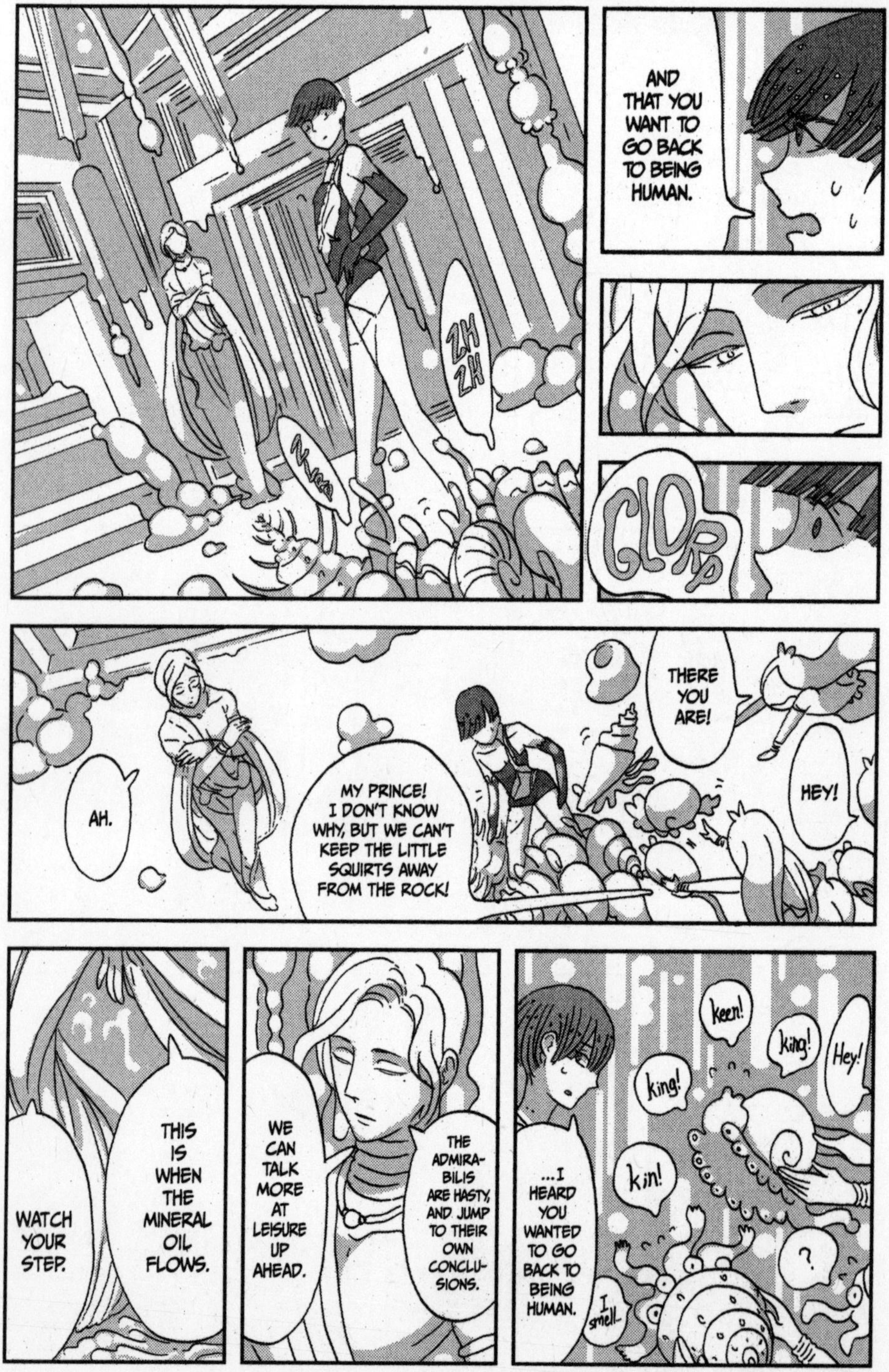
AND THAT YOU WANT TO GO BACK TO BEING HUMAN.
GLORP
ZH ZH
THERE YOU ARE!
HEY!
MY PRINCE! I DON'T KNOW WHY, BUT WE CAN'T KEEP THE LITTLE SQUIRTS AWAY FROM THE ROCK!
AH.
Hey!
king!
keen!
king!
kin!
?
...I HEARD YOU WANTED TO GO BACK TO BEING HUMAN.
I smell...
THE ADMIRA-BILIS ARE HASTY, AND JUMP TO THEIR OWN CONCLU-SIONS.
WE CAN TALK MORE AT LEISURE UP AHEAD.
THIS IS WHEN THE MINERAL OIL FLOWS.
WATCH YOUR STEP.

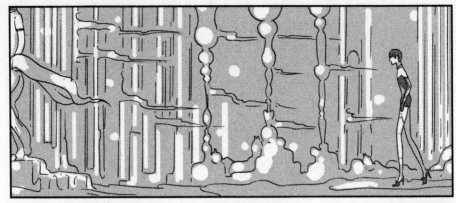

ZLRR

SLIP

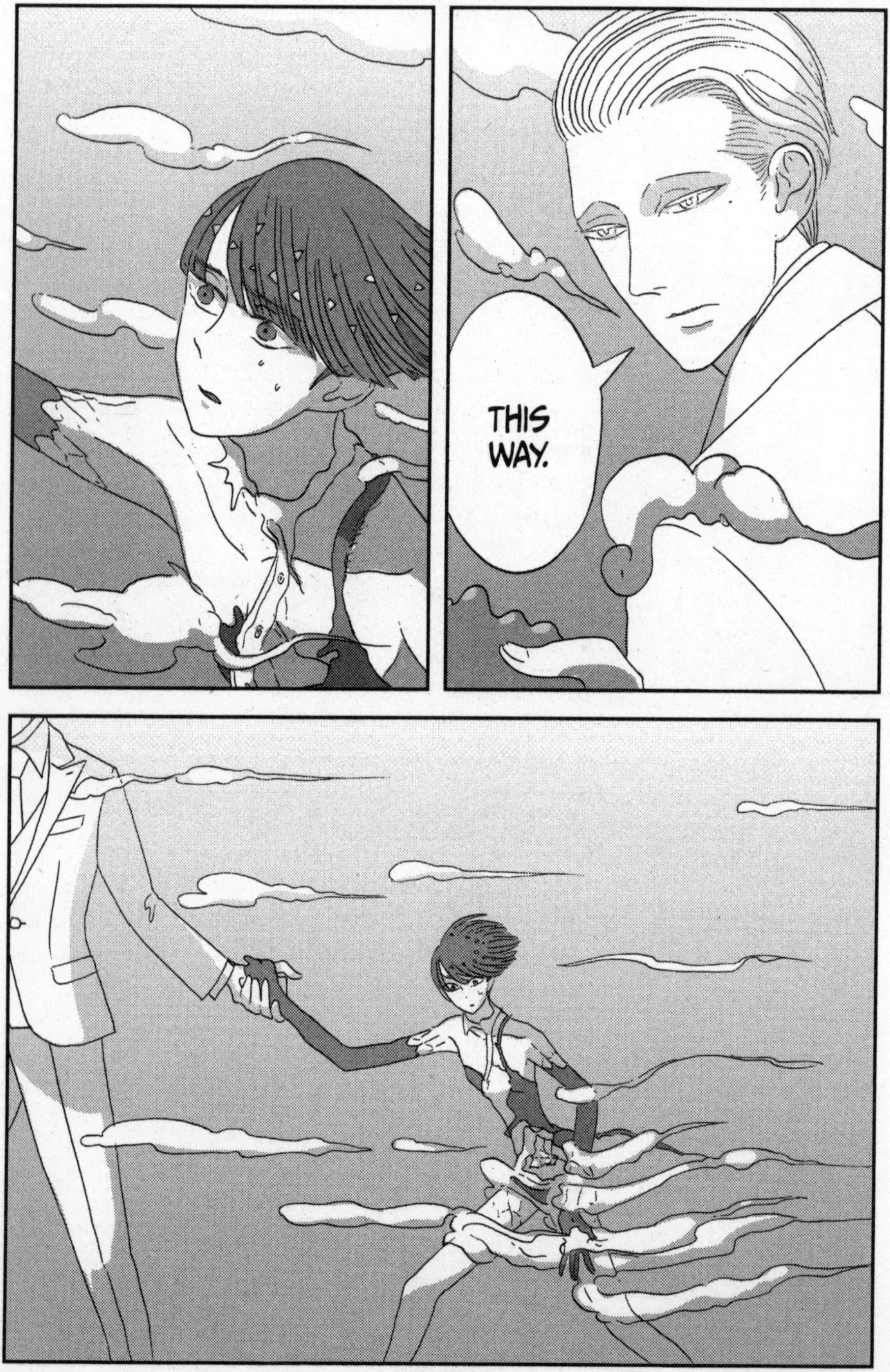
THIS WAY.

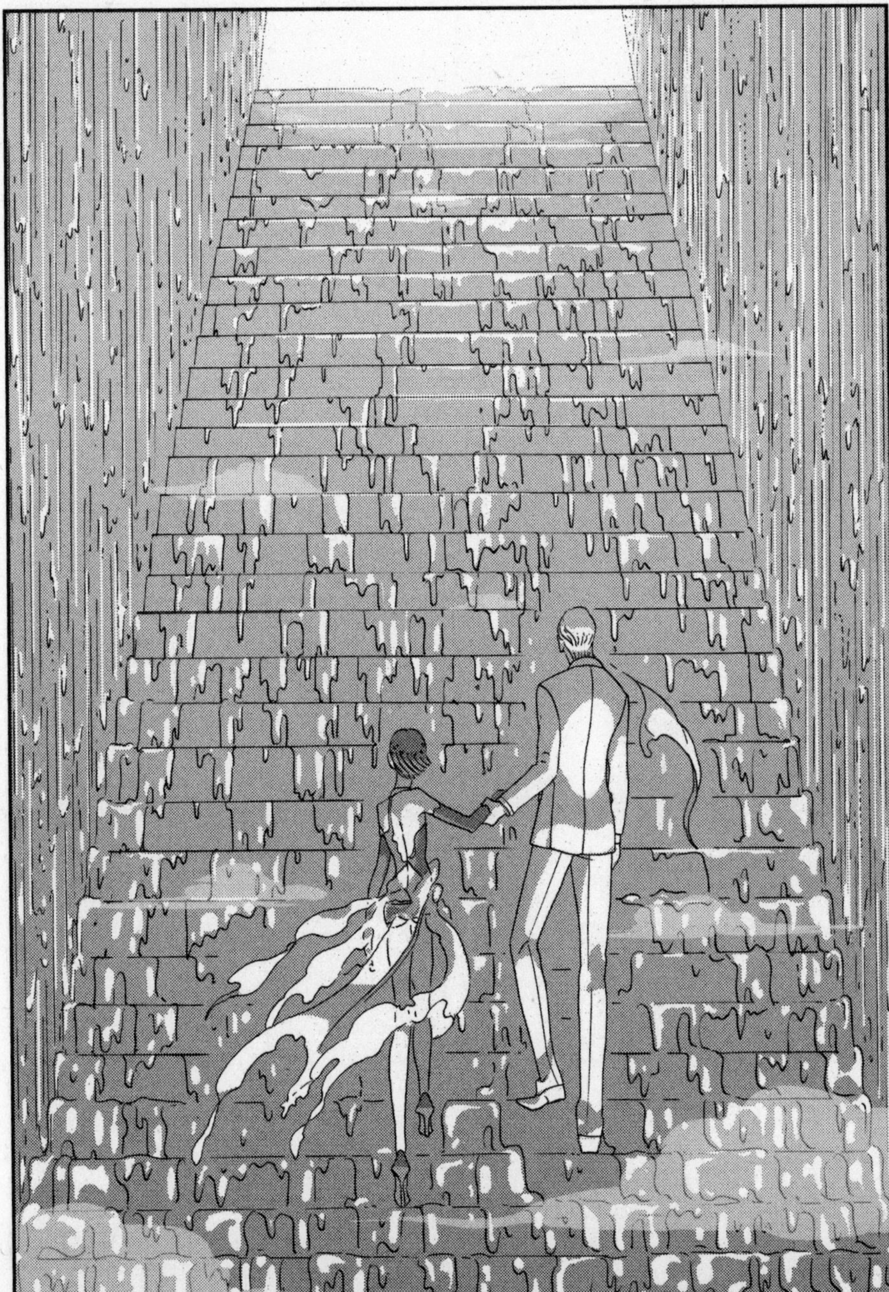

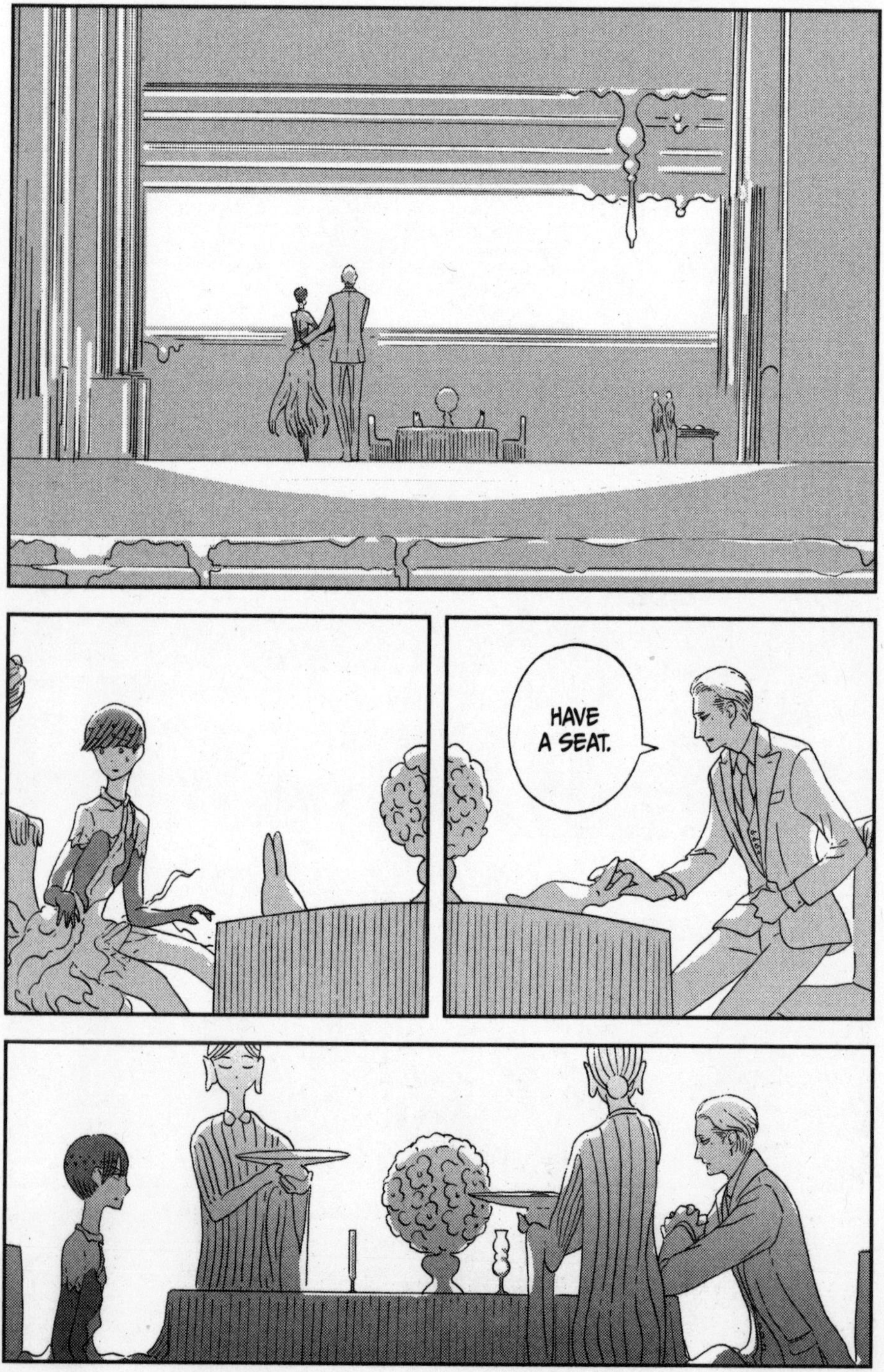
HAVE A SEAT.

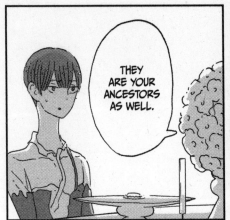

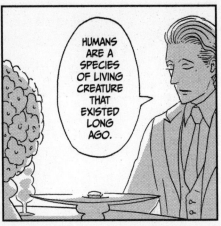

HUMANS ARE A SPECIES OF LIVING CREATURE THAT EXISTED LONG AGO.
THEY ARE YOUR ANCESTORS AS WELL.
BECAUSE THEY ARE ANIMALS, ALL THEIR FUNCTIONS EVENTUALLY SHUT DOWN AND THEY ENTER A STATE KNOWN AS DEATH, AT WHICH POINT THEIR FLESH AND BONE COMPONENTS RETURN TO THE PLANET.
MEANWHILE, THE SPIRIT— AND WE LEARNED THIS AT THE END OF HUMAN CIVILIZATION—
THE SPIRIT IS EJECTED FROM THE BODY AND THEN IS BROKEN DOWN INTO THE PUREST ELEMENTS OF SPIRIT, CONTINUING THROUGH SPACE UNTIL IT ARRIVES AT A CERTAIN POINT IN THE UNIVERSE.
FROM THERE, IT IS ABSORBED INTO A REALM KNOWN AS AN *ALTERNATE UNIVERSE.*
THIS MUCH WAS DETERMINED THROUGH ACTUAL OBSERVATION.

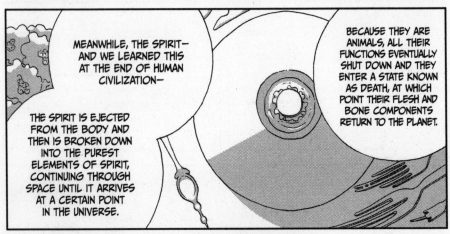

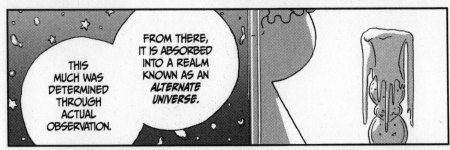

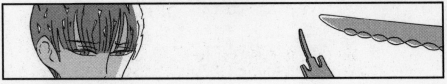

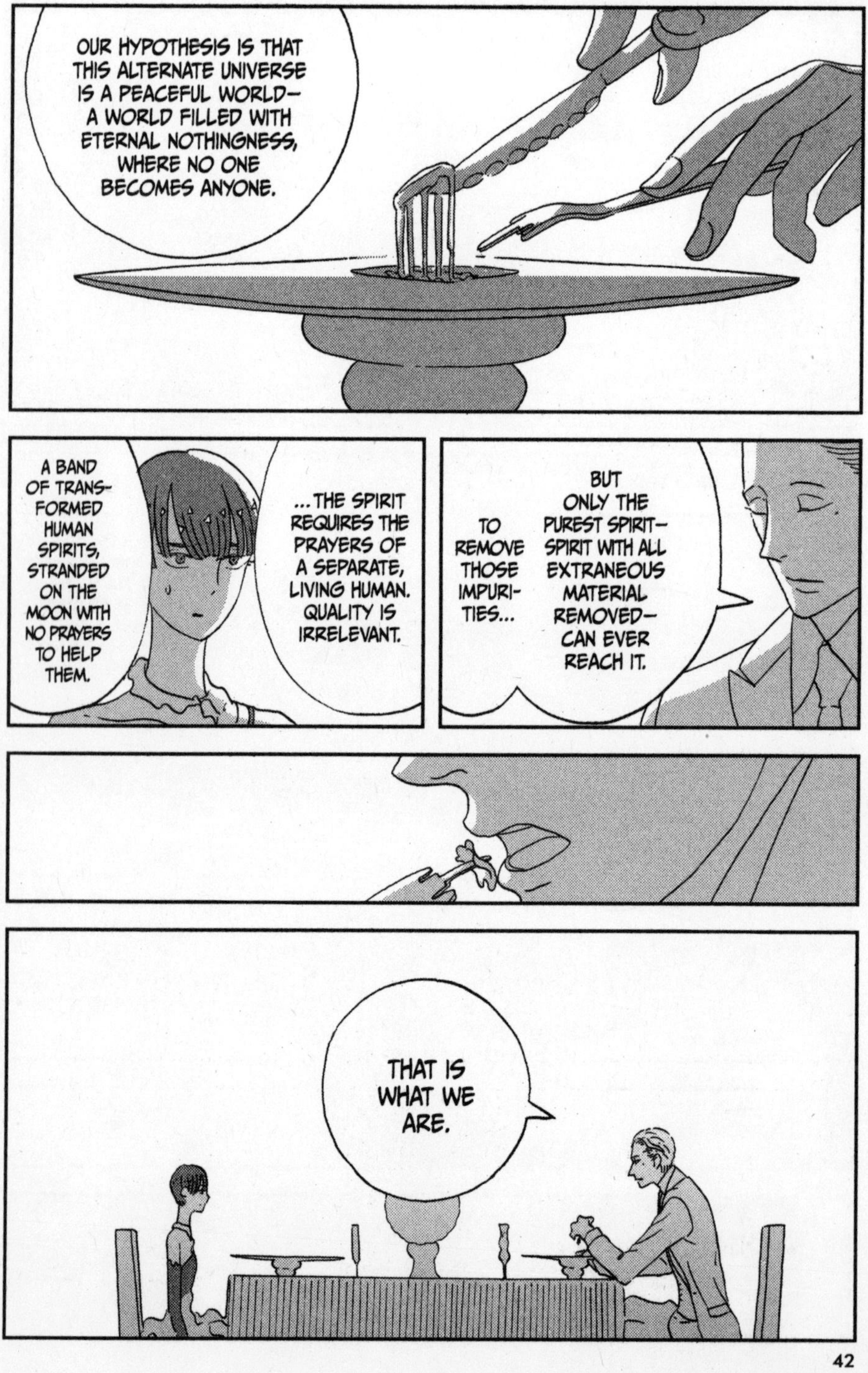
OUR HYPOTHESIS IS THAT THIS ALTERNATE UNIVERSE IS A PEACEFUL WORLD— A WORLD FILLED WITH ETERNAL NOTHINGNESS, WHERE NO ONE BECOMES ANYONE.
BUT ONLY THE PUREST SPIRIT— SPIRIT WITH ALL EXTRANEOUS MATERIAL REMOVED— CAN EVER REACH IT.
TO REMOVE THOSE IMPURITIES...
...THE SPIRIT REQUIRES THE PRAYERS OF A SEPARATE, LIVING HUMAN. QUALITY IS IRRELEVANT.
A BAND OF TRANSFORMED HUMAN SPIRITS, STRANDED ON THE MOON WITH NO PRAYERS TO HELP THEM.
THAT IS WHAT WE ARE.

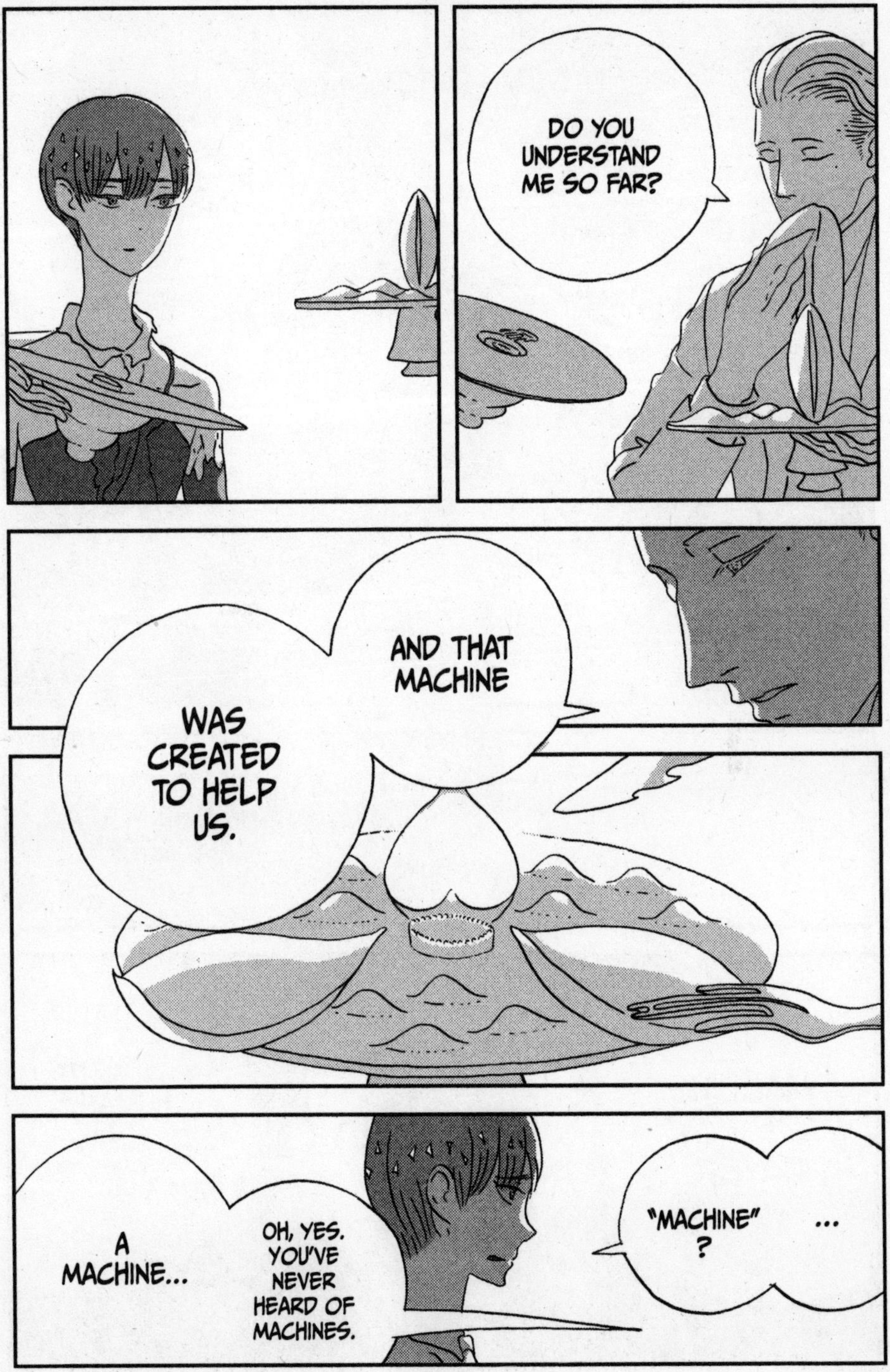
DO YOU UNDERSTAND ME SO FAR?
AND THAT MACHINE
WAS CREATED TO HELP US.
... "MACHINE" ?
OH, YES. YOU'VE NEVER HEARD OF MACHINES.
A MACHINE...

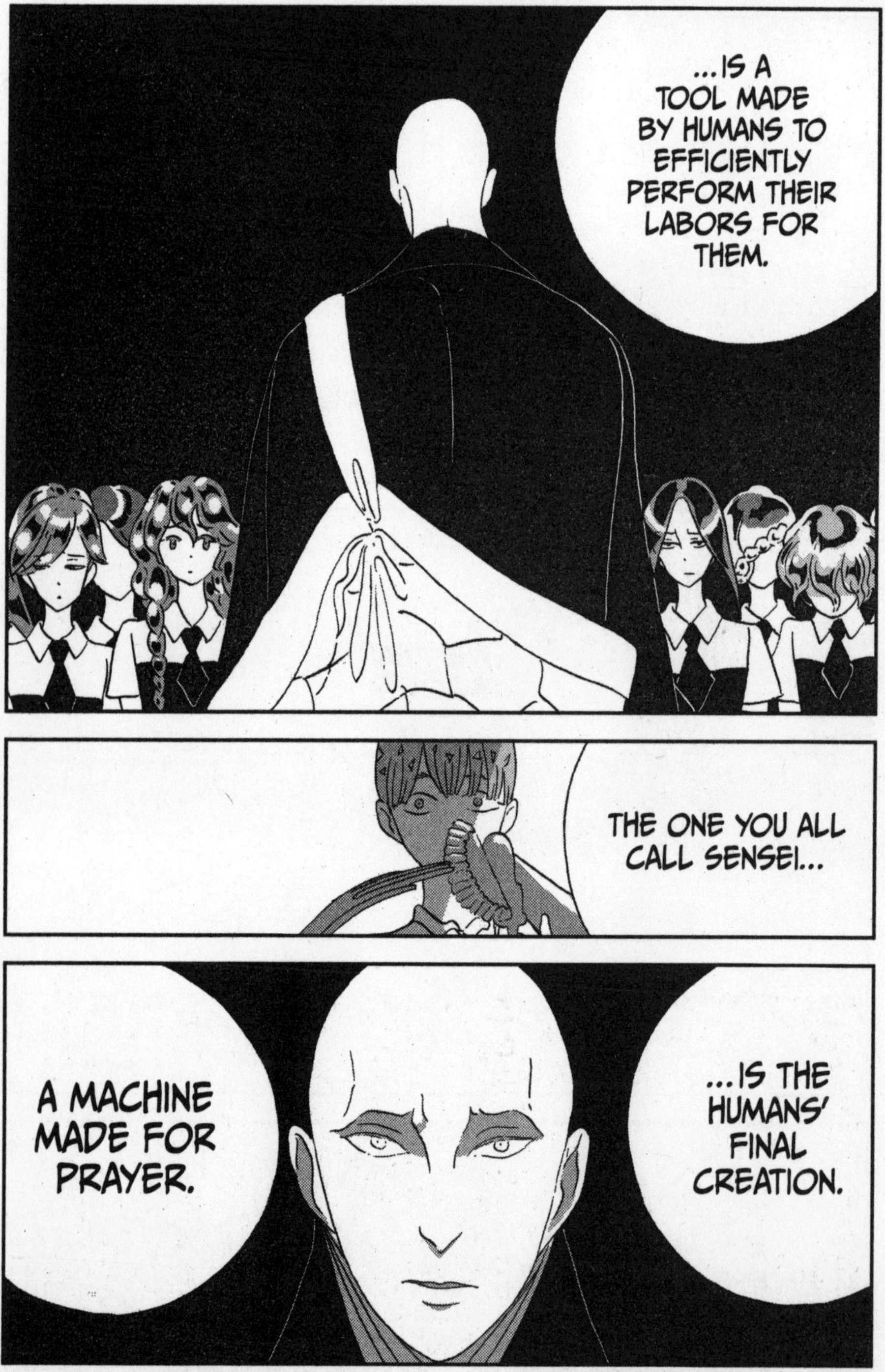
...IS A TOOL MADE BY HUMANS TO EFFICIENTLY PERFORM THEIR LABORS FOR THEM.
THE ONE YOU ALL CALL SENSEI...
...IS THE HUMANS' FINAL CREATION.
A MACHINE MADE FOR PRAYER.

...CREATION.

THE HUMANS'...

YES.

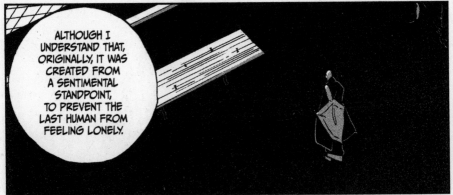

ALTHOUGH I UNDERSTAND THAT, ORIGINALLY, IT WAS CREATED FROM A SENTIMENTAL STANDPOINT, TO PREVENT THE LAST HUMAN FROM FEELING LONELY.

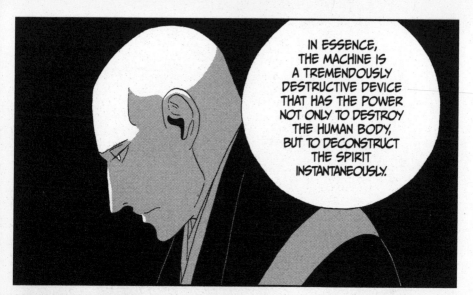

IN ESSENCE, THE MACHINE IS A TREMENDOUSLY DESTRUCTIVE DEVICE THAT HAS THE POWER NOT ONLY TO DESTROY THE HUMAN BODY, BUT TO DECONSTRUCT THE SPIRIT INSTANTANEOUSLY.

BUT AT SOME POINT IT BROKE DOWN.

IT STOPPED DOING WHAT IT WAS BUILT TO DO...

...WHILE WE REMAIN HERE, SPIRITS WHO HAVE YET TO BE DECONSTRUCTED.

AND SO...

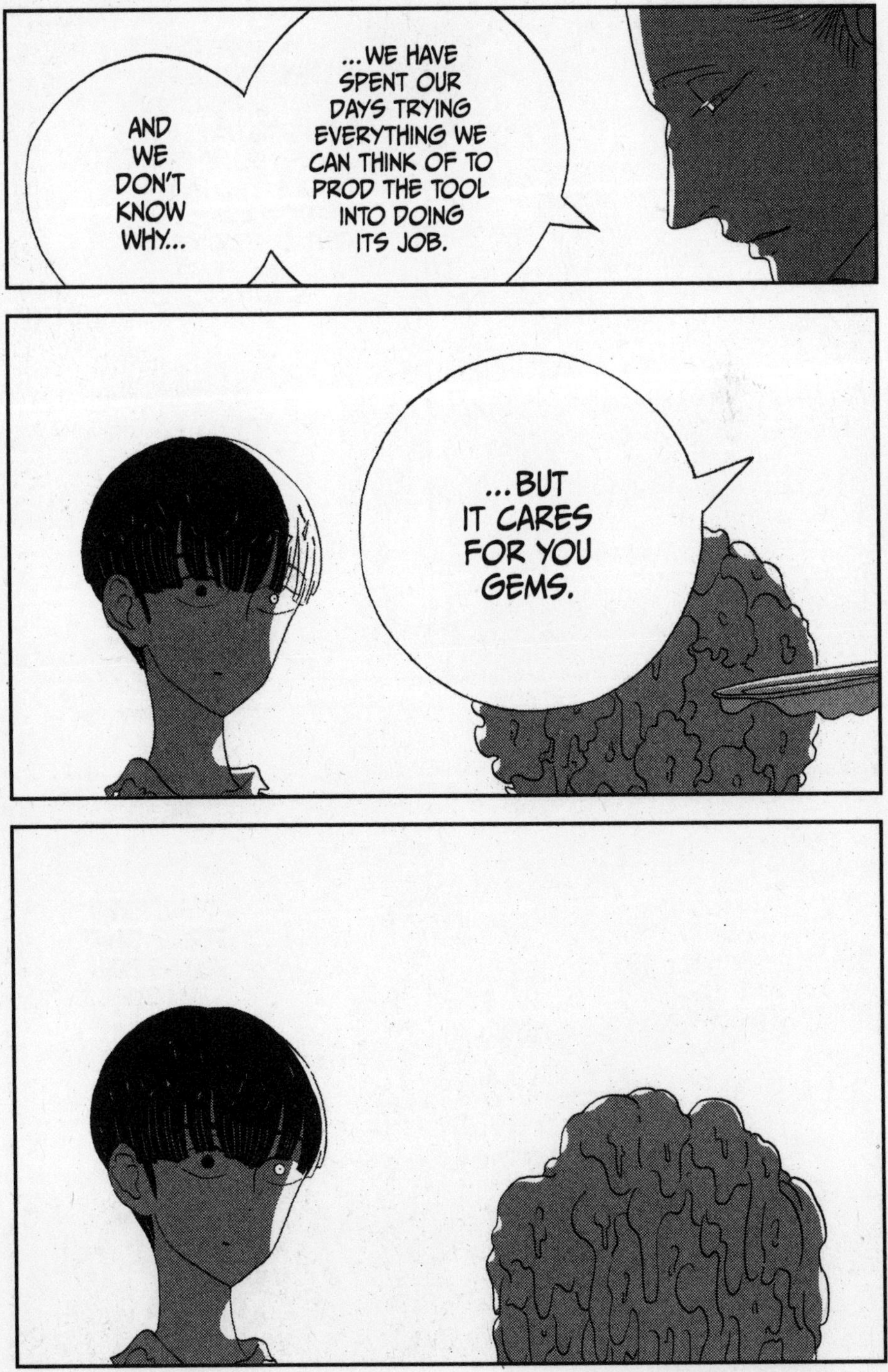
...WE HAVE SPENT OUR DAYS TRYING EVERYTHING WE CAN THINK OF TO PROD THE TOOL INTO DOING ITS JOB.
AND WE DON'T KNOW WHY...
...BUT IT CARES FOR YOU GEMS.

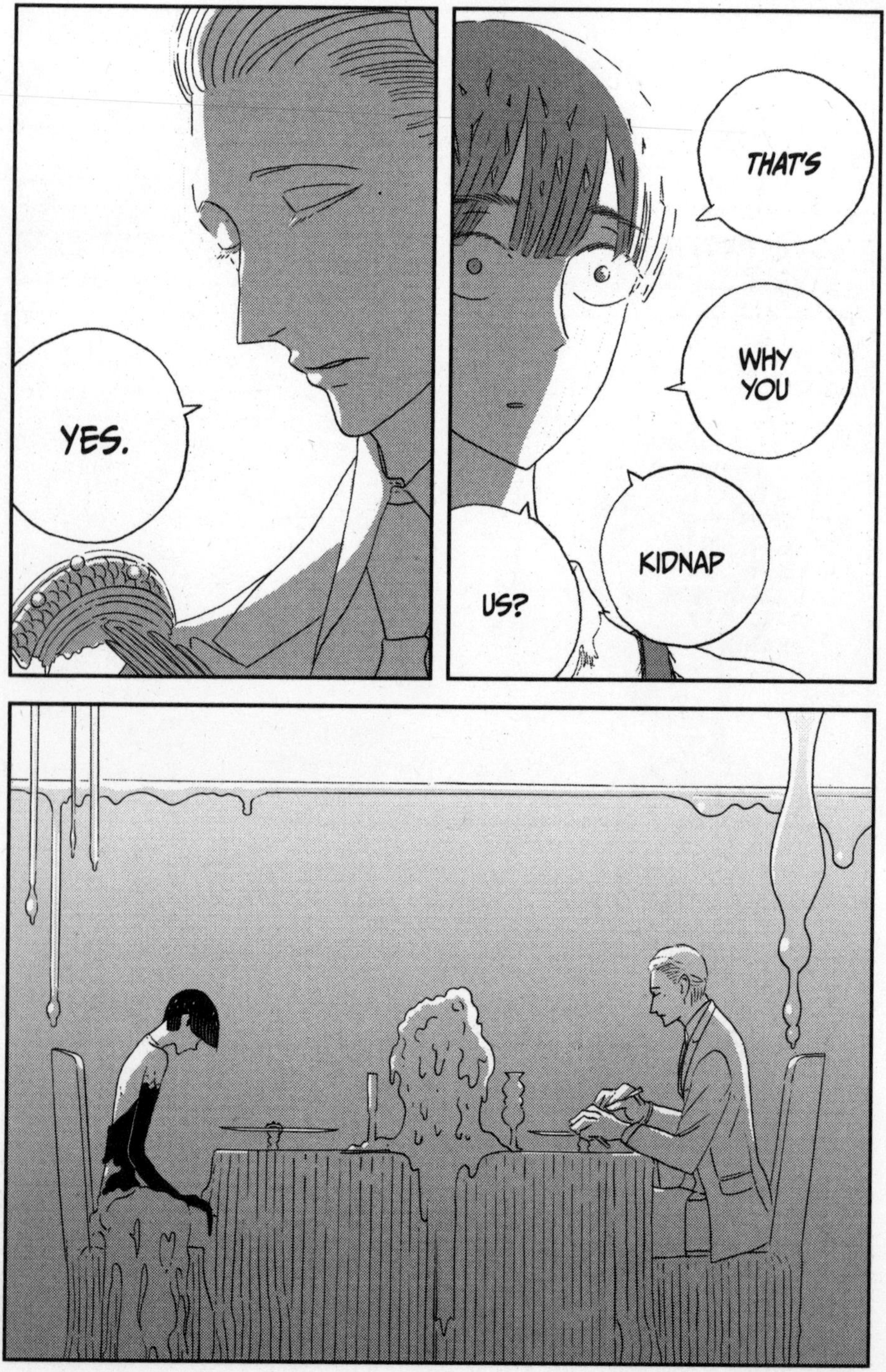
THAT'S
WHY YOU
KIDNAP
US?
YES.

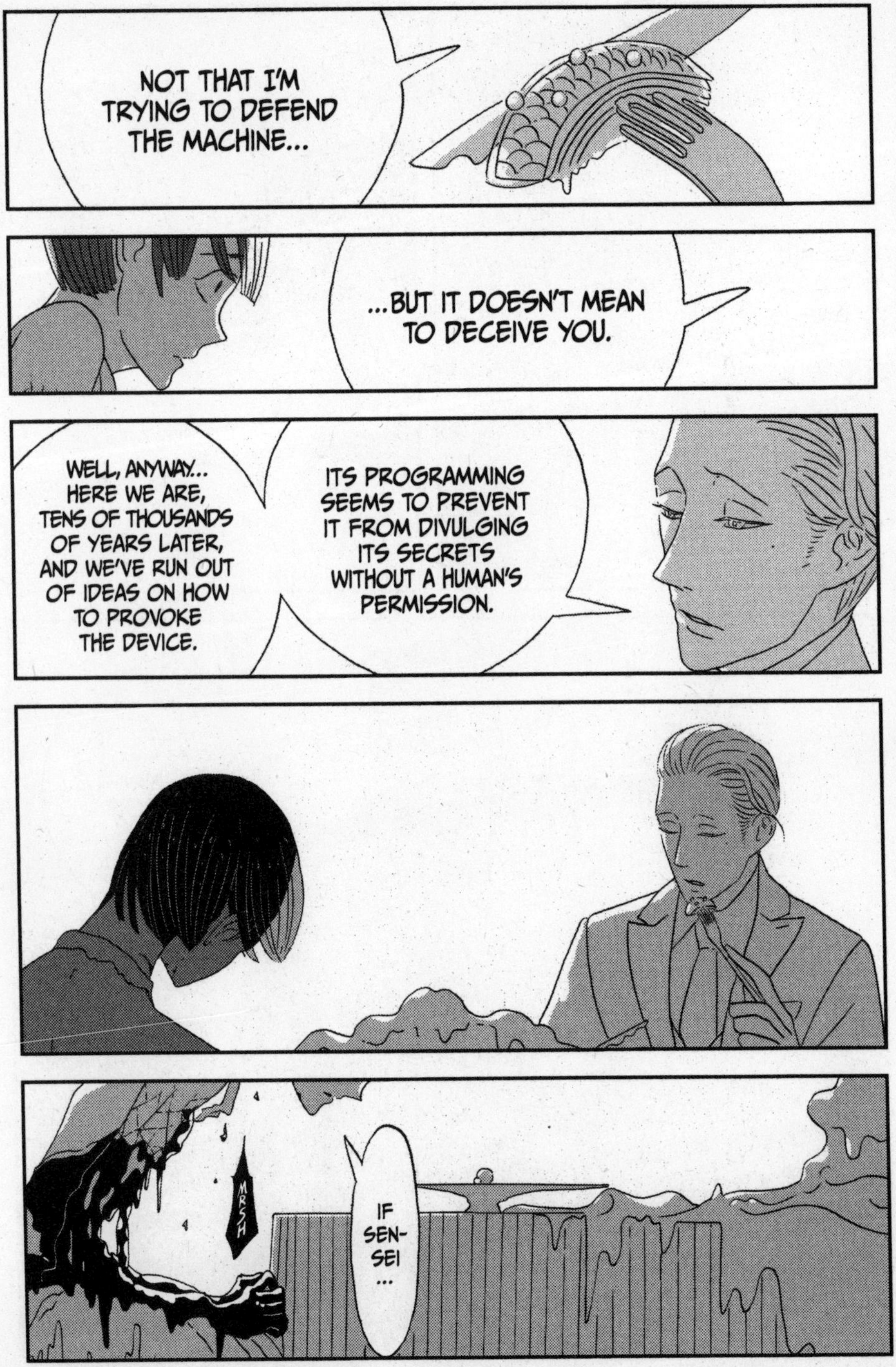
NOT THAT I'M TRYING TO DEFEND THE MACHINE...
...BUT IT DOESN'T MEAN TO DECEIVE YOU.
ITS PROGRAMMING SEEMS TO PREVENT IT FROM DIVULGING ITS SECRETS WITHOUT A HUMAN'S PERMISSION.
WELL, ANYWAY... HERE WE ARE, TENS OF THOUSANDS OF YEARS LATER, AND WE'VE RUN OUT OF IDEAS ON HOW TO PROVOKE THE DEVICE.
IF SEN-SEI ...
MRSH

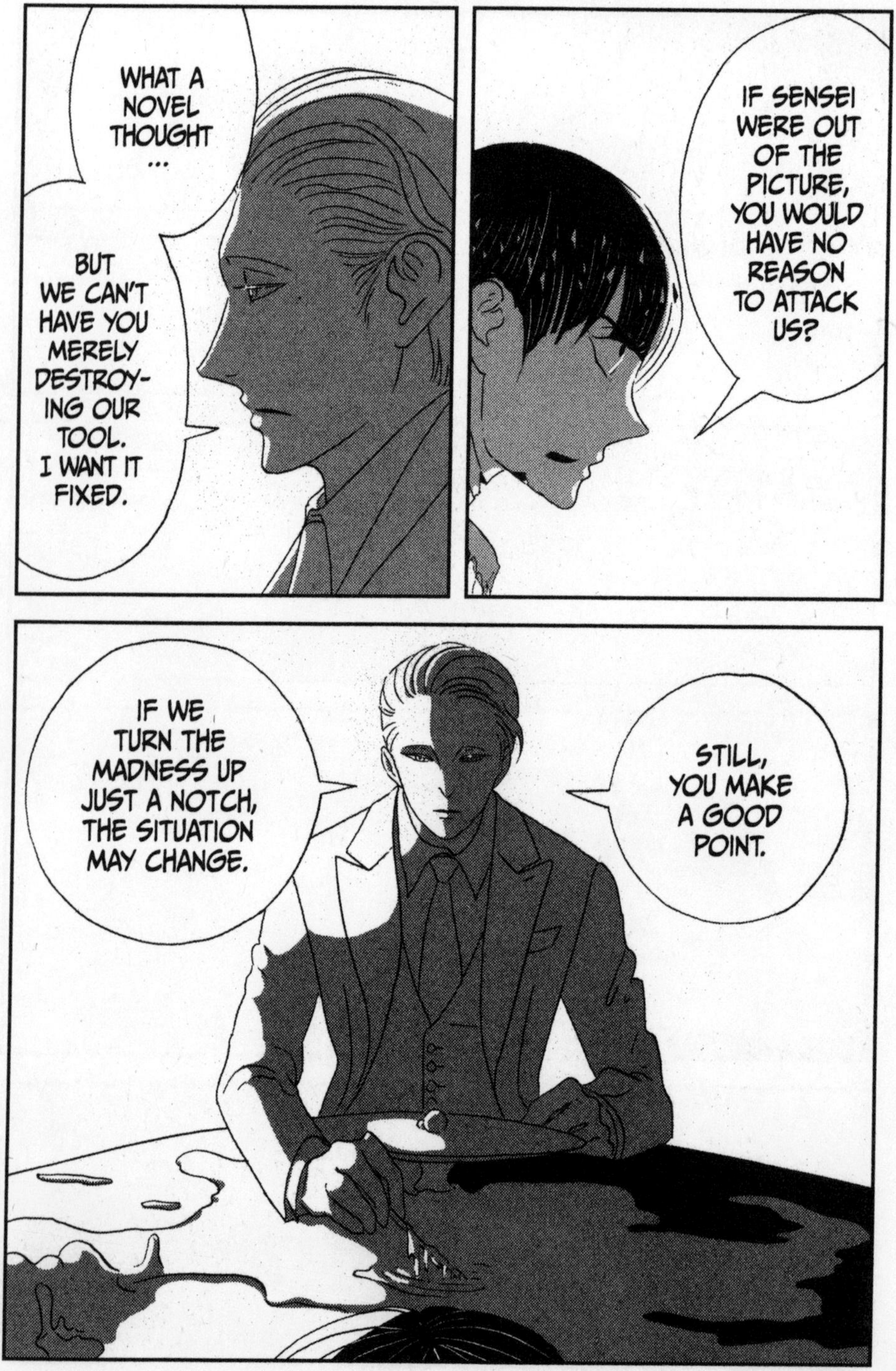
IF SENSEI WERE OUT OF THE PICTURE, YOU WOULD HAVE NO REASON TO ATTACK US?
WHAT A NOVEL THOUGHT ...
BUT WE CAN'T HAVE YOU MERELY DESTROYING OUR TOOL. I WANT IT FIXED.
STILL, YOU MAKE A GOOD POINT.
IF WE TURN THE MADNESS UP JUST A NOTCH, THE SITUATION MAY CHANGE.

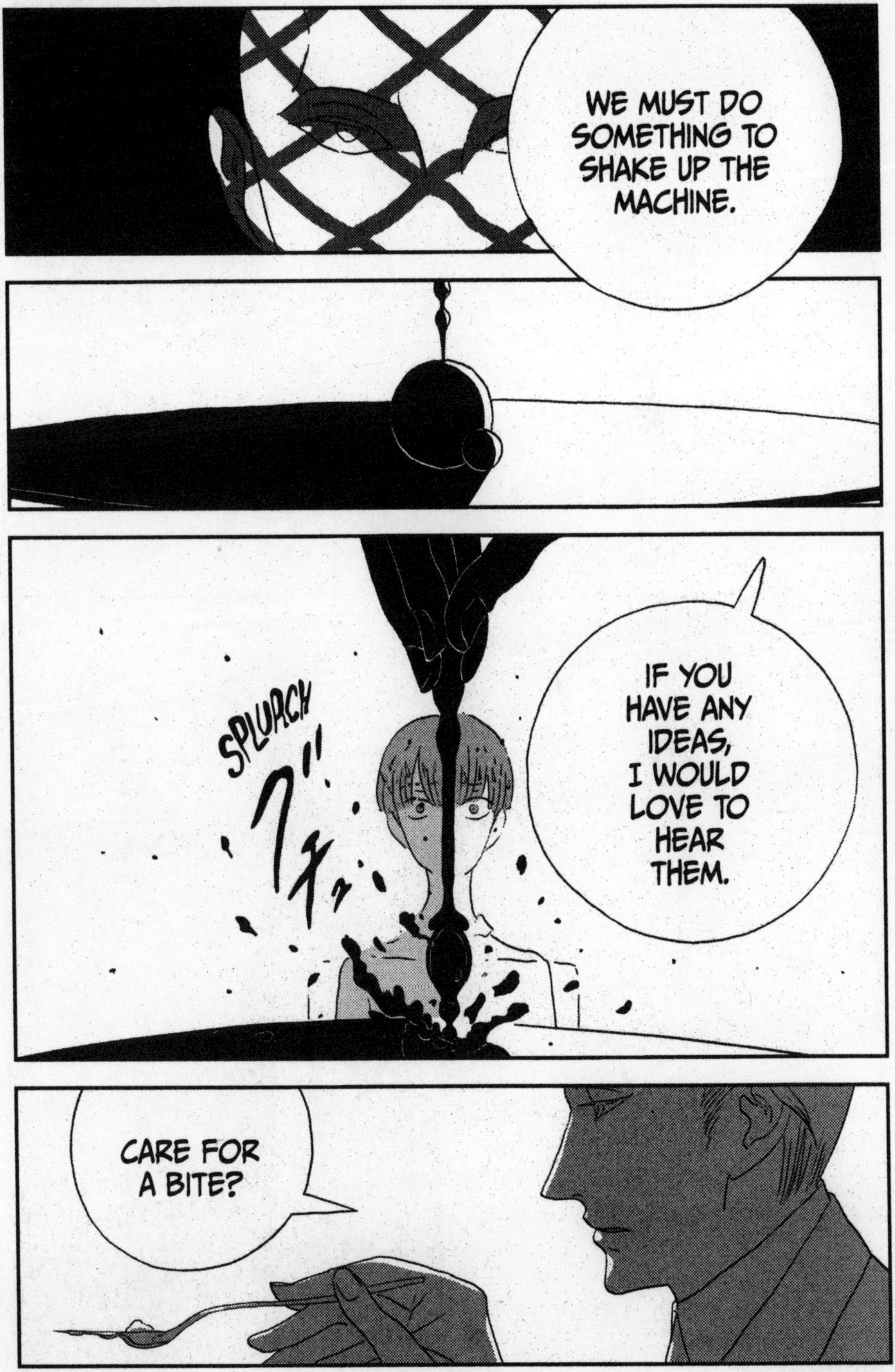
WE MUST DO SOMETHING TO SHAKE UP THE MACHINE.
IF YOU HAVE ANY IDEAS, I WOULD LOVE TO HEAR THEM.
SPLURCH
CARE FOR A BITE?

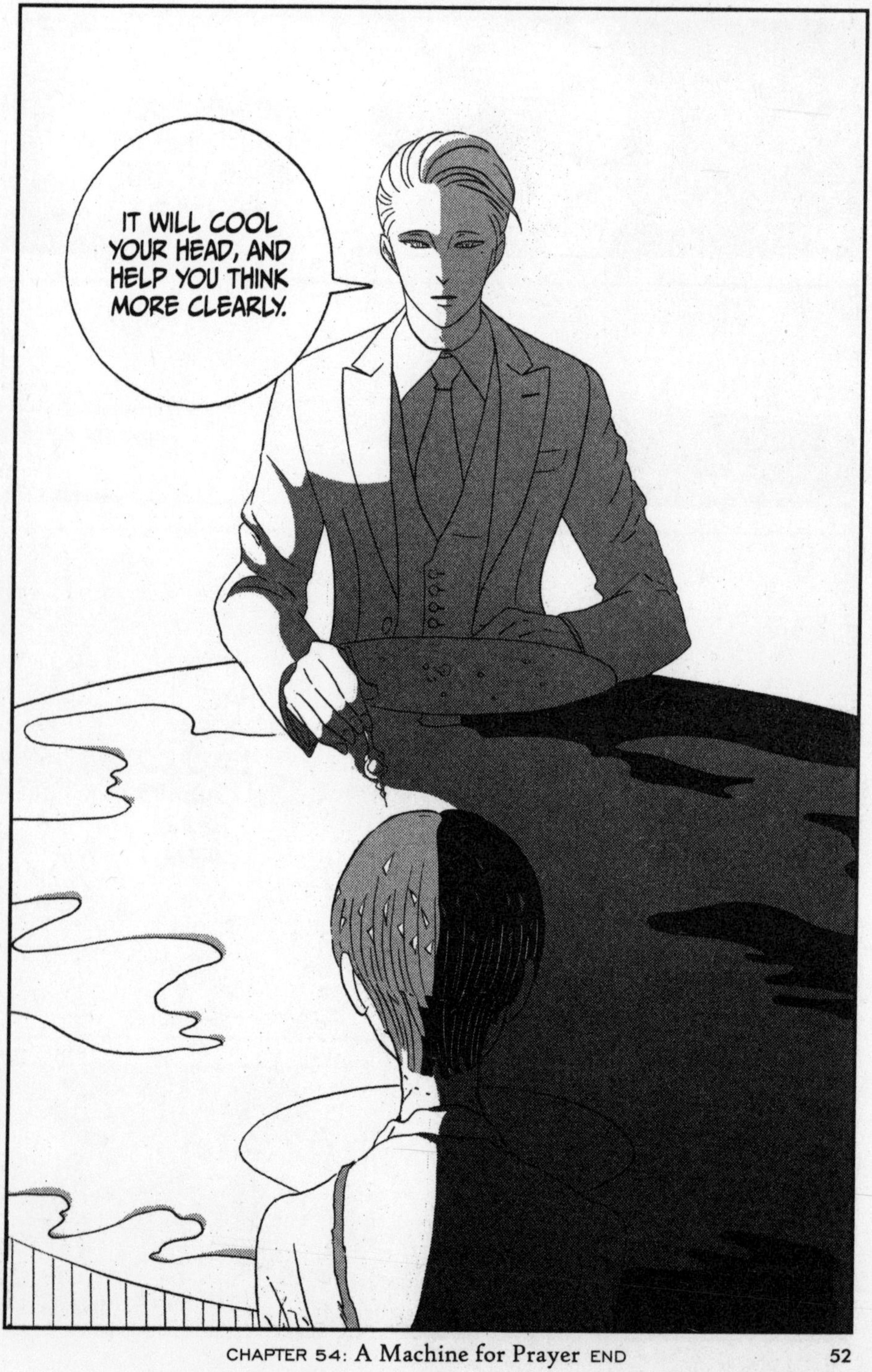
IT WILL COOL YOUR HEAD, AND HELP YOU THINK MORE CLEARLY.

CHAPTER 55:

Curse

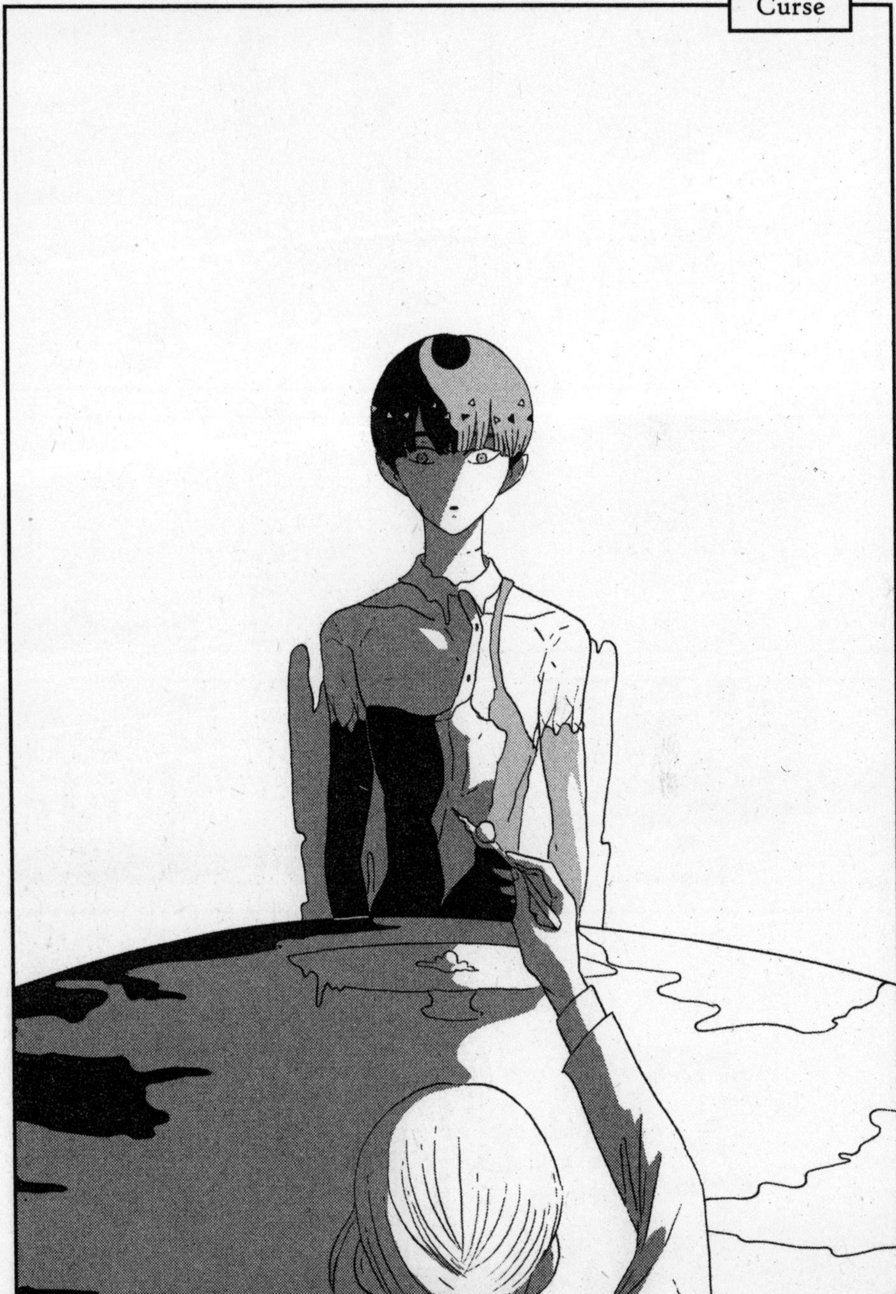

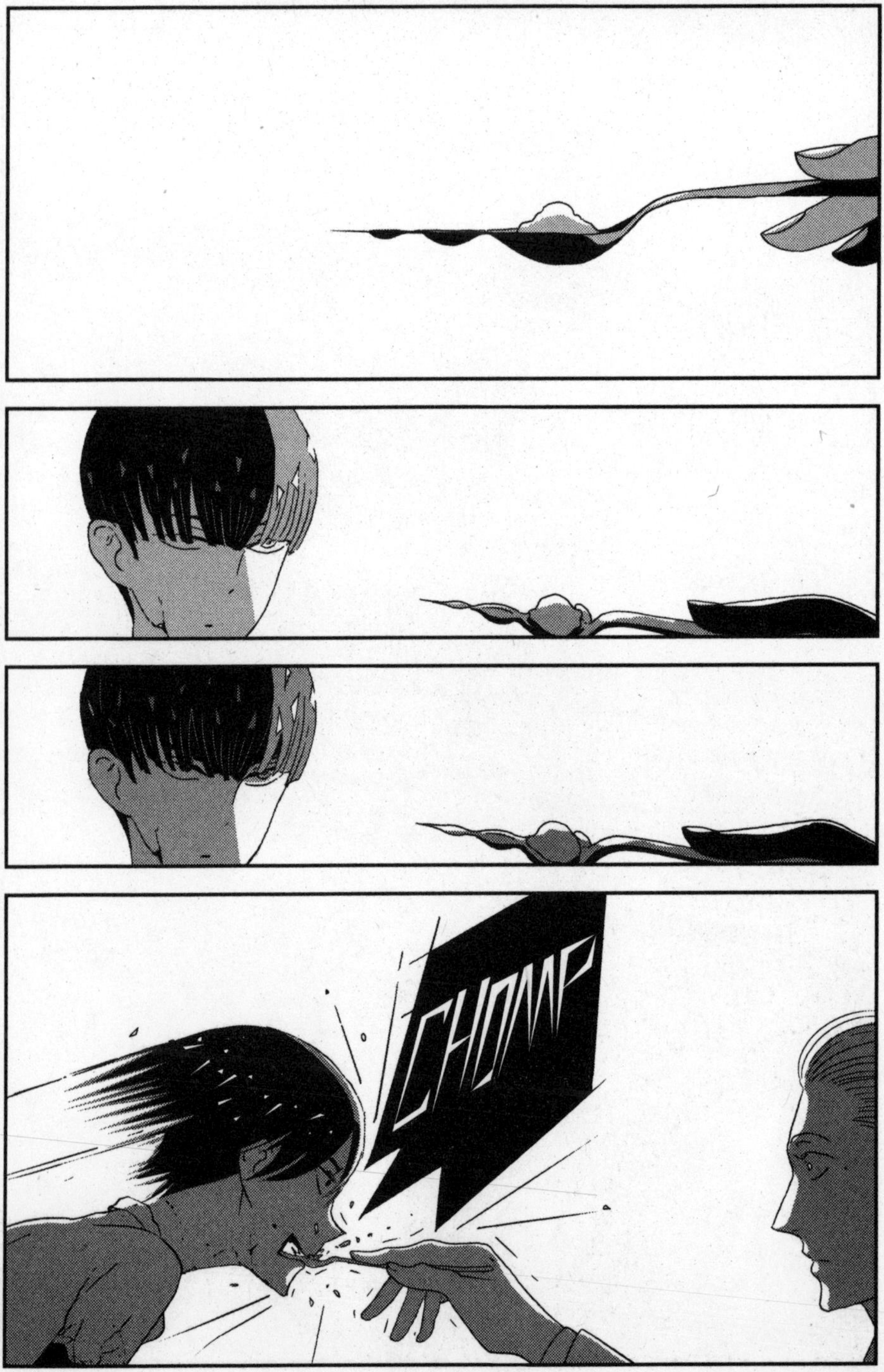
CHOMP

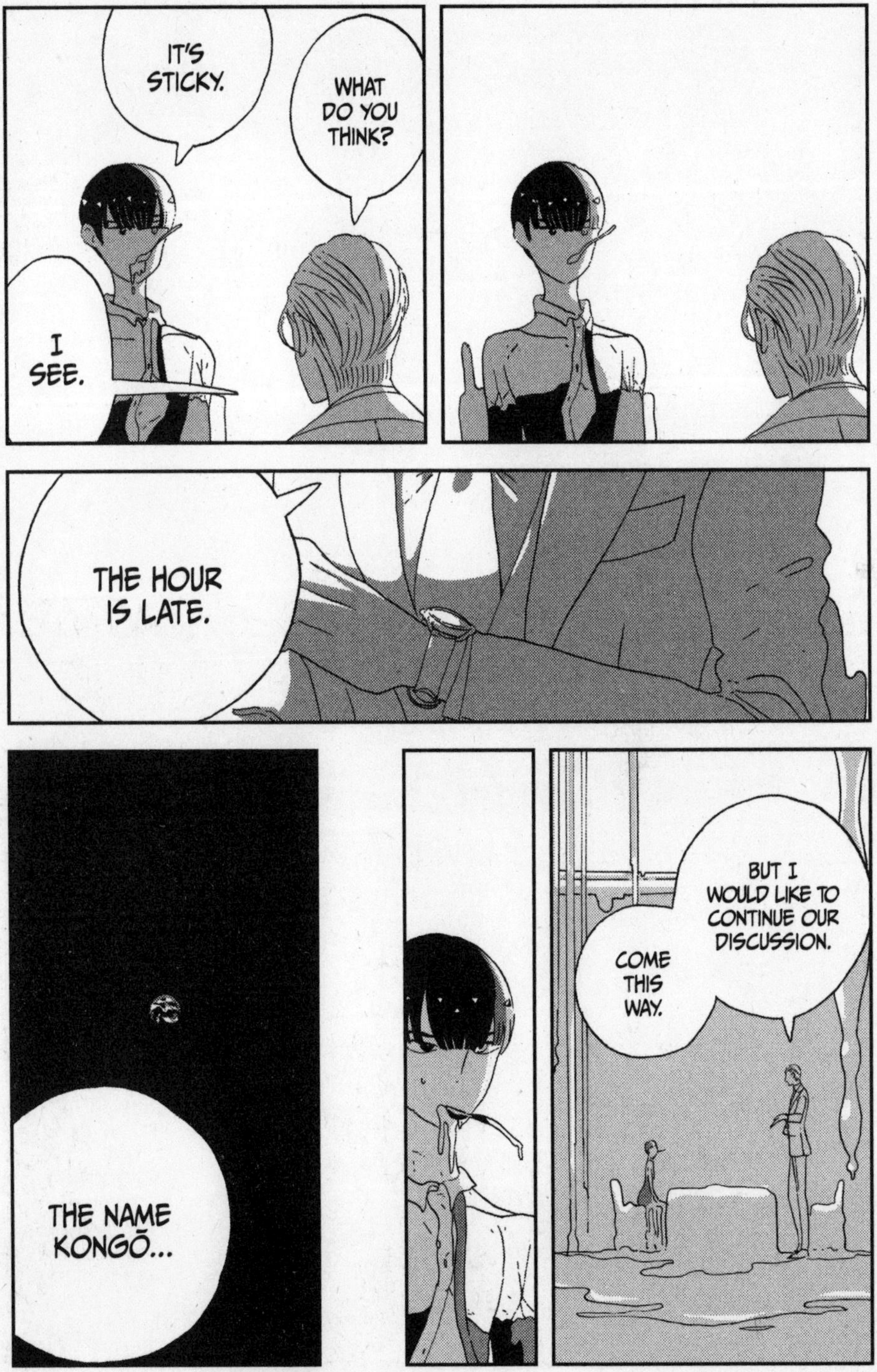
WHAT DO YOU THINK?
IT'S STICKY.
I SEE.
THE HOUR IS LATE.
BUT I WOULD LIKE TO CONTINUE OUR DISCUSSION.
COME THIS WAY.
THE NAME KONGŌ...

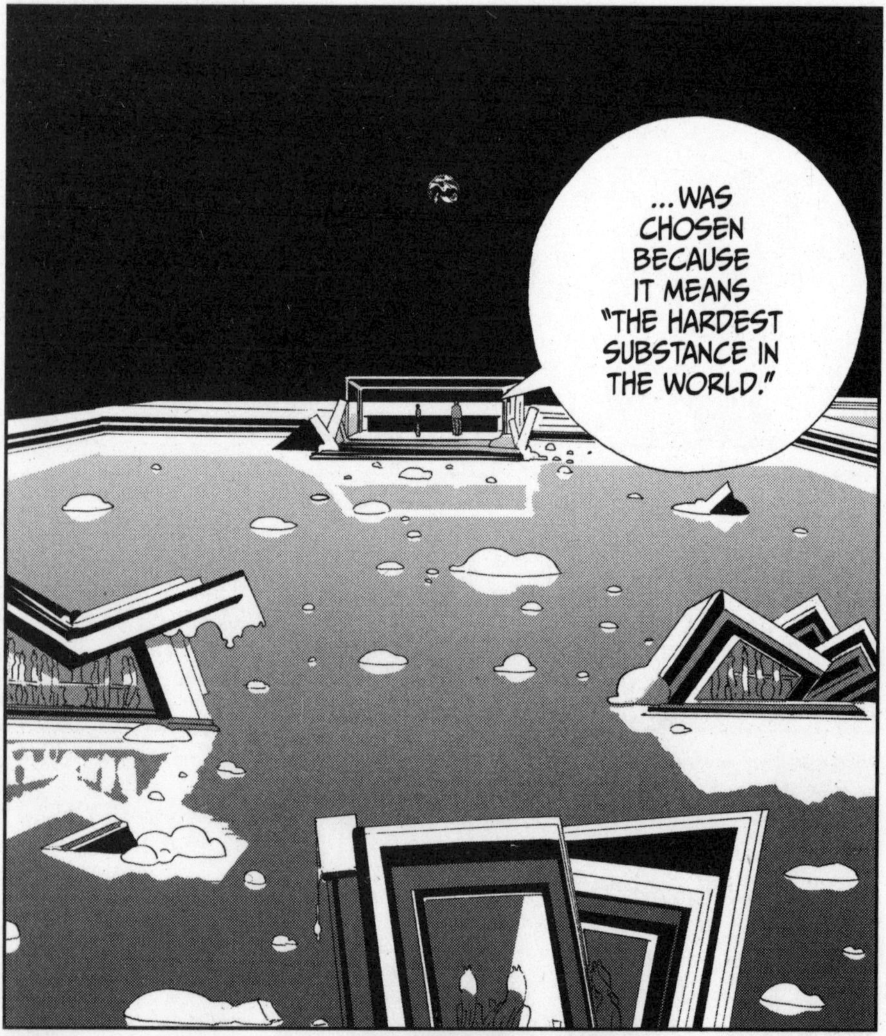
...WAS CHOSEN BECAUSE IT MEANS "THE HARDEST SUBSTANCE IN THE WORLD."

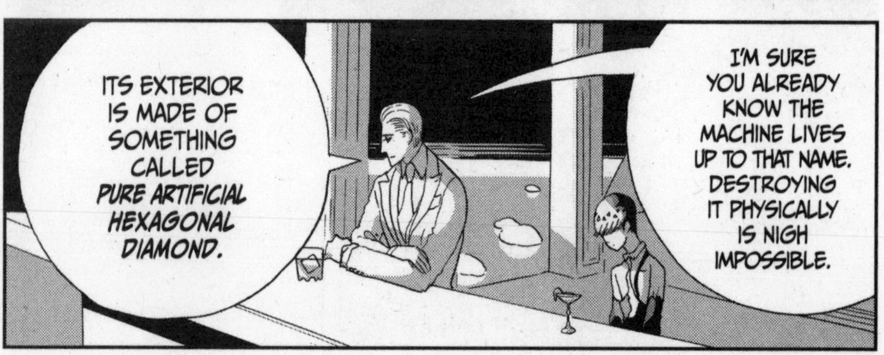
I'M SURE YOU ALREADY KNOW THE MACHINE LIVES UP TO THAT NAME. DESTROYING IT PHYSICALLY IS NIGH IMPOSSIBLE.
ITS EXTERIOR IS MADE OF SOMETHING CALLED *PURE ARTIFICIAL HEXAGONAL DIAMOND.*

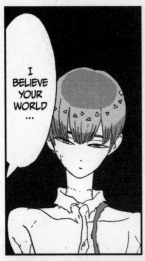

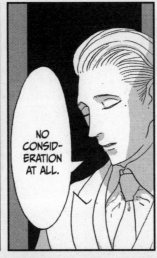

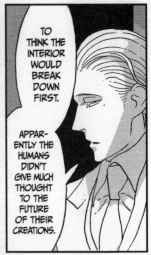

TO THINK THE INTERIOR WOULD BREAK DOWN FIRST.
APPAR-ENTLY THE HUMANS DIDN'T GIVE MUCH THOUGHT TO THE FUTURE OF THEIR CREATIONS.
NO CONSID-ERATION AT ALL.
I BELIEVE YOUR WORLD ...
...HAS NO MACHINES BECAUSE OF SOME EMOTIONAL SCARRING THAT MAKES KONGŌ UNWILLING TO ADVANCE CIVILIZATION.
IT WOULD HELP IN KEEPING THE MACHINE'S IDENTITY SECRET, AS WELL.
INCIDENTALLY, WE HAVE NOT SUCCEEDED IN SYNTHESIZING PURE HEXAGONAL DIAMOND HERE.
...
AH...
FOR YOUR REFERENCE...
...ALLOW ME TO TELL YOU SOME OF WHAT WE HAVE TRIED TO PROVOKE KONGŌ.
IN THE EARLY STAGES ...

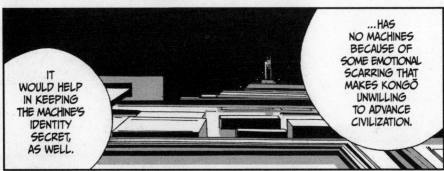

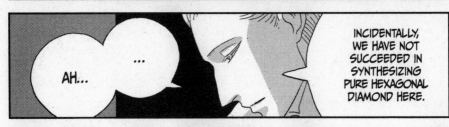

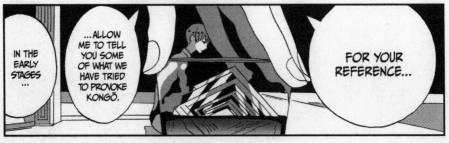

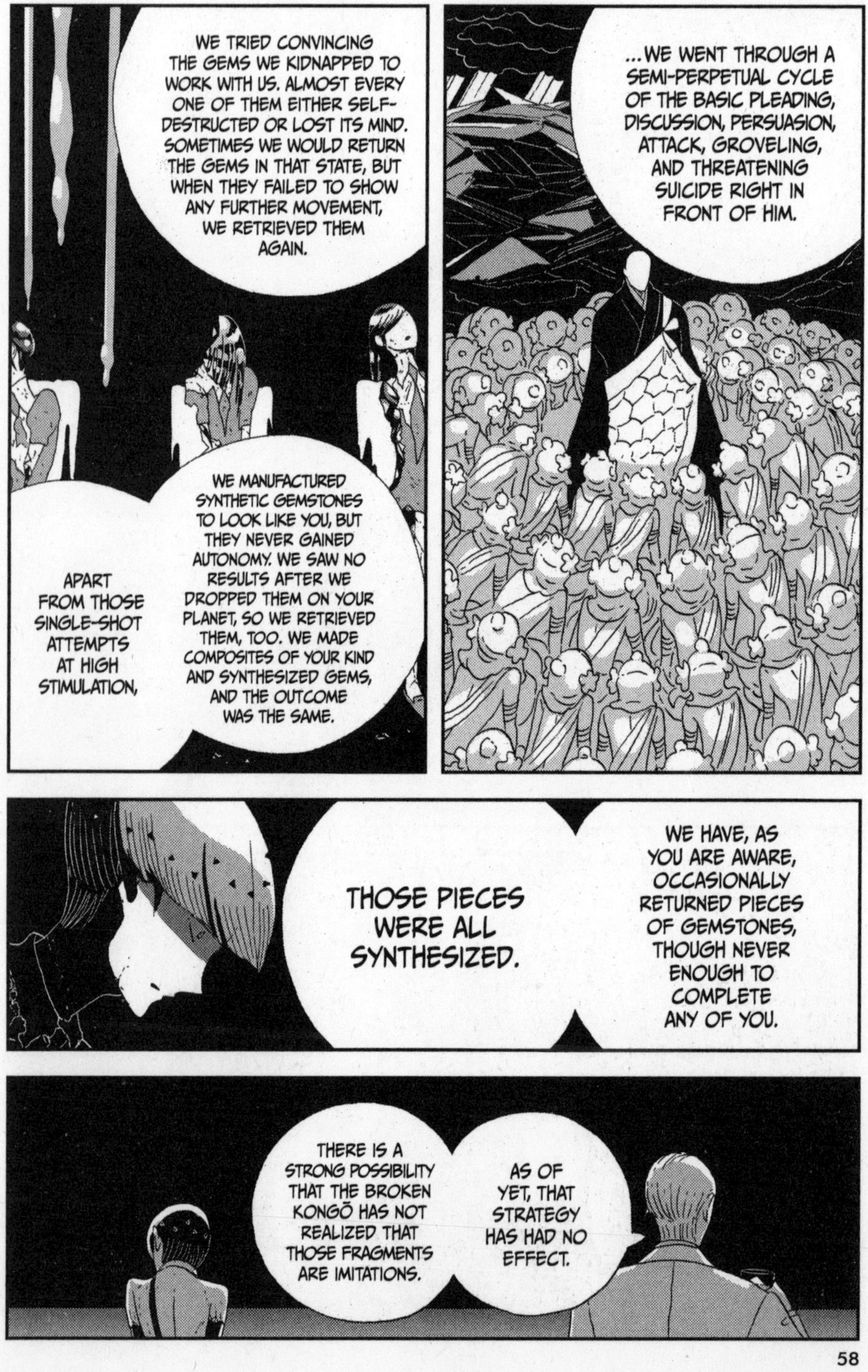
WE TRIED CONVINCING THE GEMS WE KIDNAPPED TO WORK WITH US. ALMOST EVERY ONE OF THEM EITHER SELF-DESTRUCTED OR LOST ITS MIND. SOMETIMES WE WOULD RETURN THE GEMS IN THAT STATE, BUT WHEN THEY FAILED TO SHOW ANY FURTHER MOVEMENT, WE RETRIEVED THEM AGAIN.
WE MANUFACTURED SYNTHETIC GEMSTONES TO LOOK LIKE YOU, BUT THEY NEVER GAINED AUTONOMY. WE SAW NO RESULTS AFTER WE DROPPED THEM ON YOUR PLANET, SO WE RETRIEVED THEM, TOO. WE MADE COMPOSITES OF YOUR KIND AND SYNTHESIZED GEMS, AND THE OUTCOME WAS THE SAME.
APART FROM THOSE SINGLE-SHOT ATTEMPTS AT HIGH STIMULATION,
...WE WENT THROUGH A SEMI-PERPETUAL CYCLE OF THE BASIC PLEADING, DISCUSSION, PERSUASION, ATTACK, GROVELING, AND THREATENING SUICIDE RIGHT IN FRONT OF HIM.
WE HAVE, AS YOU ARE AWARE, OCCASIONALLY RETURNED PIECES OF GEMSTONES, THOUGH NEVER ENOUGH TO COMPLETE ANY OF YOU.
THOSE PIECES WERE ALL SYNTHESIZED.
THERE IS A STRONG POSSIBILITY THAT THE BROKEN KONGŌ HAS NOT REALIZED THAT THOSE FRAGMENTS ARE IMITATIONS.
AS OF YET, THAT STRATEGY HAS HAD NO EFFECT.

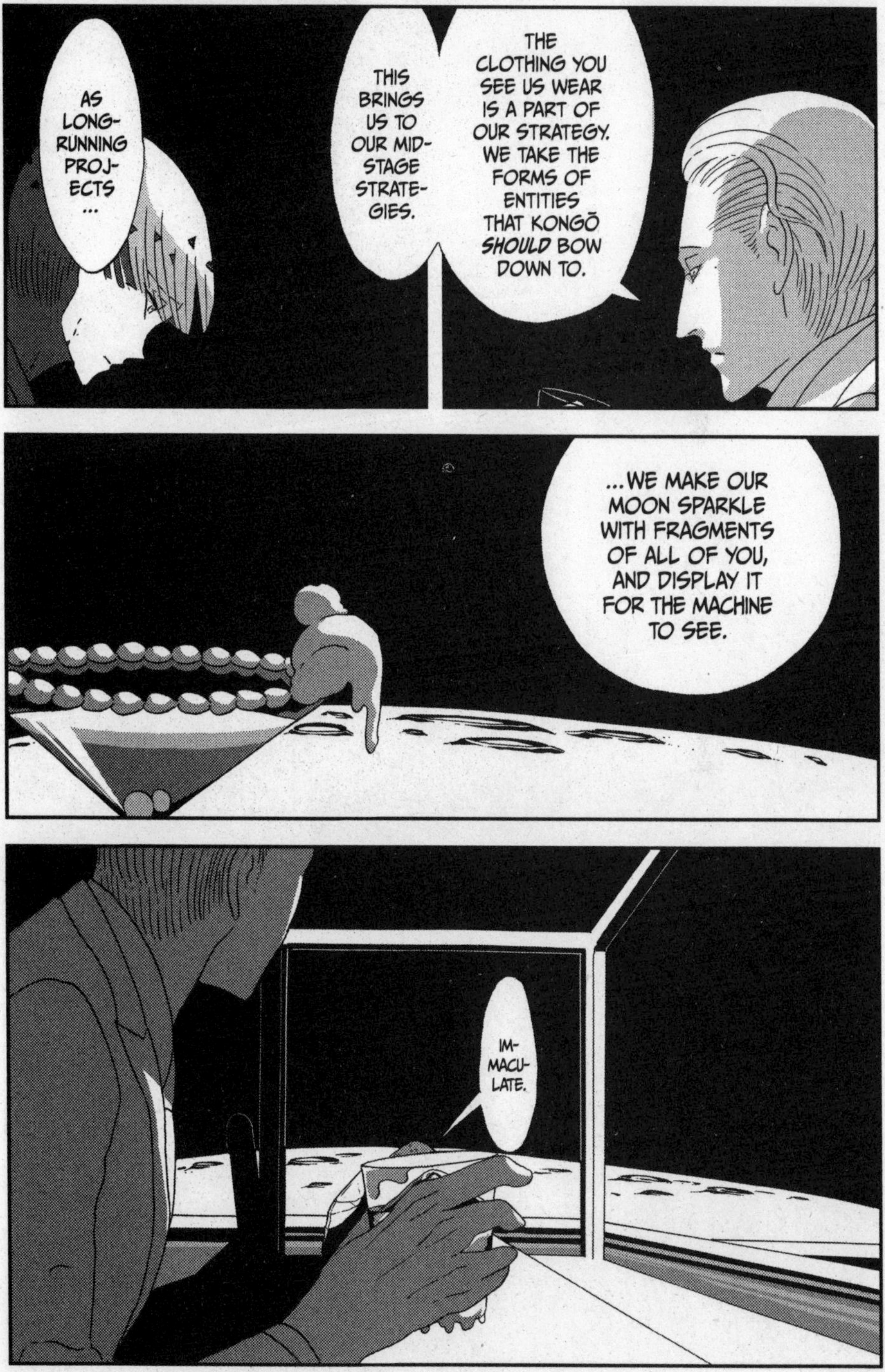
THE CLOTHING YOU SEE US WEAR IS A PART OF OUR STRATEGY. WE TAKE THE FORMS OF ENTITIES THAT KONGŌ *SHOULD* BOW DOWN TO.
THIS BRINGS US TO OUR MID-STAGE STRATEGIES.
AS LONG-RUNNING PROJECTS...
...WE MAKE OUR MOON SPARKLE WITH FRAGMENTS OF ALL OF YOU, AND DISPLAY IT FOR THE MACHINE TO SEE.
IMMACULATE.

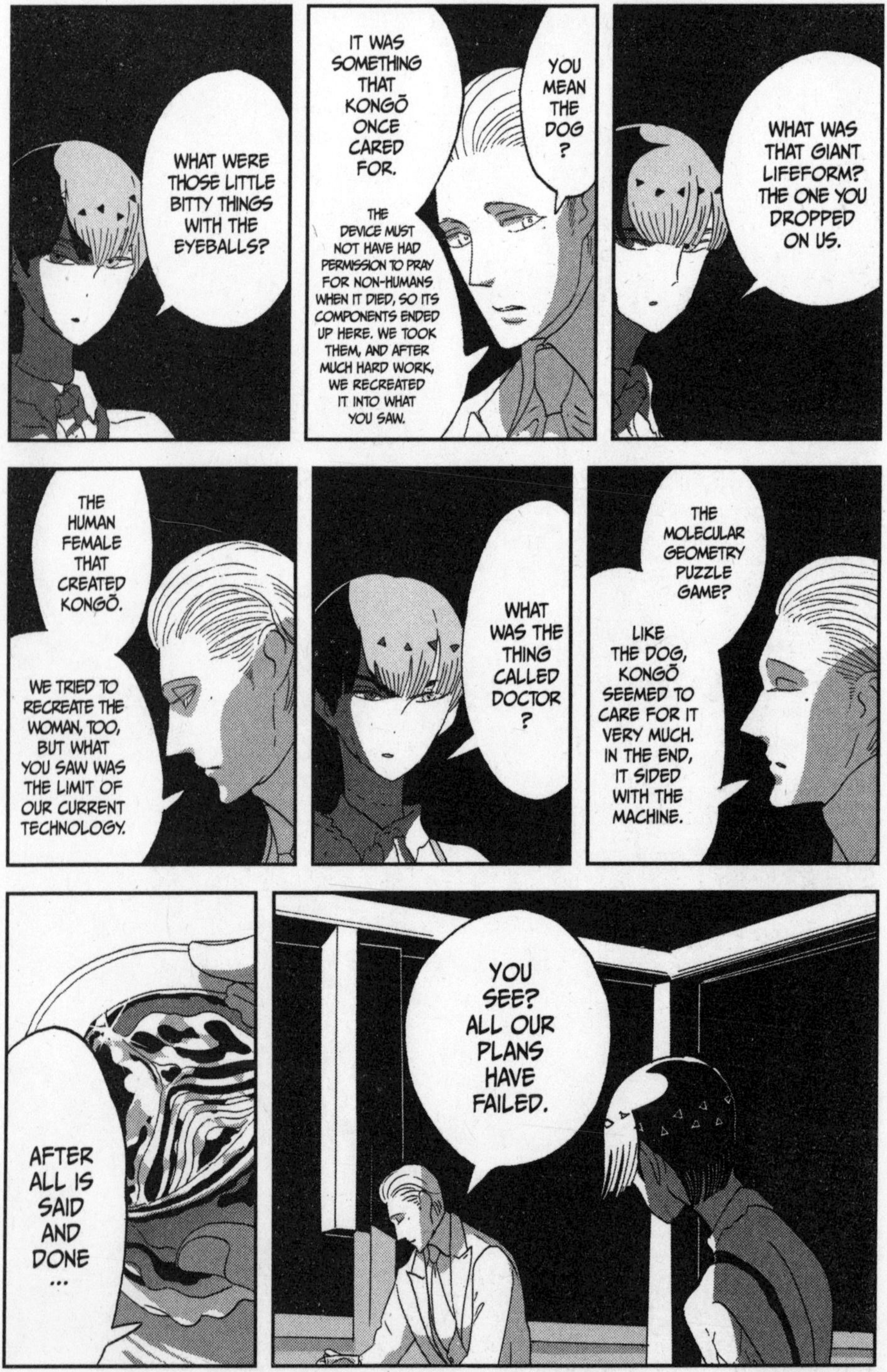
WHAT WAS THAT GIANT LIFEFORM? THE ONE YOU DROPPED ON US.
YOU MEAN THE DOG?
IT WAS SOMETHING THAT KONGŌ ONCE CARED FOR.
THE DEVICE MUST NOT HAVE HAD PERMISSION TO PRAY FOR NON-HUMANS WHEN IT DIED, SO ITS COMPONENTS ENDED UP HERE. WE TOOK THEM, AND AFTER MUCH HARD WORK, WE RECREATED IT INTO WHAT YOU SAW.
WHAT WERE THOSE LITTLE BITTY THINGS WITH THE EYEBALLS?
THE MOLECULAR GEOMETRY PUZZLE GAME?
LIKE THE DOG, KONGŌ SEEMED TO CARE FOR IT VERY MUCH. IN THE END, IT SIDED WITH THE MACHINE.
WHAT WAS THE THING CALLED DOCTOR?
THE HUMAN FEMALE THAT CREATED KONGŌ.
WE TRIED TO RECREATE THE WOMAN, TOO, BUT WHAT YOU SAW WAS THE LIMIT OF OUR CURRENT TECHNOLOGY.
YOU SEE? ALL OUR PLANS HAVE FAILED.
AFTER ALL IS SAID AND DONE ...

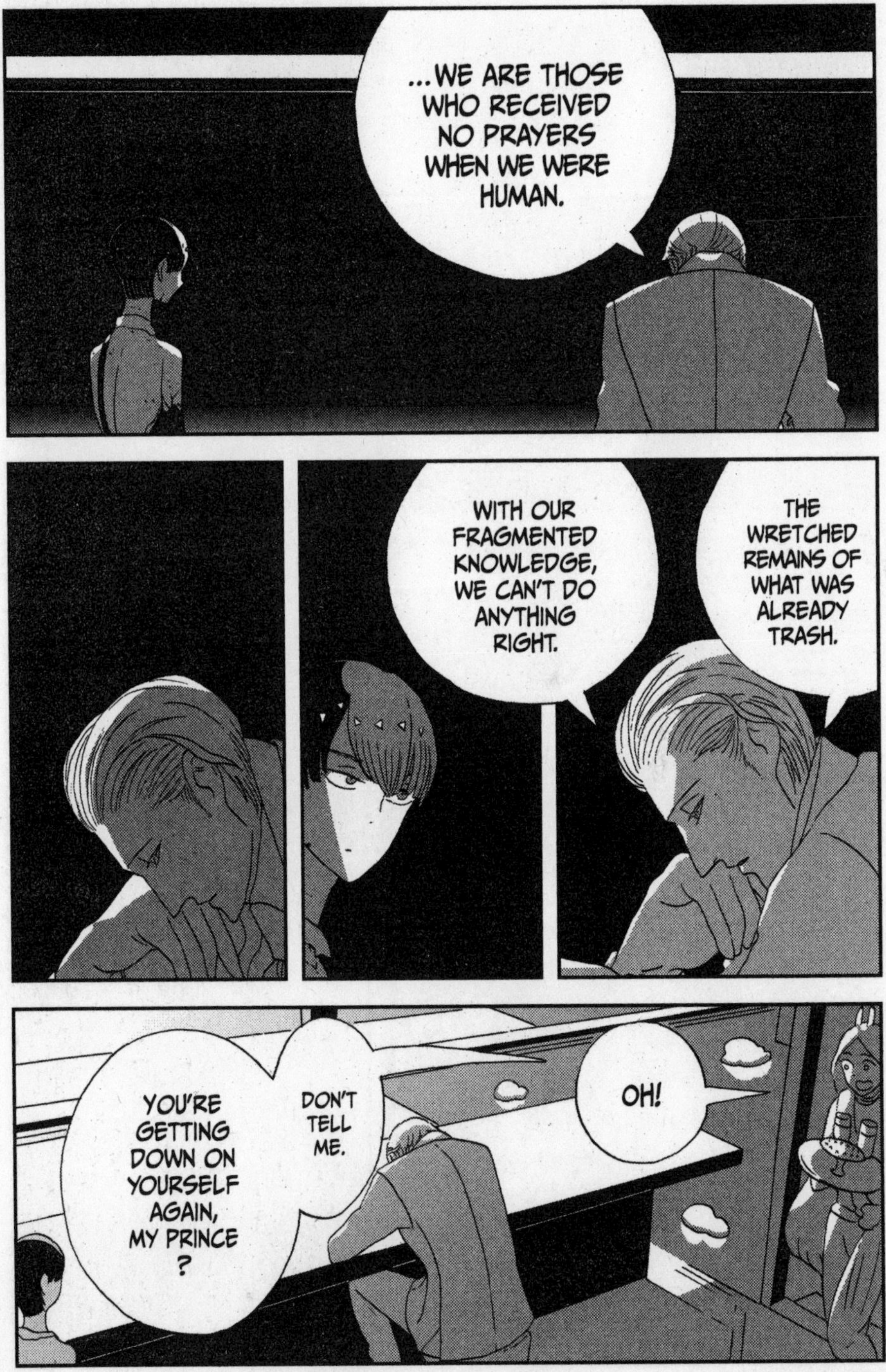
...WE ARE THOSE WHO RECEIVED NO PRAYERS WHEN WE WERE HUMAN.
THE WRETCHED REMAINS OF WHAT WAS ALREADY TRASH.
WITH OUR FRAGMENTED KNOWLEDGE, WE CAN'T DO ANYTHING RIGHT.
OH!
DON'T TELL ME.
YOU'RE GETTING DOWN ON YOURSELF AGAIN, MY PRINCE?

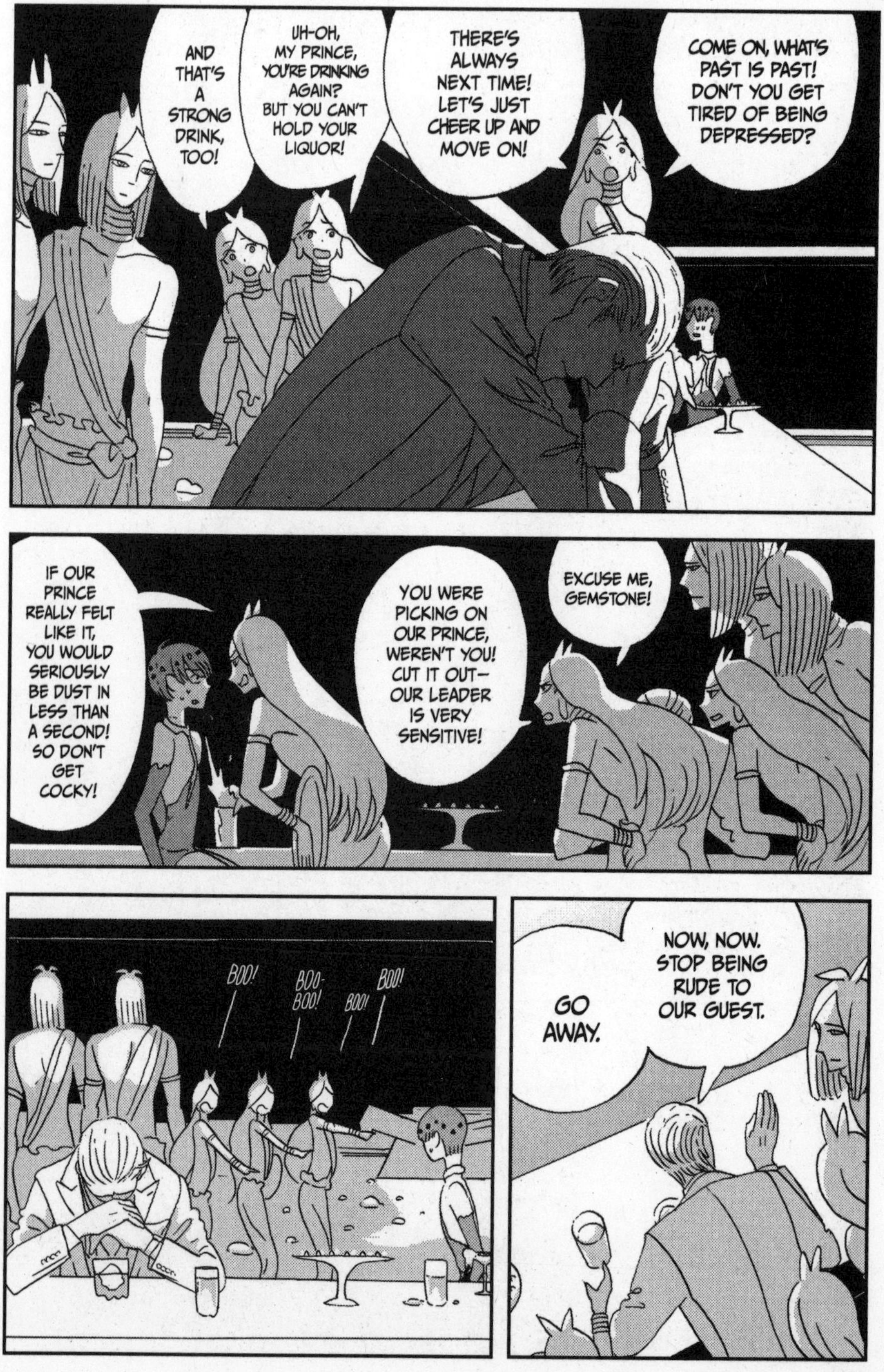
COME ON, WHAT'S PAST IS PAST! DON'T YOU GET TIRED OF BEING DEPRESSED?
THERE'S ALWAYS NEXT TIME! LET'S JUST CHEER UP AND MOVE ON!
UH-OH, MY PRINCE, YOU'RE DRINKING AGAIN? BUT YOU CAN'T HOLD YOUR LIQUOR!
AND THAT'S A STRONG DRINK, TOO!
EXCUSE ME, GEMSTONE!
YOU WERE PICKING ON OUR PRINCE, WEREN'T YOU! CUT IT OUT— OUR LEADER IS VERY SENSITIVE!
IF OUR PRINCE REALLY FELT LIKE IT, YOU WOULD SERIOUSLY BE DUST IN LESS THAN A SECOND! SO DON'T GET COCKY!
NOW, NOW. STOP BEING RUDE TO OUR GUEST.
GO AWAY.
BOO!
BOO!
BOO-BOO!
BOO!

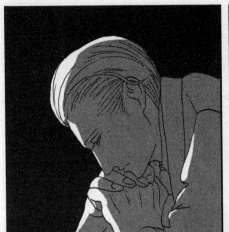

...DO YOU WANT TO BE NOTHING?

WHY...

WHY?

YES.

ARE THINGS SO BAD THE WAY THEY ARE?

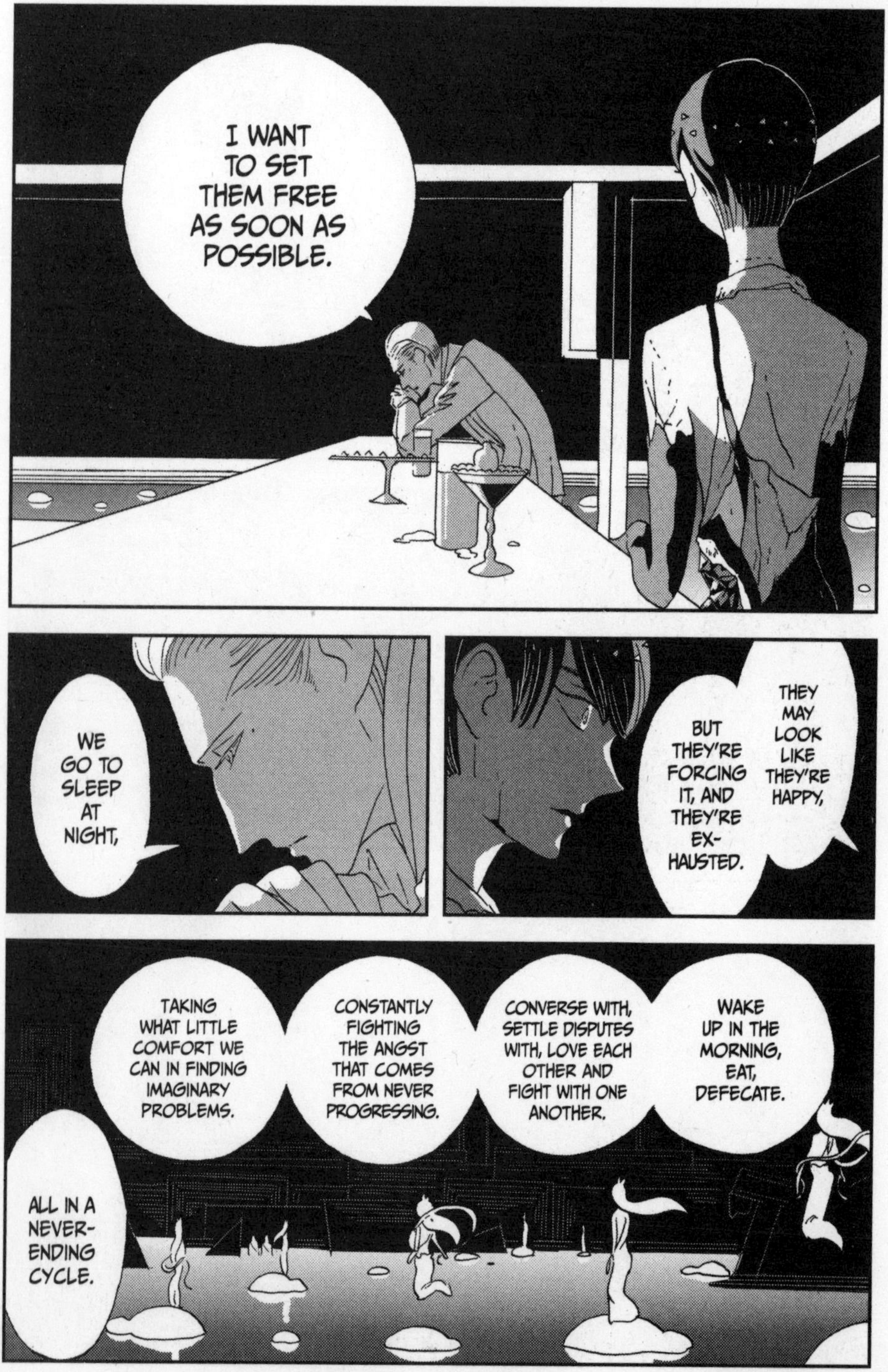
I WANT TO SET THEM FREE AS SOON AS POSSIBLE.
THEY MAY LOOK LIKE THEY'RE HAPPY,
BUT THEY'RE FORCING IT, AND THEY'RE EX-HAUSTED.
WE GO TO SLEEP AT NIGHT,
WAKE UP IN THE MORNING, EAT, DEFECATE.
CONVERSE WITH, SETTLE DISPUTES WITH, LOVE EACH OTHER AND FIGHT WITH ONE ANOTHER.
CONSTANTLY FIGHTING THE ANGST THAT COMES FROM NEVER PROGRESSING.
TAKING WHAT LITTLE COMFORT WE CAN IN FINDING IMAGINARY PROBLEMS.
ALL IN A NEVER-ENDING CYCLE.

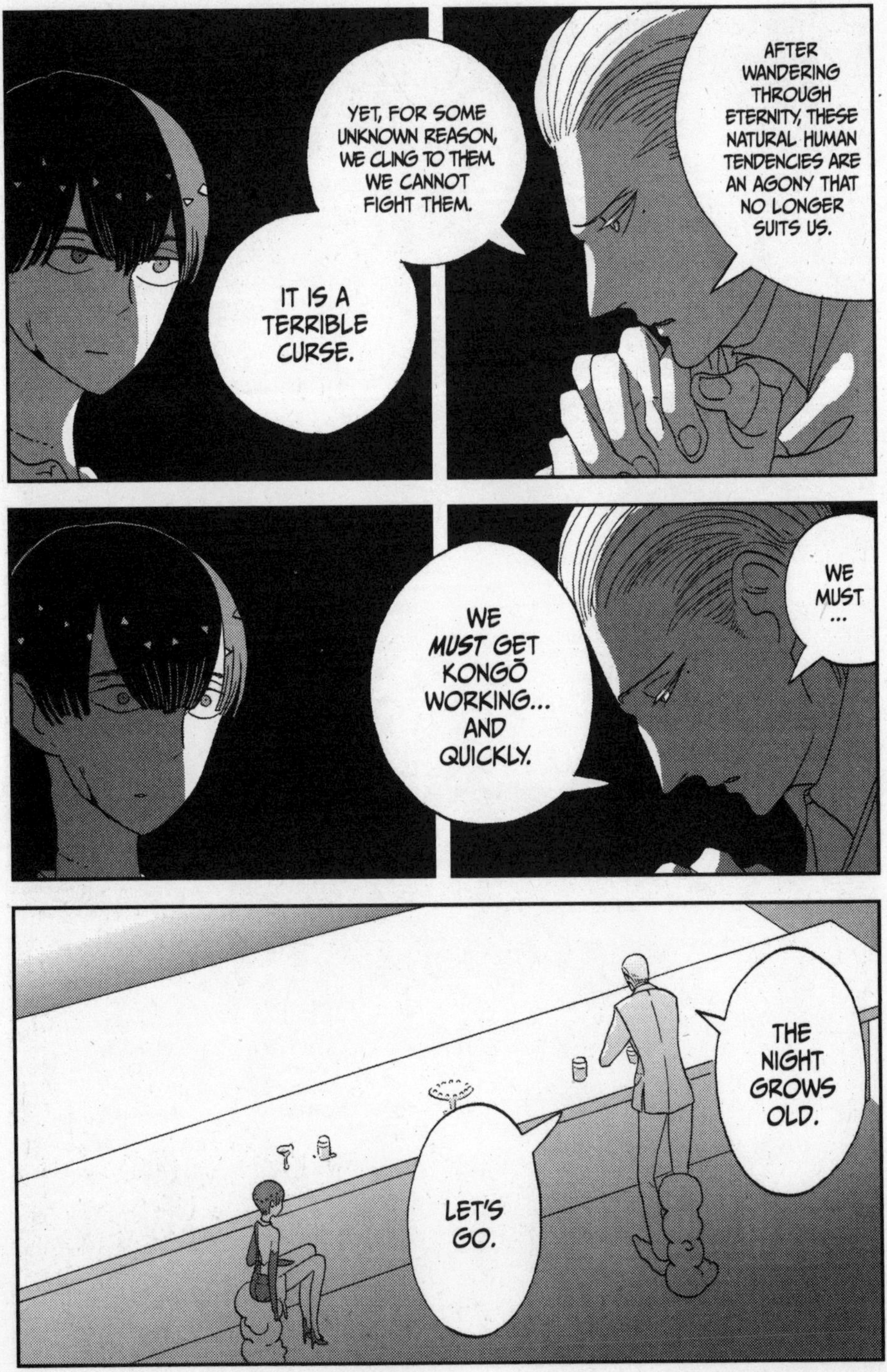
AFTER WANDERING THROUGH ETERNITY, THESE NATURAL HUMAN TENDENCIES ARE AN AGONY THAT NO LONGER SUITS US.
YET, FOR SOME UNKNOWN REASON, WE CLING TO THEM. WE CANNOT FIGHT THEM.
IT IS A TERRIBLE CURSE.
WE MUST ...
WE *MUST* GET KONGŌ WORKING... AND QUICKLY.
THE NIGHT GROWS OLD.
LET'S GO.

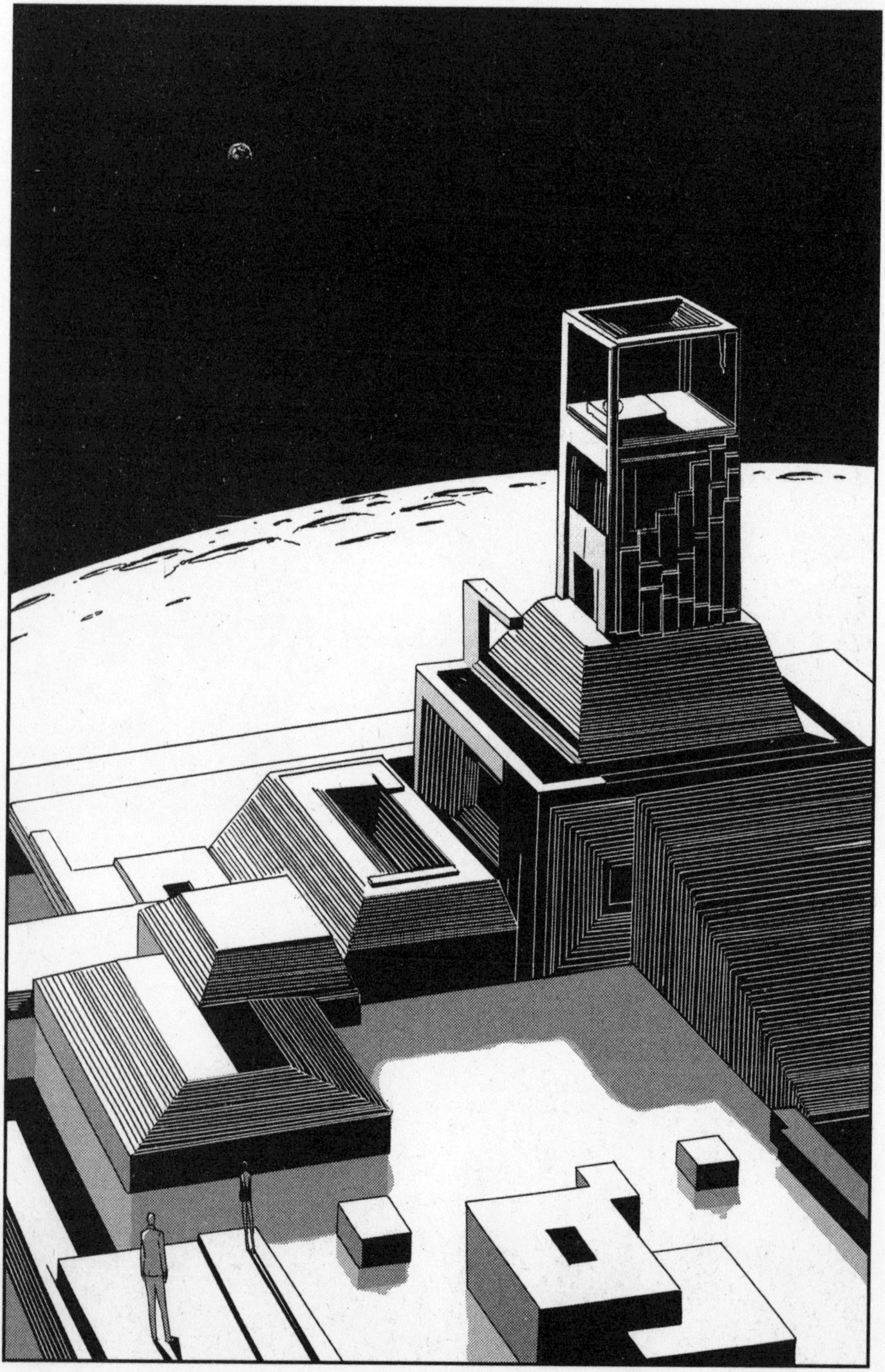

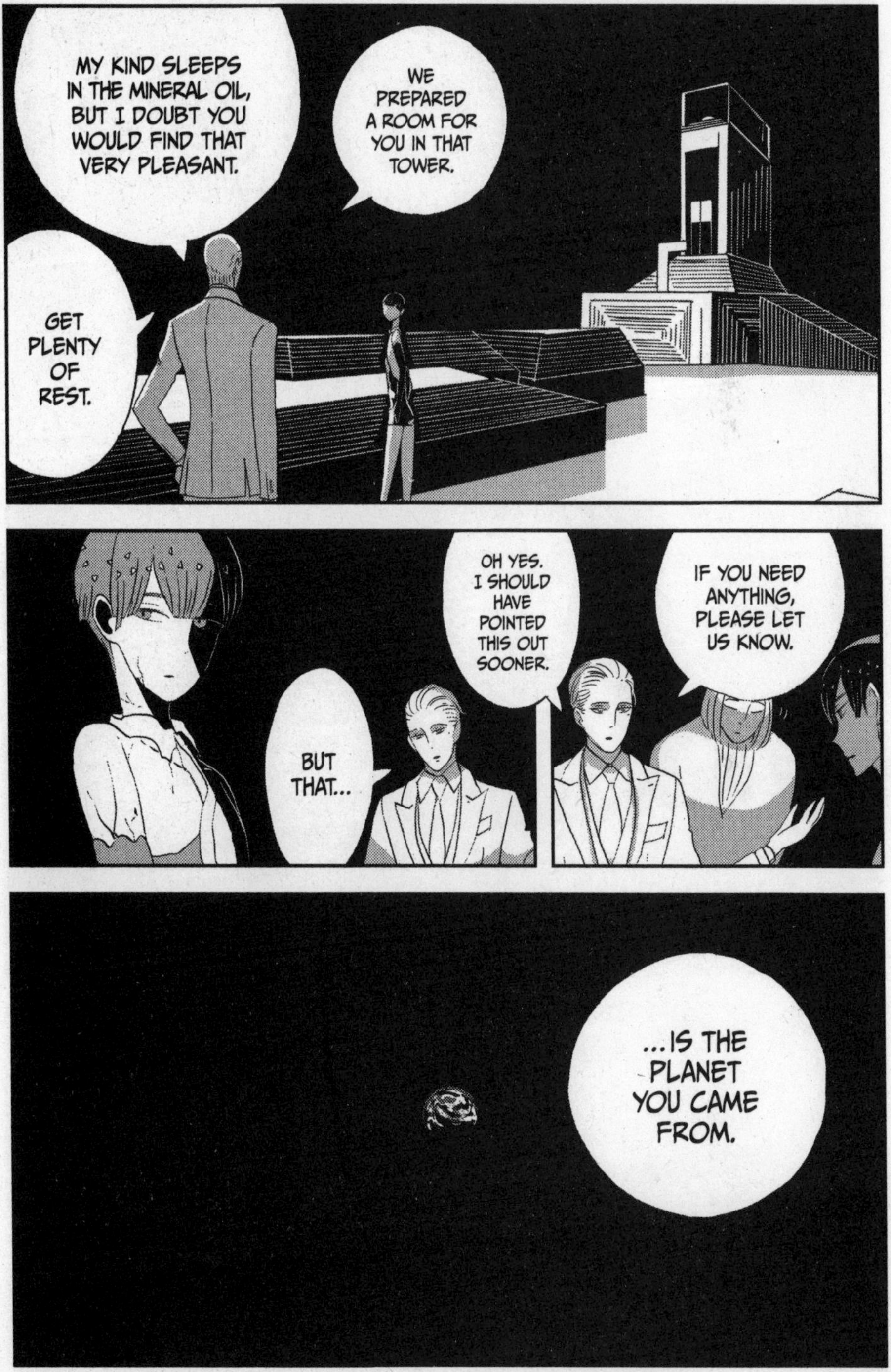
MY KIND SLEEPS IN THE MINERAL OIL, BUT I DOUBT YOU WOULD FIND THAT VERY PLEASANT.
WE PREPARED A ROOM FOR YOU IN THAT TOWER.
GET PLENTY OF REST.
IF YOU NEED ANYTHING, PLEASE LET US KNOW.
OH YES. I SHOULD HAVE POINTED THIS OUT SOONER.
BUT THAT...
...IS THE PLANET YOU CAME FROM.

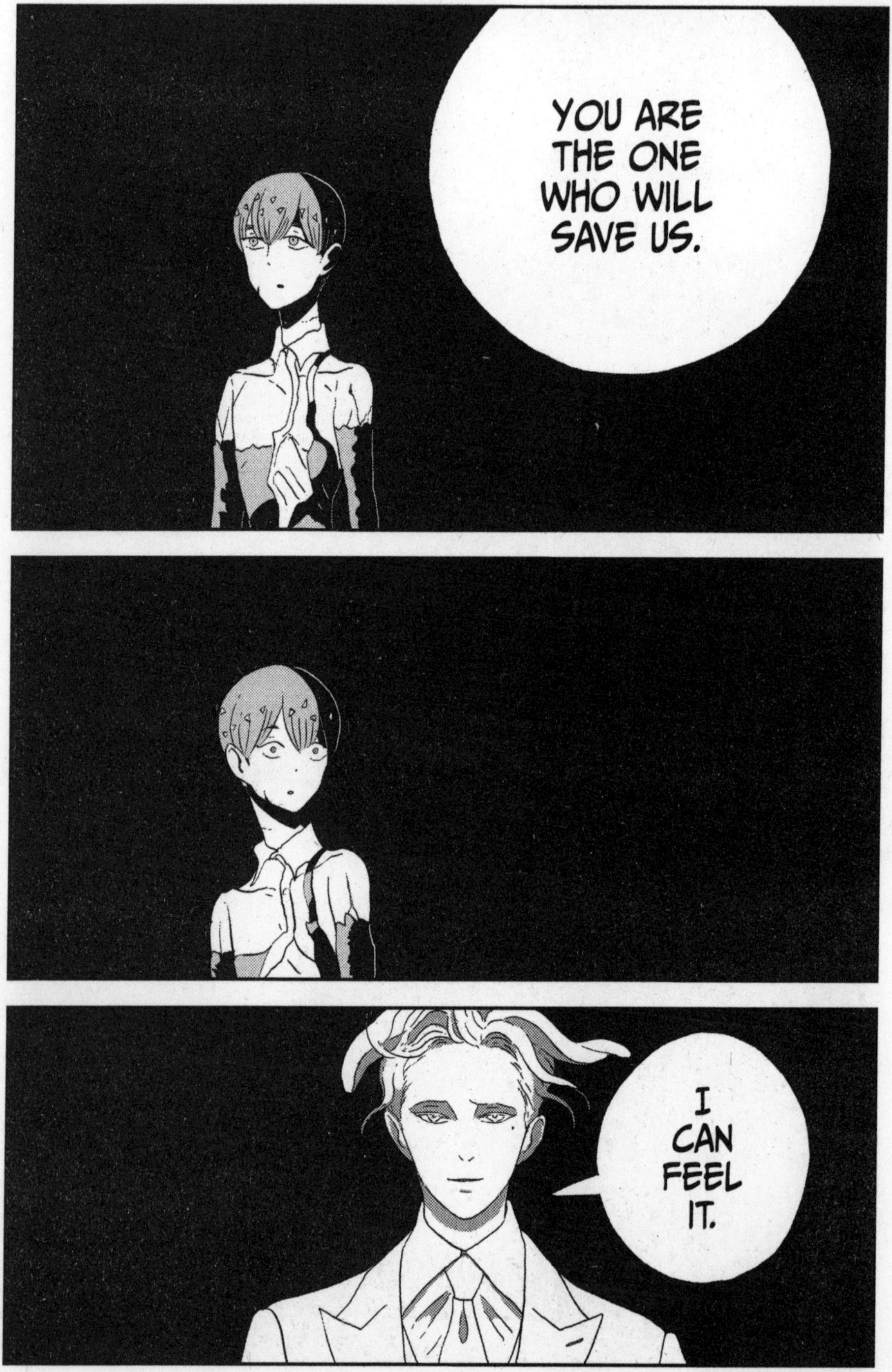
YOU ARE THE ONE WHO WILL SAVE US.
I CAN FEEL IT.

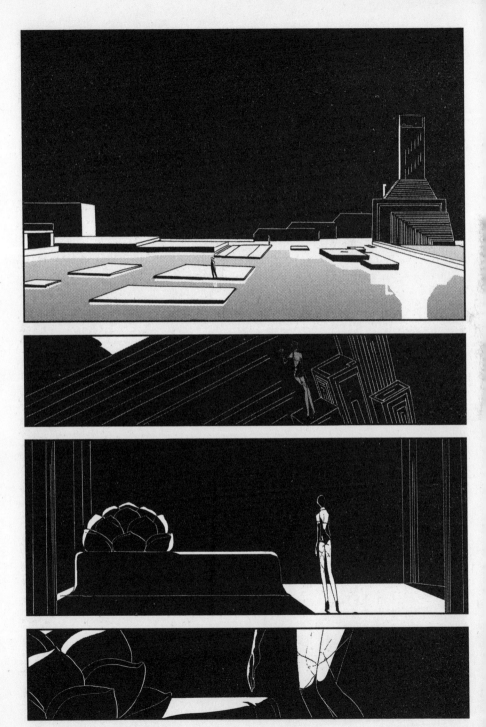

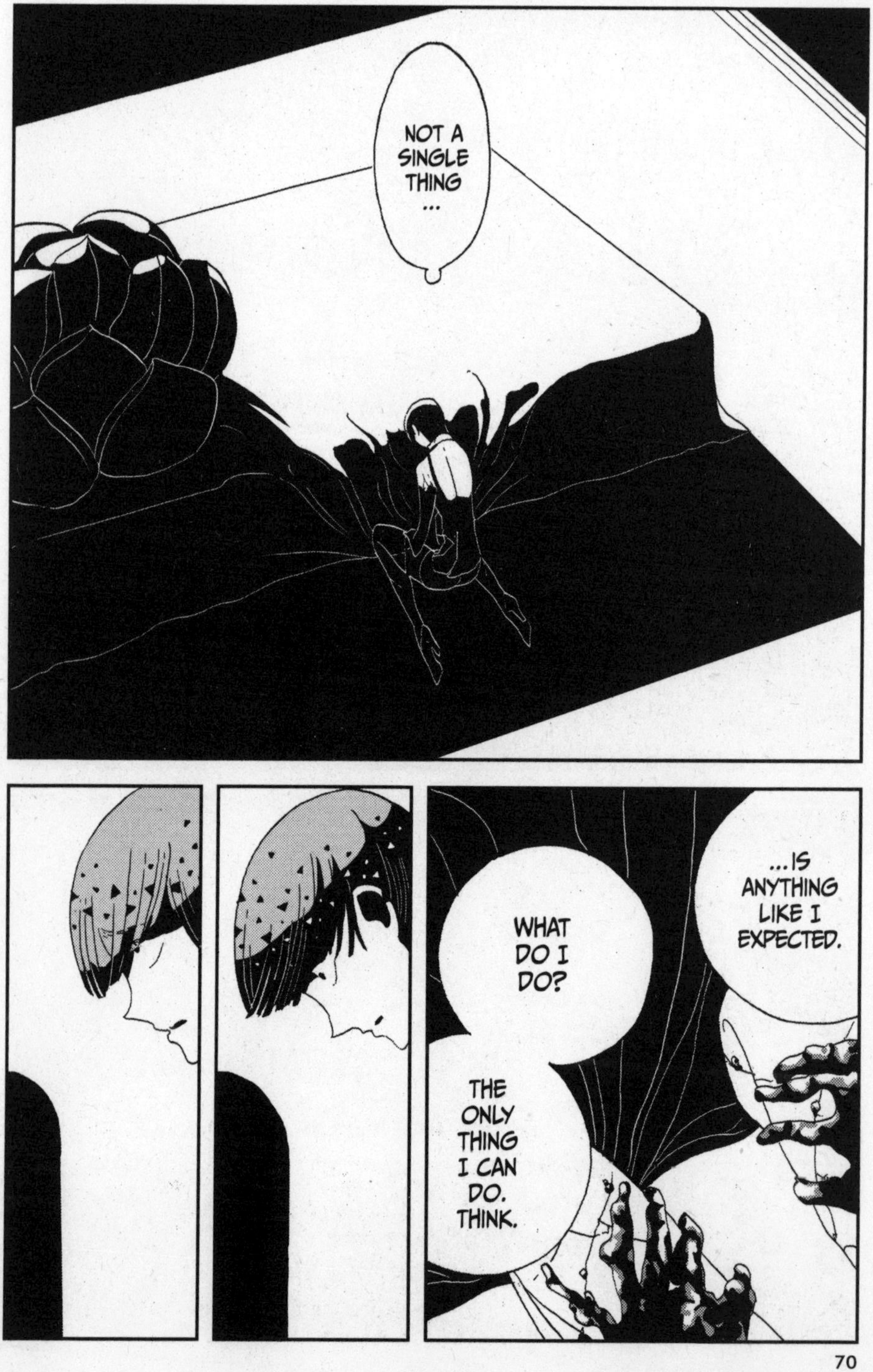
NOT A SINGLE THING ...
...IS ANYTHING LIKE I EXPECTED.
WHAT DO I DO?
THE ONLY THING I CAN DO. THINK.

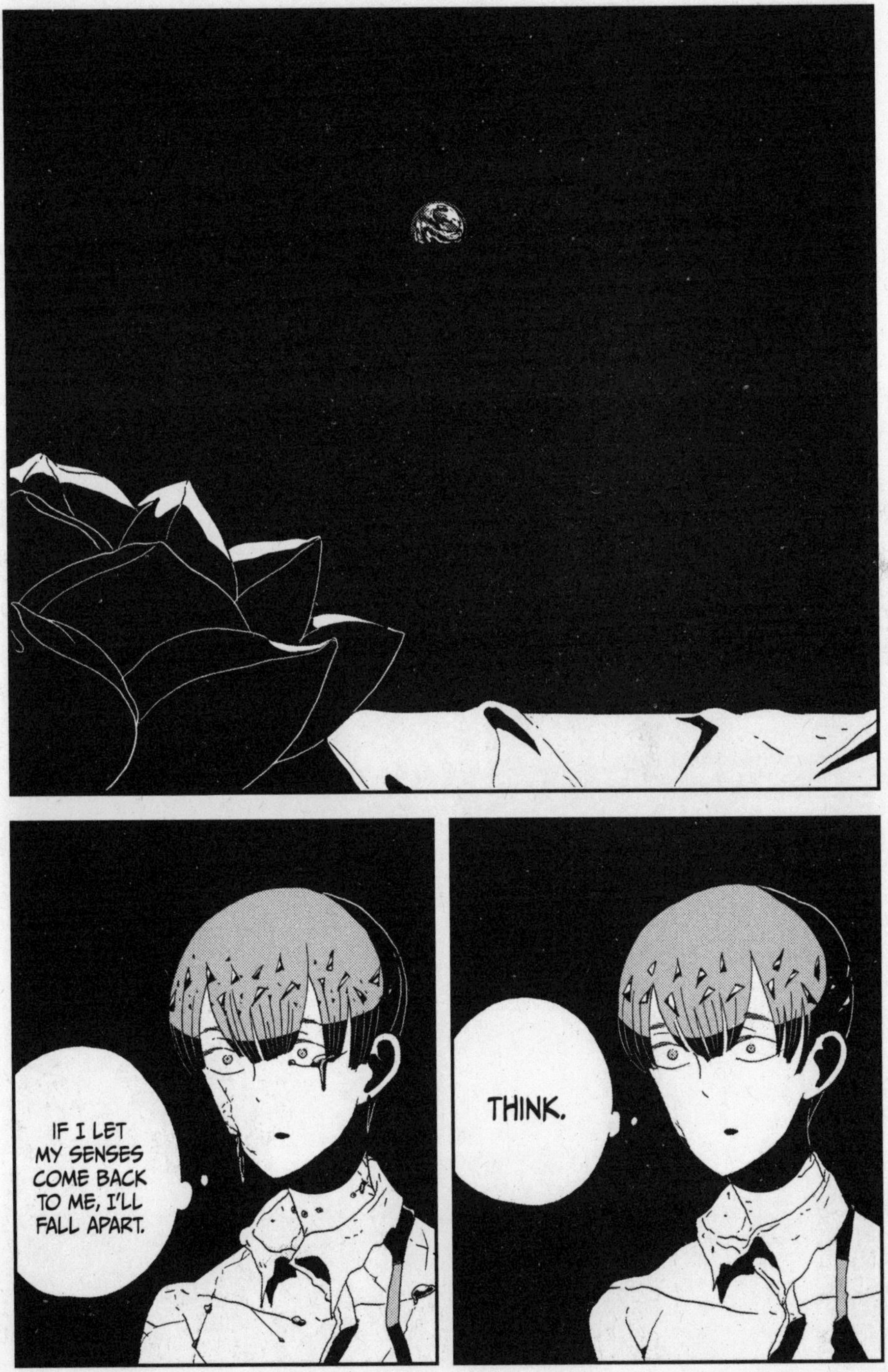
THINK.
IF I LET MY SENSES COME BACK TO ME, I'LL FALL APART.

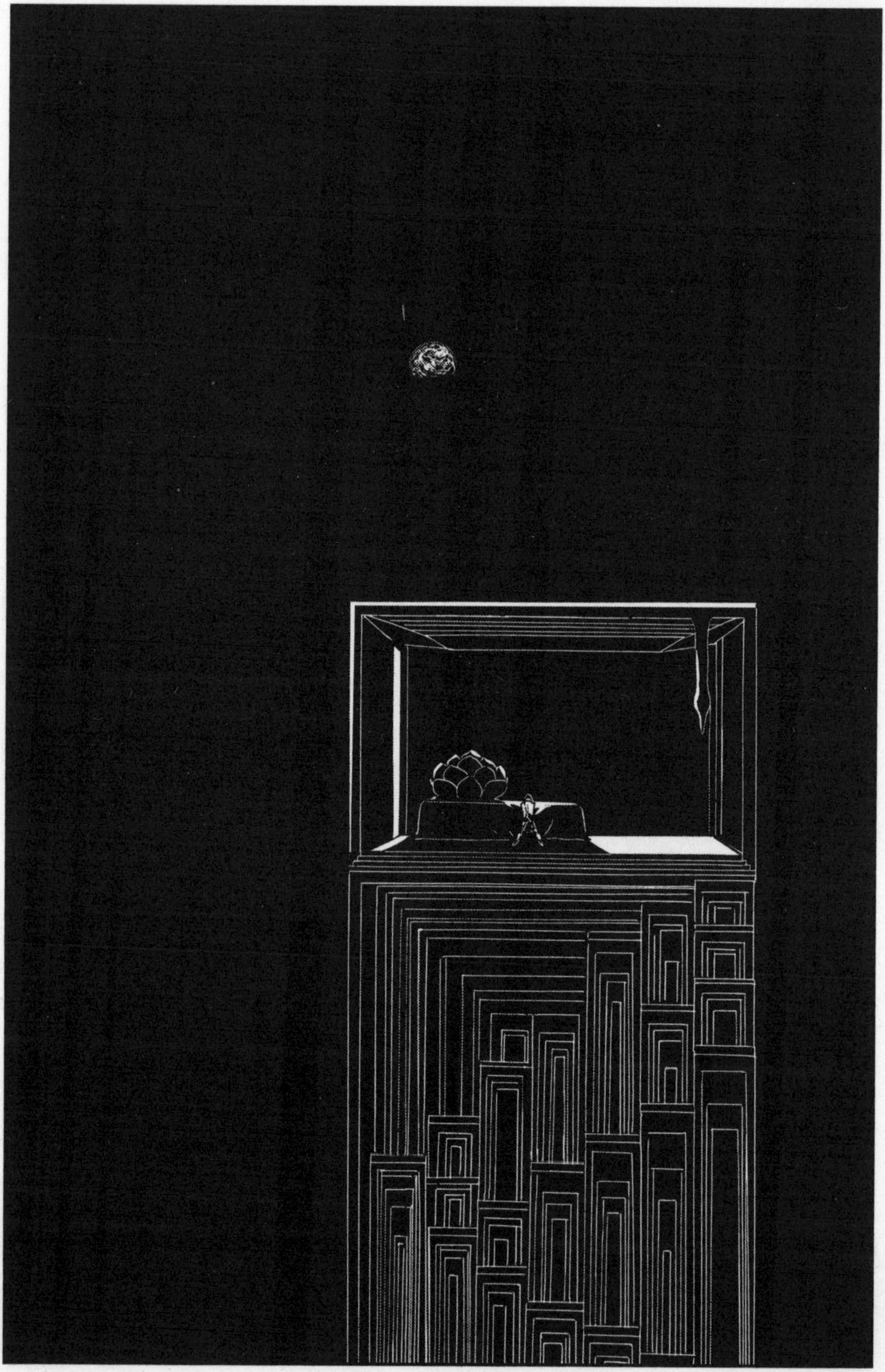

CHAPTER 55: Curse END

CHAPTER 56:

Synthetic Pearl

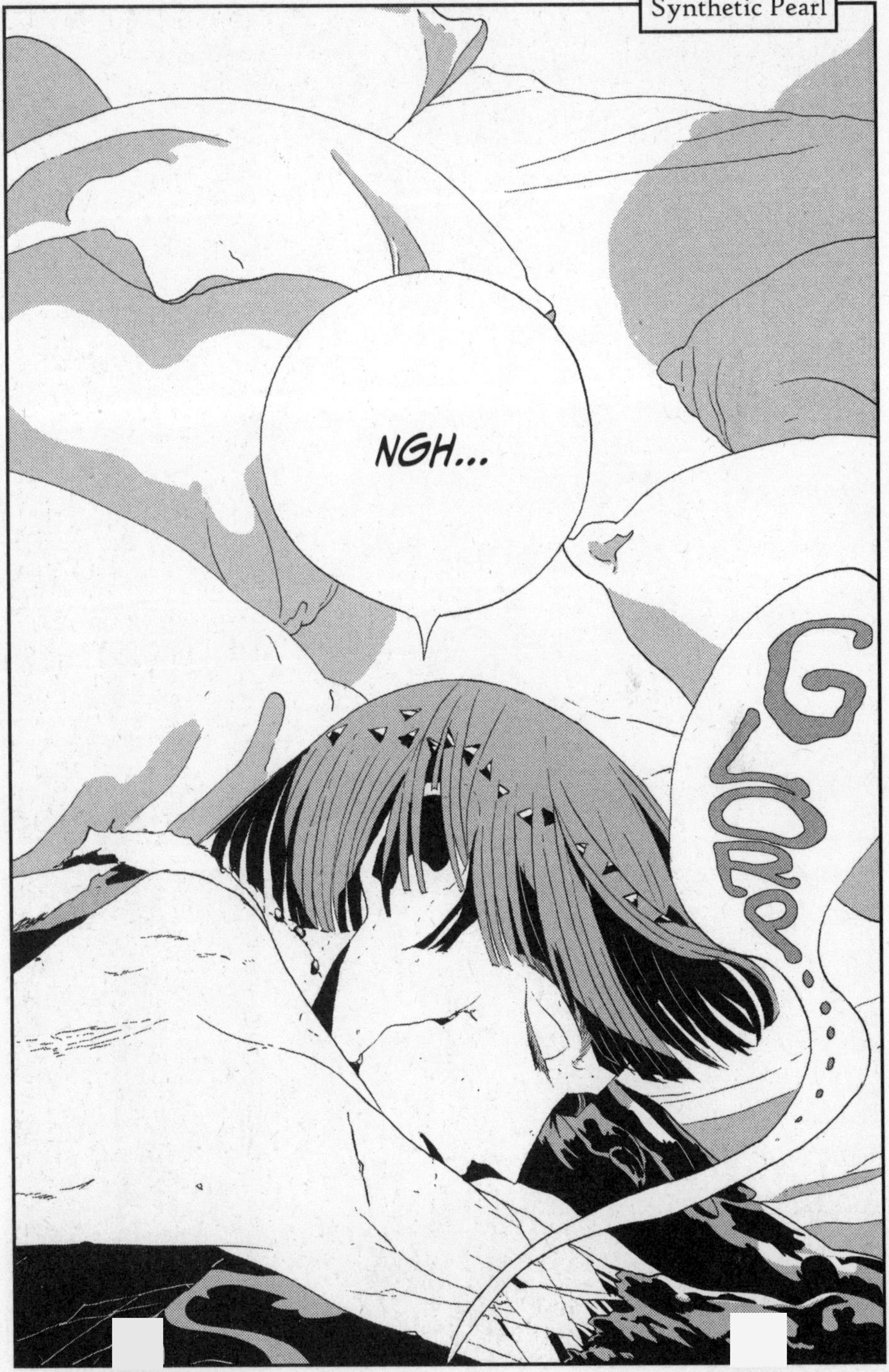
NGH...
GLORP......

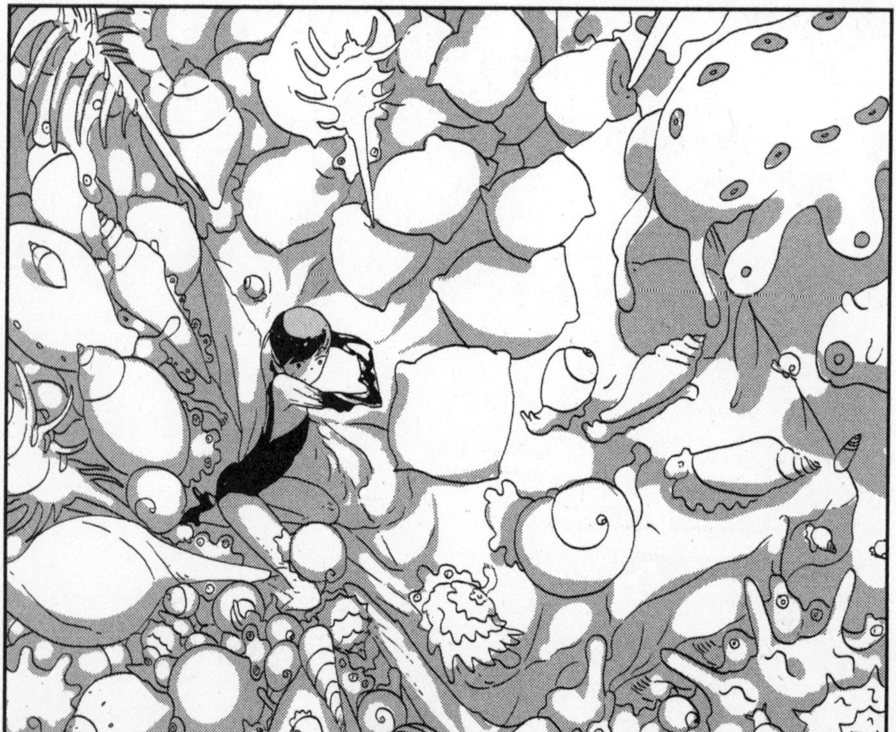

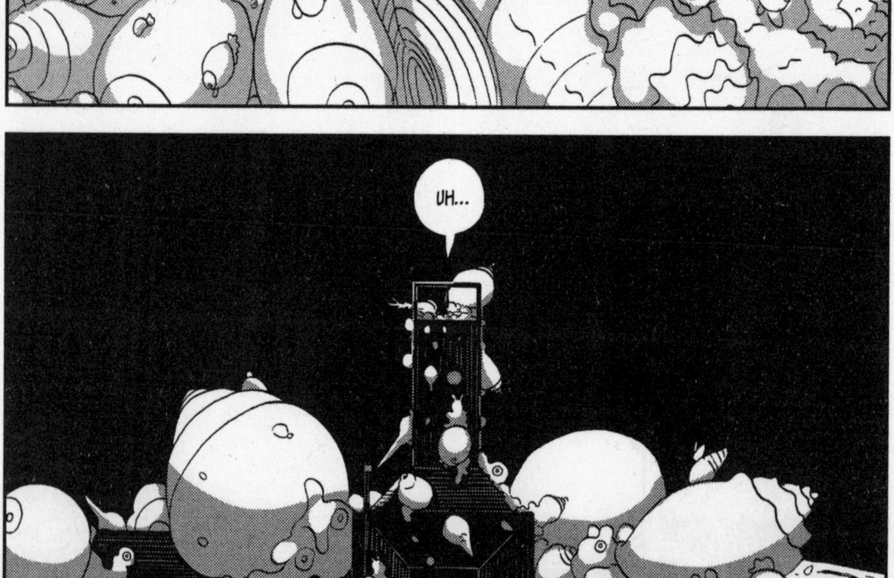
UH...

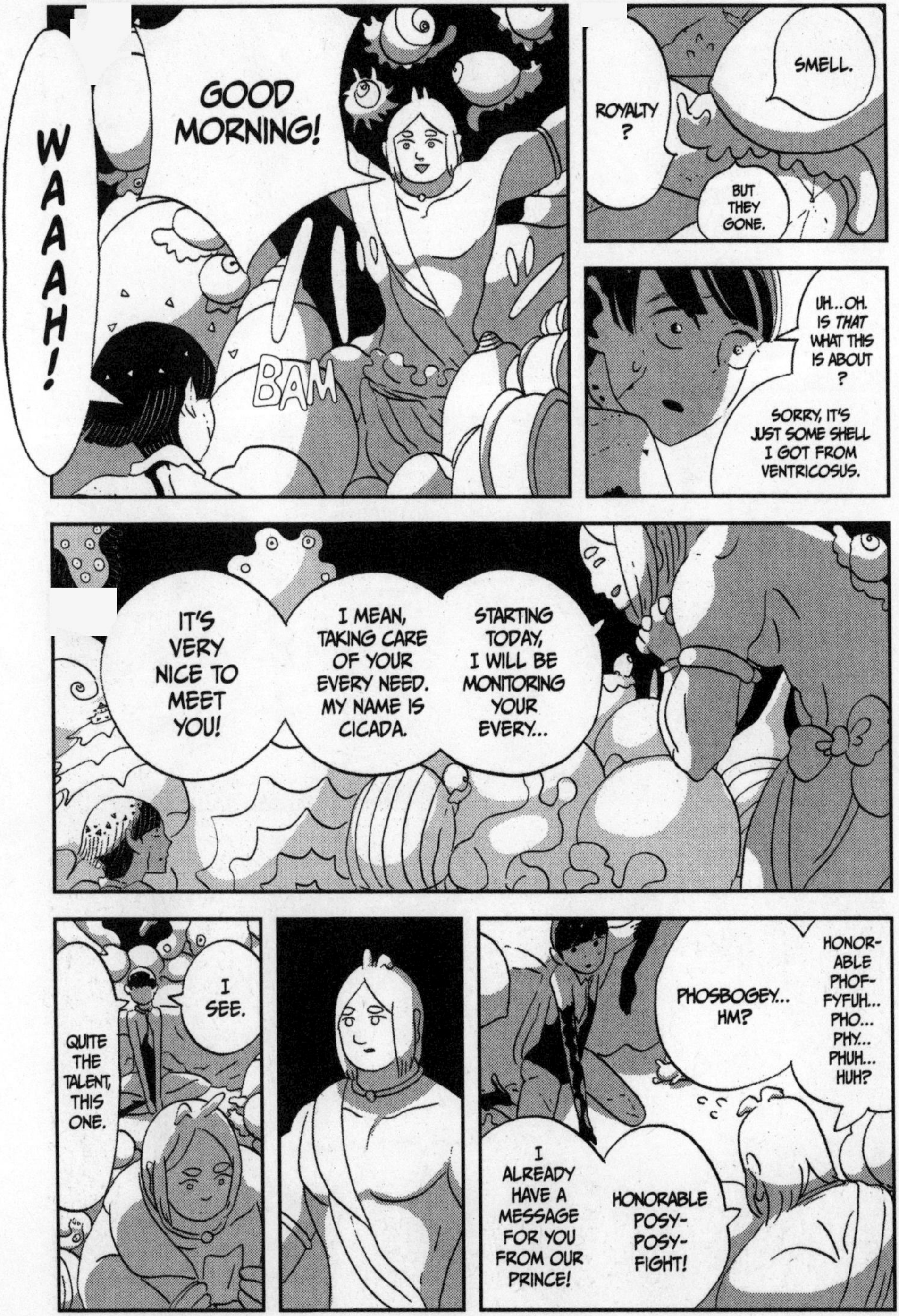
SMELL.
ROYALTY ?
BUT THEY GONE.
UH...OH. IS *THAT* WHAT THIS IS ABOUT ?
SORRY, IT'S JUST SOME SHELL I GOT FROM VENTRICOSUS.
GOOD MORNING!
WAAAAH!
BAM
STARTING TODAY, I WILL BE MONITORING YOUR EVERY...
I MEAN, TAKING CARE OF YOUR EVERY NEED. MY NAME IS CICADA.
IT'S VERY NICE TO MEET YOU!
HONOR-ABLE PHOF-FYFUH... PHO... PHY... PHUH... HUH?
PHOSBOGEY... HM?
HONORABLE POSY-POSY-FIGHT!
I ALREADY HAVE A MESSAGE FOR YOU FROM OUR PRINCE!
I SEE.
QUITE THE TALENT, THIS ONE.

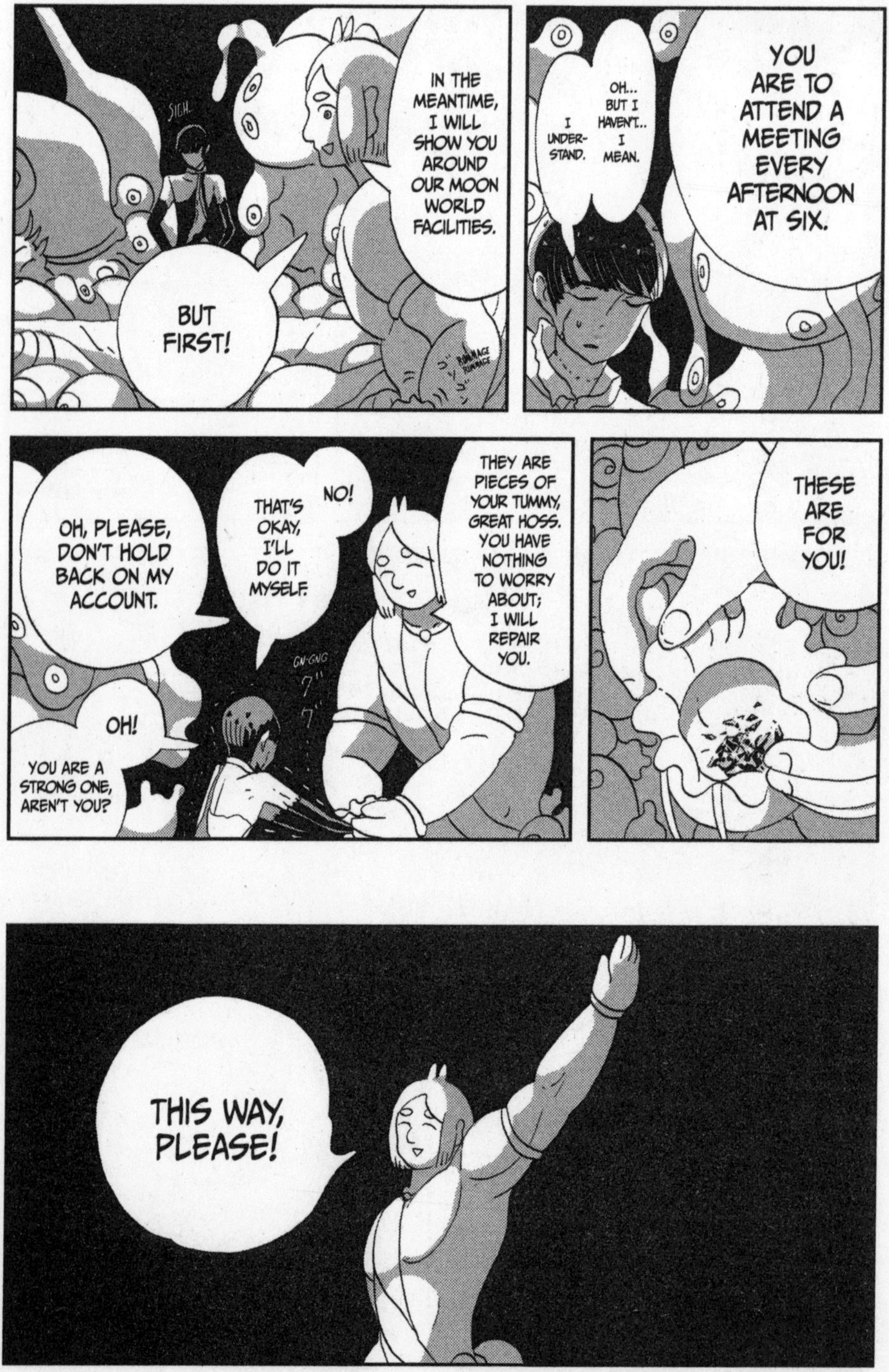
YOU ARE TO ATTEND A MEETING EVERY AFTERNOON AT SIX.
OH... BUT I HAVEN'T.. I MEAN.
I UNDER-STAND.
IN THE MEANTIME, I WILL SHOW YOU AROUND OUR MOON WORLD FACILITIES.
SIGH.
BUT FIRST!
RUMMAGE RUMMAGE
THESE ARE FOR YOU!
THEY ARE PIECES OF YOUR TUMMY, GREAT HOSS. YOU HAVE NOTHING TO WORRY ABOUT; I WILL REPAIR YOU.
NO!
THAT'S OKAY, I'LL DO IT MYSELF.
OH, PLEASE, DON'T HOLD BACK ON MY ACCOUNT.
GN-GNG
OH!
YOU ARE A STRONG ONE, AREN'T YOU?
THIS WAY, PLEASE!

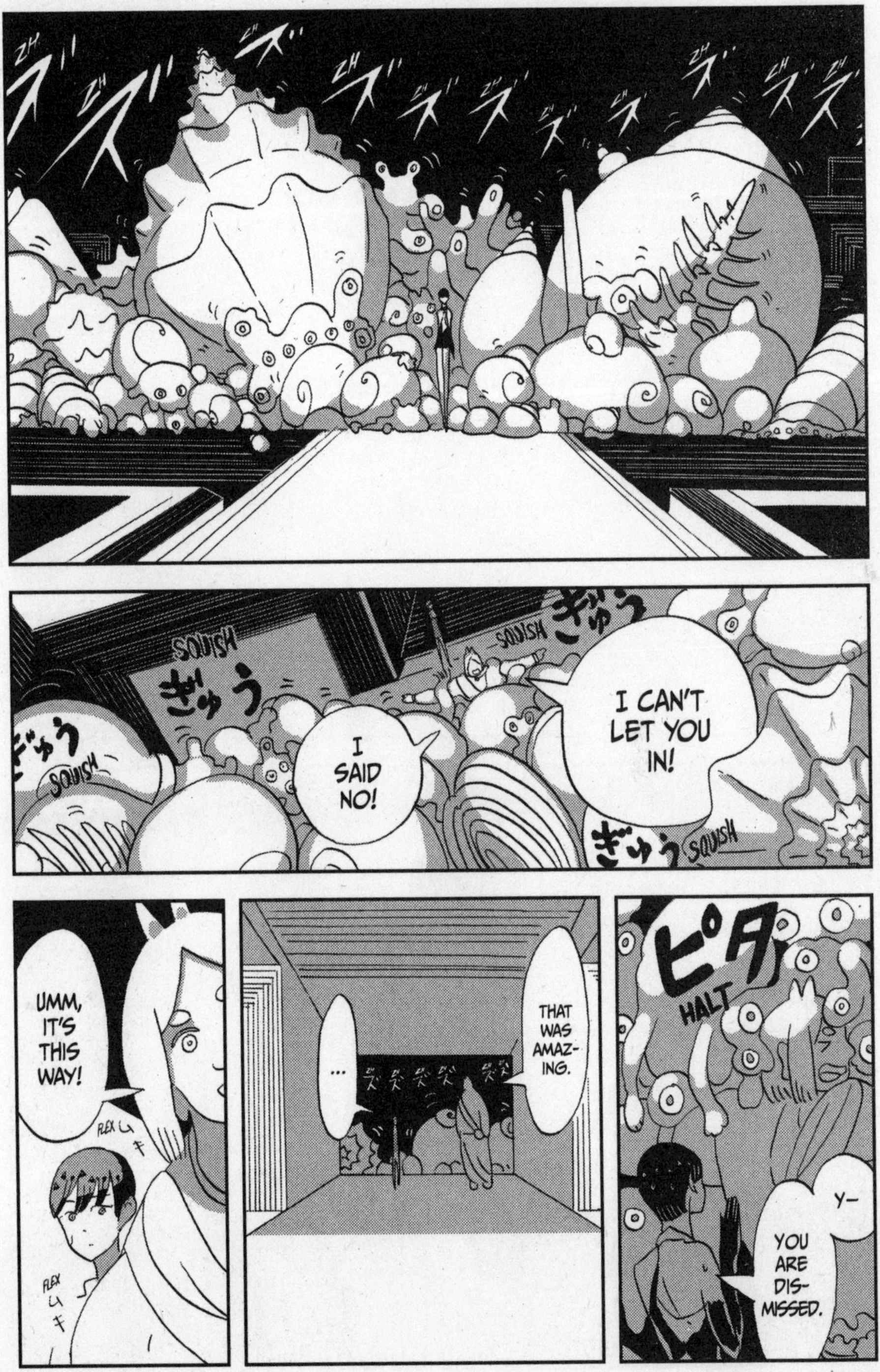
ZH ズ
SQUISH ぎゅう
I CAN'T LET YOU IN!
I SAID NO!
SQUISH ぎゅう
SQUISH ぎゅう
SQUISH ぎゅう
ピタ HALT
Y—
YOU ARE DIS-MISSED.
THAT WAS AMAZ-ING.
...
UMM, IT'S THIS WAY!
FLEX ムキ
FLEX ムキ

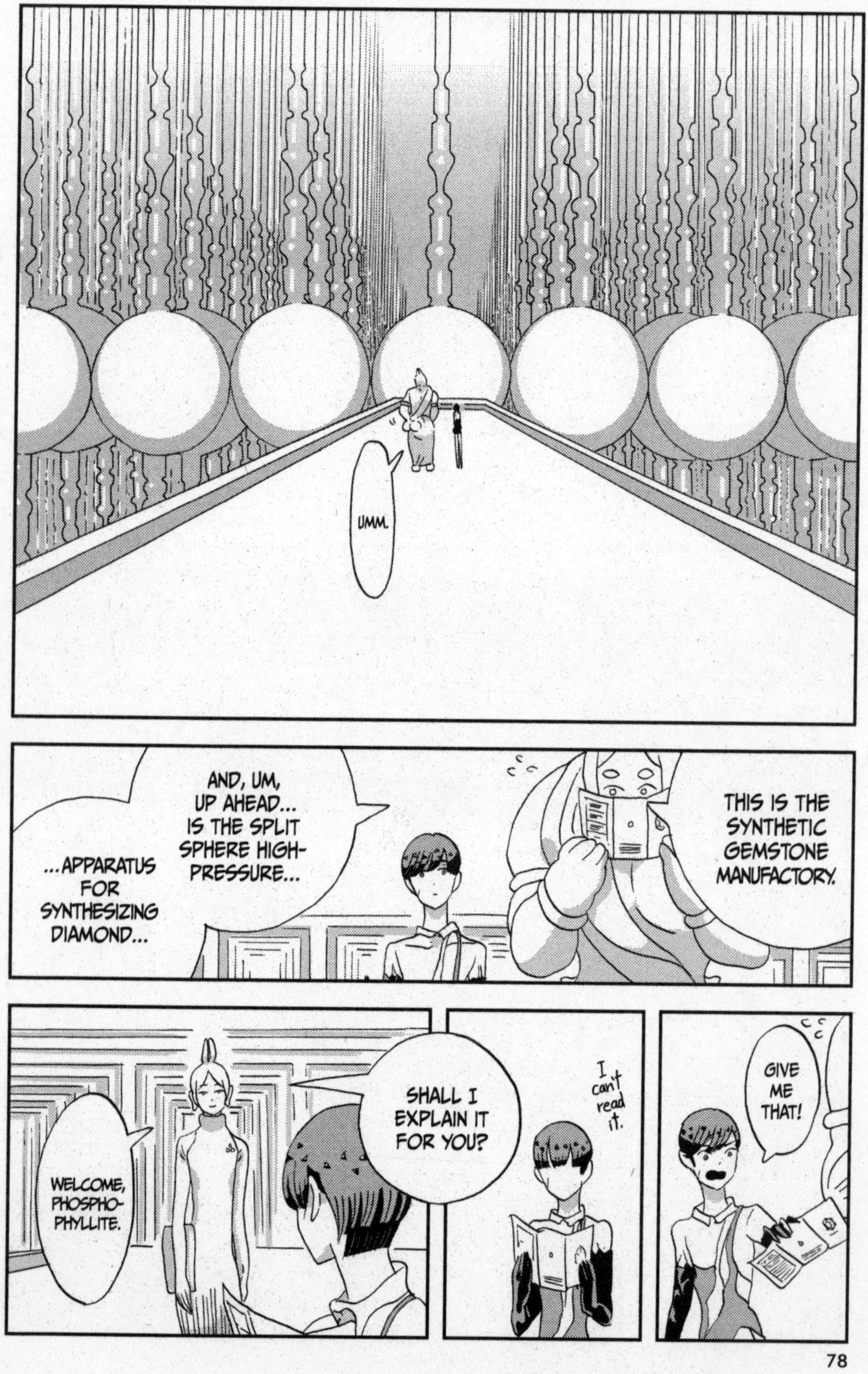
UMM.
THIS IS THE SYNTHETIC GEMSTONE MANUFACTORY.
AND, UM, UP AHEAD... IS THE SPLIT SPHERE HIGH-PRESSURE...
...APPARATUS FOR SYNTHESIZING DIAMOND...
GIVE ME THAT!
I can't read it.
SHALL I EXPLAIN IT FOR YOU?
WELCOME, PHOSPHO-PHYLLITE.

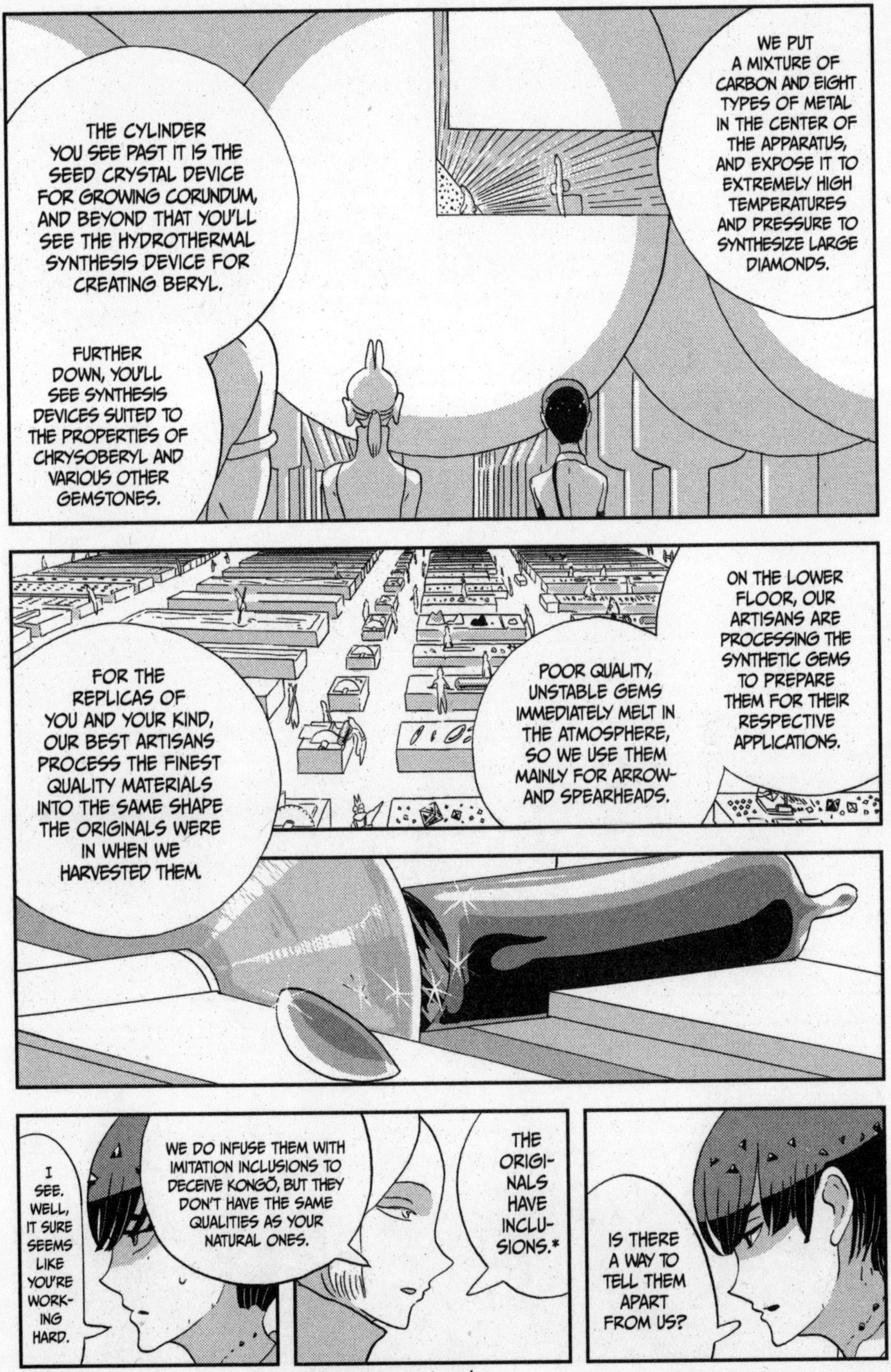

WE PUT A MIXTURE OF CARBON AND EIGHT TYPES OF METAL IN THE CENTER OF THE APPARATUS, AND EXPOSE IT TO EXTREMELY HIGH TEMPERATURES AND PRESSURE TO SYNTHESIZE LARGE DIAMONDS.
THE CYLINDER YOU SEE PAST IT IS THE SEED CRYSTAL DEVICE FOR GROWING CORUNDUM, AND BEYOND THAT YOU'LL SEE THE HYDROTHERMAL SYNTHESIS DEVICE FOR CREATING BERYL.
FURTHER DOWN, YOU'LL SEE SYNTHESIS DEVICES SUITED TO THE PROPERTIES OF CHRYSOBERYL AND VARIOUS OTHER GEMSTONES.
ON THE LOWER FLOOR, OUR ARTISANS ARE PROCESSING THE SYNTHETIC GEMS TO PREPARE THEM FOR THEIR RESPECTIVE APPLICATIONS.
POOR QUALITY, UNSTABLE GEMS IMMEDIATELY MELT IN THE ATMOSPHERE, SO WE USE THEM MAINLY FOR ARROW- AND SPEARHEADS.
FOR THE REPLICAS OF YOU AND YOUR KIND, OUR BEST ARTISANS PROCESS THE FINEST QUALITY MATERIALS INTO THE SAME SHAPE THE ORIGINALS WERE IN WHEN WE HARVESTED THEM.
IS THERE A WAY TO TELL THEM APART FROM US?
THE ORIGI-NALS HAVE INCLU-SIONS.*
WE DO INFUSE THEM WITH IMITATION INCLUSIONS TO DECEIVE KONGŌ, BUT THEY DON'T HAVE THE SAME QUALITIES AS YOUR NATURAL ONES.
I SEE. WELL, IT SURE SEEMS LIKE YOU'RE WORK-ING HARD.

*Microscopic organisms that live inside the Lustrous.

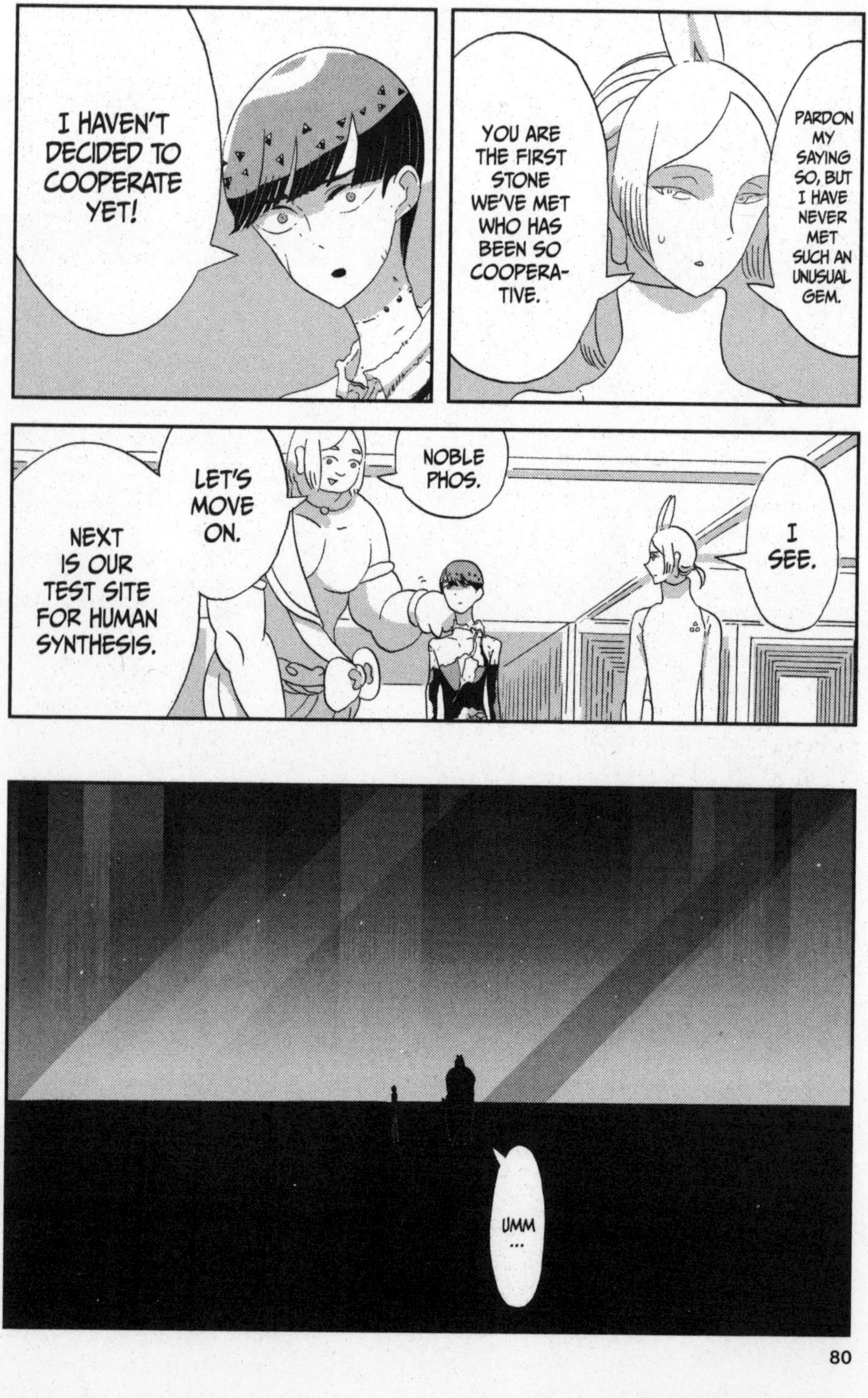

PARDON MY SAYING SO, BUT I HAVE NEVER MET SUCH AN UNUSUAL GEM.
YOU ARE THE FIRST STONE WE'VE MET WHO HAS BEEN SO COOPERA-TIVE.
I HAVEN'T DECIDED TO COOPERATE YET!
I SEE.
NOBLE PHOS.
LET'S MOVE ON.
NEXT IS OUR TEST SITE FOR HUMAN SYNTHESIS.
UMM ...

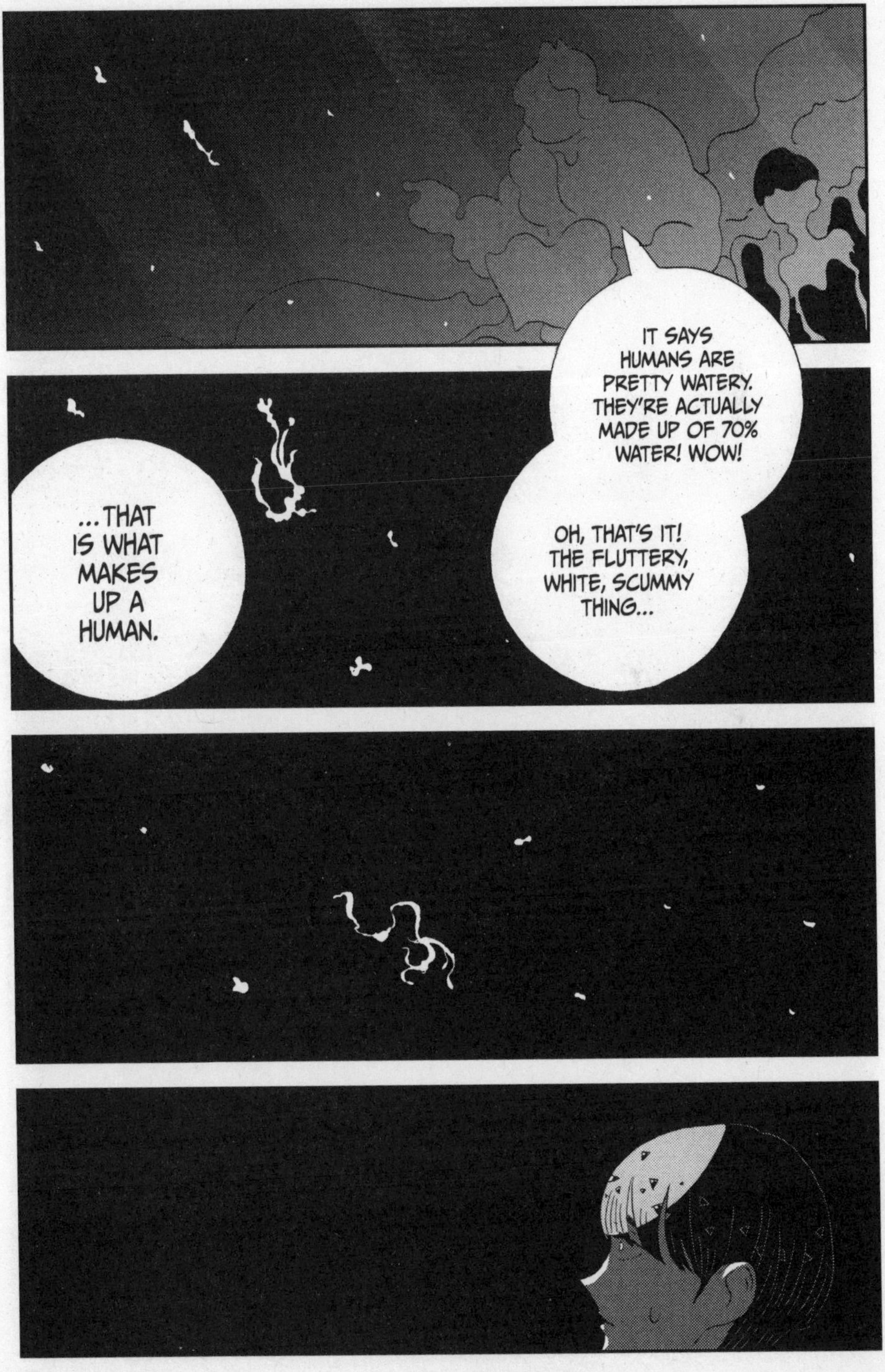
IT SAYS HUMANS ARE PRETTY WATERY. THEY'RE ACTUALLY MADE UP OF 70% WATER! WOW!
OH, THAT'S IT! THE FLUTTERY, WHITE, SCUMMY THING...
...THAT IS WHAT MAKES UP A HUMAN.

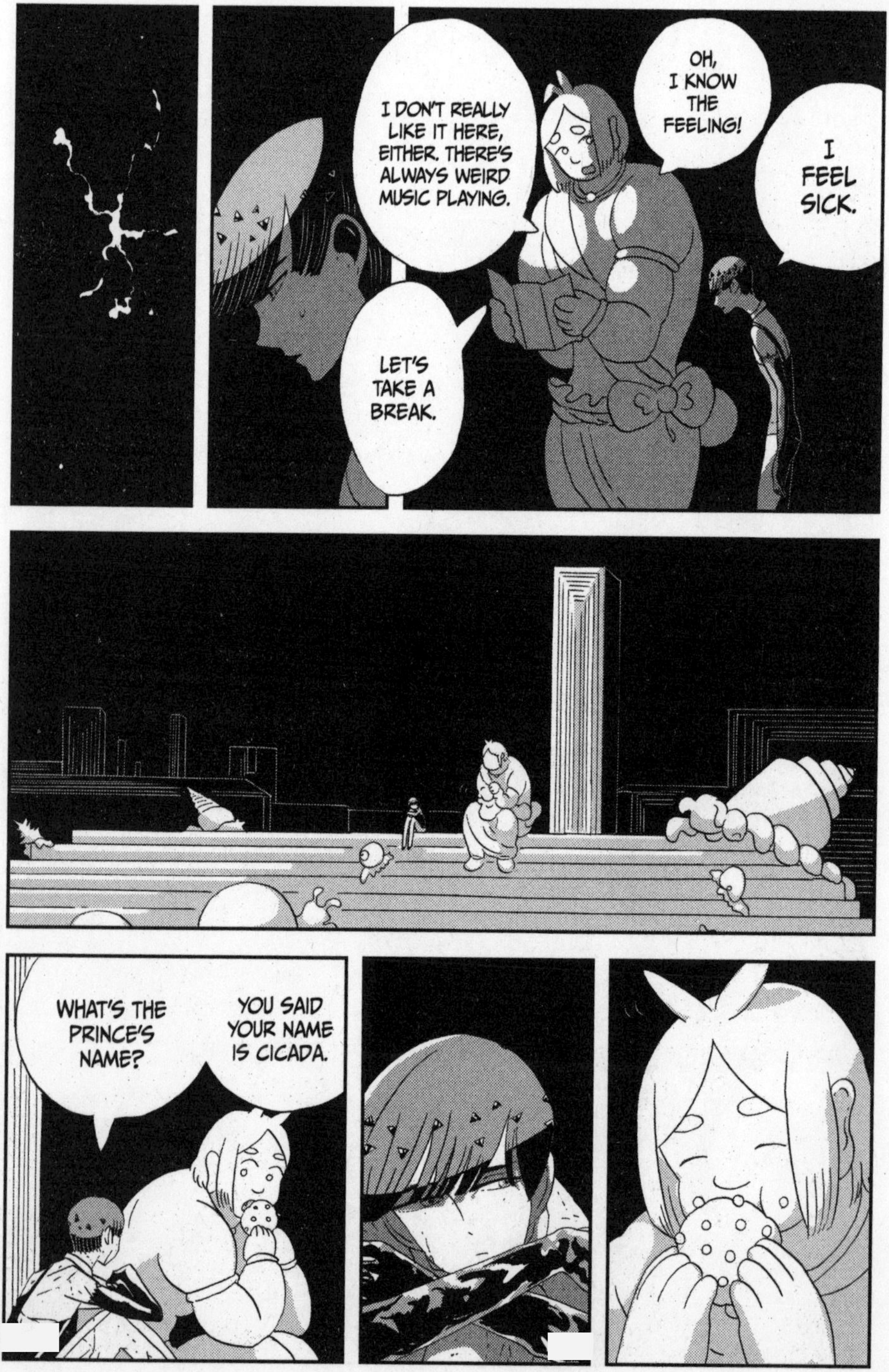
I FEEL SICK.
OH, I KNOW THE FEELING!
I DON'T REALLY LIKE IT HERE, EITHER. THERE'S ALWAYS WEIRD MUSIC PLAYING.
LET'S TAKE A BREAK.
YOU SAID YOUR NAME IS CICADA.
WHAT'S THE PRINCE'S NAME?

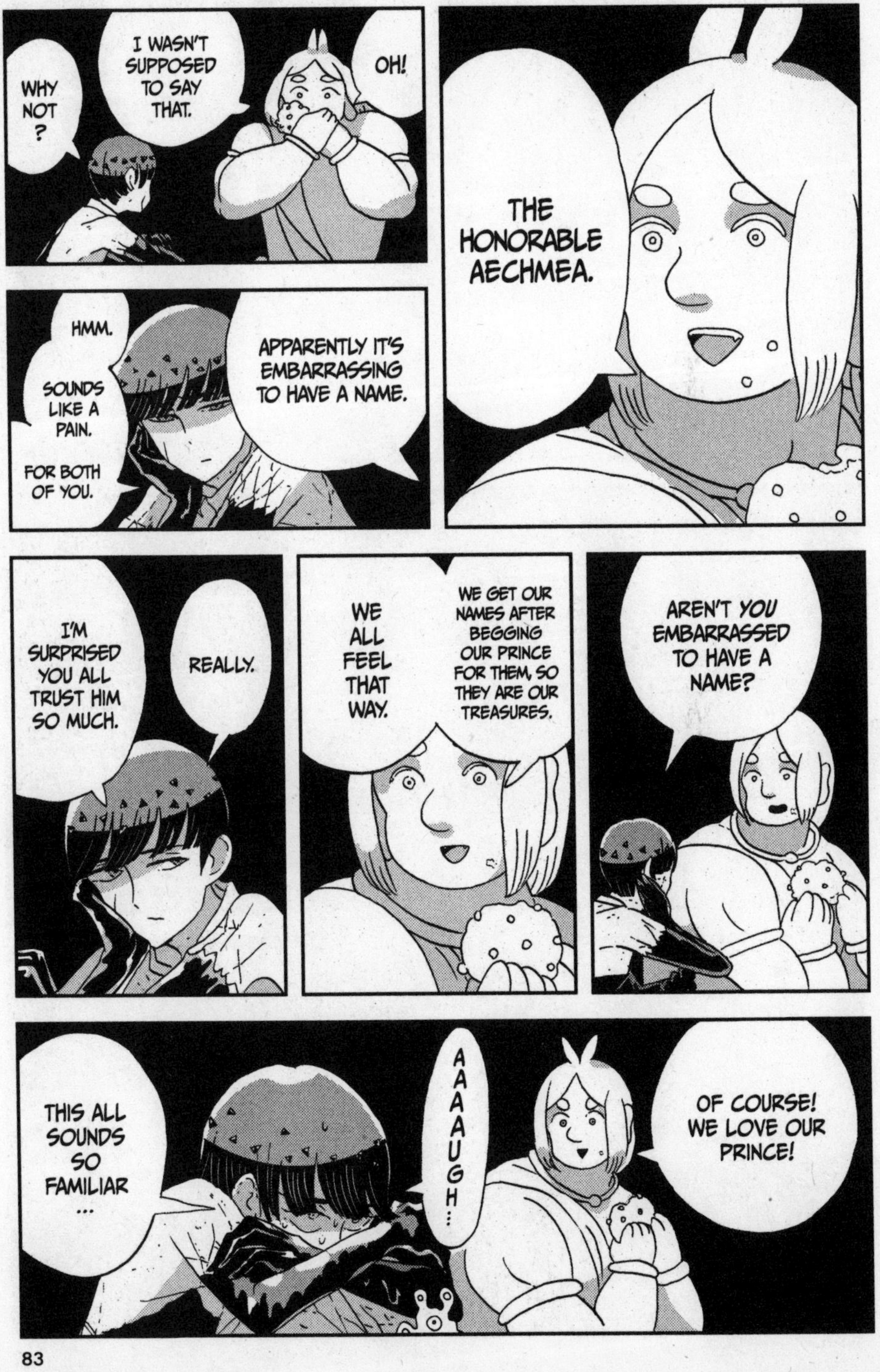
THE HONORABLE AECHMEA.
OH!
I WASN'T SUPPOSED TO SAY THAT.
WHY NOT?
APPARENTLY IT'S EMBARRASSING TO HAVE A NAME.
HMM.
SOUNDS LIKE A PAIN.
FOR BOTH OF YOU.
AREN'T *YOU* EMBARRASSED TO HAVE A NAME?
WE GET OUR NAMES AFTER BEGGING OUR PRINCE FOR THEM, SO THEY ARE OUR TREASURES.
WE ALL FEEL THAT WAY.
REALLY.
I'M SURPRISED YOU ALL TRUST HIM SO MUCH.
OF COURSE! WE LOVE OUR PRINCE!
AAAAAUGH...
THIS ALL SOUNDS SO FAMILIAR...

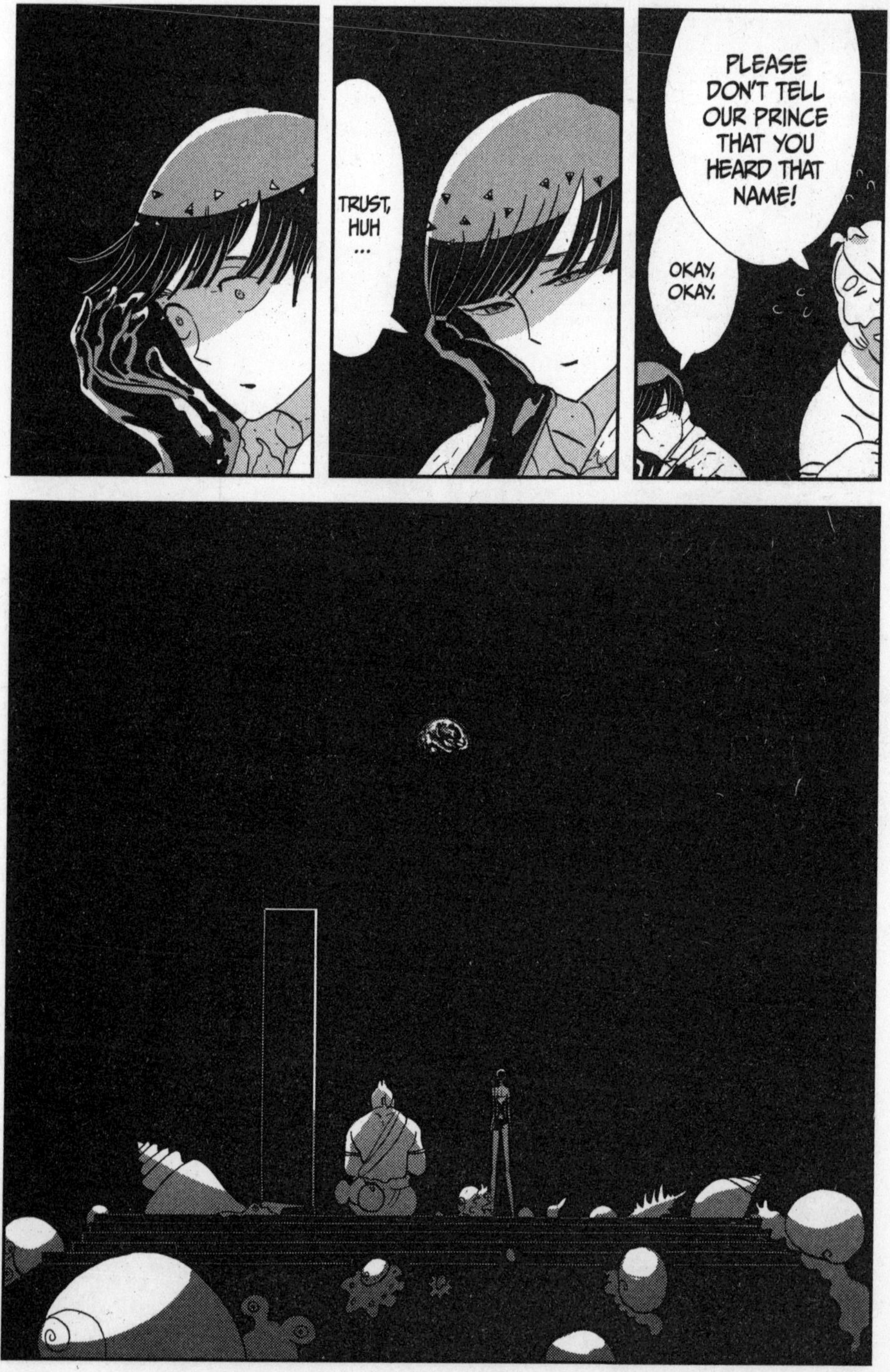
PLEASE DON'T TELL OUR PRINCE THAT YOU HEARD THAT NAME!
OKAY, OKAY.
TRUST, HUH ...

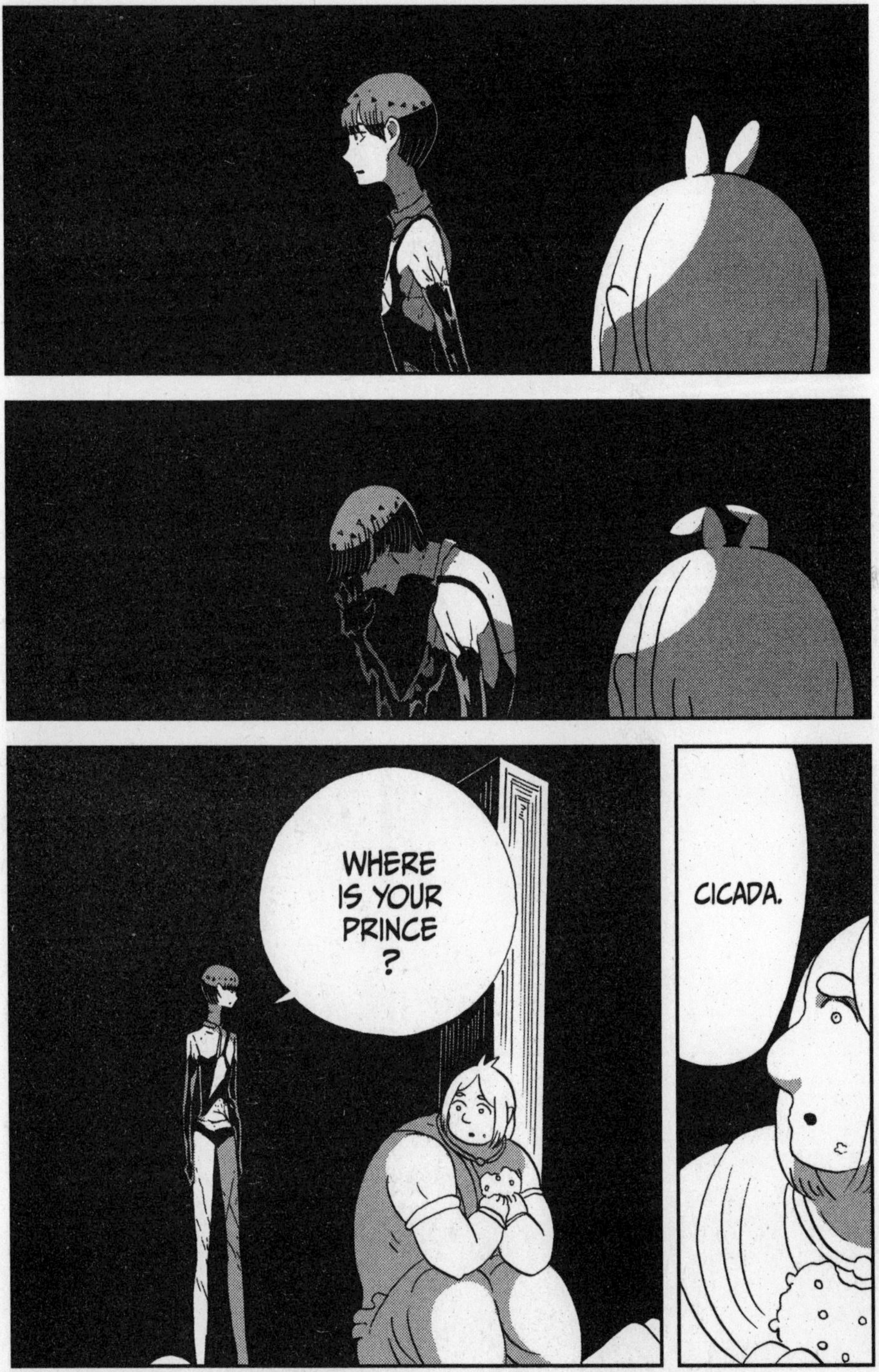
CICADA.
WHERE IS YOUR PRINCE?

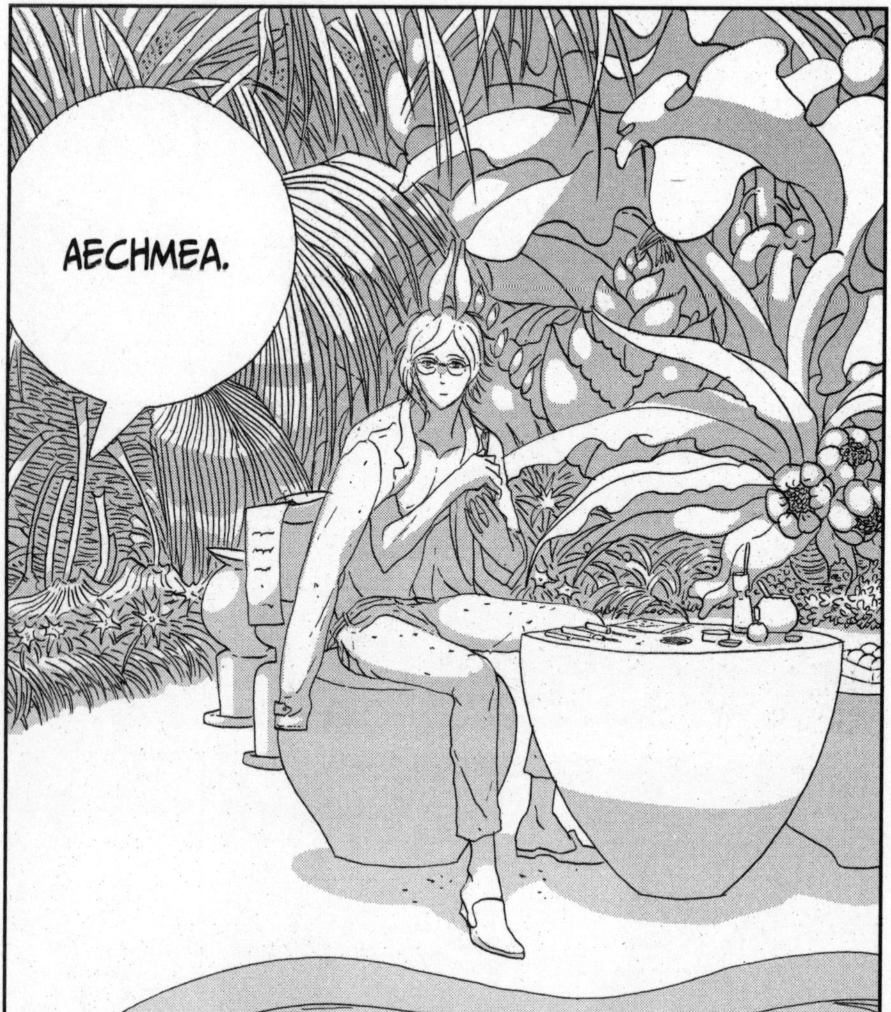
AECHMEA.
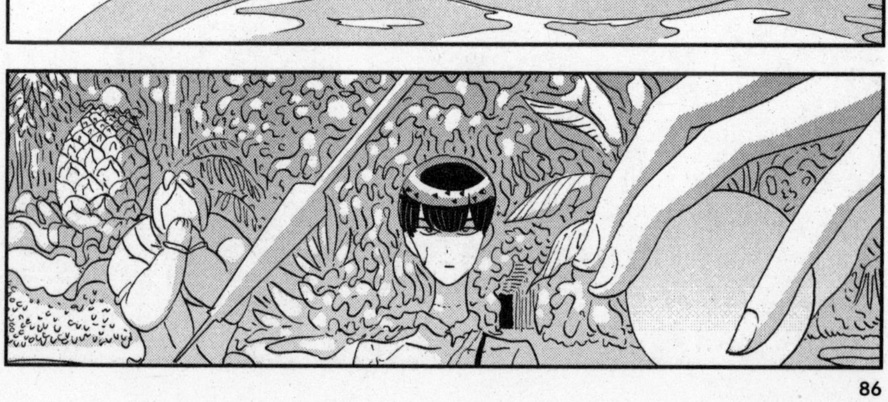

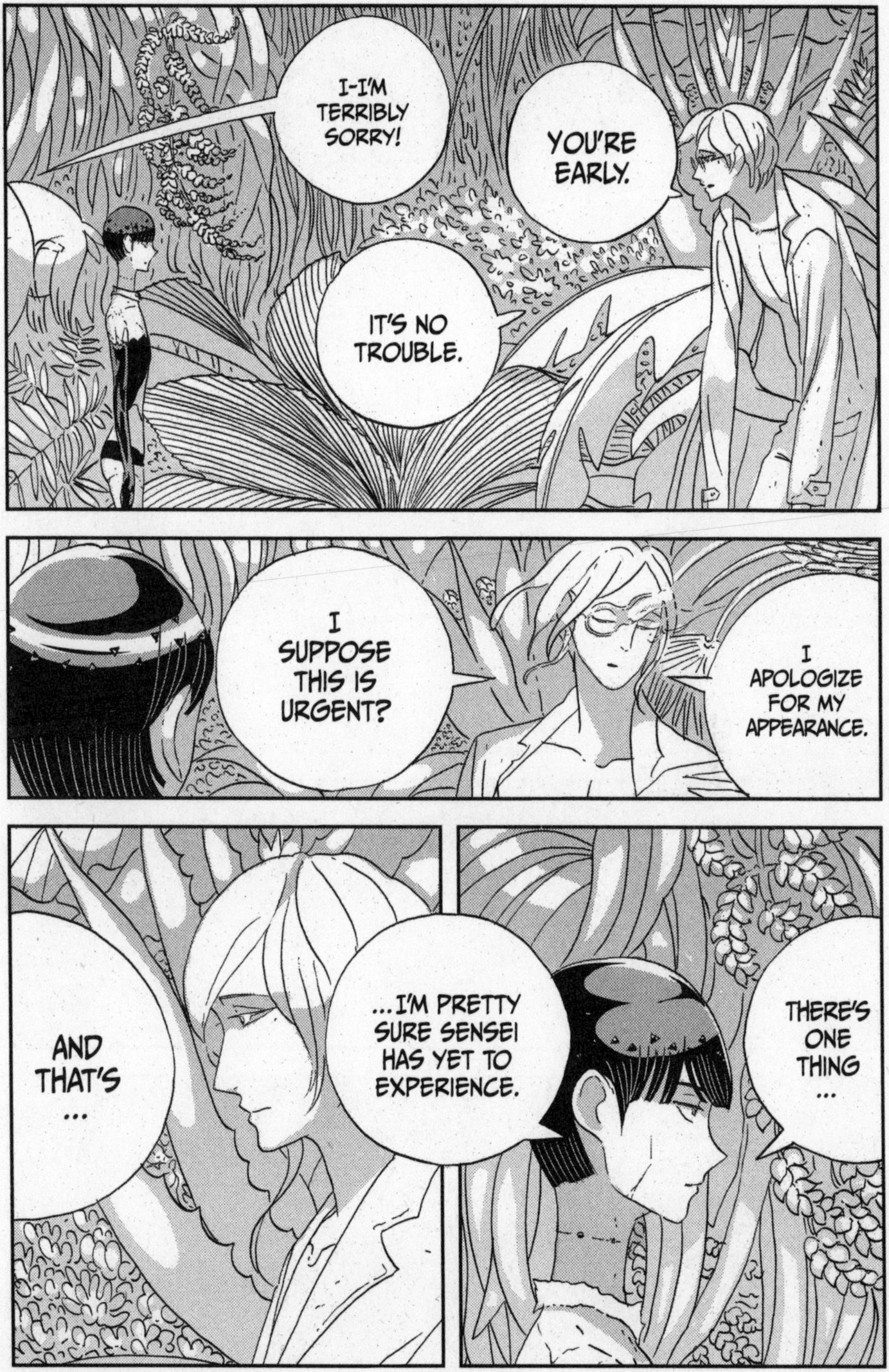
YOU'RE EARLY.
I-I'M TERRIBLY SORRY!
IT'S NO TROUBLE.
I APOLOGIZE FOR MY APPEARANCE.
I SUPPOSE THIS IS URGENT?
THERE'S ONE THING ...
...I'M PRETTY SURE SENSEI HAS YET TO EXPERIENCE.
AND THAT'S ...

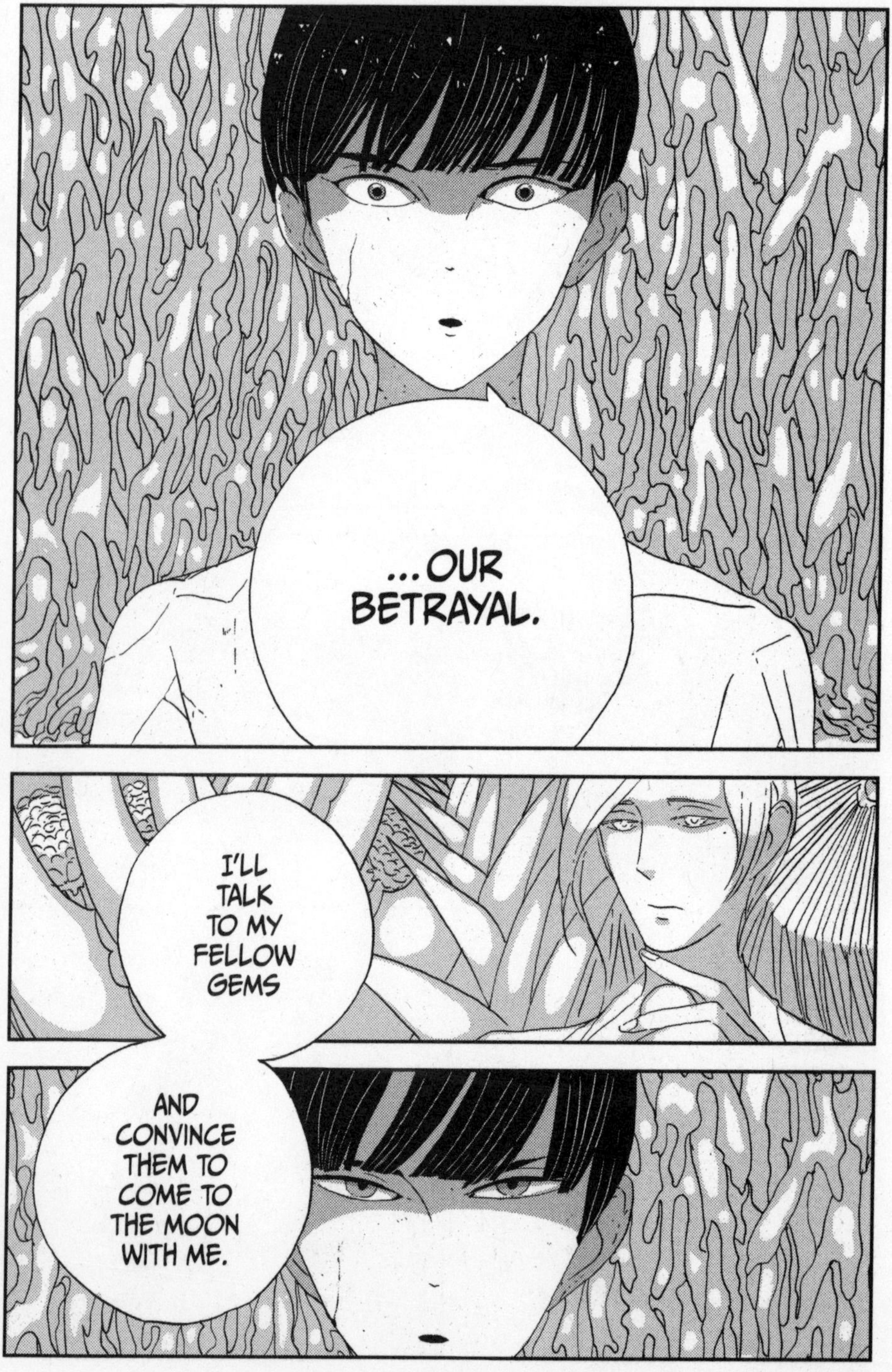
...OUR BETRAYAL.
I'LL TALK TO MY FELLOW GEMS
AND CONVINCE THEM TO COME TO THE MOON WITH ME.

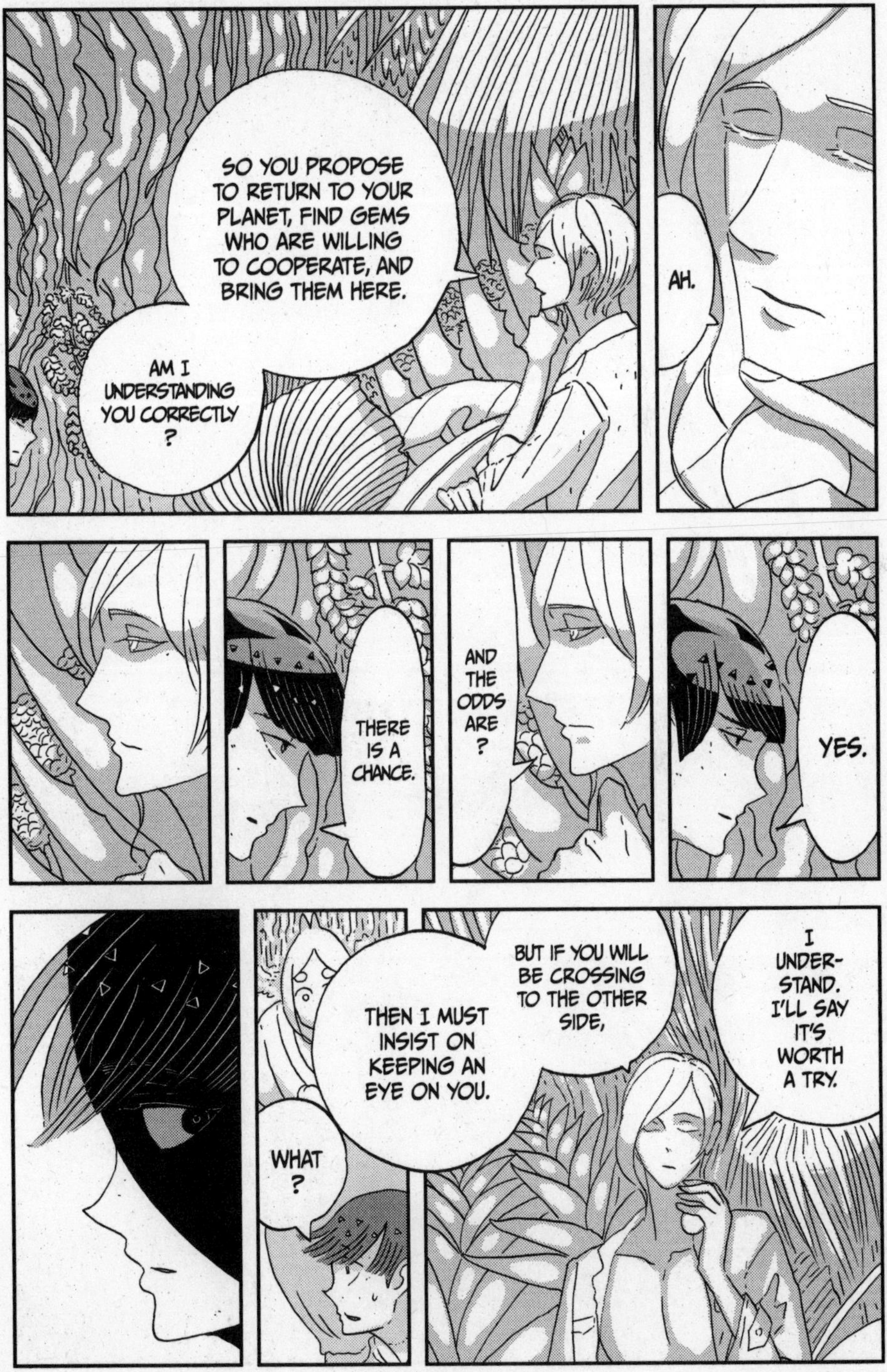
AH.
SO YOU PROPOSE TO RETURN TO YOUR PLANET, FIND GEMS WHO ARE WILLING TO COOPERATE, AND BRING THEM HERE.
AM I UNDERSTANDING YOU CORRECTLY ?
YES.
AND THE ODDS ARE ?
THERE IS A CHANCE.
I UNDER-STAND. I'LL SAY IT'S WORTH A TRY.
BUT IF YOU WILL BE CROSSING TO THE OTHER SIDE,
THEN I MUST INSIST ON KEEPING AN EYE ON YOU.
WHAT ?

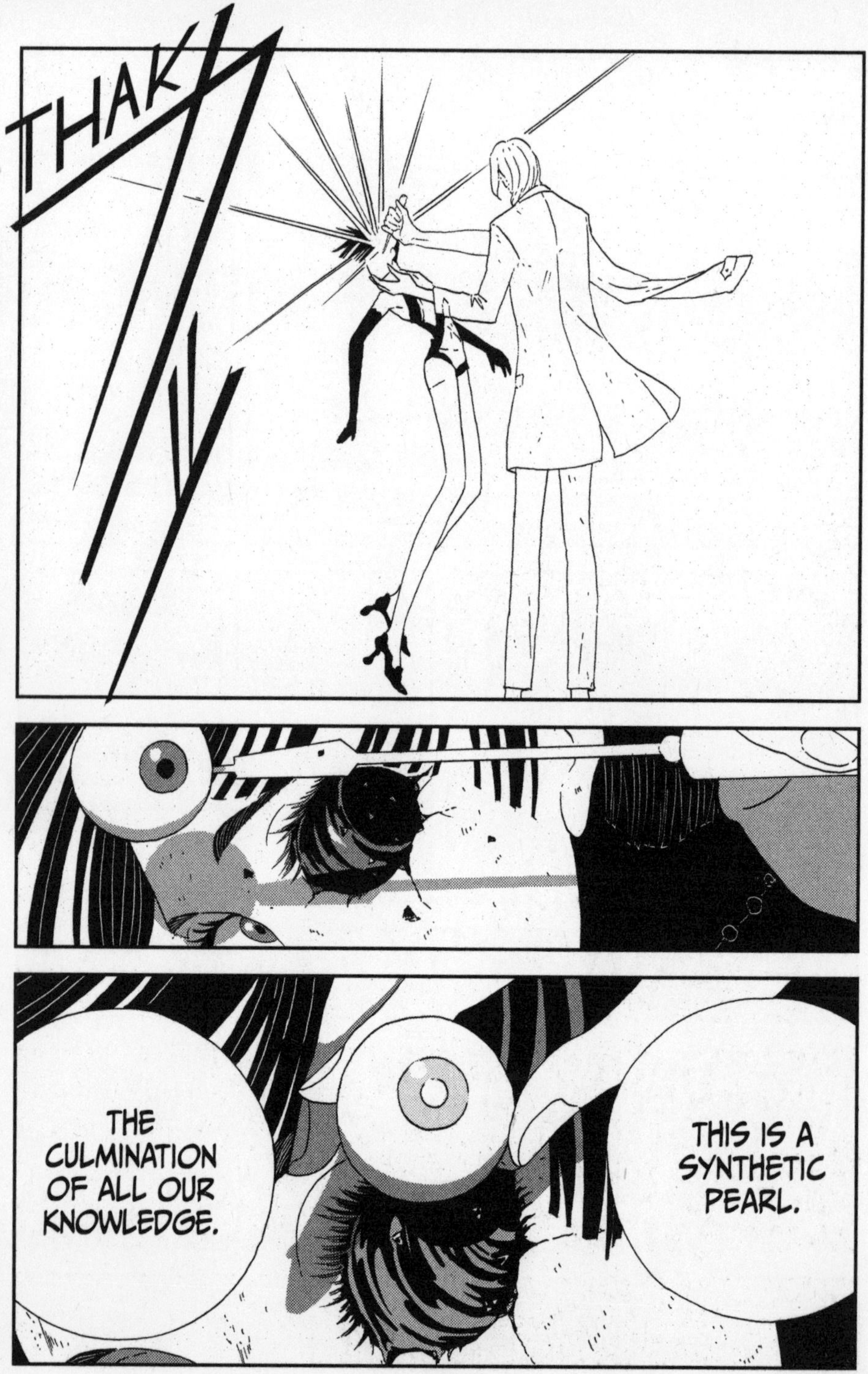
THAK
THIS IS A SYNTHETIC PEARL.
THE CULMINATION OF ALL OUR KNOWLEDGE.

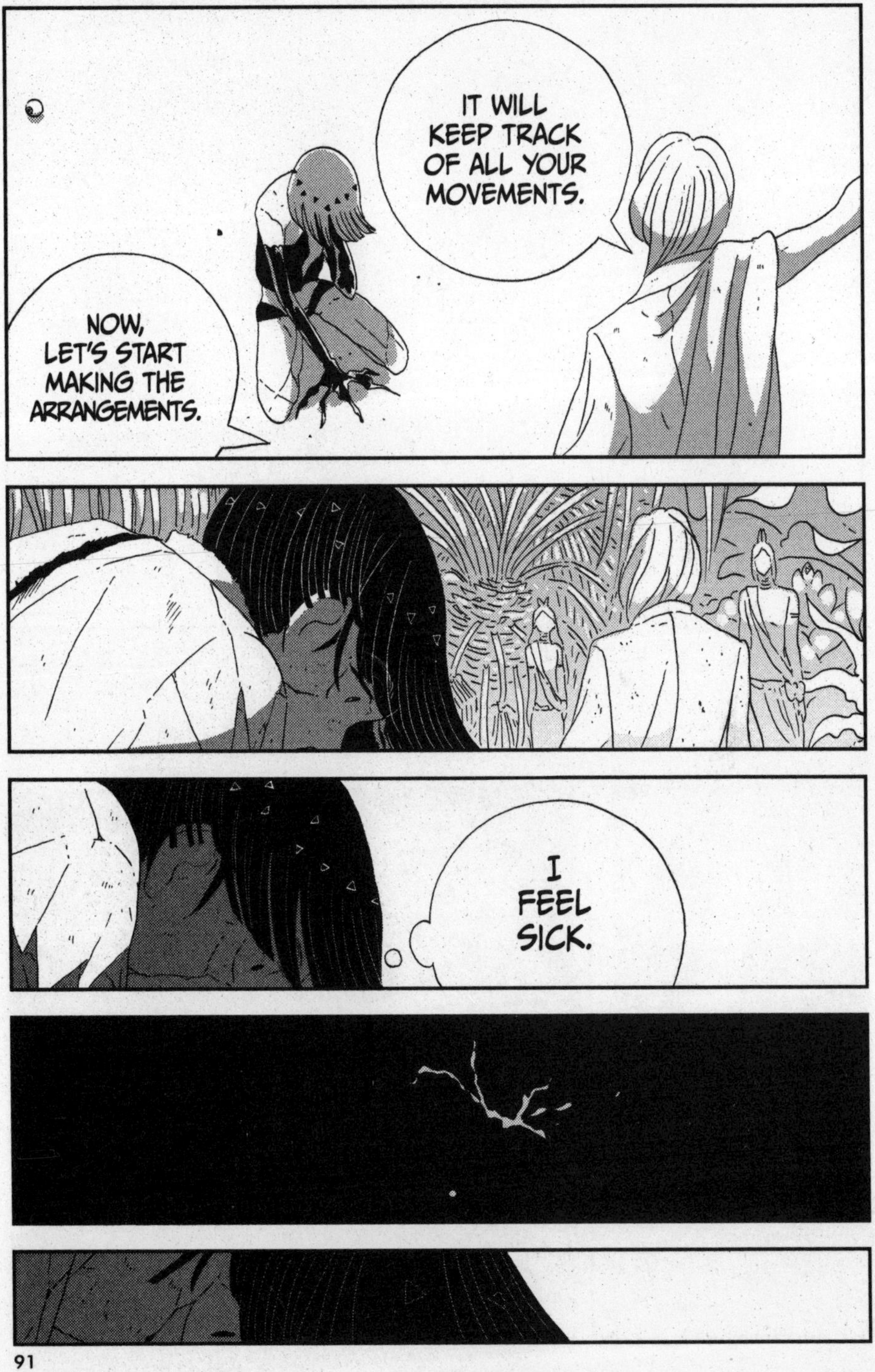
IT WILL KEEP TRACK OF ALL YOUR MOVEMENTS.
NOW, LET'S START MAKING THE ARRANGEMENTS.
I FEEL SICK.

GREAT PHOS!
CLACK

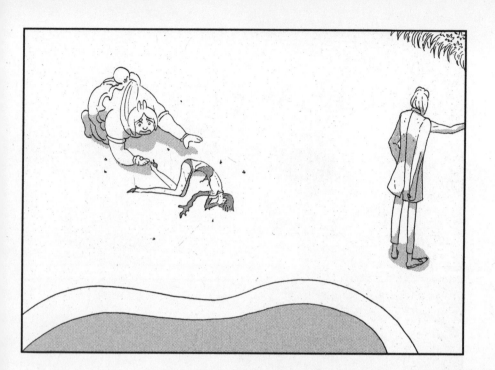

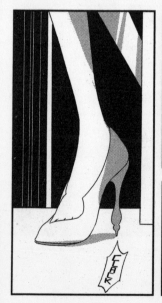

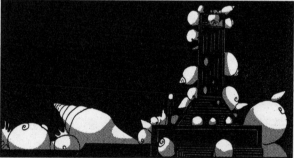

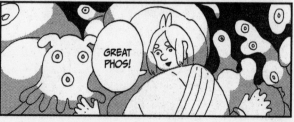

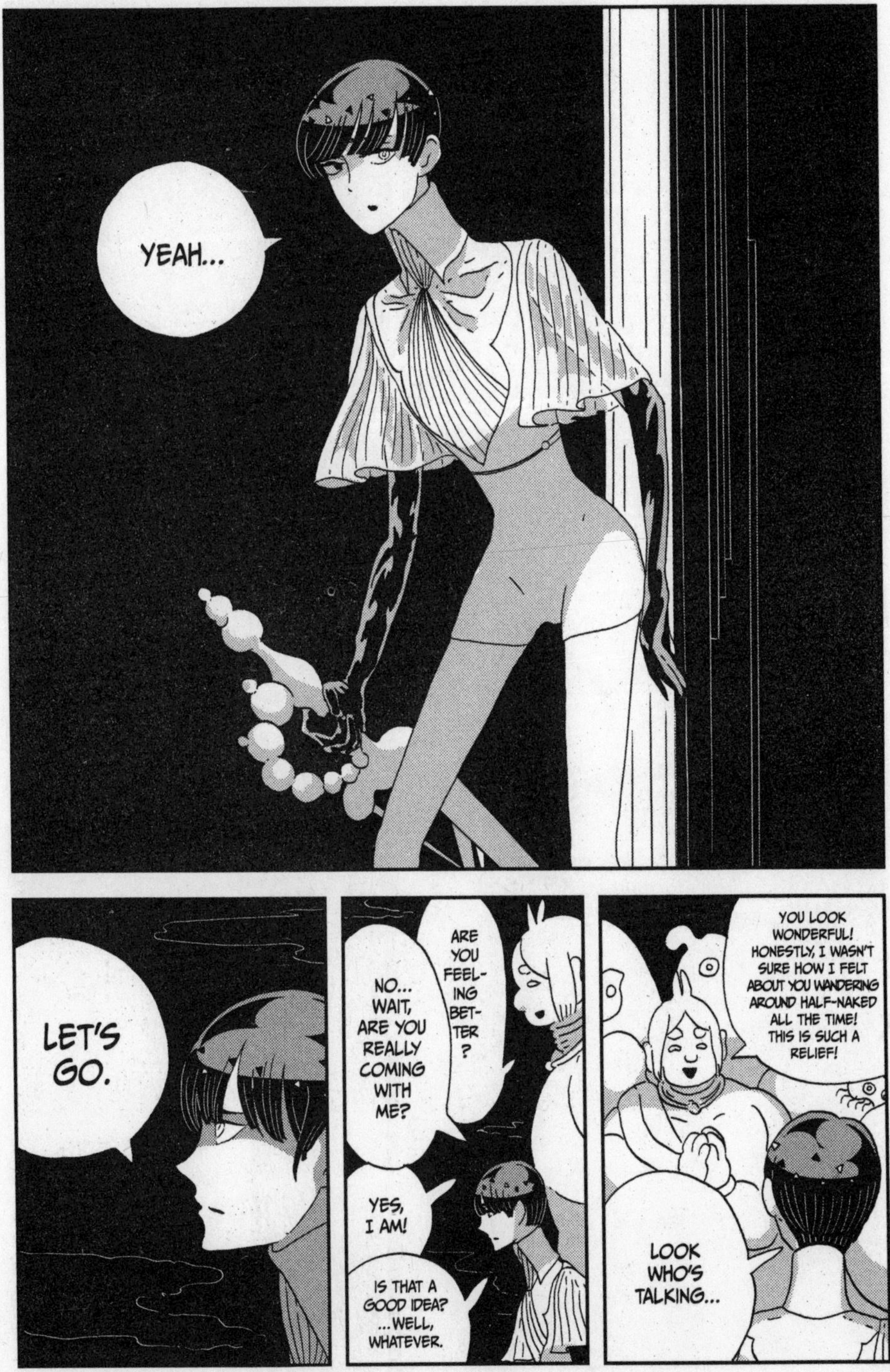
YEAH...
YOU LOOK WONDERFUL! HONESTLY, I WASN'T SURE HOW I FELT ABOUT YOU WANDERING AROUND HALF-NAKED ALL THE TIME! THIS IS SUCH A RELIEF!
LOOK WHO'S TALKING...
ARE YOU FEELING BETTER?
NO... WAIT, ARE YOU REALLY COMING WITH ME?
YES, I AM!
IS THAT A GOOD IDEA? ...WELL, WHATEVER.
LET'S GO.

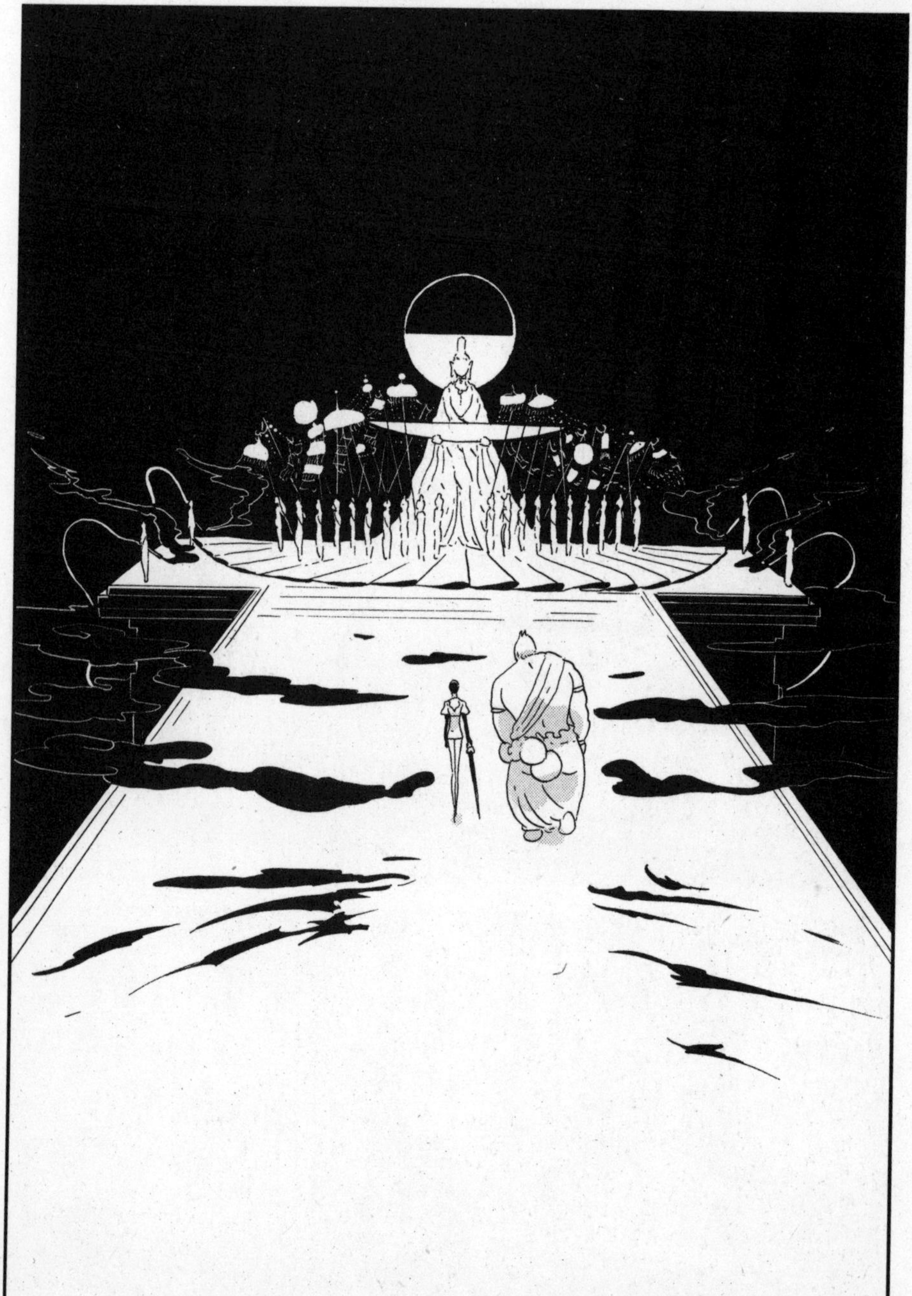

CHAPTER 56: Synthetic Pearl END

CHAPTER 57: Crossroads

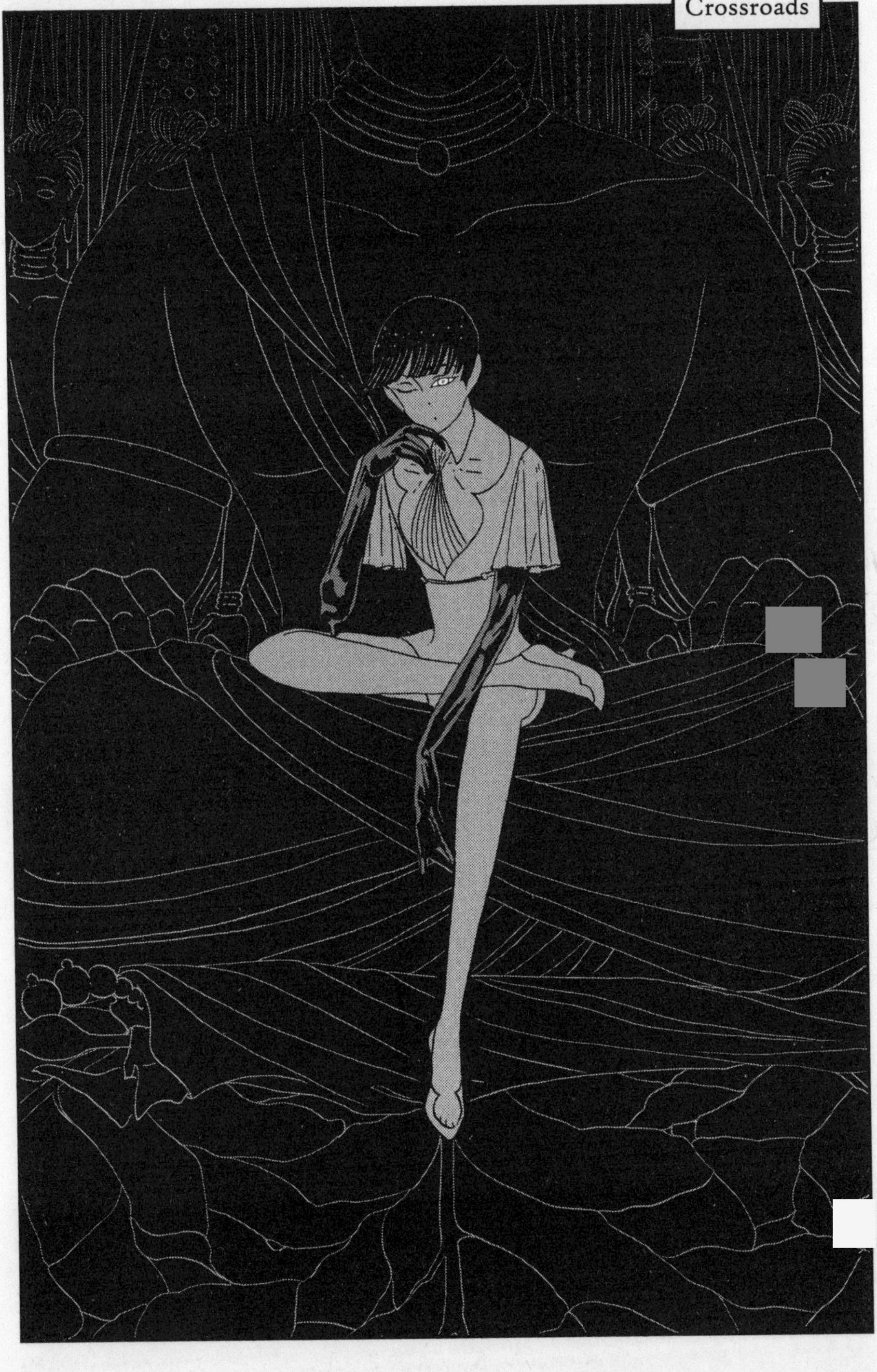

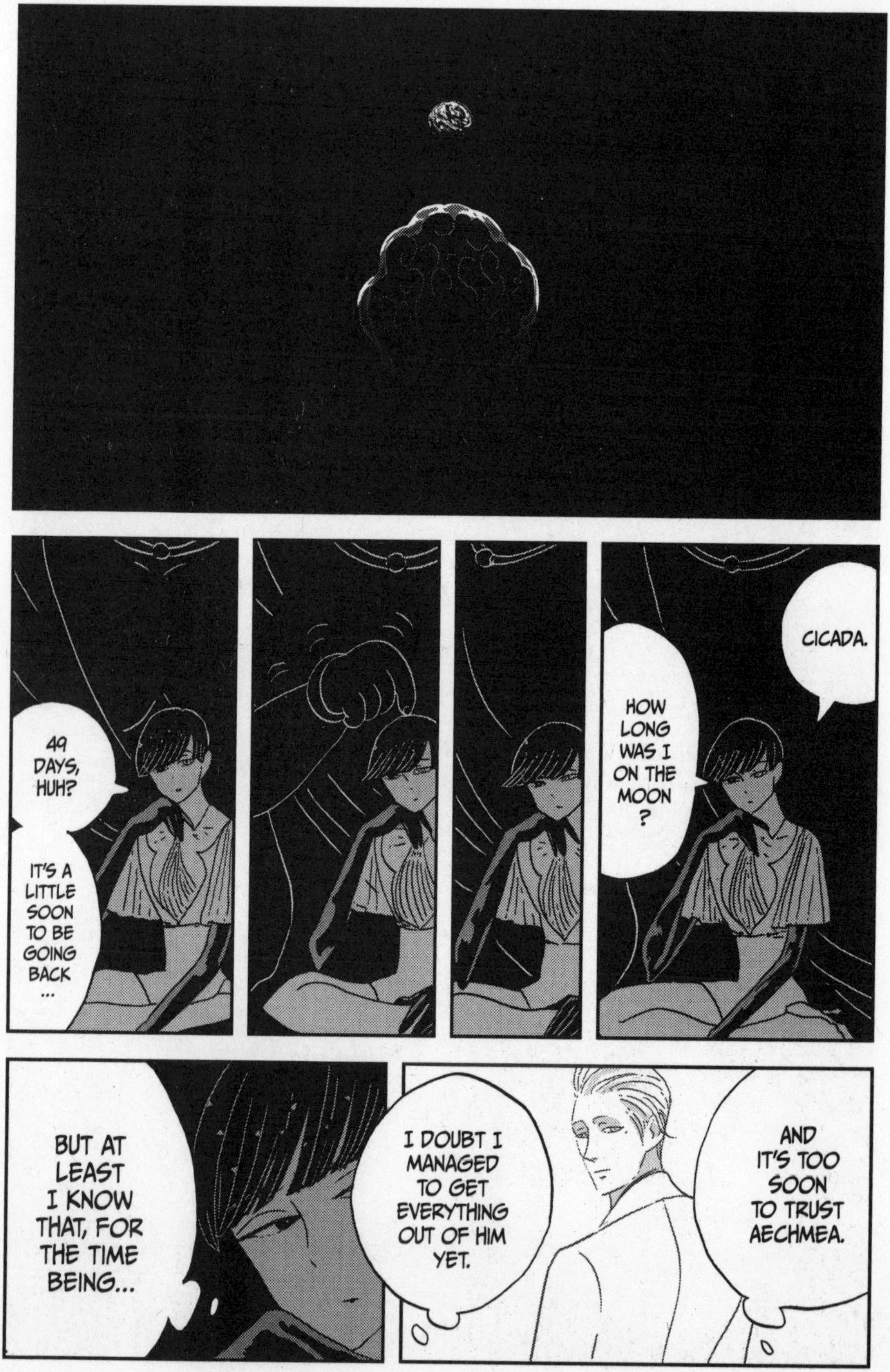
CICADA.
HOW LONG WAS I ON THE MOON?
49 DAYS, HUH?
IT'S A LITTLE SOON TO BE GOING BACK...
AND IT'S TOO SOON TO TRUST AECHMEA.
I DOUBT I MANAGED TO GET EVERYTHING OUT OF HIM YET.
BUT AT LEAST I KNOW THAT, FOR THE TIME BEING...

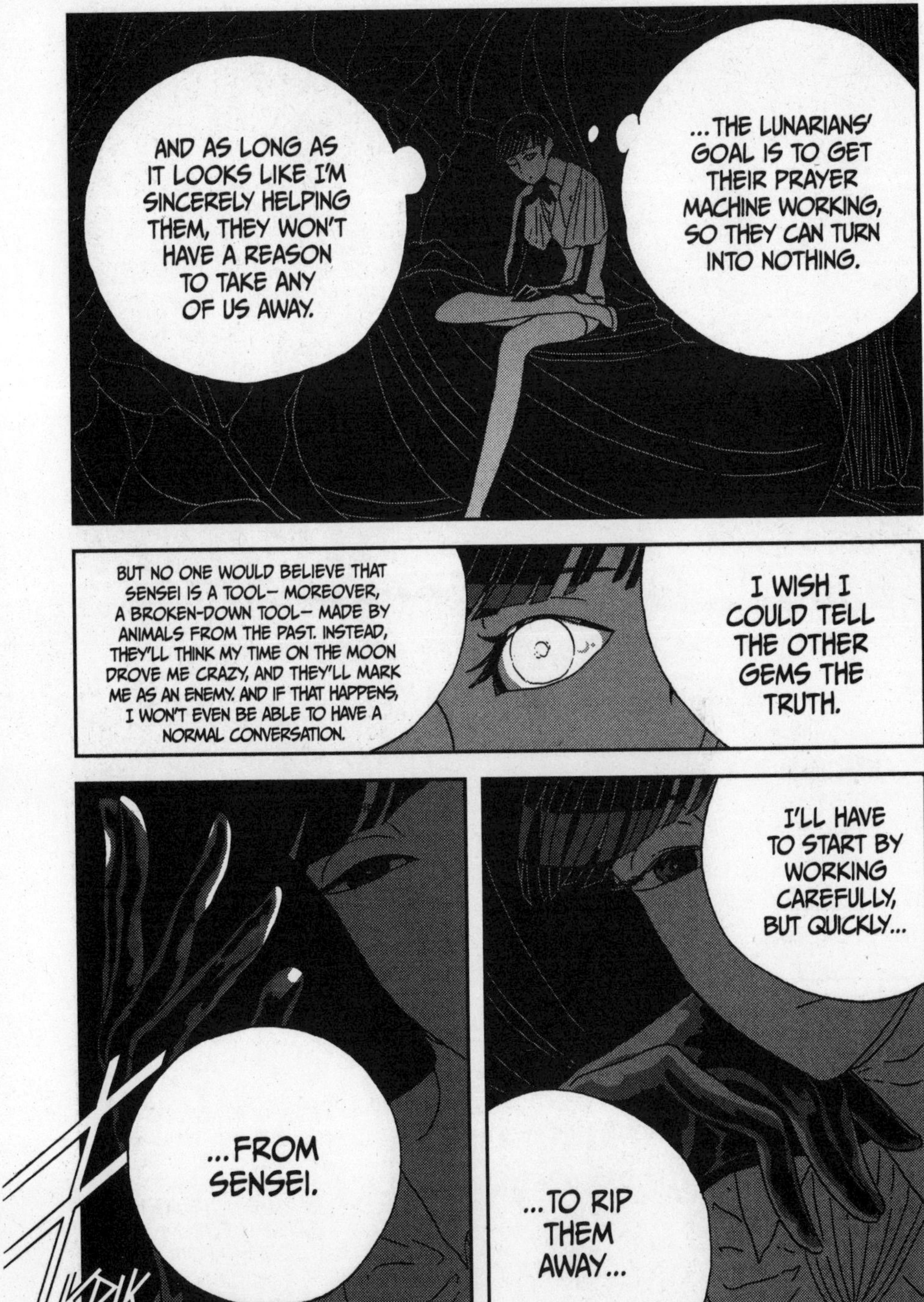
...THE LUNARIANS' GOAL IS TO GET THEIR PRAYER MACHINE WORKING, SO THEY CAN TURN INTO NOTHING.
AND AS LONG AS IT LOOKS LIKE I'M SINCERELY HELPING THEM, THEY WON'T HAVE A REASON TO TAKE ANY OF US AWAY.
I WISH I COULD TELL THE OTHER GEMS THE TRUTH.
BUT NO ONE WOULD BELIEVE THAT SENSEI IS A TOOL— MOREOVER, A BROKEN-DOWN TOOL— MADE BY ANIMALS FROM THE PAST. INSTEAD, THEY'LL THINK MY TIME ON THE MOON DROVE ME CRAZY, AND THEY'LL MARK ME AS AN ENEMY. AND IF THAT HAPPENS, I WON'T EVEN BE ABLE TO HAVE A NORMAL CONVERSATION.
I'LL HAVE TO START BY WORKING CAREFULLY, BUT QUICKLY...
...TO RIP THEM AWAY...
...FROM SENSEI.
KRIK

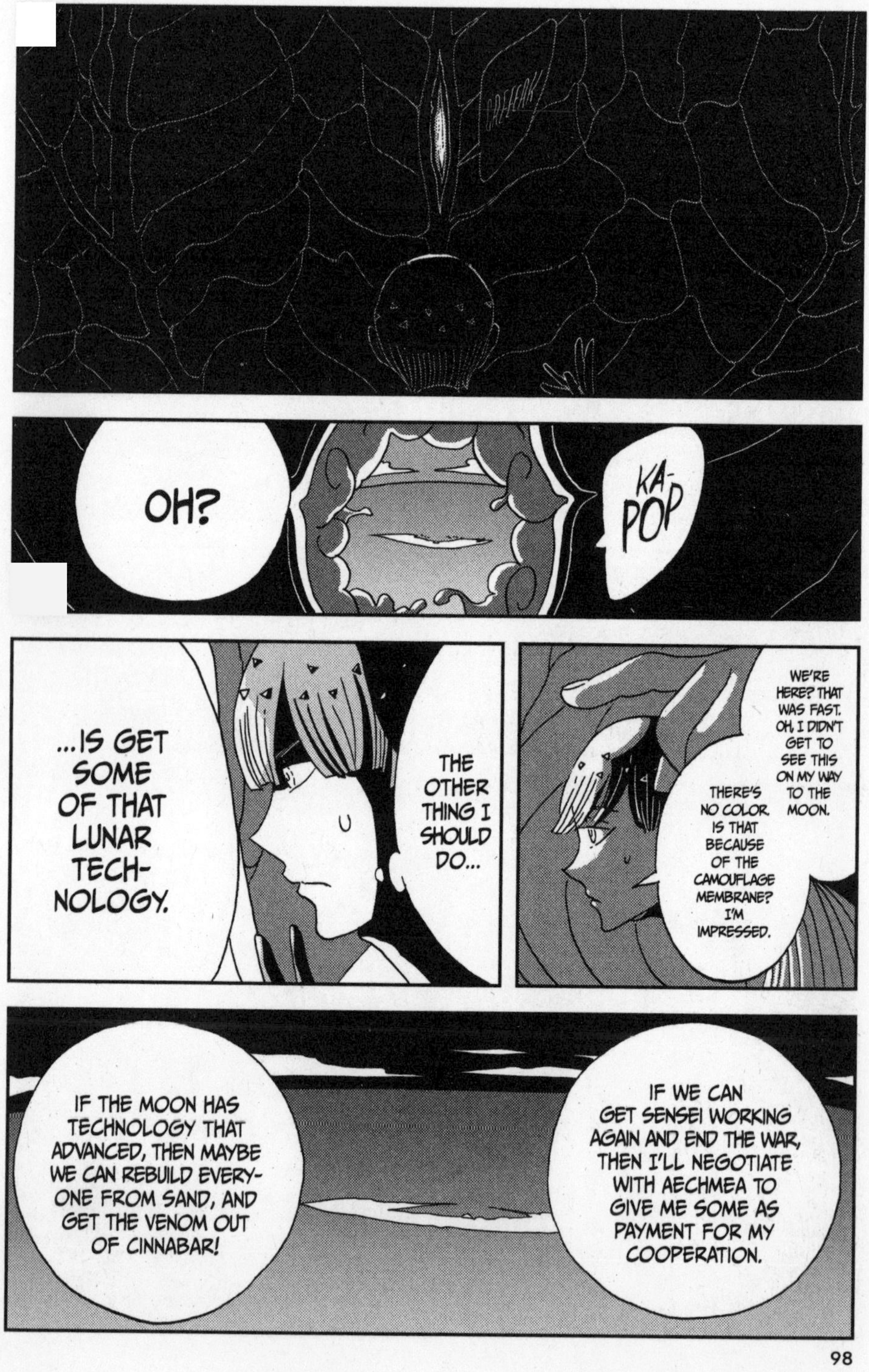
KA-POP
OH?
WE'RE HERE? THAT WAS FAST. OH, I DIDN'T GET TO SEE THIS ON MY WAY TO THE MOON.
THERE'S NO COLOR. IS THAT BECAUSE OF THE CAMOUFLAGE MEMBRANE? I'M IMPRESSED.
THE OTHER THING I SHOULD DO...
...IS GET SOME OF THAT LUNAR TECH-NOLOGY.
IF WE CAN GET SENSEI WORKING AGAIN AND END THE WAR, THEN I'LL NEGOTIATE WITH AECHMEA TO GIVE ME SOME AS PAYMENT FOR MY COOPERATION.
IF THE MOON HAS TECHNOLOGY THAT ADVANCED, THEN MAYBE WE CAN REBUILD EVERY-ONE FROM SAND, AND GET THE VENOM OUT OF CINNABAR!

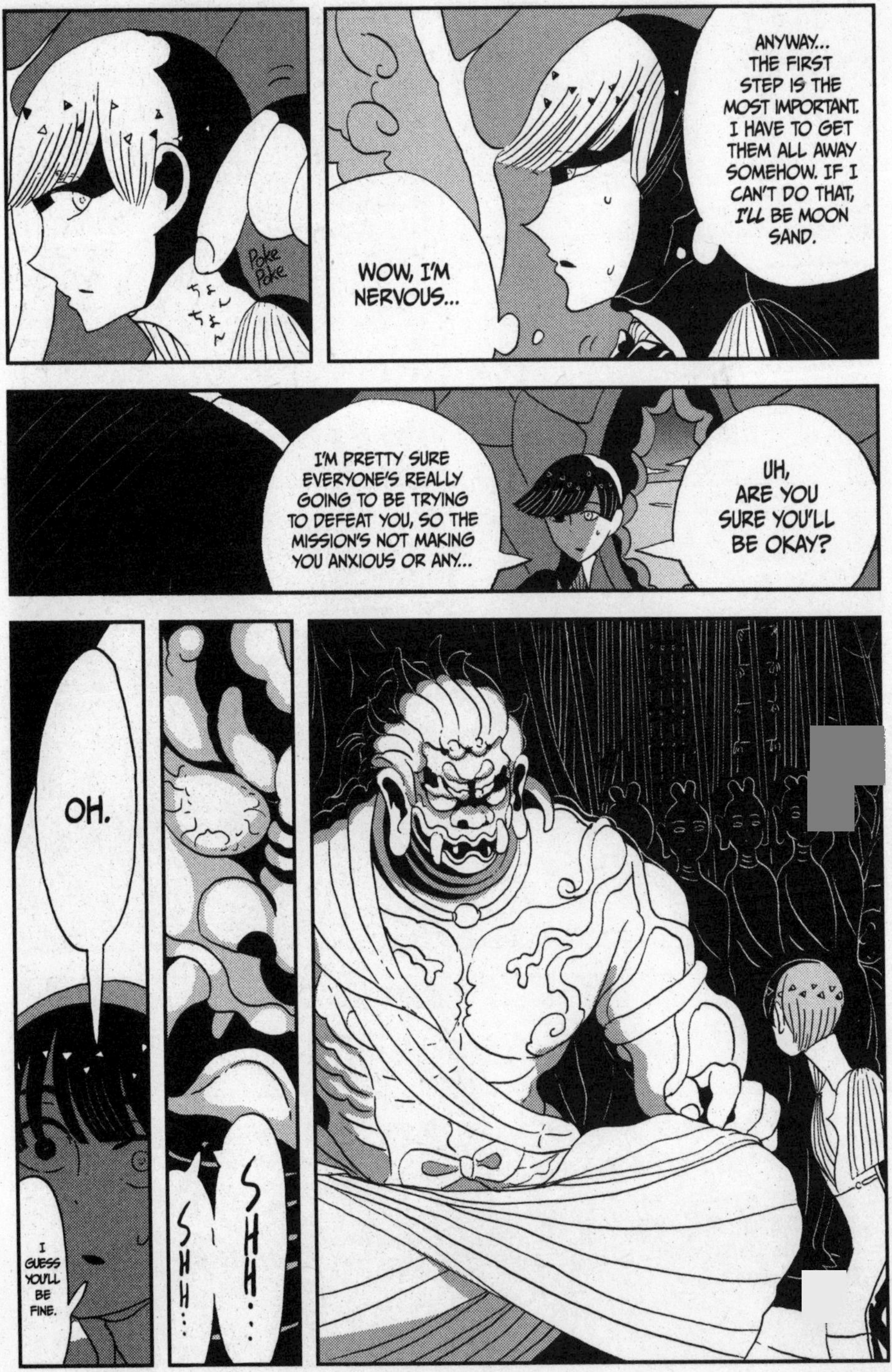
ANYWAY... THE FIRST STEP IS THE MOST IMPORTANT. I HAVE TO GET THEM ALL AWAY SOMEHOW. IF I CAN'T DO THAT, I'LL BE MOON SAND.
WOW, I'M NERVOUS...
Poke Poke
ちょんちょん~
UH, ARE YOU SURE YOU'LL BE OKAY?
I'M PRETTY SURE EVERYONE'S REALLY GOING TO BE TRYING TO DEFEAT YOU, SO THE MISSION'S NOT MAKING YOU ANXIOUS OR ANY...
SHH...
SHH...
OH.
I GUESS YOU'LL BE FINE.

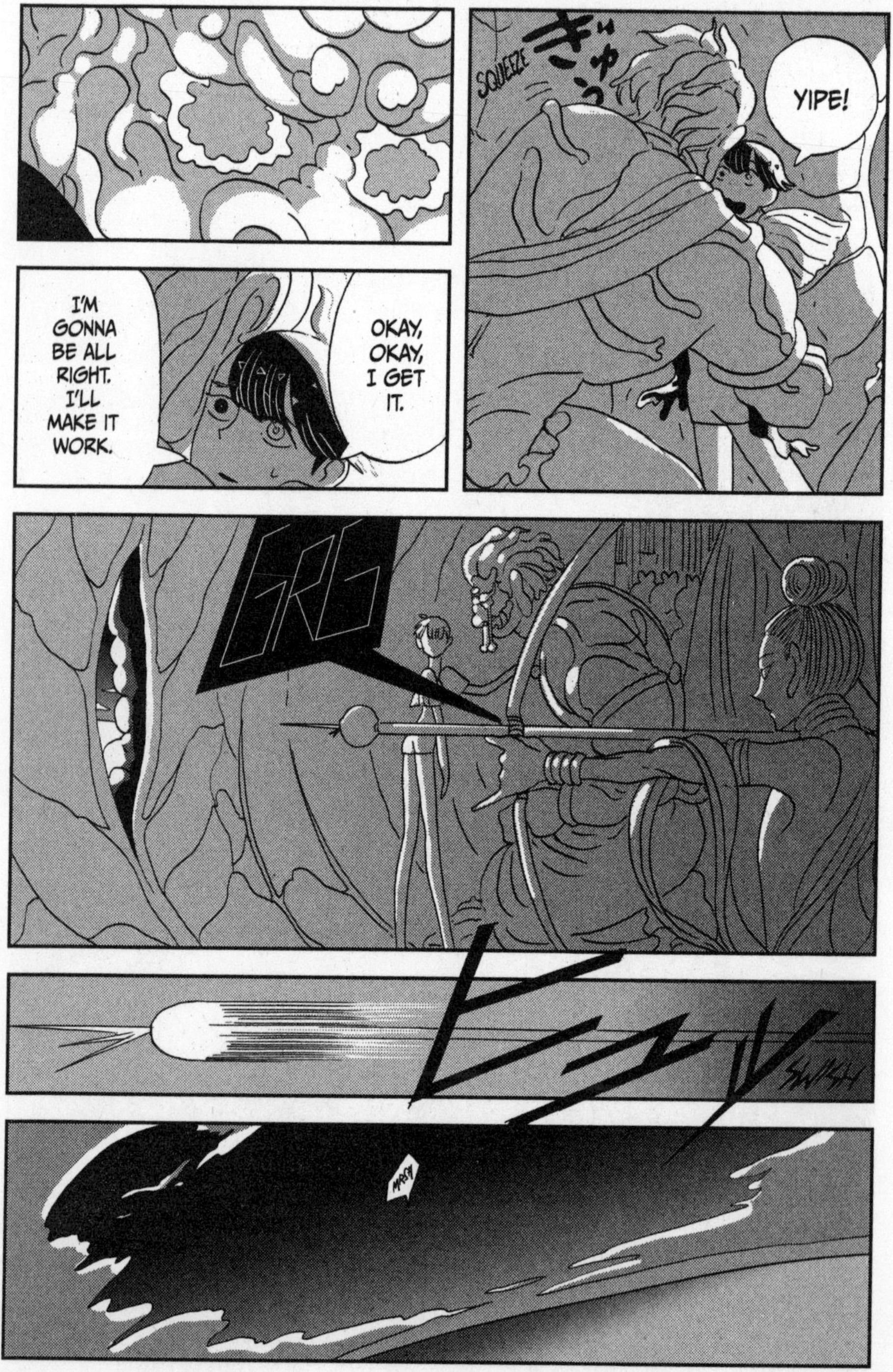
SQUEEZE
YIPE!
OKAY, OKAY, I GET IT.
I'M GONNA BE ALL RIGHT. I'LL MAKE IT WORK.
GRG
SWISH
MRSH

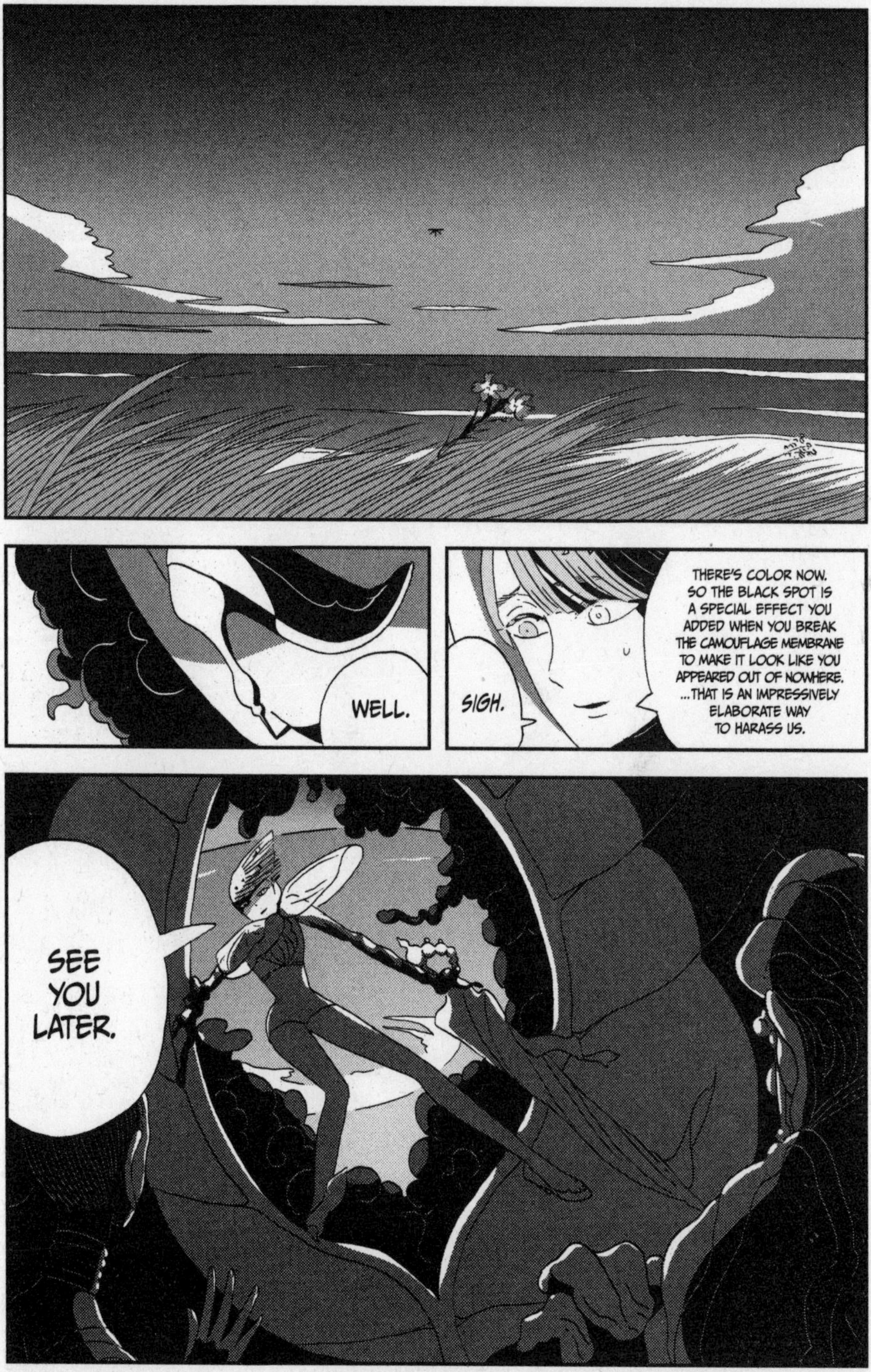

THERE'S COLOR NOW. SO THE BLACK SPOT IS A SPECIAL EFFECT YOU ADDED WHEN YOU BREAK THE CAMOUFLAGE MEMBRANE TO MAKE IT LOOK LIKE YOU APPEARED OUT OF NOWHERE. ...THAT IS AN IMPRESSIVELY ELABORATE WAY TO HARASS US.
SIGH.
WELL.
SEE YOU LATER.

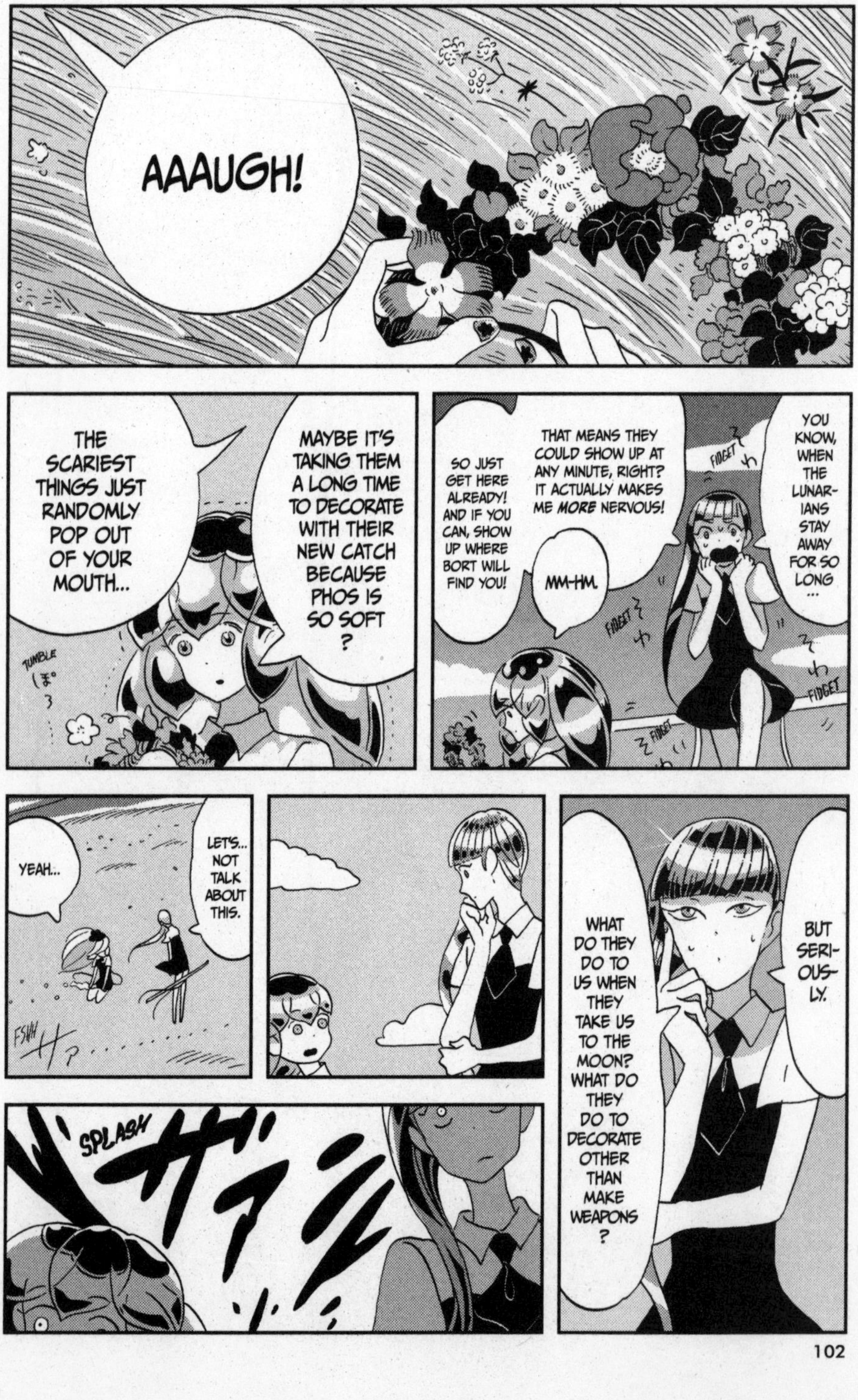

AAAUGH!
YOU KNOW, WHEN THE LUNARIANS STAY AWAY FOR SO LONG ...
THAT MEANS THEY COULD SHOW UP AT ANY MINUTE, RIGHT? IT ACTUALLY MAKES ME *MORE* NERVOUS!
MM-HM.
SO JUST GET HERE ALREADY! AND IF YOU CAN, SHOW UP WHERE BORT WILL FIND YOU!
FIDGET
FIDGET
FIDGET
FIDGET
MAYBE IT'S TAKING THEM A LONG TIME TO DECORATE WITH THEIR NEW CATCH BECAUSE PHOS IS SO SOFT ?
THE SCARIEST THINGS JUST RANDOMLY POP OUT OF YOUR MOUTH...
TUMBLE
BUT SERIOUSLY.
WHAT DO THEY DO TO US WHEN THEY TAKE US TO THE MOON? WHAT DO THEY DO TO DECORATE OTHER THAN MAKE WEAPONS ?
LET'S... NOT TALK ABOUT THIS.
YEAH...
FSHH
SPLASH

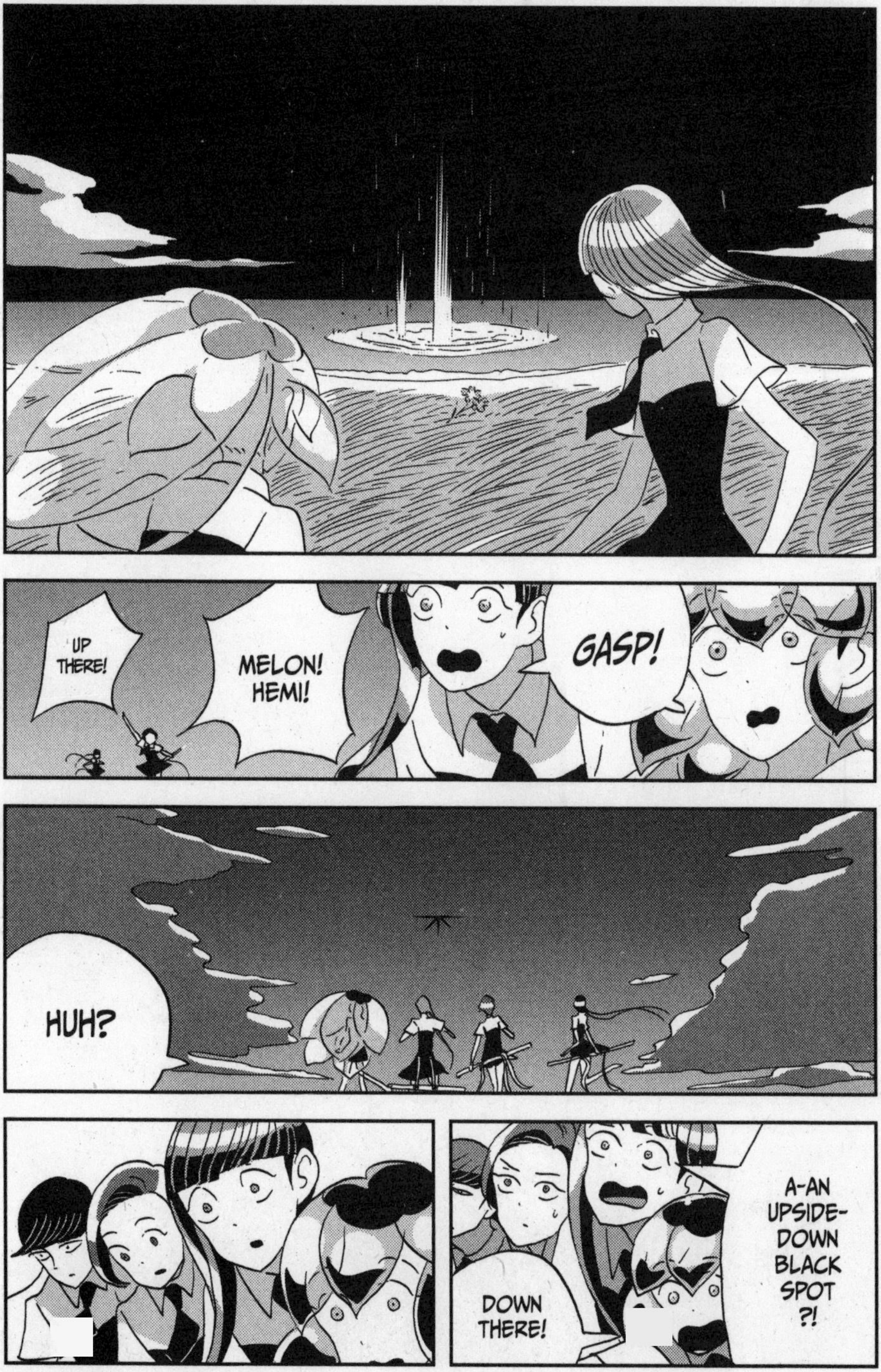
GASP!
MELON! HEMI!
UP THERE!
HUH?
A-AN UPSIDE-DOWN BLACK SPOT ?!
DOWN THERE!

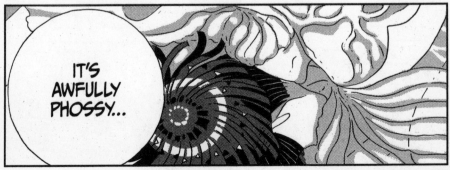

IT'S AWFULLY PHOSSY...

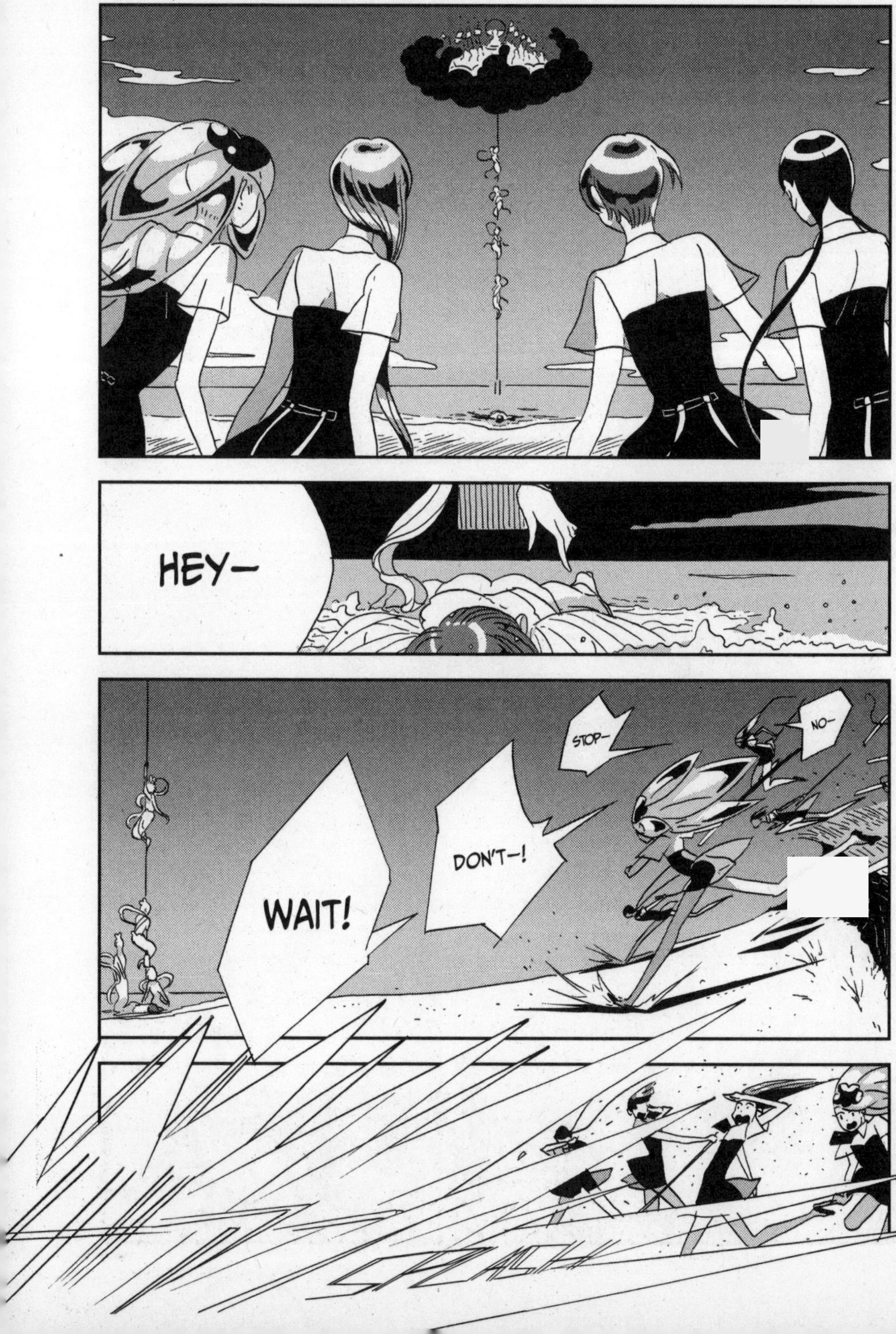
HEY–
NO–
STOP–
DON'T–!
WAIT!

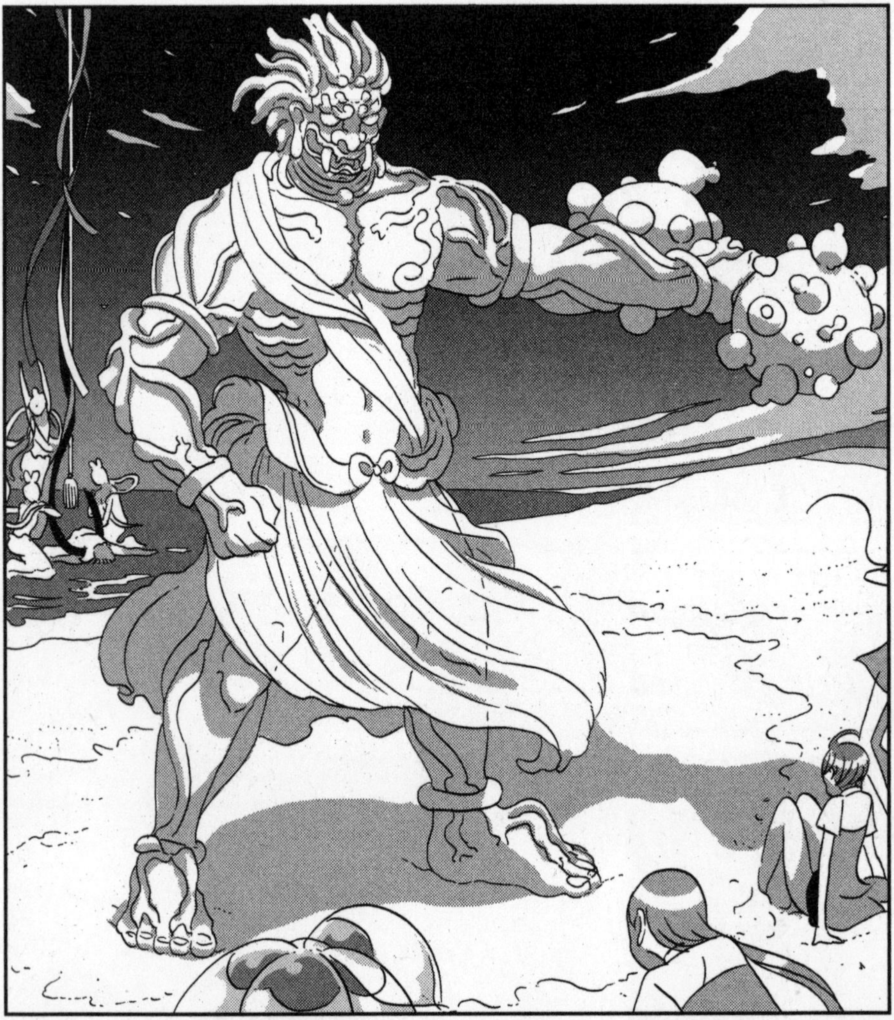

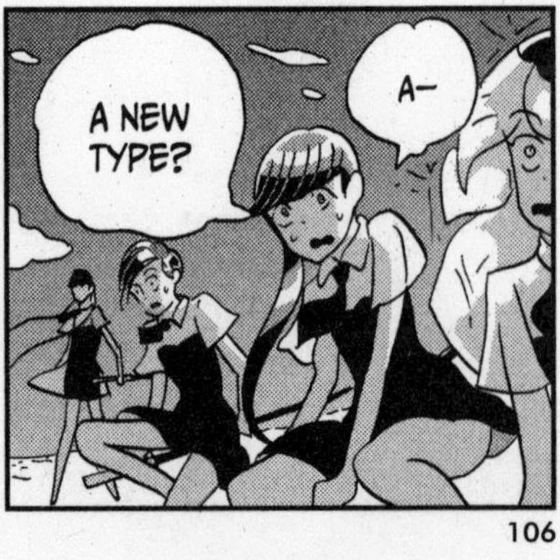
A—
A NEW TYPE?

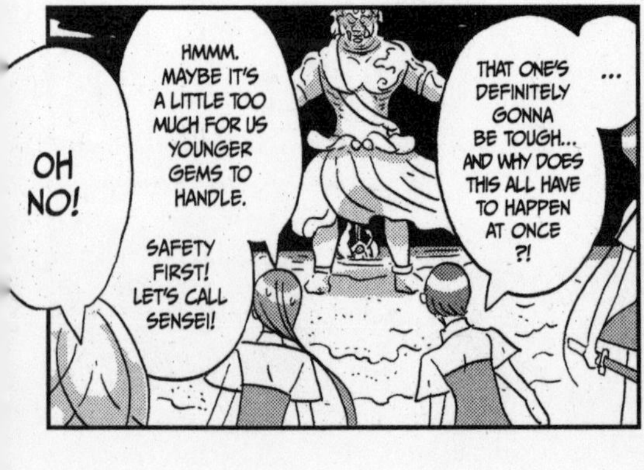
...
THAT ONE'S DEFINITELY GONNA BE TOUGH... AND WHY DOES THIS ALL HAVE TO HAPPEN AT ONCE ?!
HMMM. MAYBE IT'S A LITTLE TOO MUCH FOR US YOUNGER GEMS TO HANDLE.
SAFETY FIRST! LET'S CALL SENSEI!
OH NO!

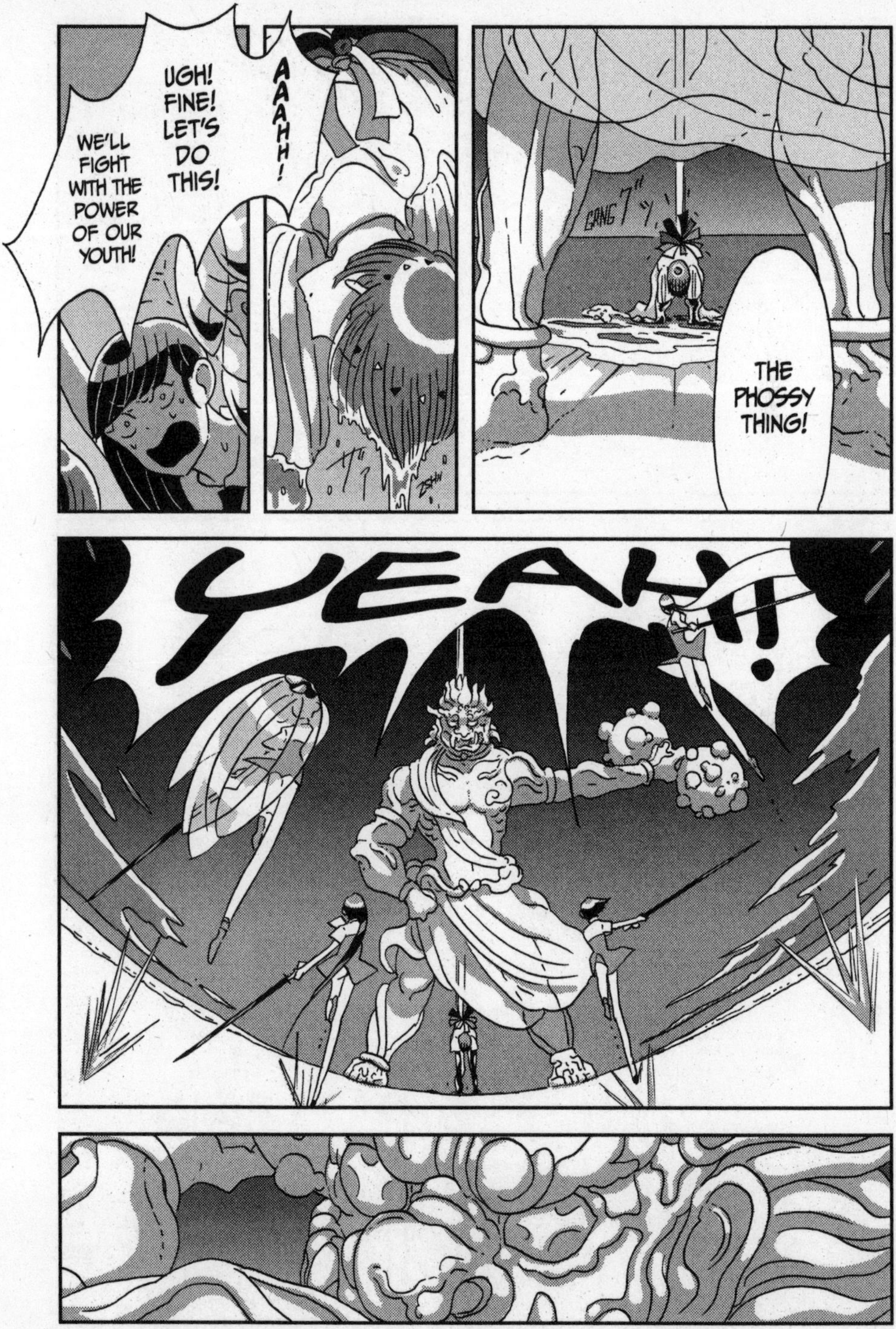
THE PHOSSY THING!
AAAHH!
UGH! FINE! LET'S DO THIS!
WE'LL FIGHT WITH THE POWER OF OUR YOUTH!
YEAH!!

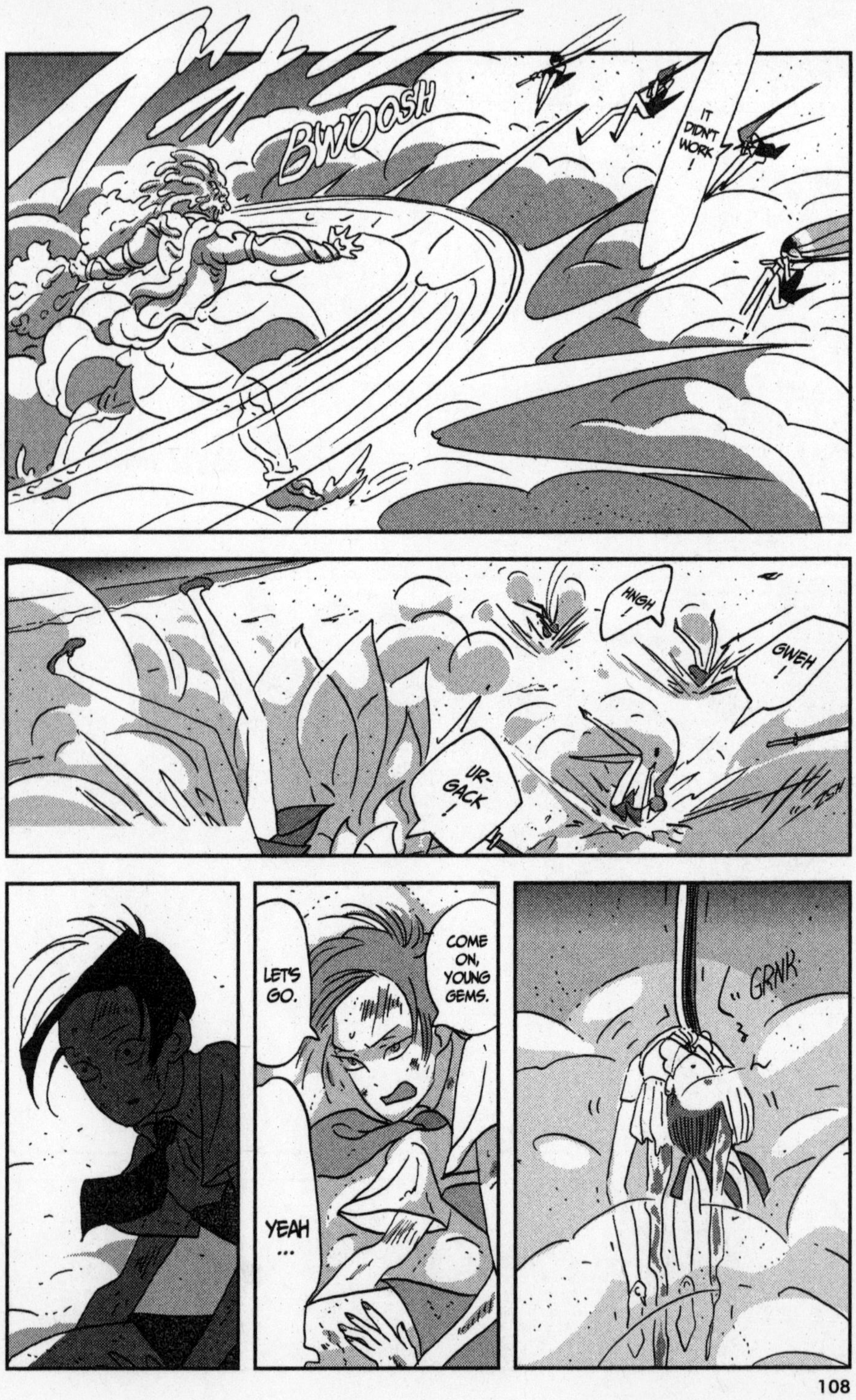

IT DIDN'T WORK!
BWOOSH
GWEH!
HNGH!
ZSH
UR-GACK!
GRNK
COME ON, YOUNG GEMS.
LET'S GO.
YEAH...

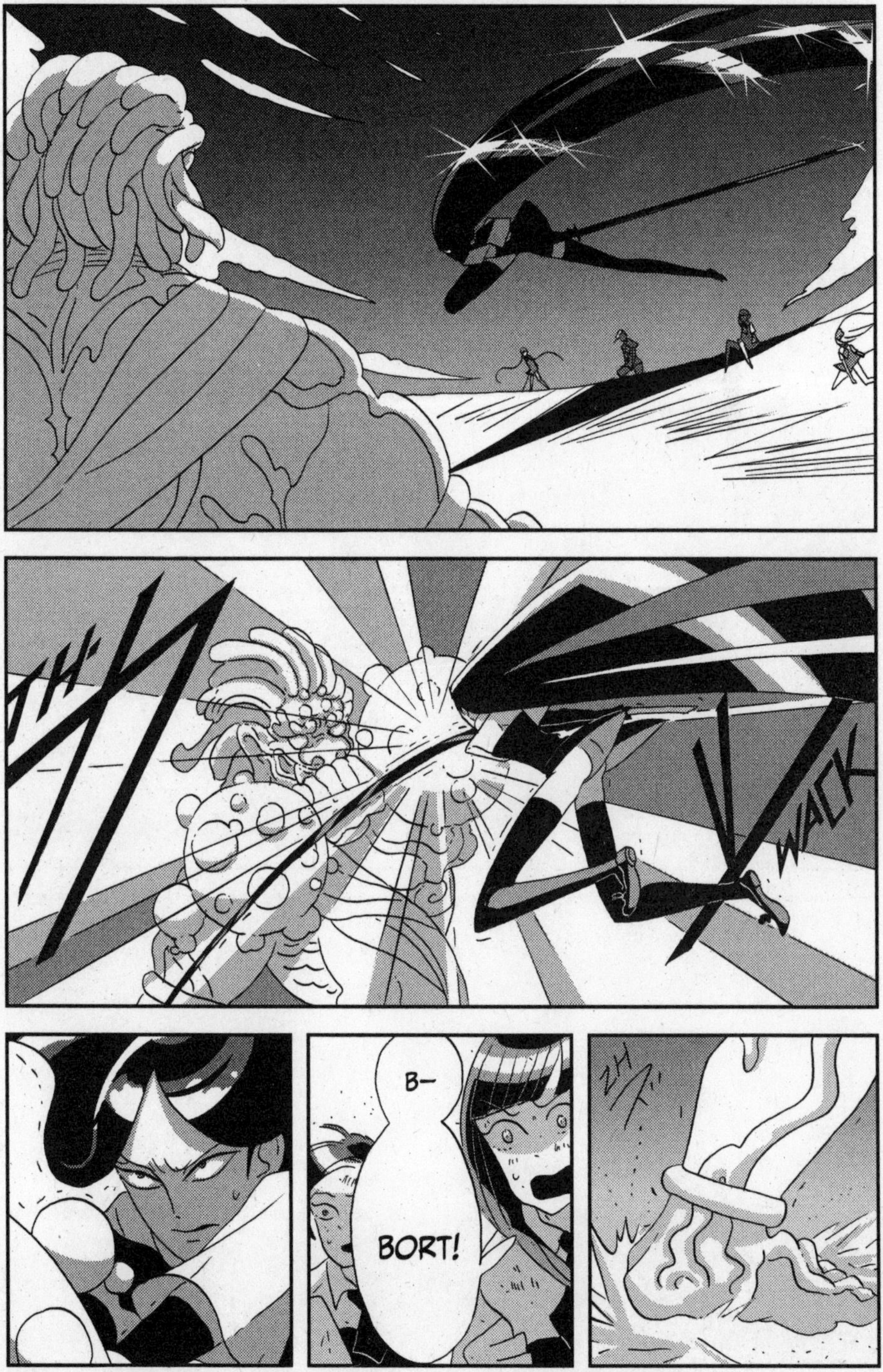
WACK
B—
BORT!

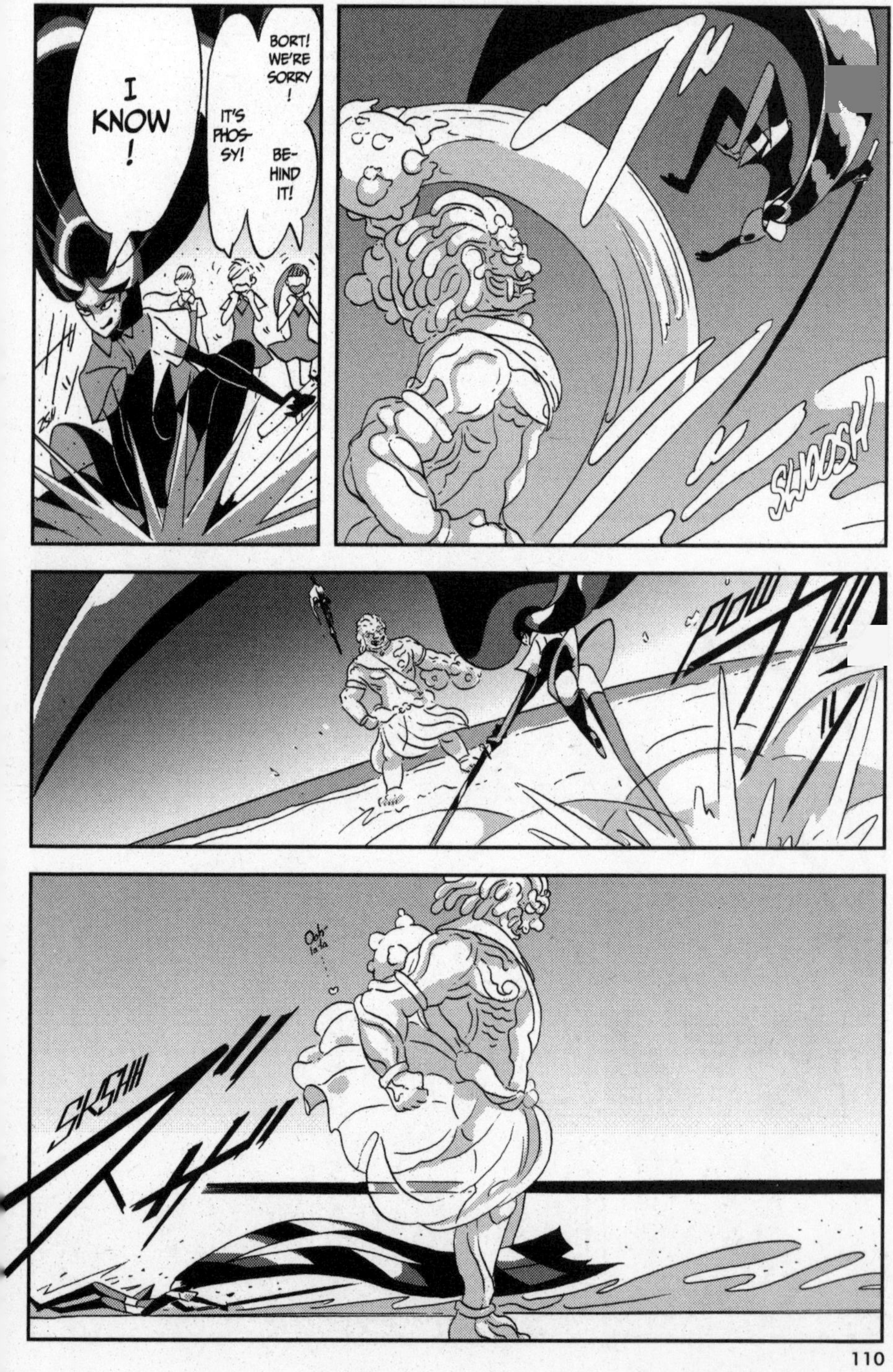
SWOOSH
BORT! WE'RE SORRY!
IT'S PHOS-SY!
BE-HIND IT!
I KNOW!
POW
Ooh la la...
SKSH

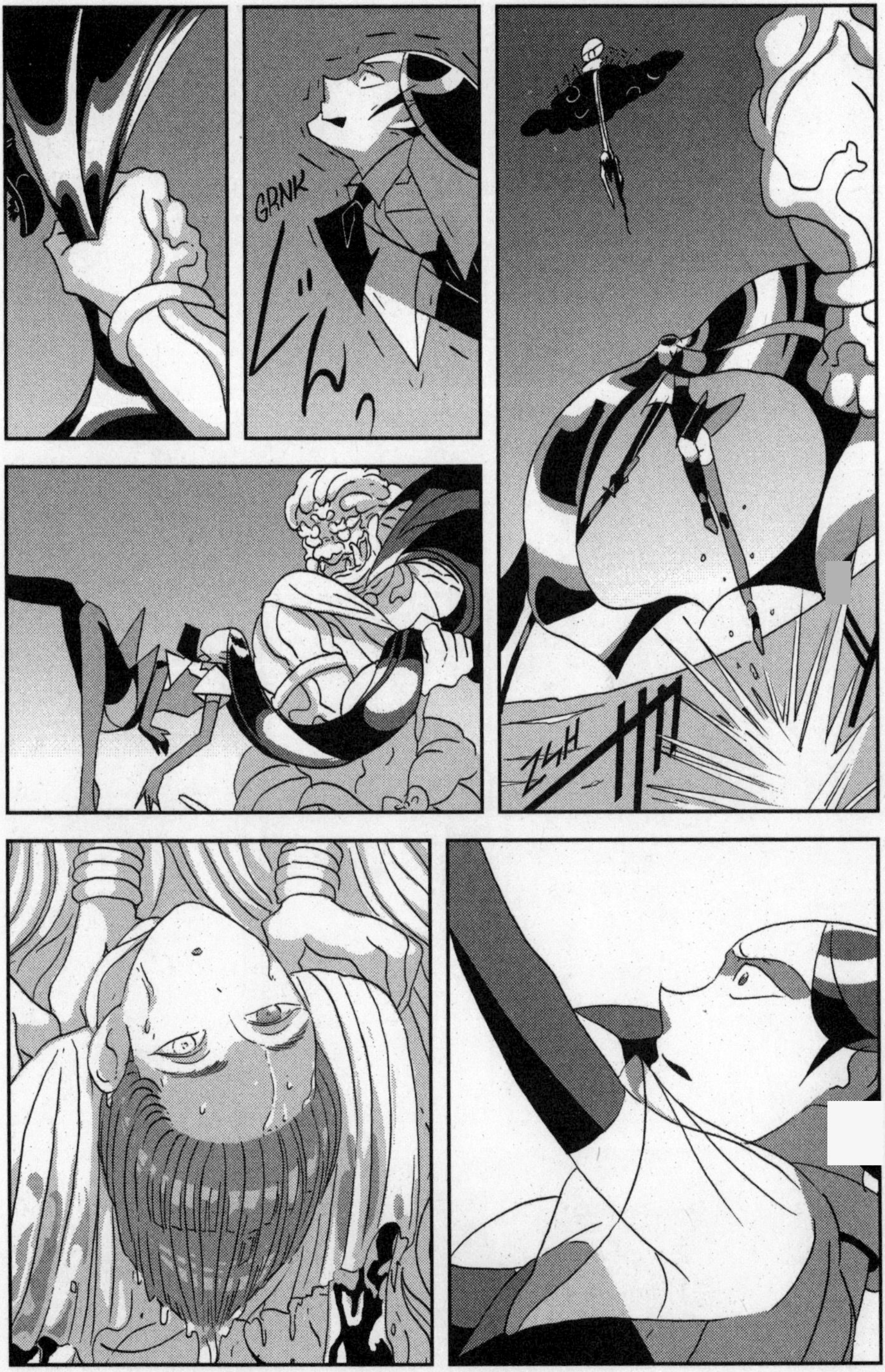
ZSH
GRNK

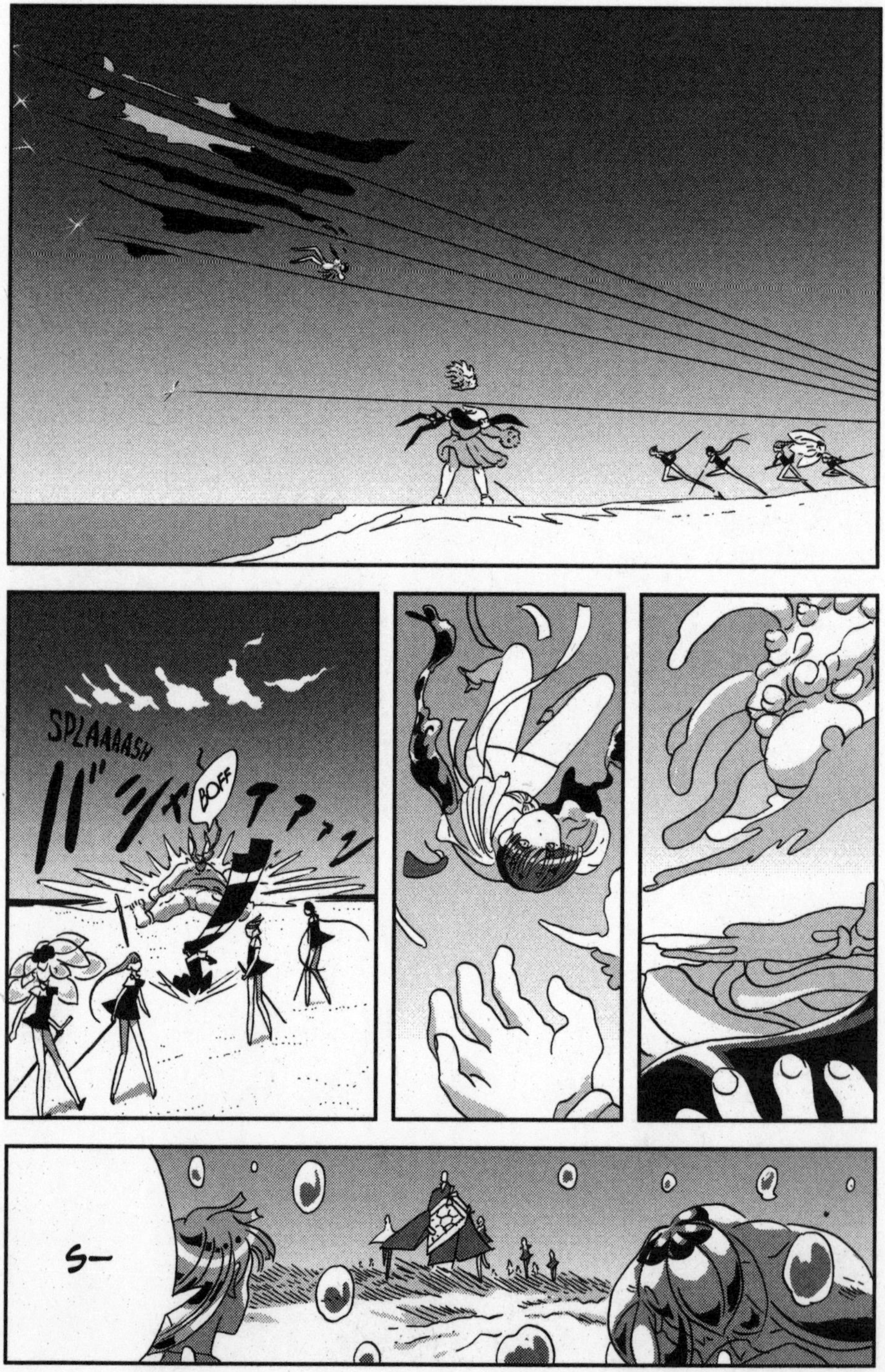
SPLAAAASH
バシャアァァン
BOFF
S—

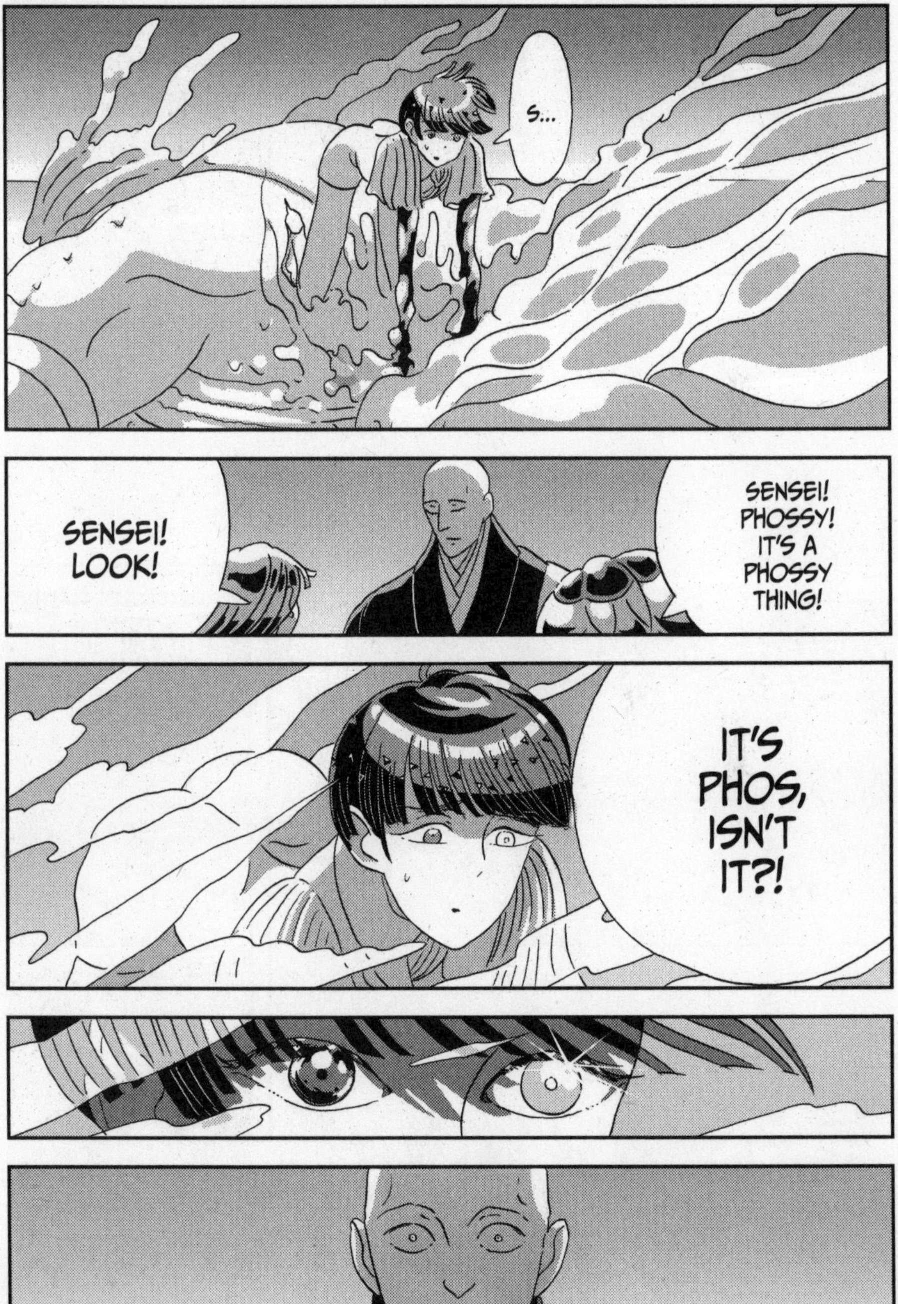
S...
SENSEI! PHOSSY! IT'S A PHOSSY THING!
SENSEI! LOOK!
IT'S PHOS, ISN'T IT?!

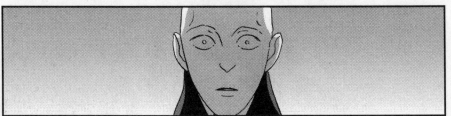

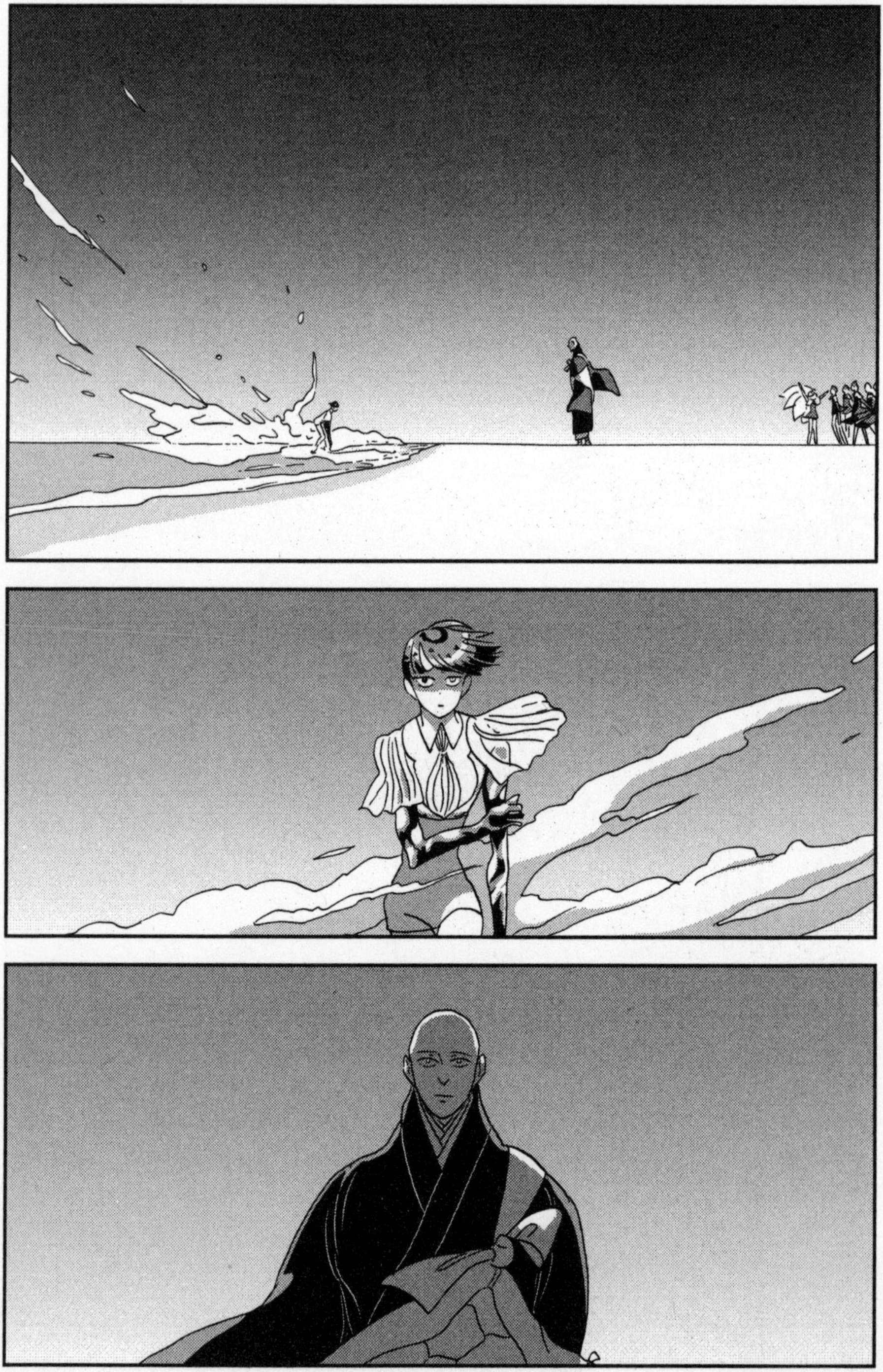

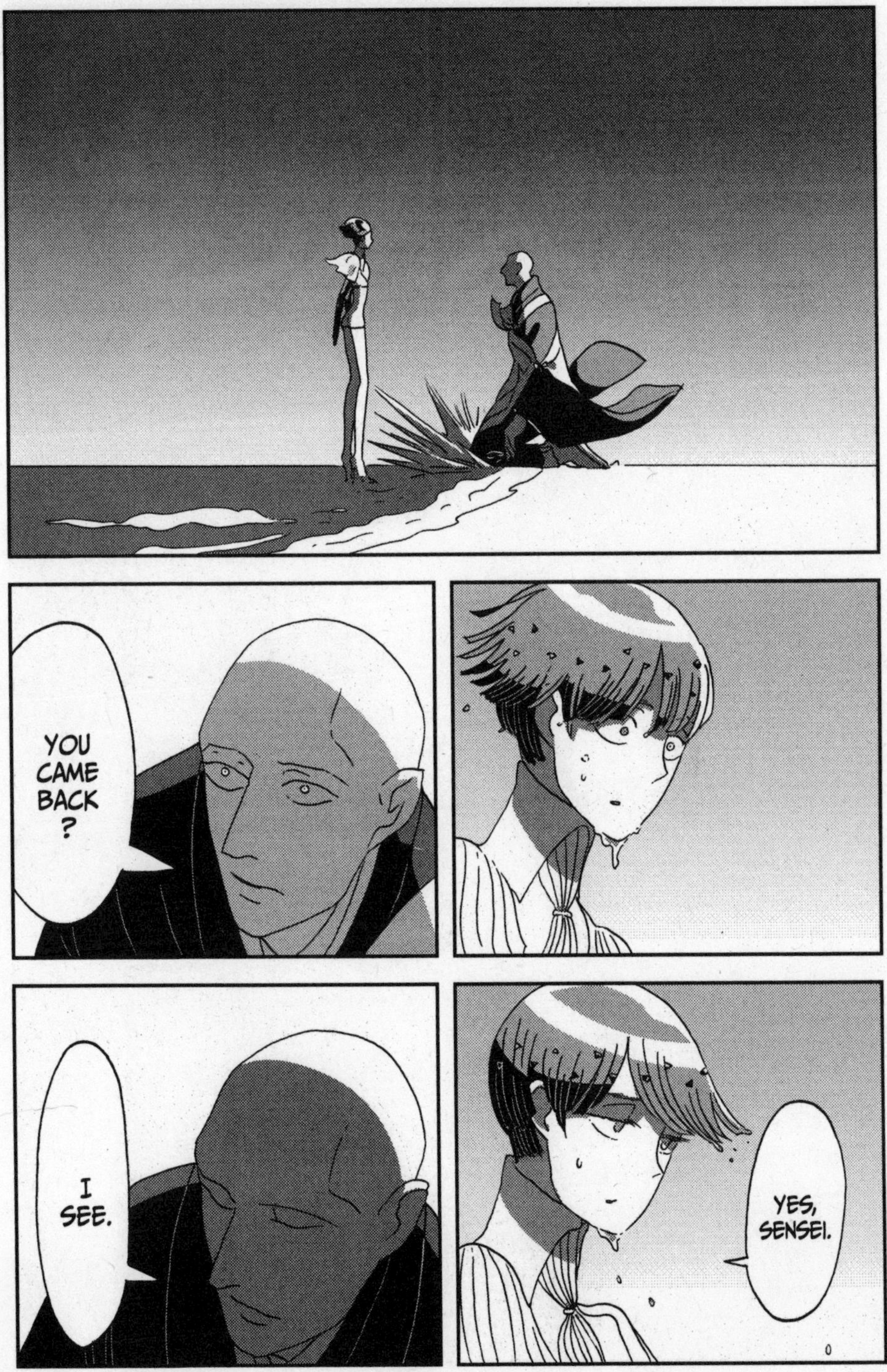
YOU CAME BACK?
YES, SENSEI.
I SEE.

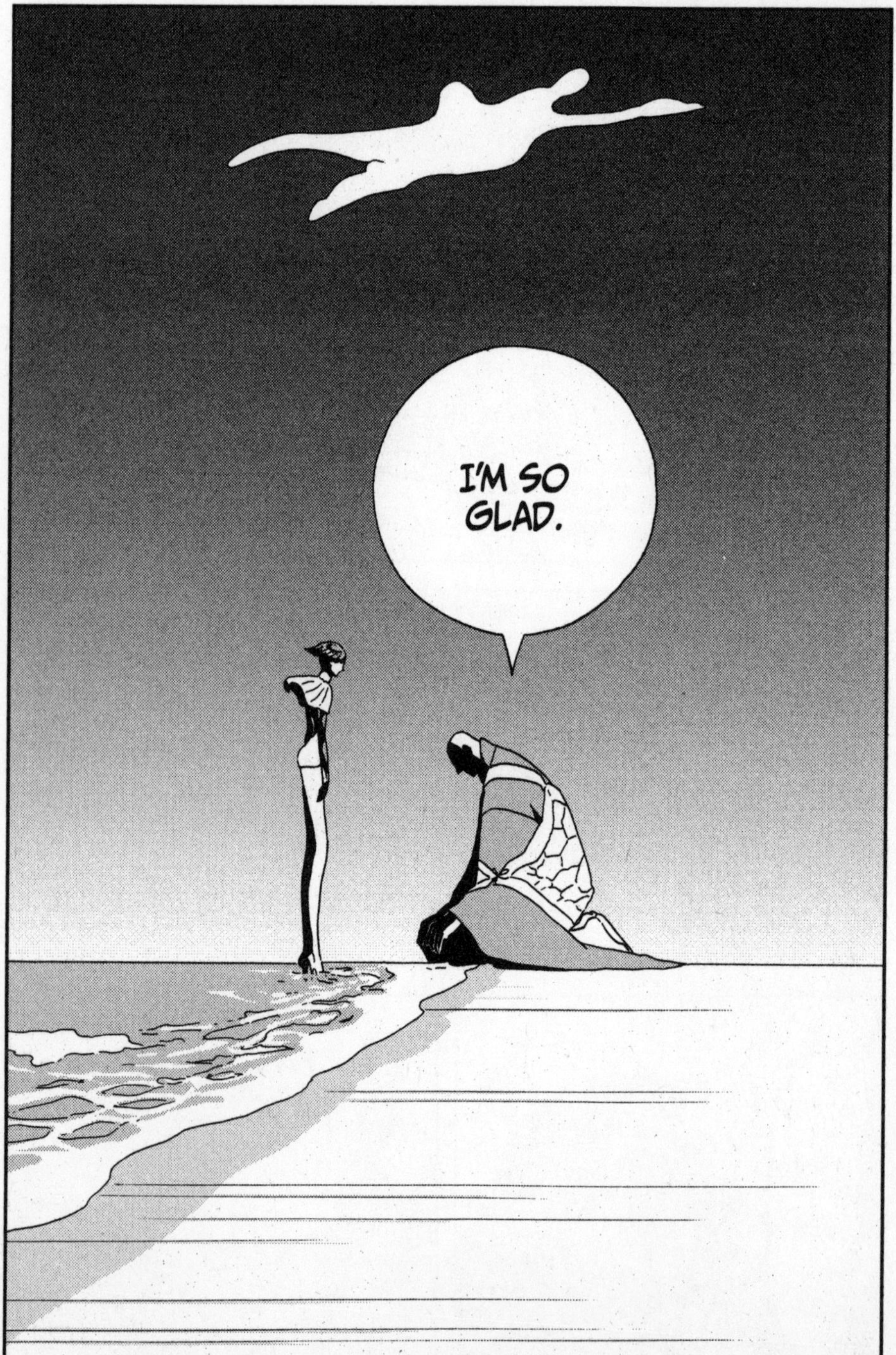
I'M SO GLAD.

CHAPTER 58:

Hope

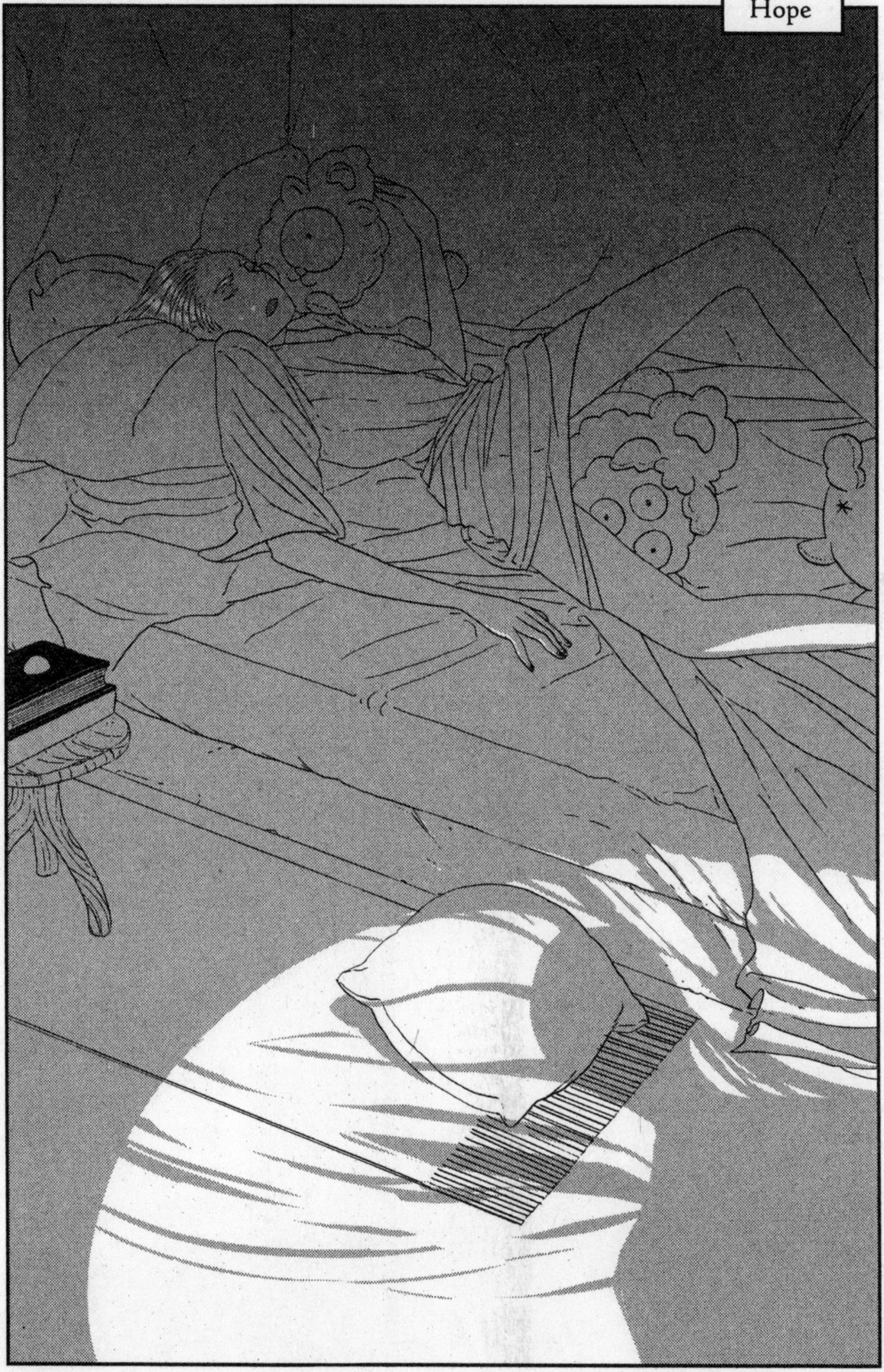

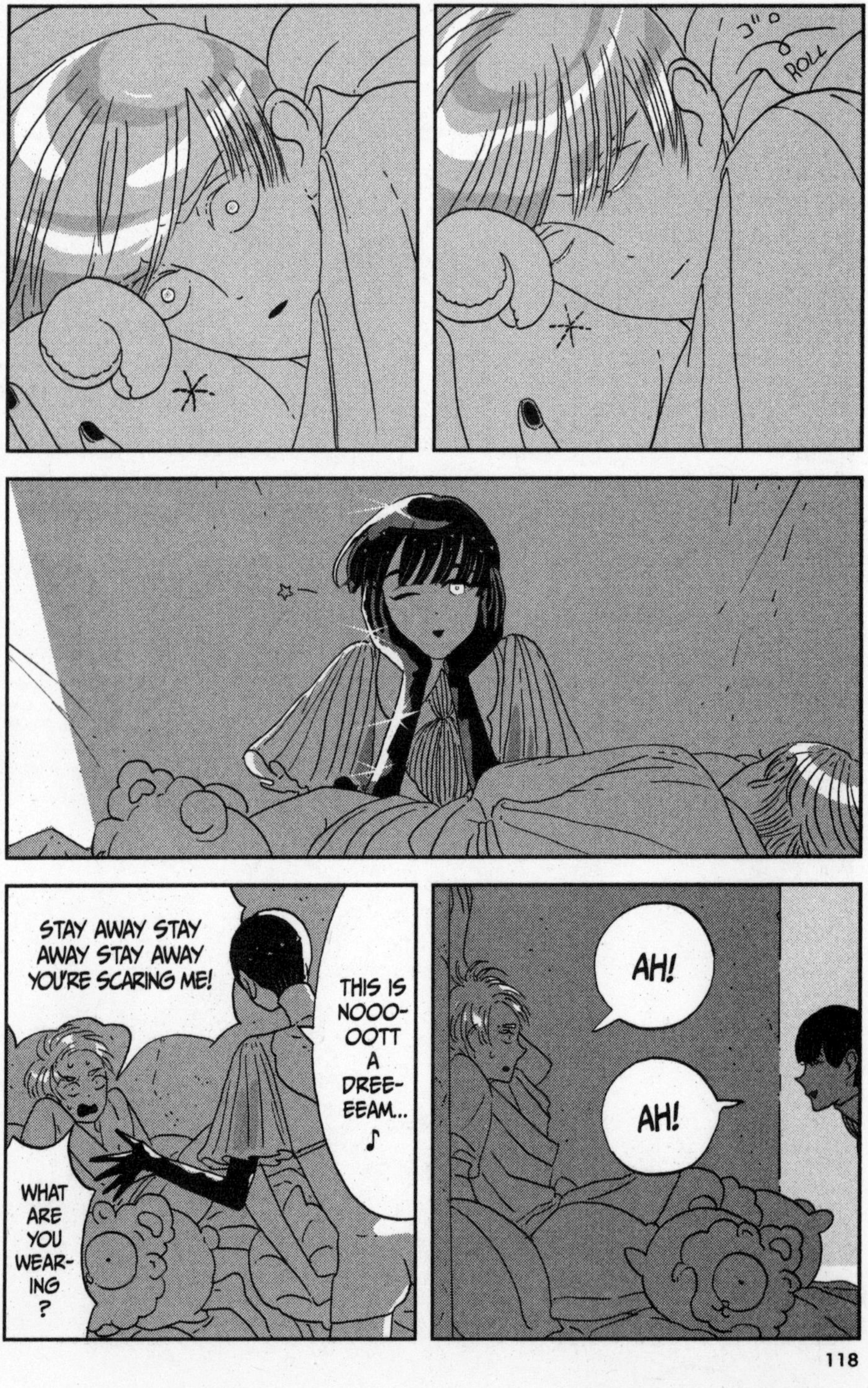
ゴロ
ROLL
AH!
AH!
THIS IS NOOOO-OOTT A DREE-EEAM... ♪
STAY AWAY STAY AWAY STAY AWAY YOU'RE SCARING ME!
WHAT ARE YOU WEAR-ING?

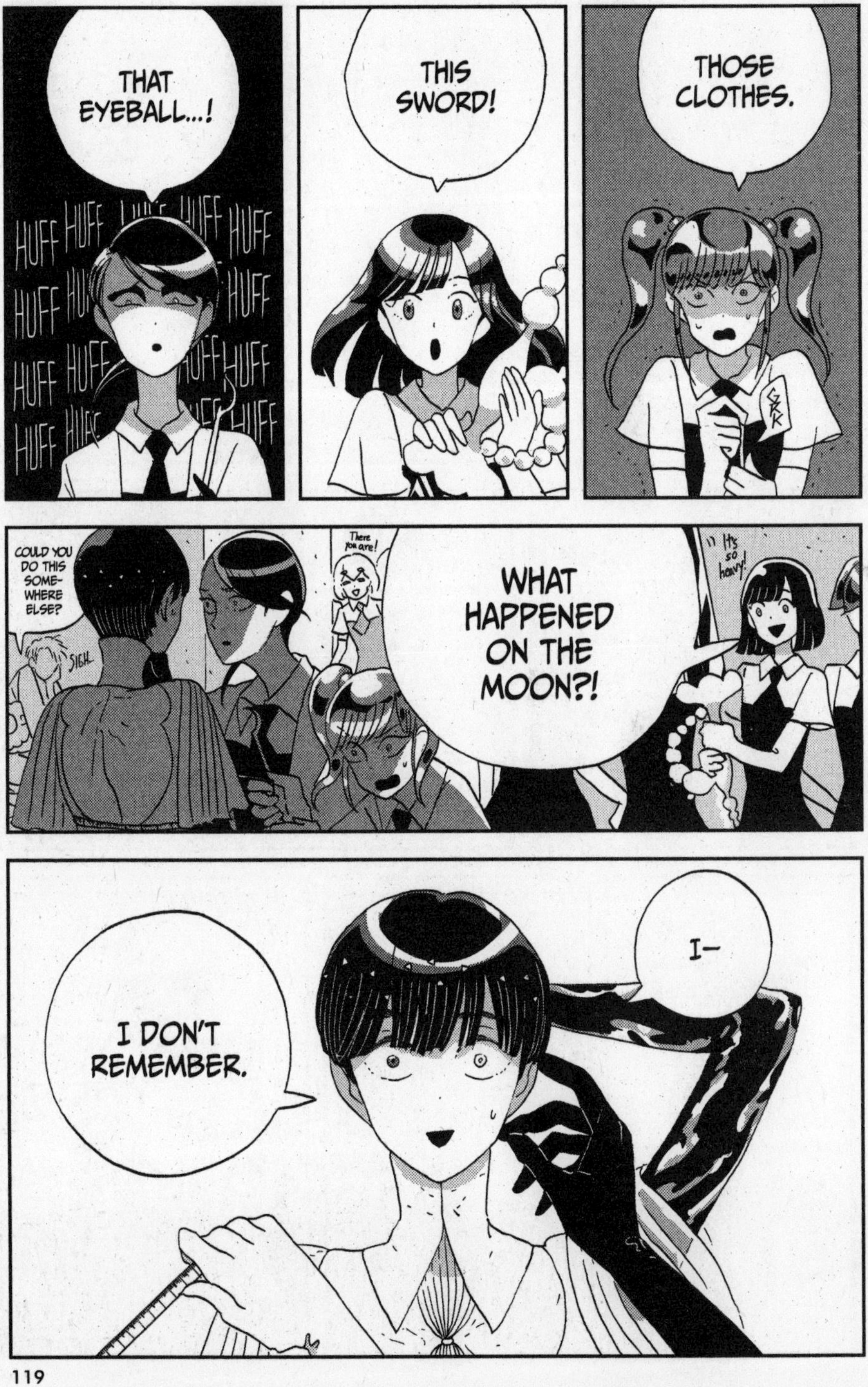
THOSE CLOTHES.
THIS SWORD!
THAT EYEBALL...!
HUFF HUFF HUFF HUFF
It's so heavy!
WHAT HAPPENED ON THE MOON?!
There you are!
SIGH
COULD YOU DO THIS SOMEWHERE ELSE?
I—
I DON'T REMEMBER.

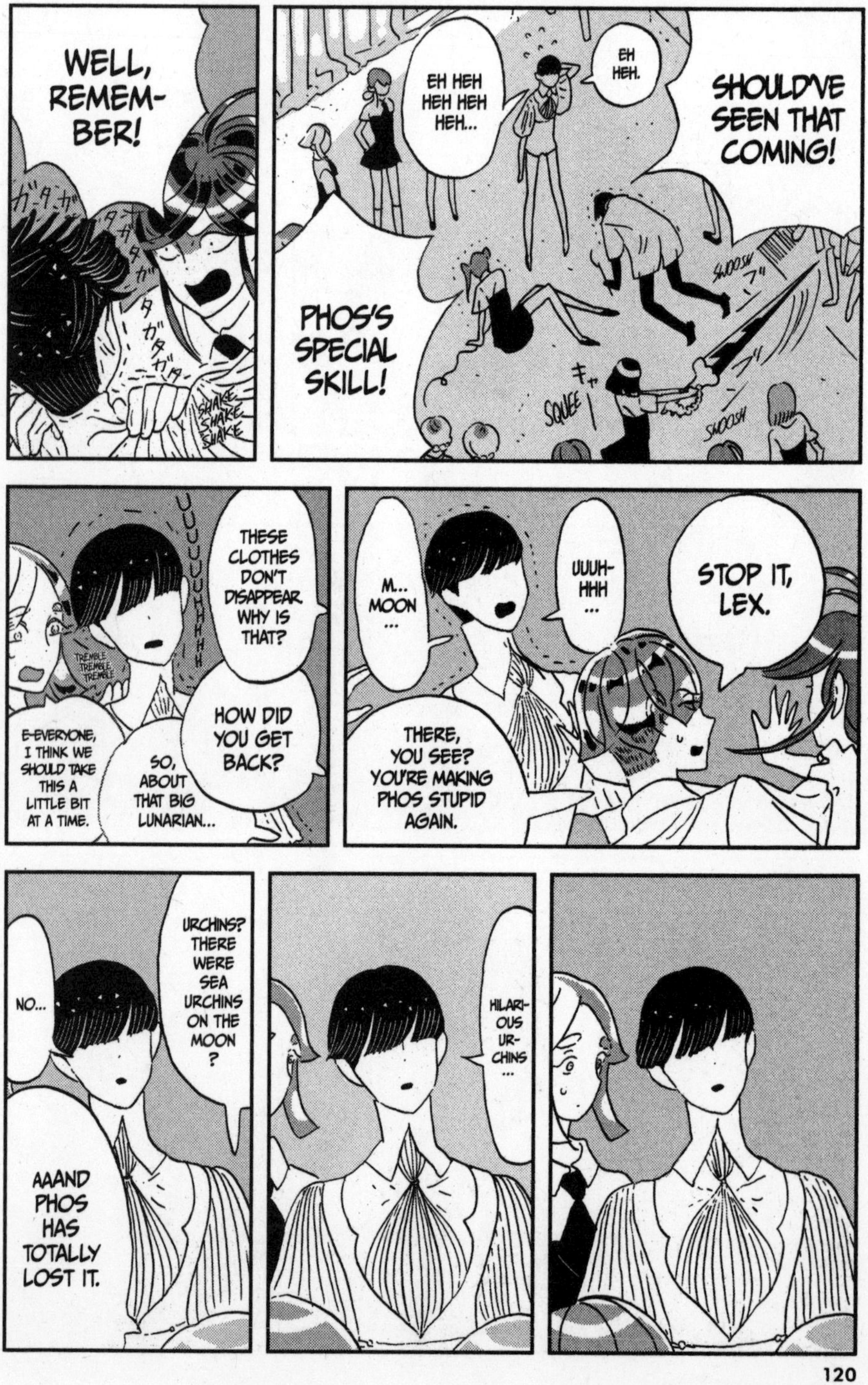
SHOULD'VE SEEN THAT COMING!
EH HEH.
EH HEH HEH HEH HEH...
PHOS'S SPECIAL SKILL!
SWOOSH
SQUEE
SWOOSH
WELL, REMEMBER!
SHAKE SHAKE SHAKE
STOP IT, LEX.
UUUH-HHH...
M... MOON...
THERE, YOU SEE? YOU'RE MAKING PHOS STUPID AGAIN.
THESE CLOTHES DON'T DISAPPEAR WHY IS THAT?
HOW DID YOU GET BACK?
SO, ABOUT THAT BIG LUNARIAN...
TREMBLE TREMBLE TREMBLE
E-EVERYONE, I THINK WE SHOULD TAKE THIS A LITTLE BIT AT A TIME.
HILARIOUS URCHINS...
URCHINS? THERE WERE SEA URCHINS ON THE MOON?
NO...
AAAND PHOS HAS TOTALLY LOST IT.

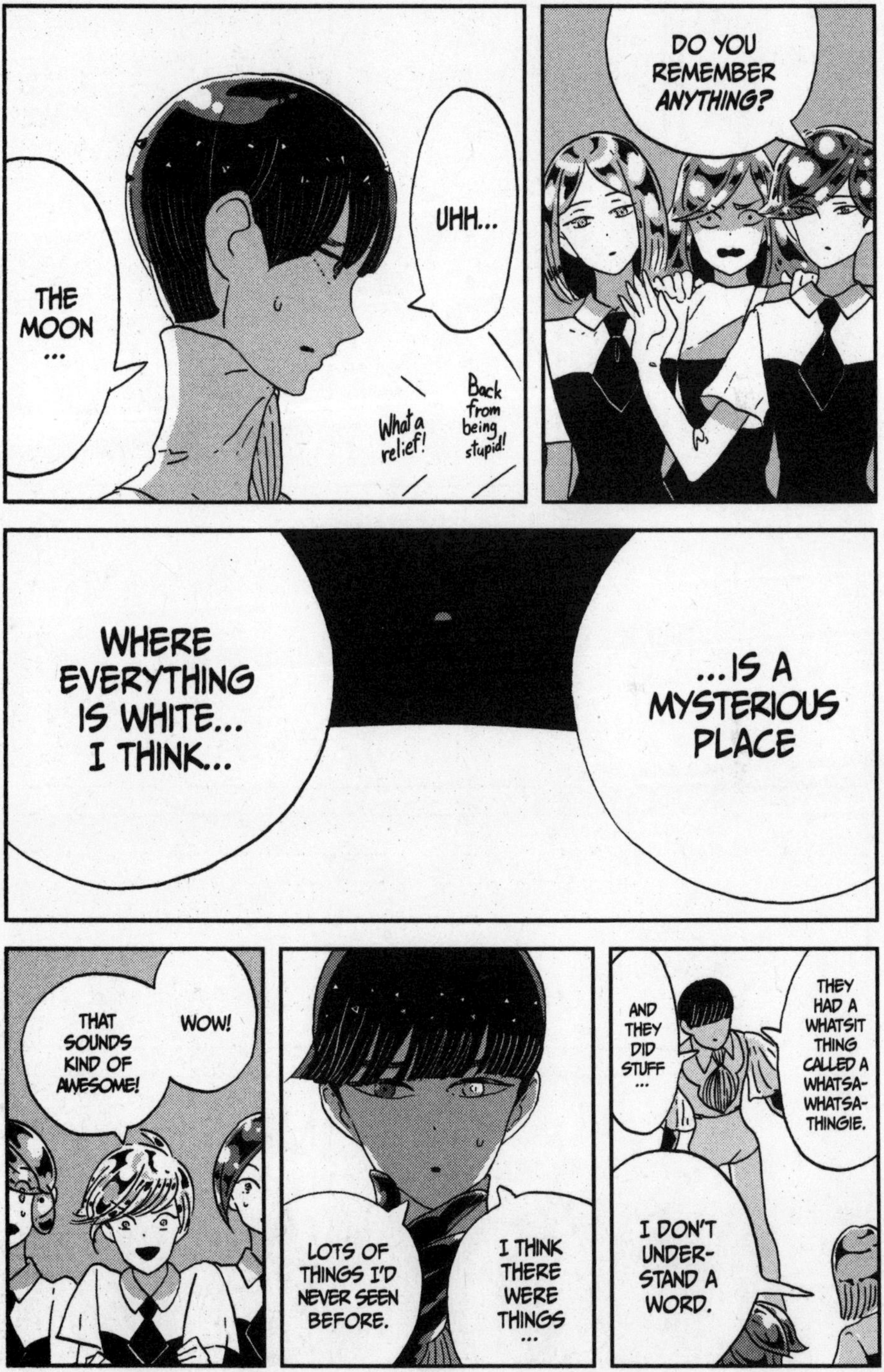

DO YOU REMEMBER ANYTHING?
UHH...
Back from being stupid!
What a relief!
THE MOON ...
WHERE EVERYTHING IS WHITE... I THINK...
...IS A MYSTERIOUS PLACE
THEY HAD A WHATSIT THING CALLED A WHATSA-WHATSA-THINGIE.
AND THEY DID STUFF ...
I DON'T UNDER-STAND A WORD.
I THINK THERE WERE THINGS ...
LOTS OF THINGS I'D NEVER SEEN BEFORE.
WOW!
THAT SOUNDS KIND OF AWESOME!

...SEE ANY OTHER GEMS?

DID YOU...

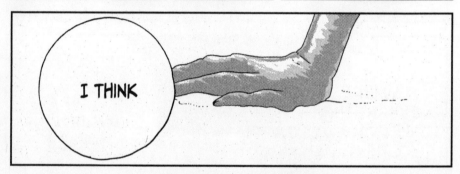

I THINK

I SAW SOME.

YOU

...DID?

OH, BUT IT'S NOT LIKE I TALKED TO THEM...

...OR ANYTHING...

I CAN'T GIVE YOU ANY BETTER INFORMATION.

I'M SORRY.

COME TO THINK OF IT, SENSEI...

THAT'S OKAY...

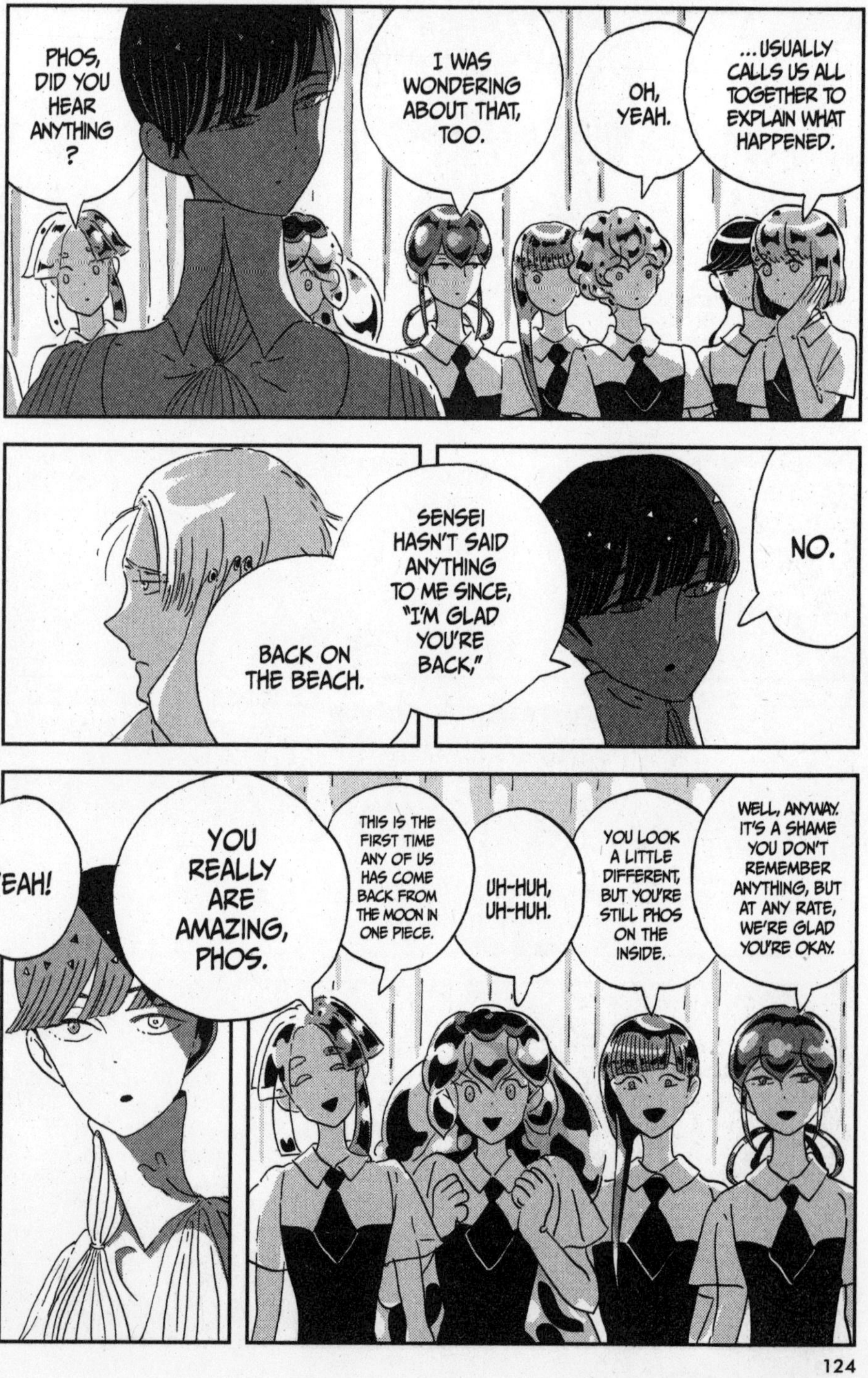
...USUALLY CALLS US ALL TOGETHER TO EXPLAIN WHAT HAPPENED.
OH, YEAH.
I WAS WONDERING ABOUT THAT, TOO.
PHOS, DID YOU HEAR ANYTHING ?
NO.
SENSEI HASN'T SAID ANYTHING TO ME SINCE, "I'M GLAD YOU'RE BACK,"
BACK ON THE BEACH.
WELL, ANYWAY. IT'S A SHAME YOU DON'T REMEMBER ANYTHING, BUT AT ANY RATE, WE'RE GLAD YOU'RE OKAY.
YOU LOOK A LITTLE DIFFERENT, BUT YOU'RE STILL PHOS ON THE INSIDE.
UH-HUH, UH-HUH.
THIS IS THE FIRST TIME ANY OF US HAS COME BACK FROM THE MOON IN ONE PIECE.
YOU REALLY ARE AMAZING, PHOS.
YEAH!

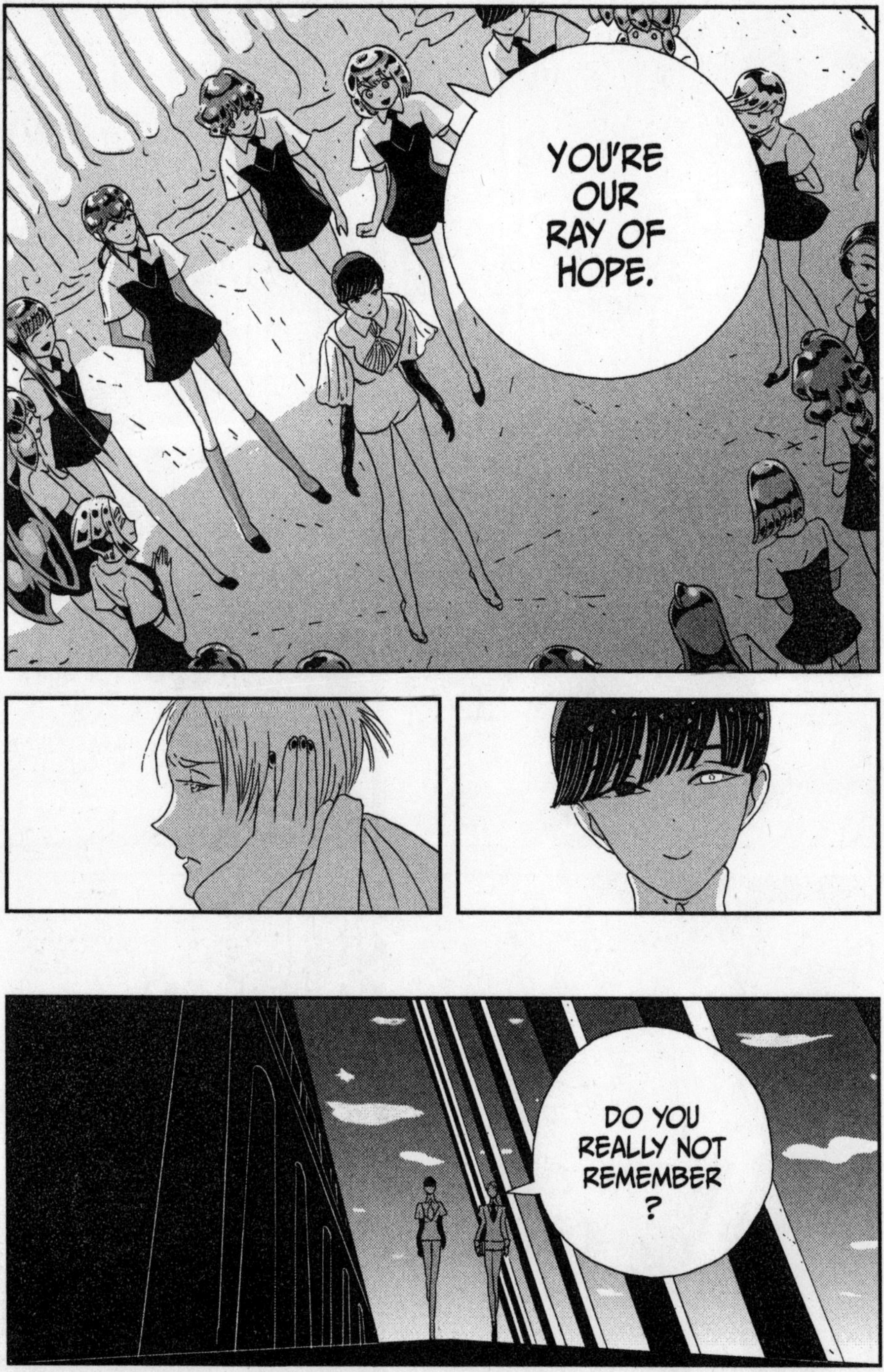
YOU'RE OUR RAY OF HOPE.
DO YOU REALLY NOT REMEMBER ?

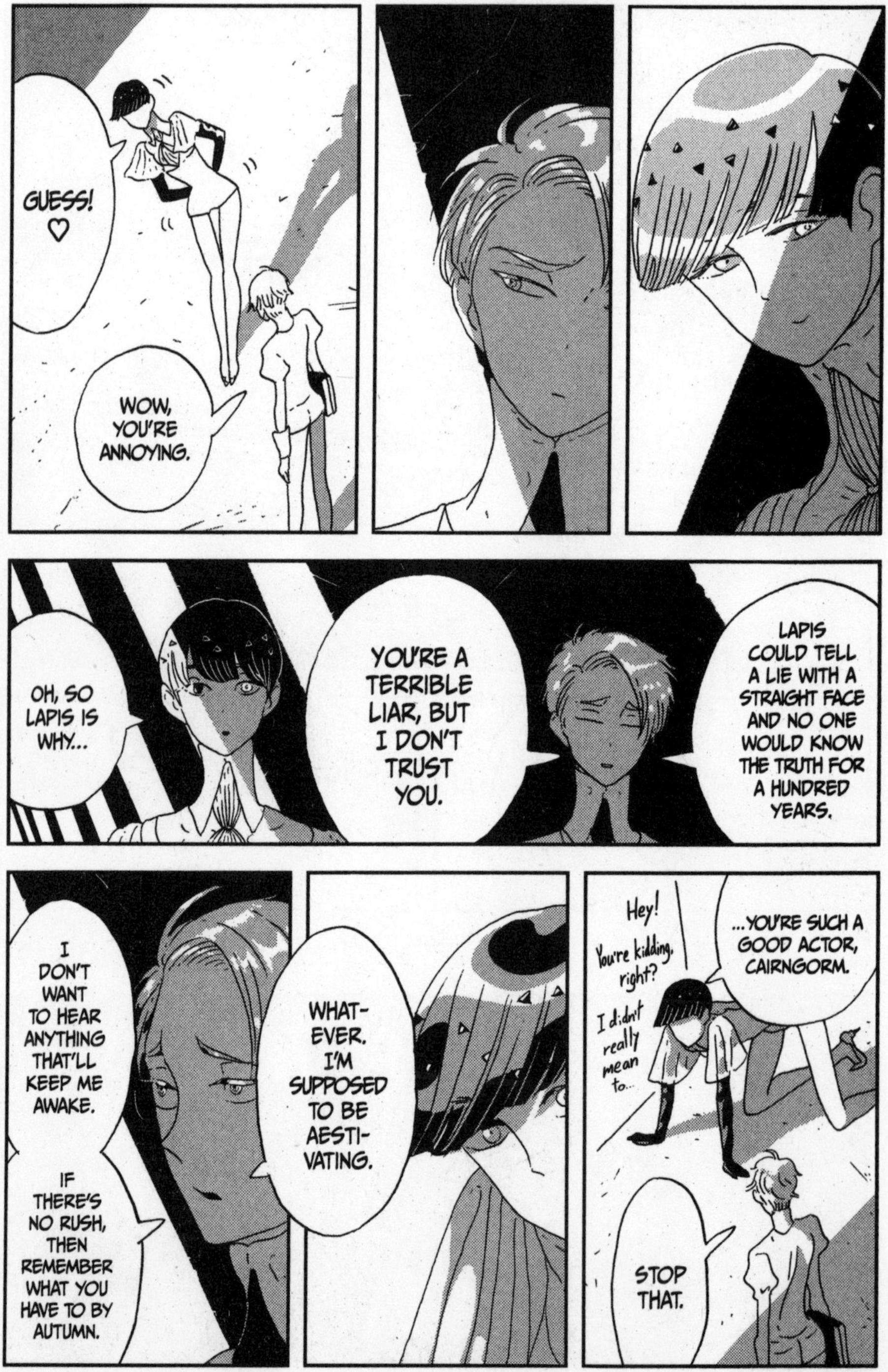
GUESS! ♡
WOW, YOU'RE ANNOYING.
LAPIS COULD TELL A LIE WITH A STRAIGHT FACE AND NO ONE WOULD KNOW THE TRUTH FOR A HUNDRED YEARS.
YOU'RE A TERRIBLE LIAR, BUT I DON'T TRUST YOU.
OH, SO LAPIS IS WHY...
...YOU'RE SUCH A GOOD ACTOR, CAIRNGORM.
Hey! You're kidding, right? I didn't really mean to...
STOP THAT.
WHAT-EVER. I'M SUPPOSED TO BE AESTI-VATING.
I DON'T WANT TO HEAR ANYTHING THAT'LL KEEP ME AWAKE.
IF THERE'S NO RUSH, THEN REMEMBER WHAT YOU HAVE TO BY AUTUMN.

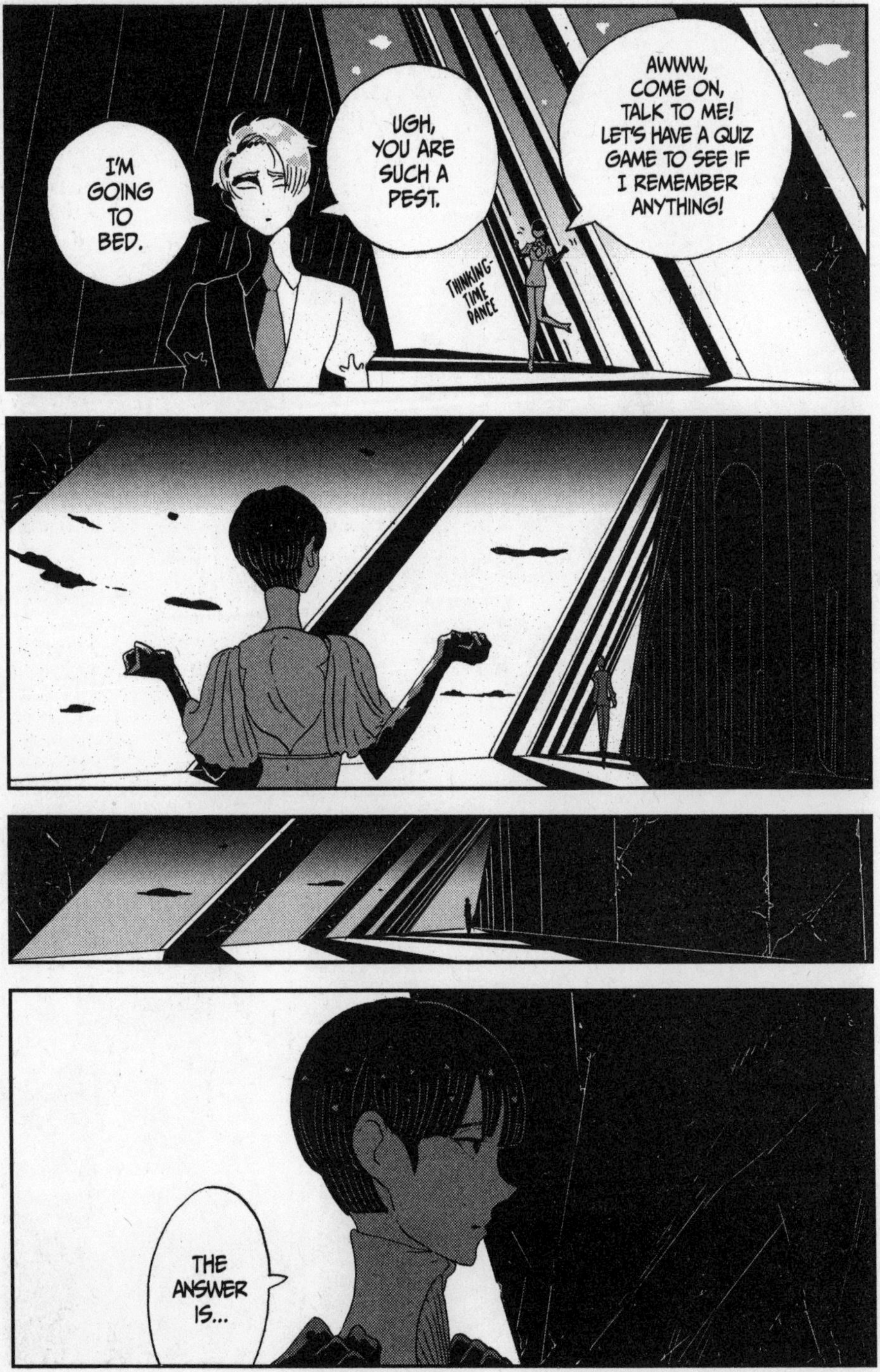
AWWW, COME ON, TALK TO ME! LET'S HAVE A QUIZ GAME TO SEE IF I REMEMBER ANYTHING!
THINKING-TIME DANCE
UGH, YOU ARE SUCH A PEST.
I'M GOING TO BED.
THE ANSWER IS...

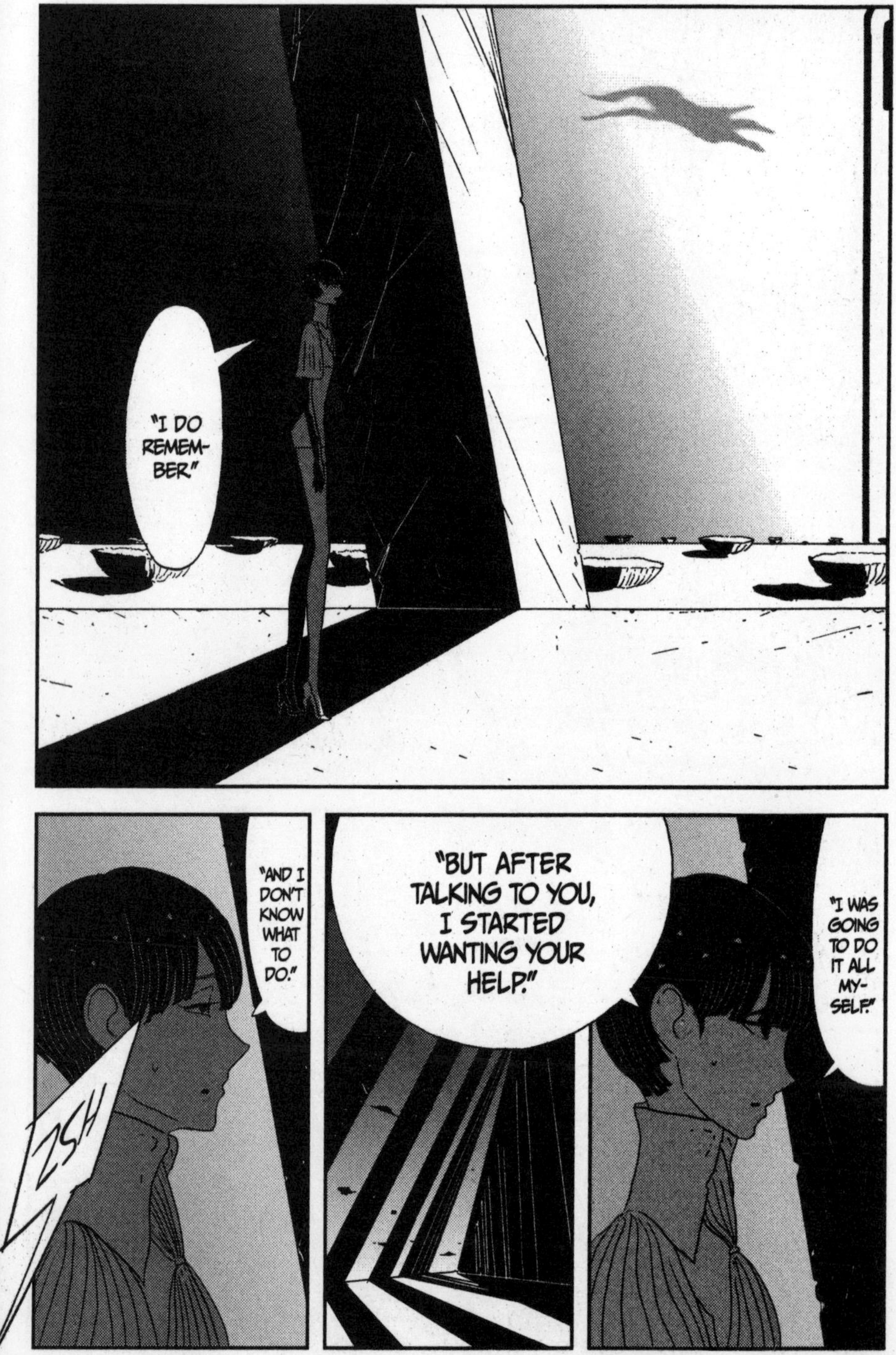
"I DO REMEMBER"
"I WAS GOING TO DO IT ALL MYSELF."
"BUT AFTER TALKING TO YOU, I STARTED WANTING YOUR HELP."
"AND I DON'T KNOW WHAT TO DO."
ZSH

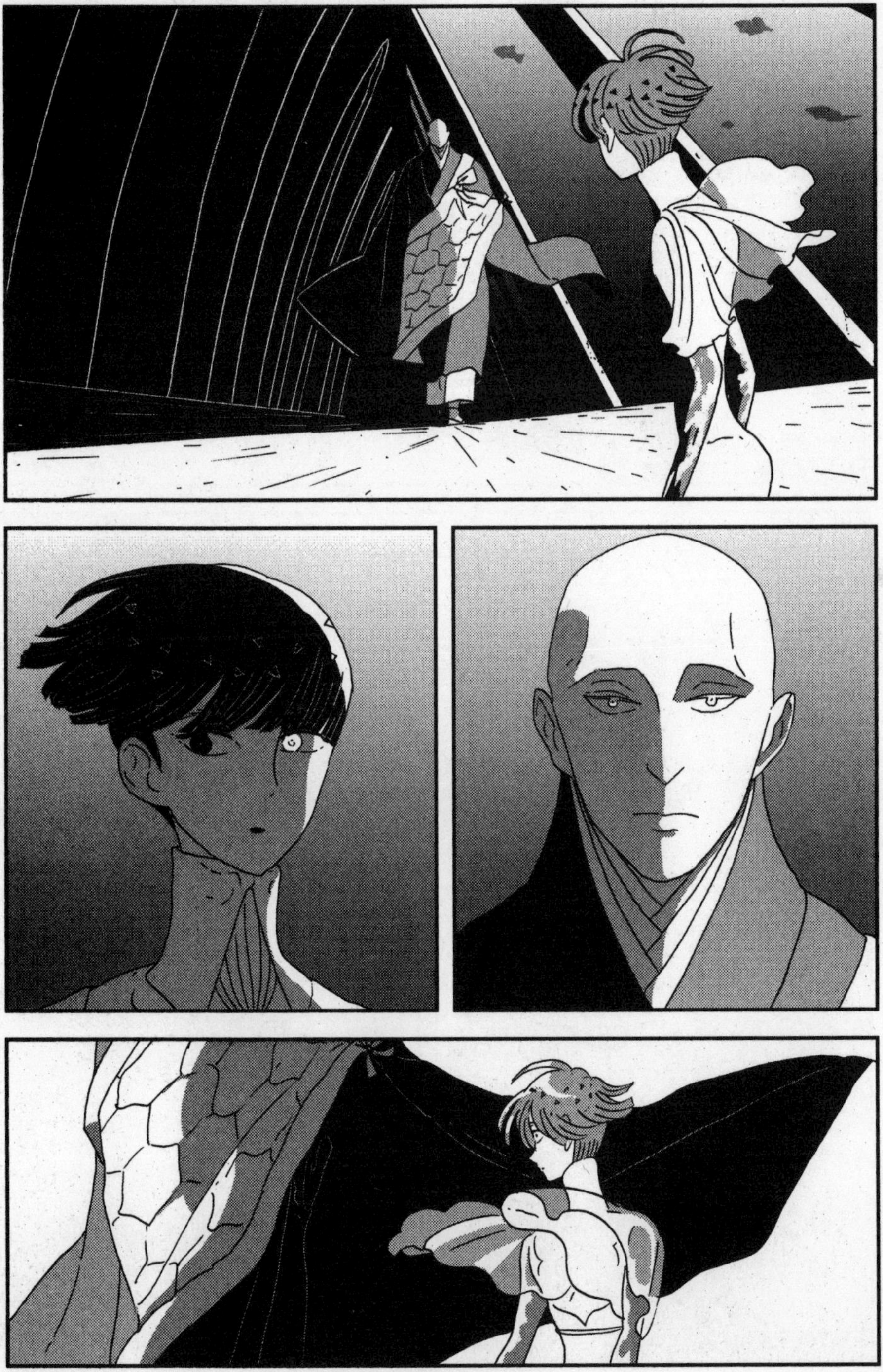

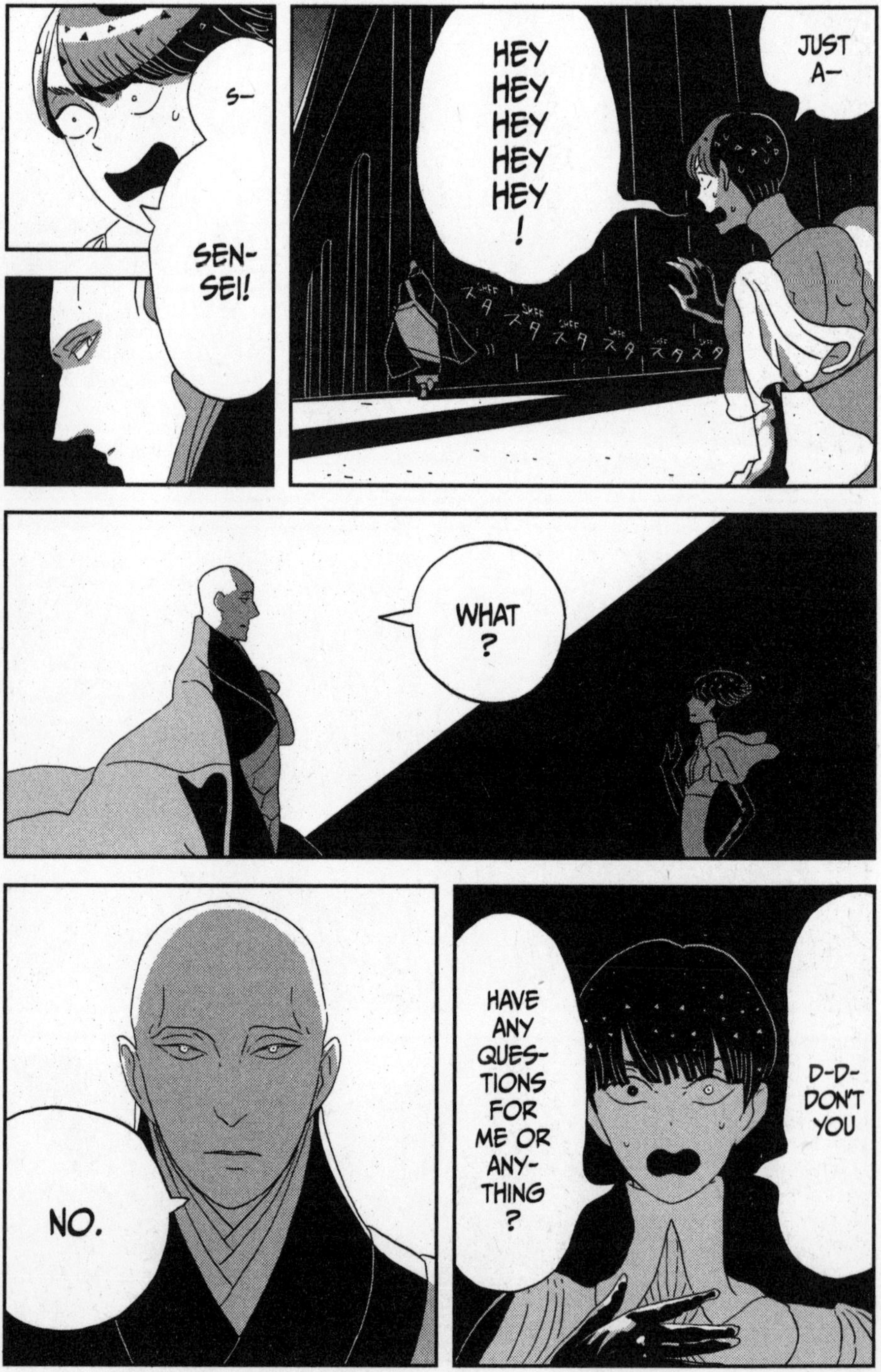
JUST A—
HEY HEY HEY HEY HEY!
S—
SEN-SEI!
WHAT?
D-D-DON'T YOU
HAVE ANY QUES-TIONS FOR ME OR ANY-THING?
NO.

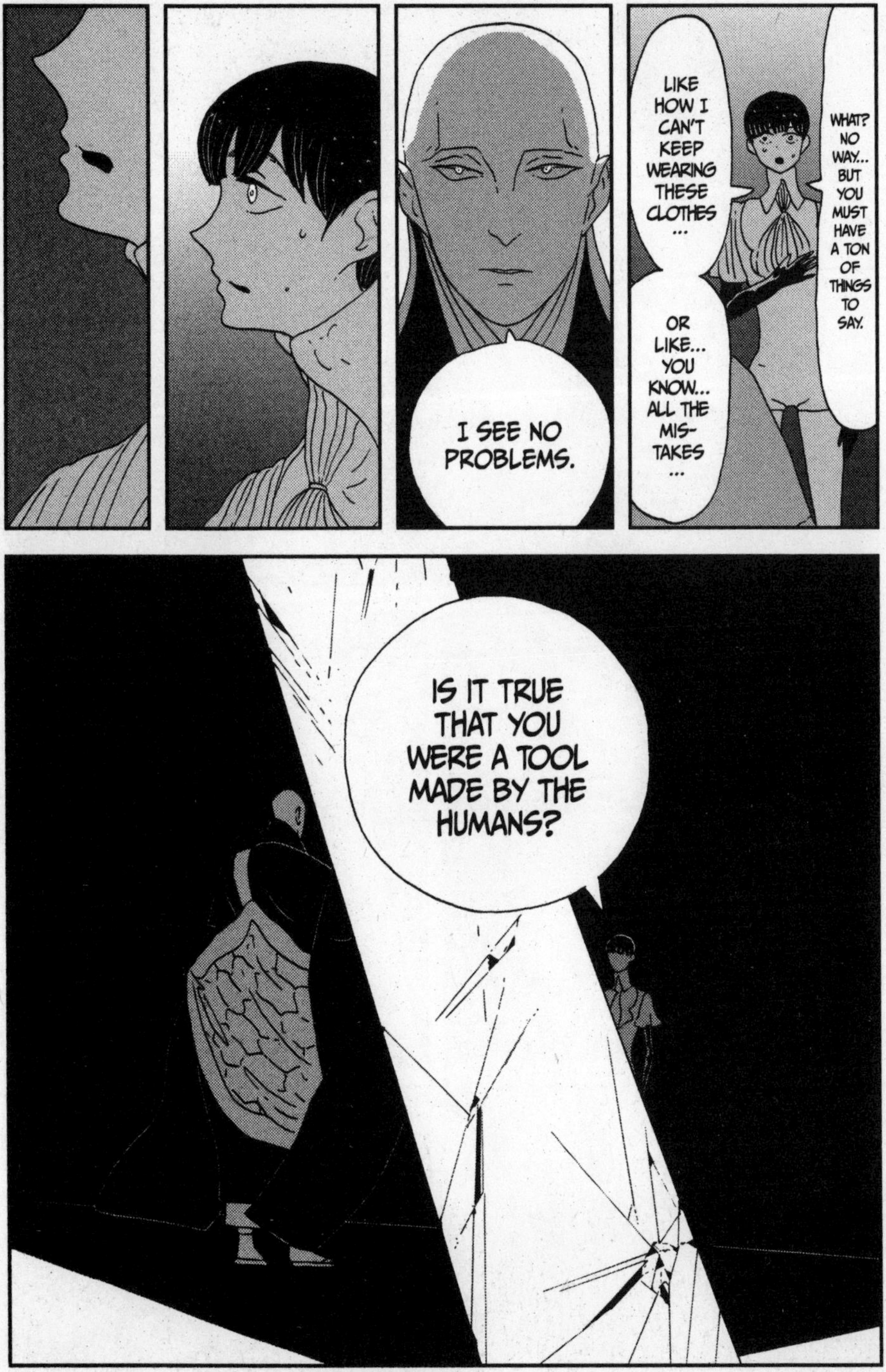
WHAT? NO WAY... BUT YOU MUST HAVE A TON OF THINGS TO SAY.
LIKE HOW I CAN'T KEEP WEARING THESE CLOTHES ...
OR LIKE... YOU KNOW... ALL THE MIS-TAKES ...
I SEE NO PROBLEMS.
IS IT TRUE THAT YOU WERE A TOOL MADE BY THE HUMANS?

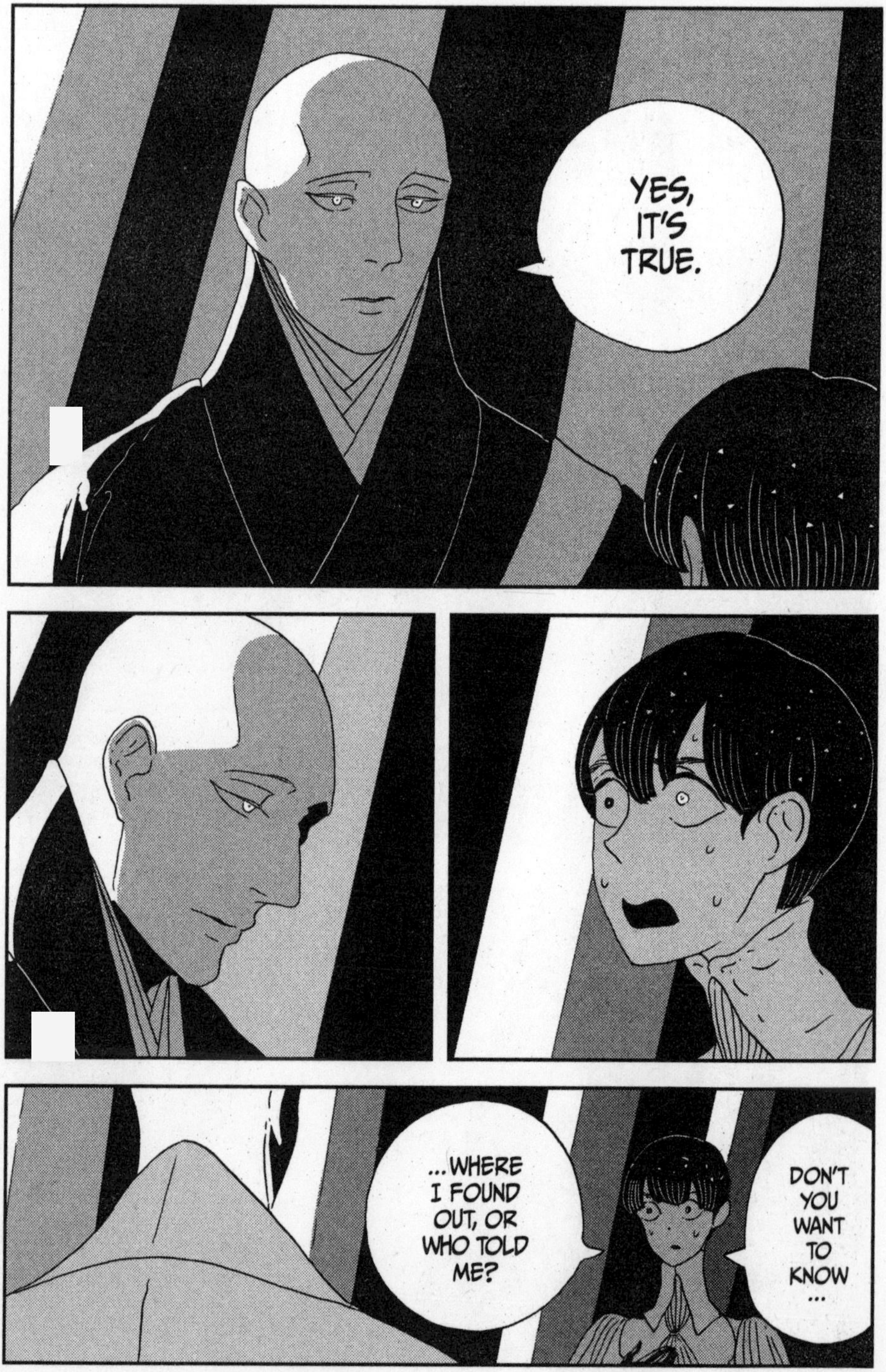
YES, IT'S TRUE.
DON'T YOU WANT TO KNOW ...
...WHERE I FOUND OUT, OR WHO TOLD ME?

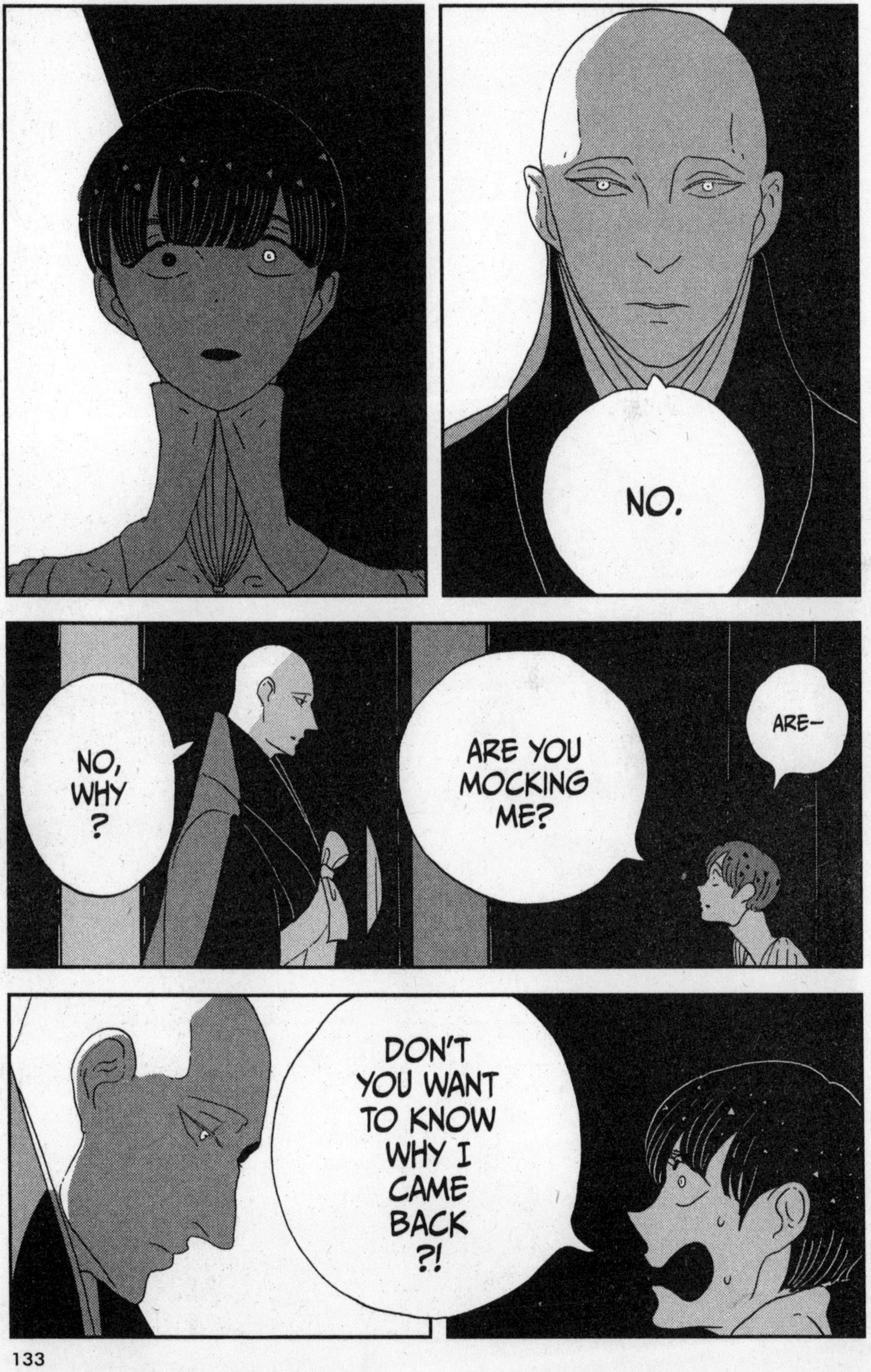
NO.
ARE—
ARE YOU MOCKING ME?
NO, WHY ?
DON'T YOU WANT TO KNOW WHY I CAME BACK ?!

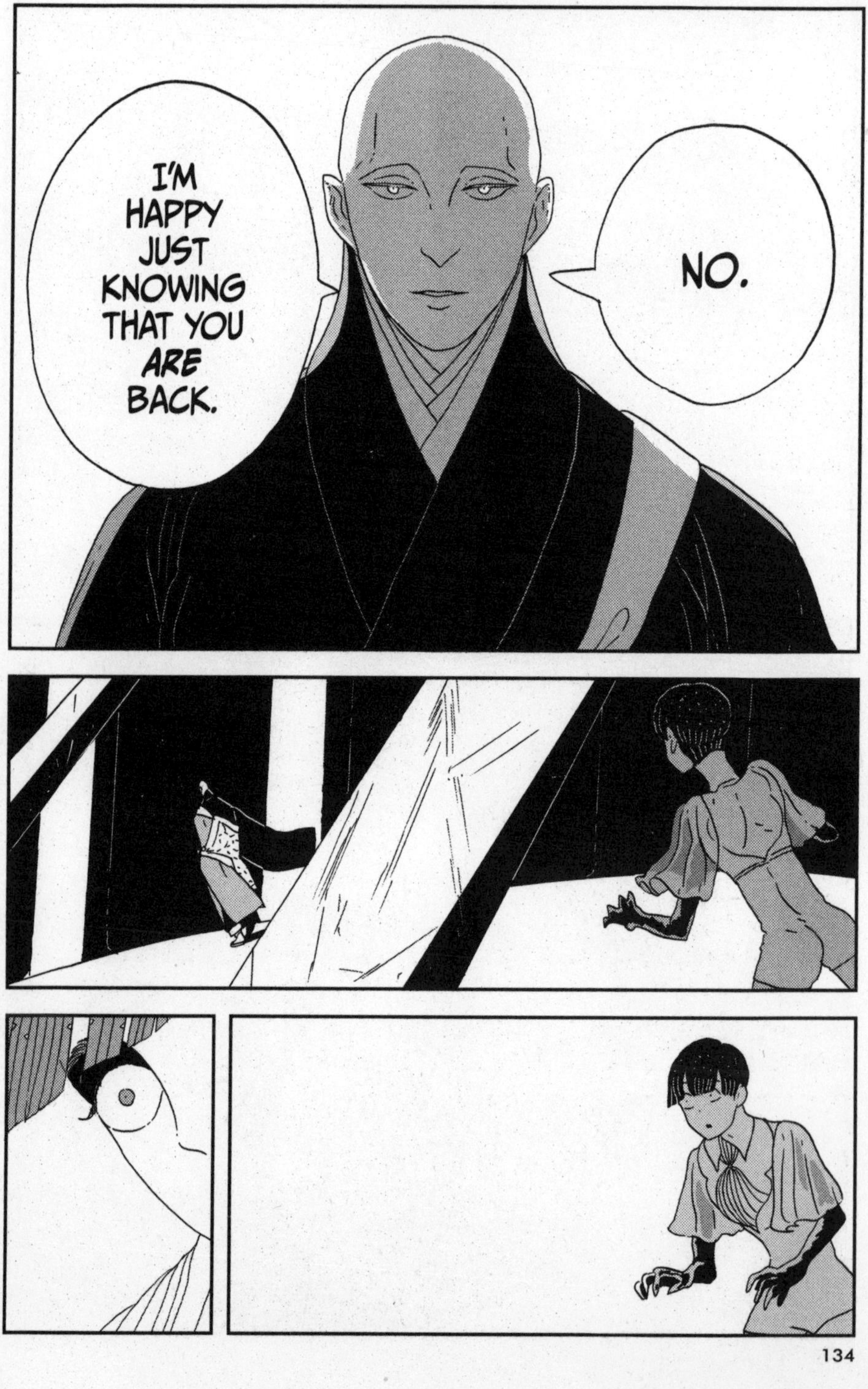
NO.
I'M HAPPY JUST KNOWING THAT YOU ARE BACK.

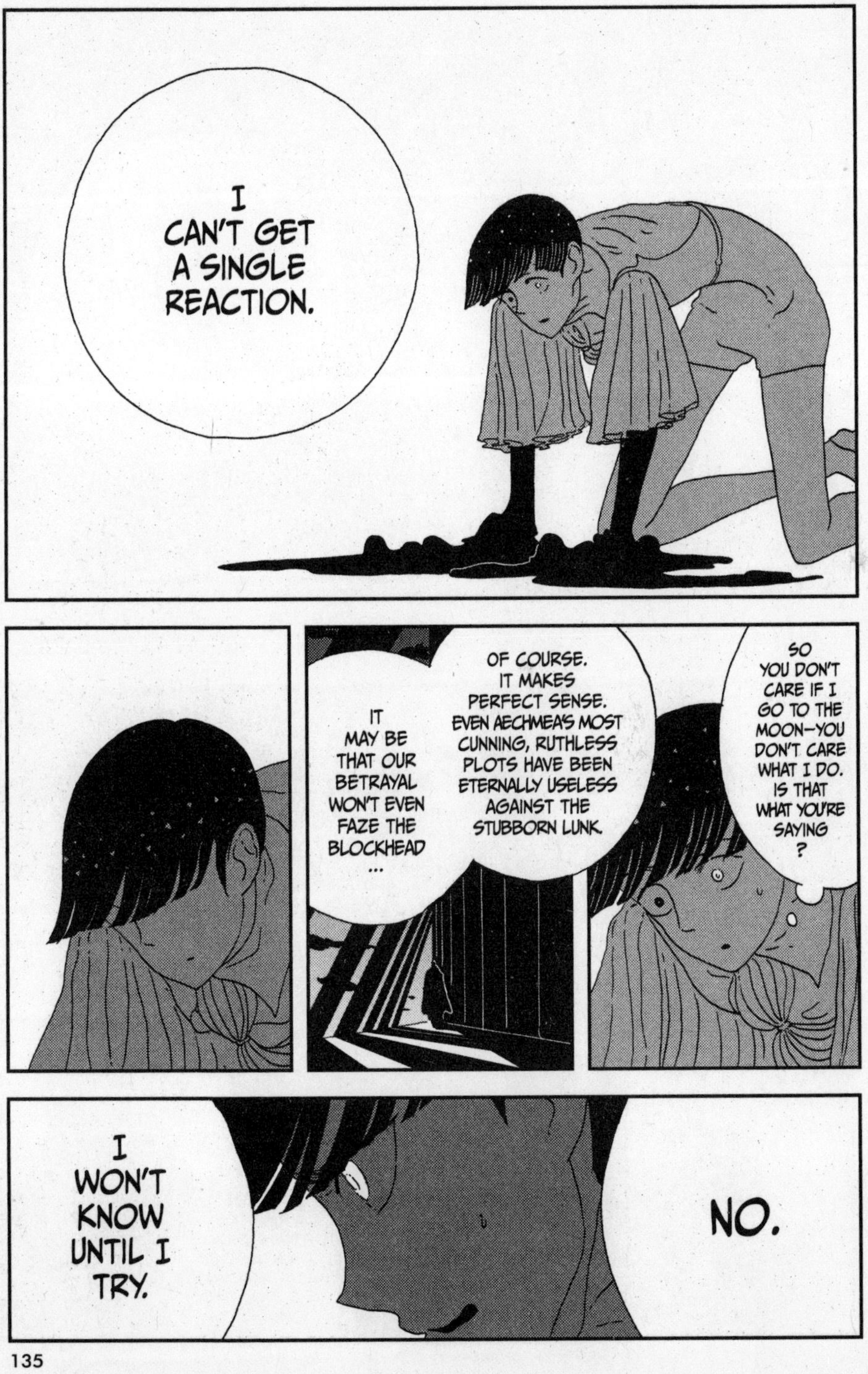
I CAN'T GET A SINGLE REACTION.
SO YOU DON'T CARE IF I GO TO THE MOON—YOU DON'T CARE WHAT I DO. IS THAT WHAT YOU'RE SAYING ?
OF COURSE. IT MAKES PERFECT SENSE. EVEN AECHMEA'S MOST CUNNING, RUTHLESS PLOTS HAVE BEEN ETERNALLY USELESS AGAINST THE STUBBORN LUNK.
IT MAY BE THAT OUR BETRAYAL WON'T EVEN FAZE THE BLOCKHEAD ...
NO.
I WON'T KNOW UNTIL I TRY.

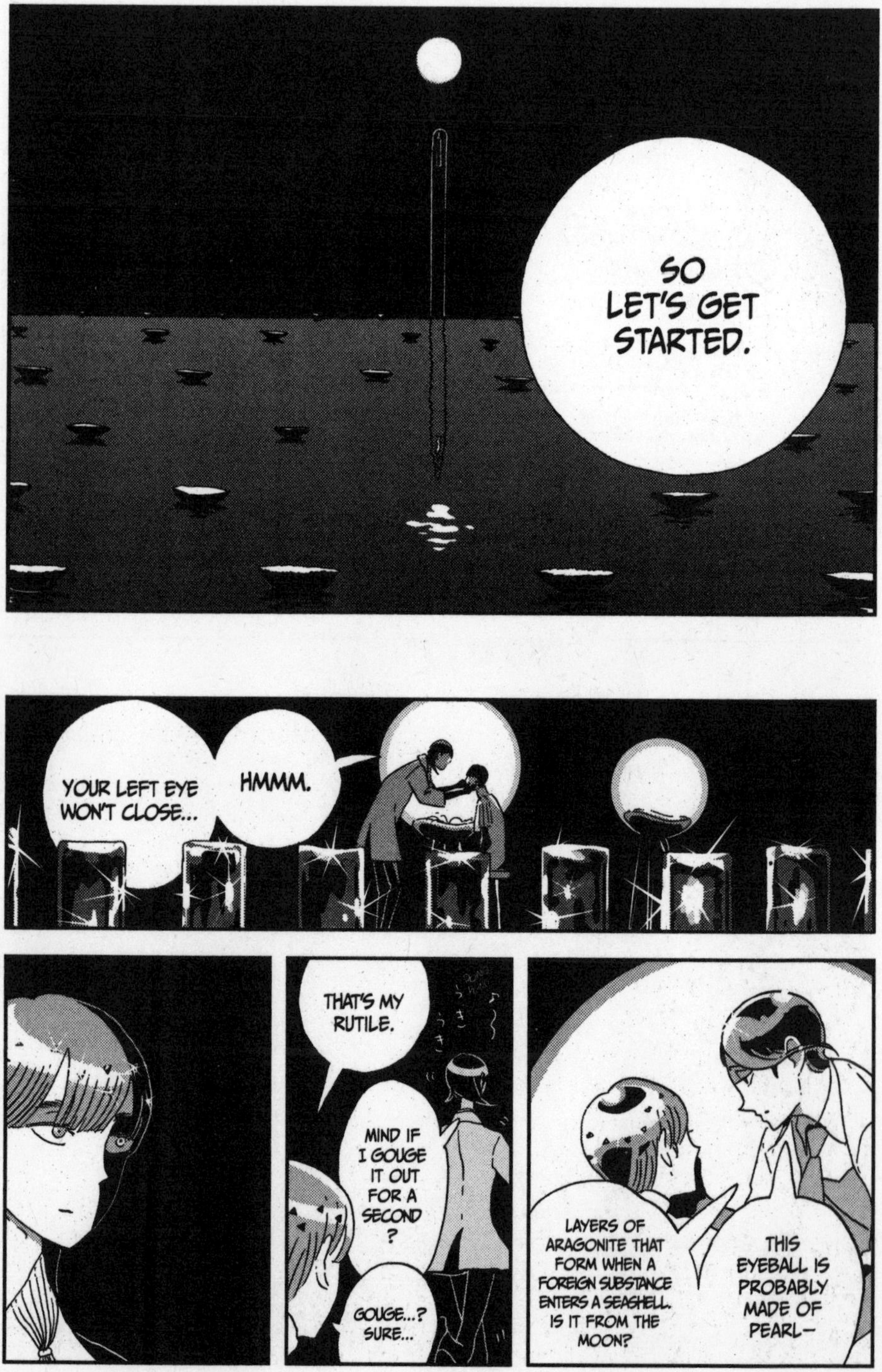
SO LET'S GET STARTED.
HMMM.
YOUR LEFT EYE WON'T CLOSE...
THIS EYEBALL IS PROBABLY MADE OF PEARL—
LAYERS OF ARAGONITE THAT FORM WHEN A FOREIGN SUBSTANCE ENTERS A SEASHELL. IS IT FROM THE MOON?
THAT'S MY RUTILE.
MIND IF I GOUGE IT OUT FOR A SECOND?
GOUGE...? SURE...

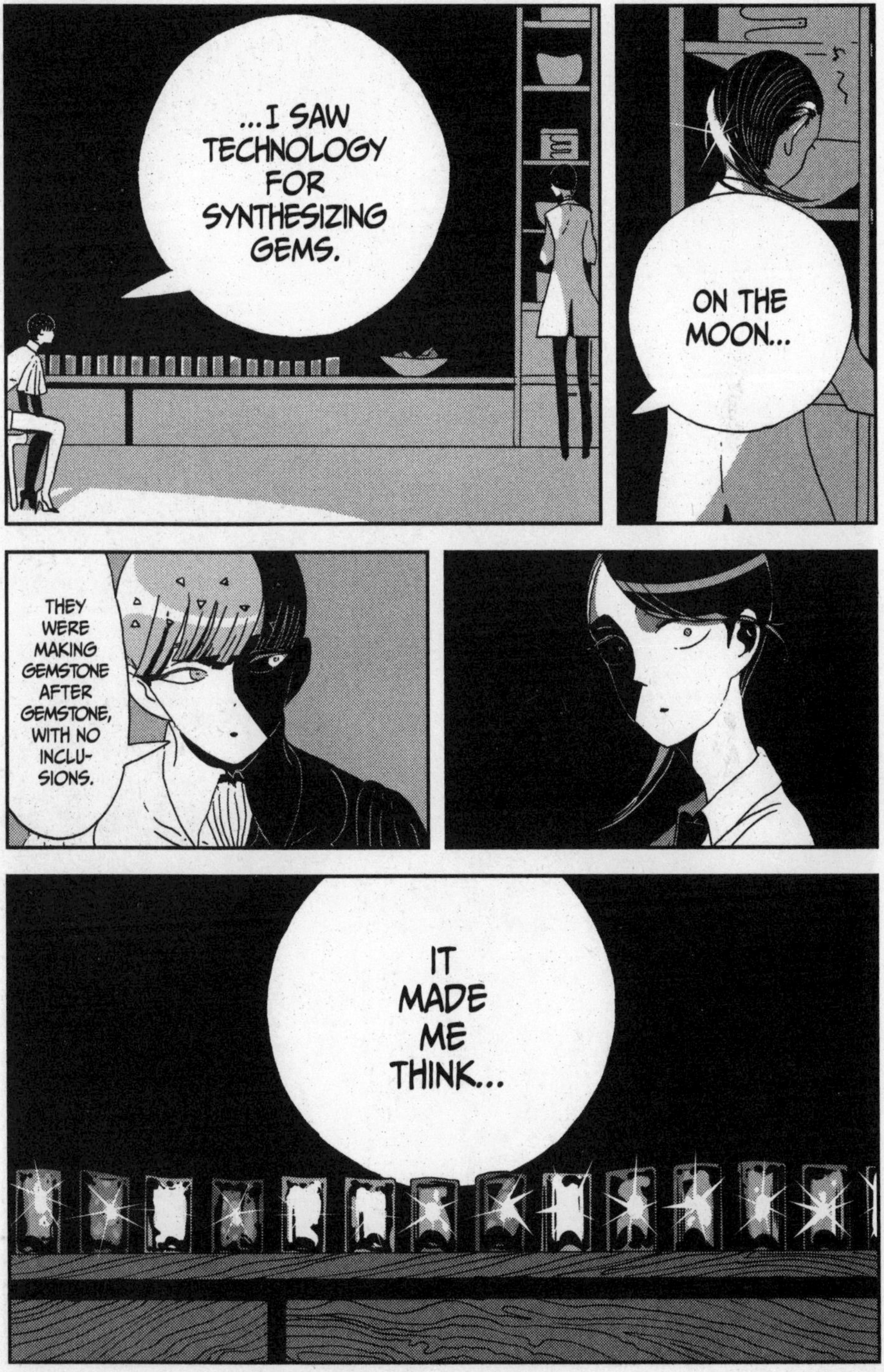
ON THE MOON...
...I SAW TECHNOLOGY FOR SYNTHESIZING GEMS.
THEY WERE MAKING GEMSTONE AFTER GEMSTONE, WITH NO INCLUSIONS.
IT MADE ME THINK...

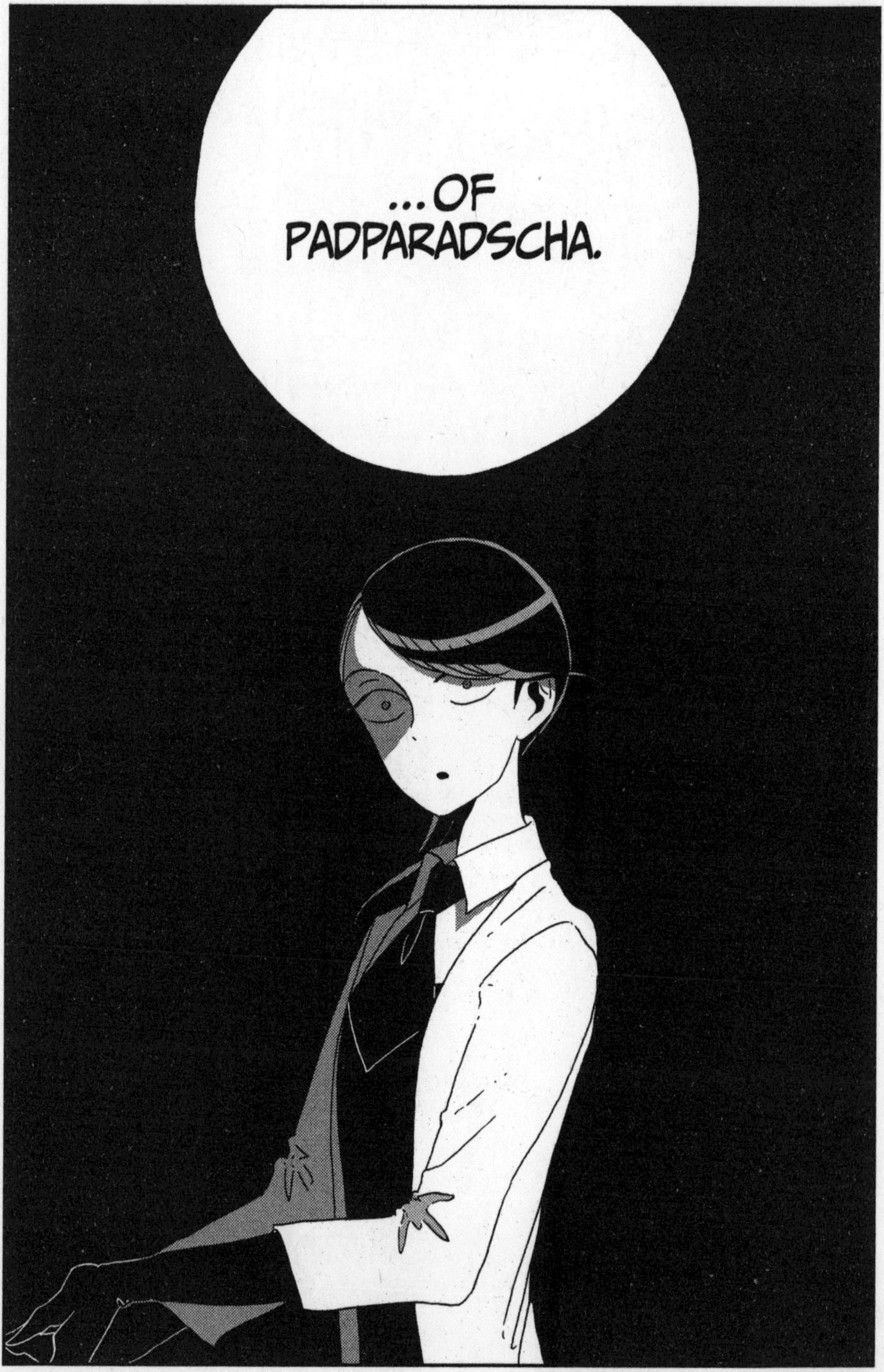
...OF PADPARADSCHA.

CHAPTER 59:

Unrest

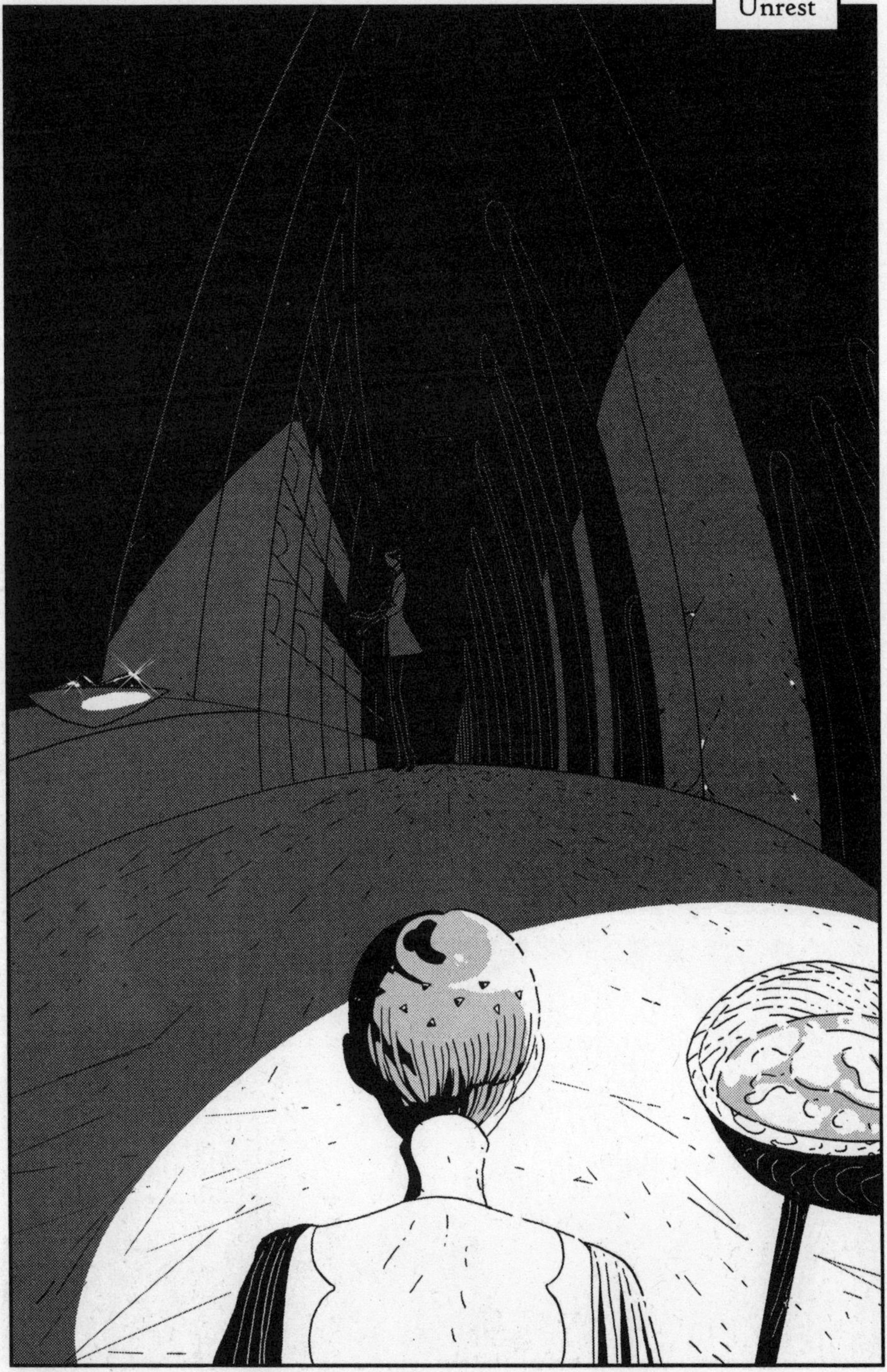

THAT'S SOMETHING I JUST REMEMBERED.

ER...

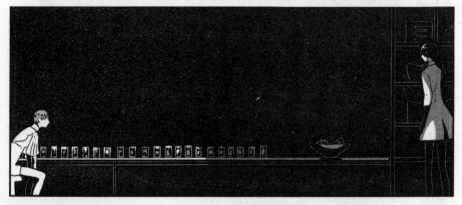

ARE YOU SAYING PADPARADSCHA COULD GET TREATMENT ON THE MOON?

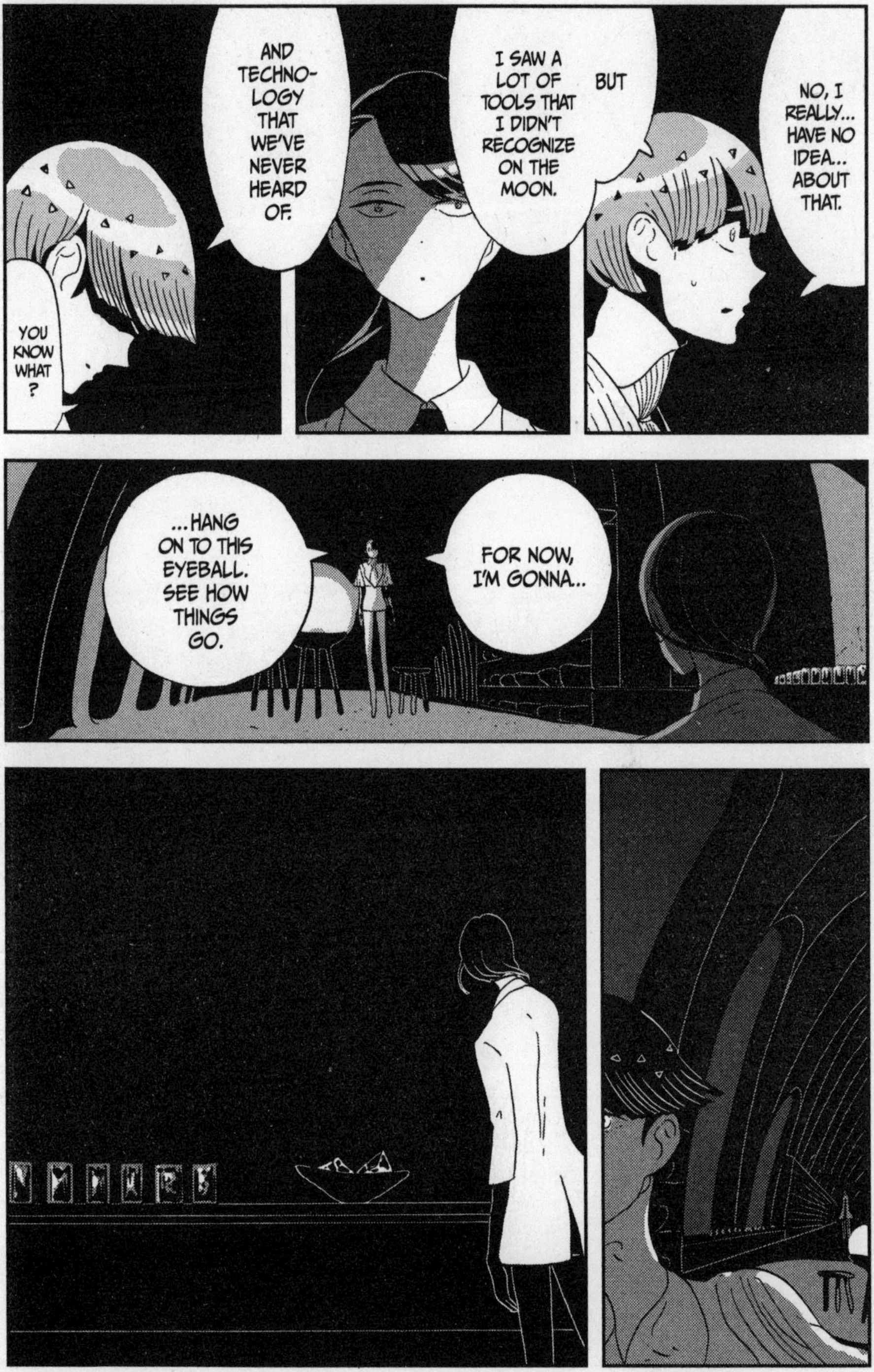
NO, I REALLY... HAVE NO IDEA... ABOUT THAT.
BUT
I SAW A LOT OF TOOLS THAT I DIDN'T RECOGNIZE ON THE MOON.
AND TECHNOLOGY THAT WE'VE NEVER HEARD OF.
YOU KNOW WHAT?
FOR NOW, I'M GONNA...
...HANG ON TO THIS EYEBALL. SEE HOW THINGS GO.

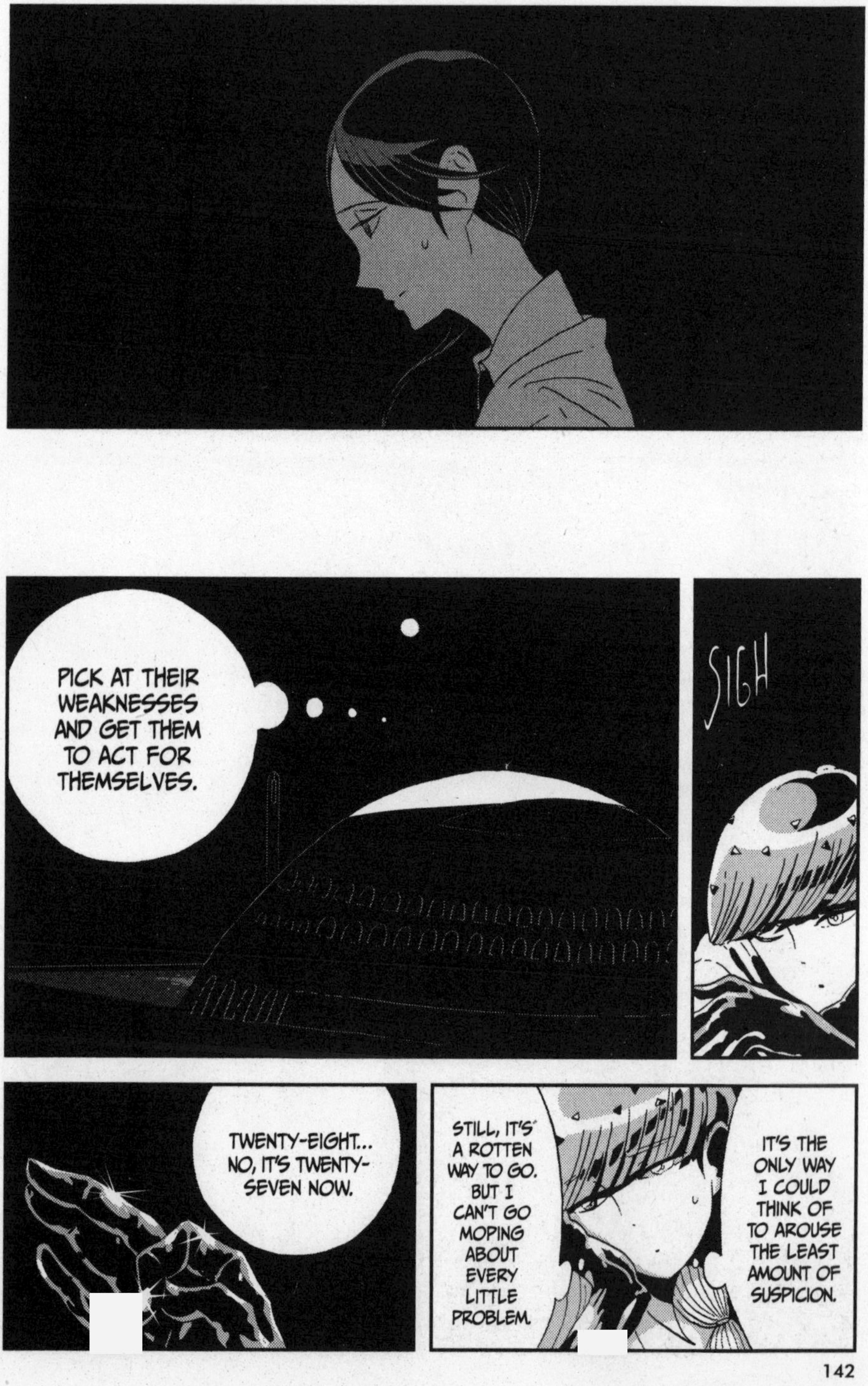
SIGH
PICK AT THEIR WEAKNESSES AND GET THEM TO ACT FOR THEMSELVES.
IT'S THE ONLY WAY I COULD THINK OF TO AROUSE THE LEAST AMOUNT OF SUSPICION.
STILL, IT'S A ROTTEN WAY TO GO. BUT I CAN'T GO MOPING ABOUT EVERY LITTLE PROBLEM.
TWENTY-EIGHT... NO, IT'S TWENTY-SEVEN NOW.

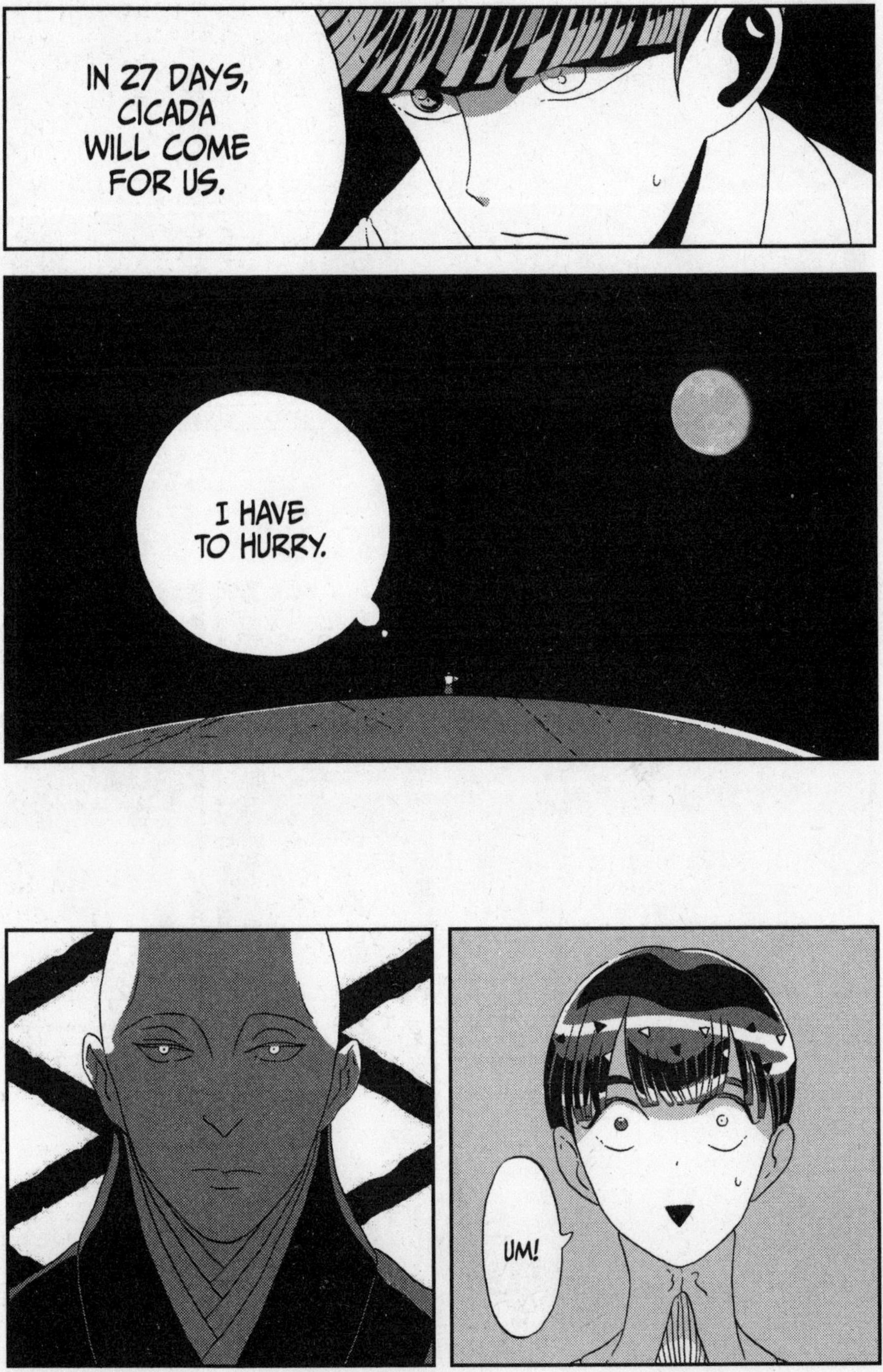
IN 27 DAYS, CICADA WILL COME FOR US.
I HAVE TO HURRY.
UM!

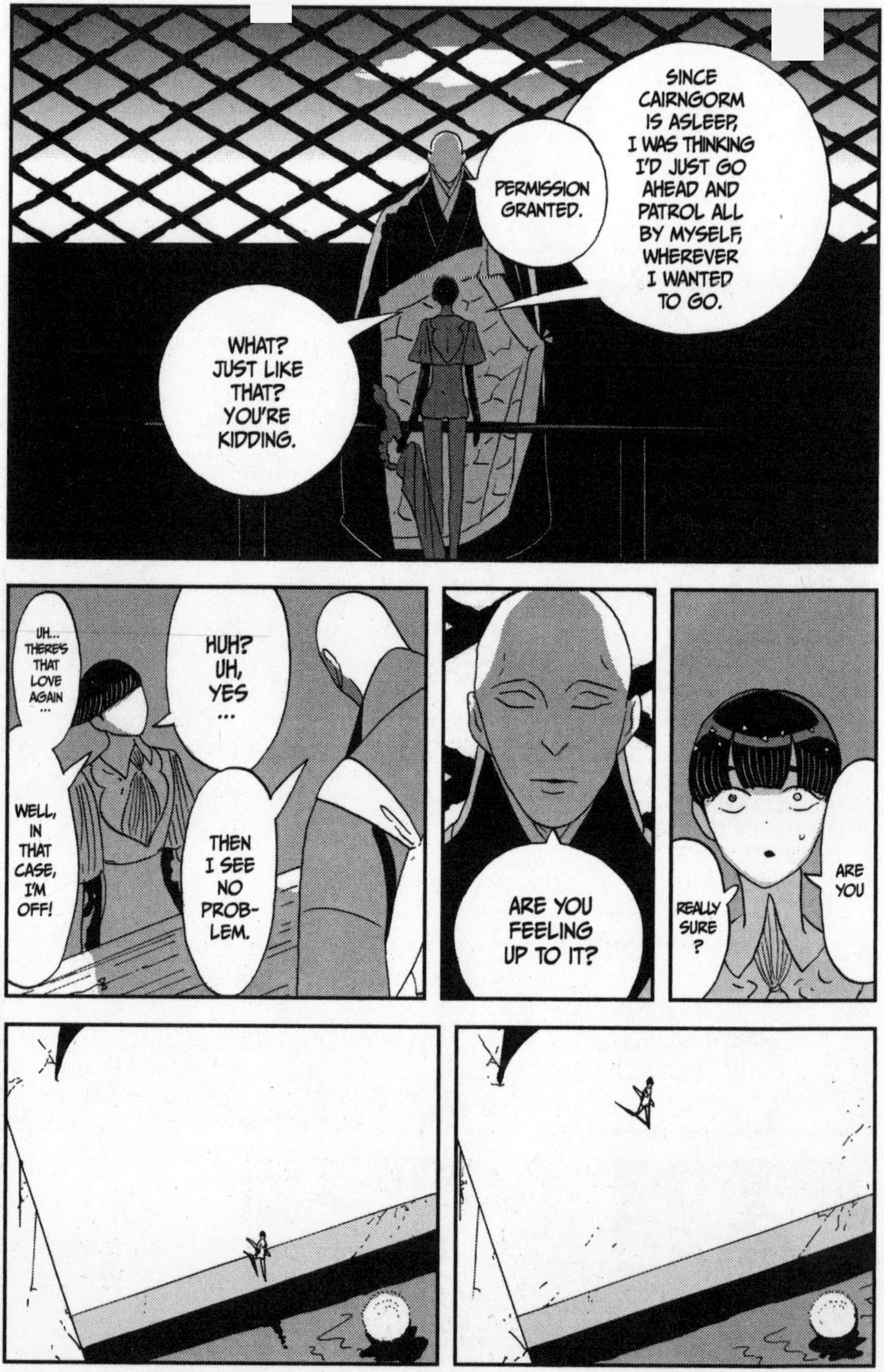
SINCE CAIRNGORM IS ASLEEP, I WAS THINKING I'D JUST GO AHEAD AND PATROL ALL BY MYSELF, WHEREVER I WANTED TO GO.
PERMISSION GRANTED.
WHAT? JUST LIKE THAT? YOU'RE KIDDING.
ARE YOU
REALLY SURE ?
ARE YOU FEELING UP TO IT?
HUH? UH, YES ...
UH... THERE'S THAT LOVE AGAIN ...
THEN I SEE NO PROB- LEM.
WELL, IN THAT CASE, I'M OFF!

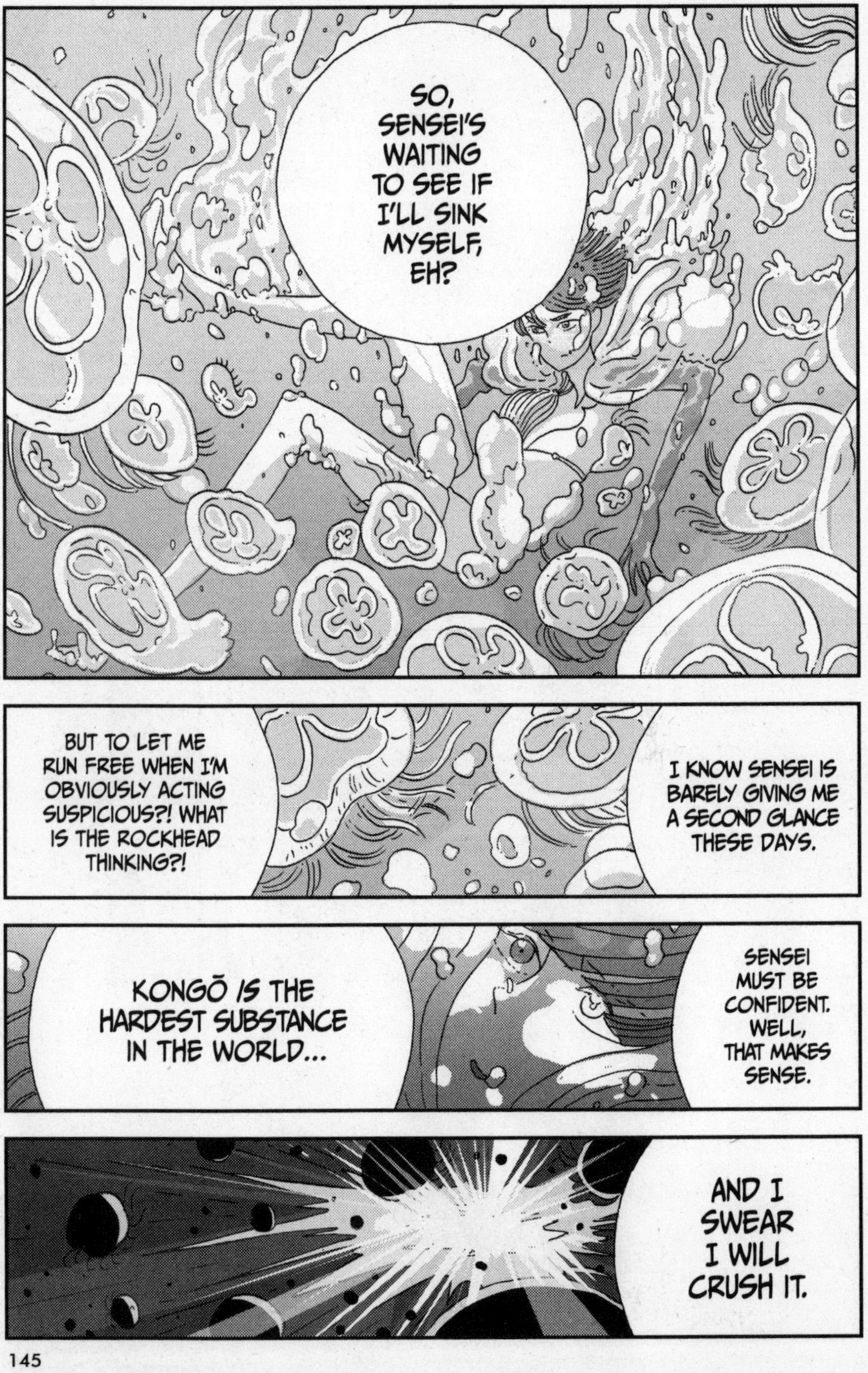
SO, SENSEI'S WAITING TO SEE IF I'LL SINK MYSELF, EH?
I KNOW SENSEI IS BARELY GIVING ME A SECOND GLANCE THESE DAYS.
BUT TO LET ME RUN FREE WHEN I'M OBVIOUSLY ACTING SUSPICIOUS?! WHAT IS THE ROCKHEAD THINKING?!
SENSEI MUST BE CONFIDENT. WELL, THAT MAKES SENSE.
KONGŌ *IS* THE HARDEST SUBSTANCE IN THE WORLD...
AND I SWEAR I WILL CRUSH IT.

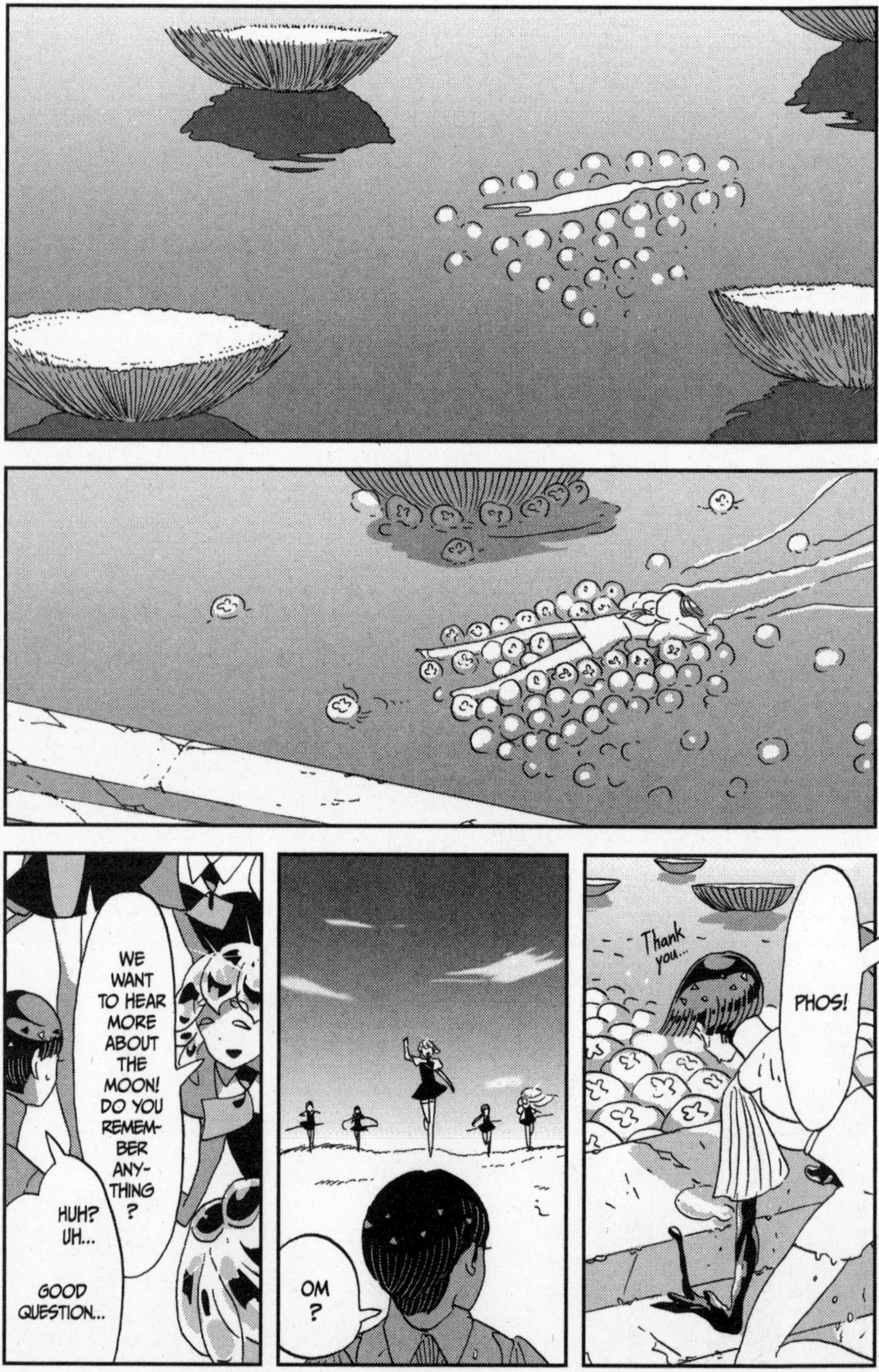
PHOS!
Thank you...
OM ?
WE WANT TO HEAR MORE ABOUT THE MOON! DO YOU REMEMBER ANYTHING ?
HUH? UH...
GOOD QUESTION...

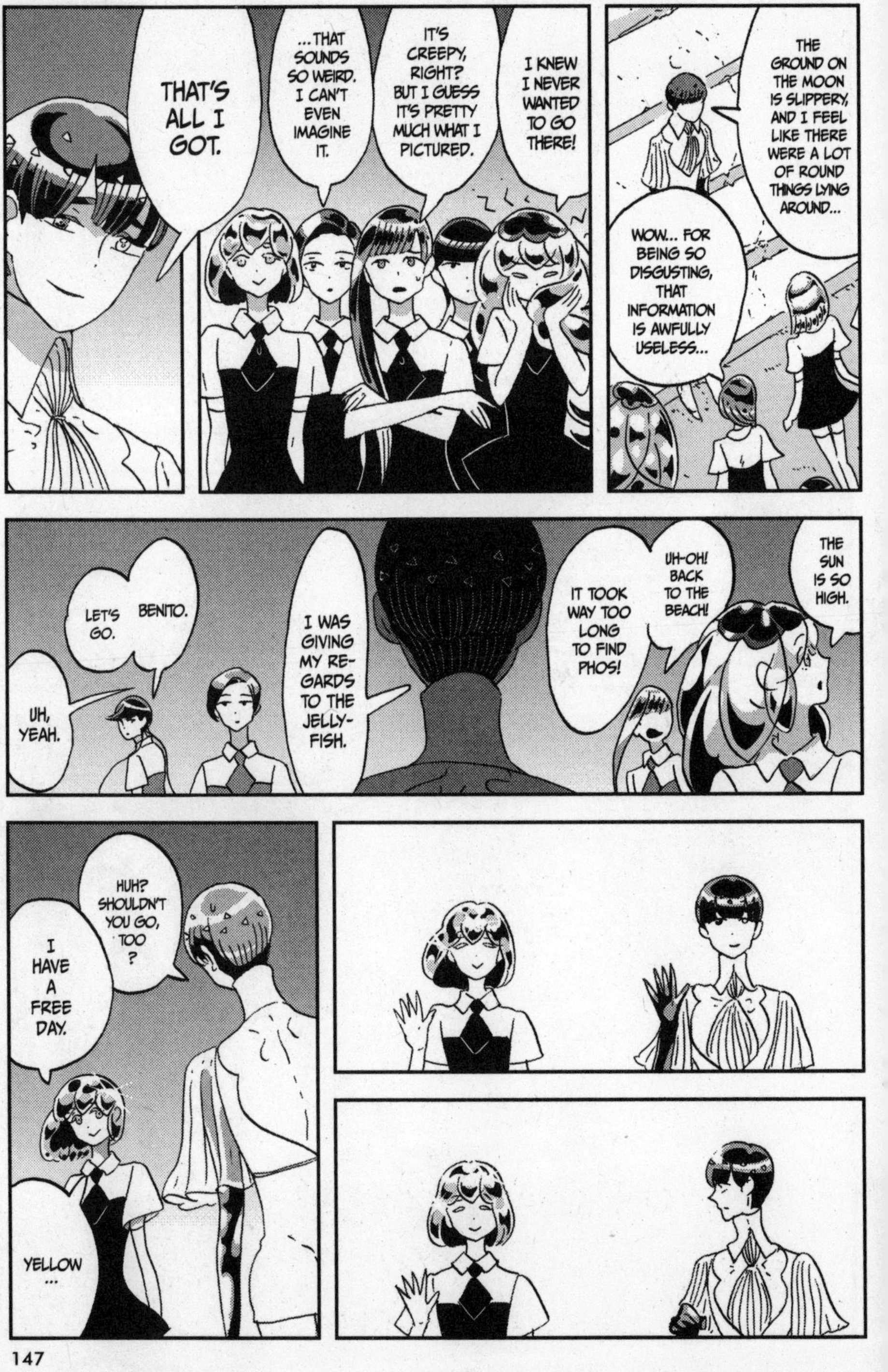
THE GROUND ON THE MOON IS SLIPPERY, AND I FEEL LIKE THERE WERE A LOT OF ROUND THINGS LYING AROUND...
WOW... FOR BEING SO DISGUSTING, THAT INFORMATION IS AWFULLY USELESS...
I KNEW I NEVER WANTED TO GO THERE!
IT'S CREEPY, RIGHT? BUT I GUESS IT'S PRETTY MUCH WHAT I PICTURED.
...THAT SOUNDS SO WEIRD. I CAN'T EVEN IMAGINE IT.
THAT'S ALL I GOT.
THE SUN IS SO HIGH.
UH-OH! BACK TO THE BEACH!
IT TOOK WAY TOO LONG TO FIND PHOS!
I WAS GIVING MY RE-GARDS TO THE JELLY-FISH.
BENITO.
LET'S GO.
UH, YEAH.
HUH? SHOULDN'T YOU GO, TOO?
I HAVE A FREE DAY.
YELLOW ...

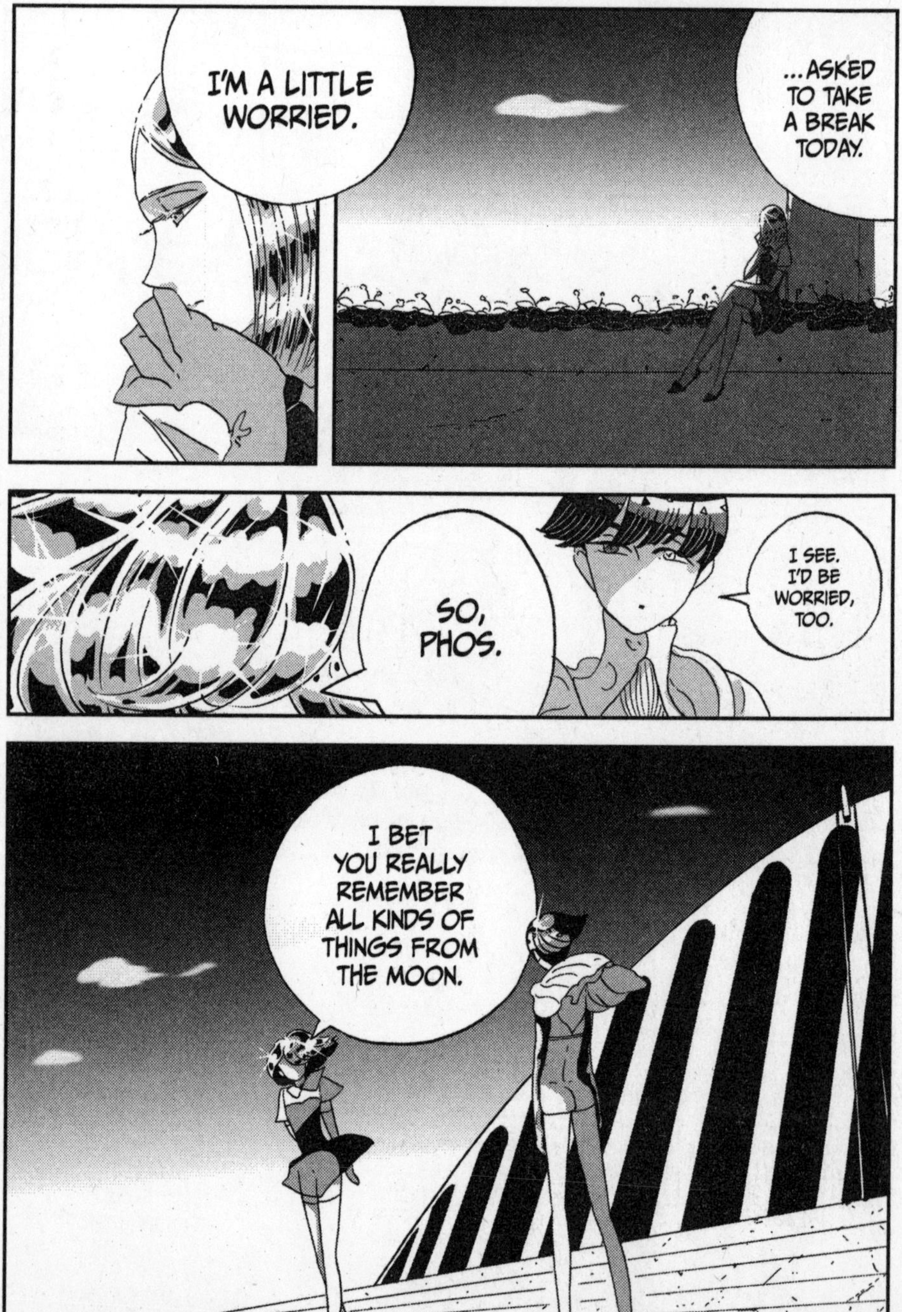
...ASKED TO TAKE A BREAK TODAY.
I'M A LITTLE WORRIED.
I SEE. I'D BE WORRIED, TOO.
SO, PHOS.
I BET YOU REALLY REMEMBER ALL KINDS OF THINGS FROM THE MOON.

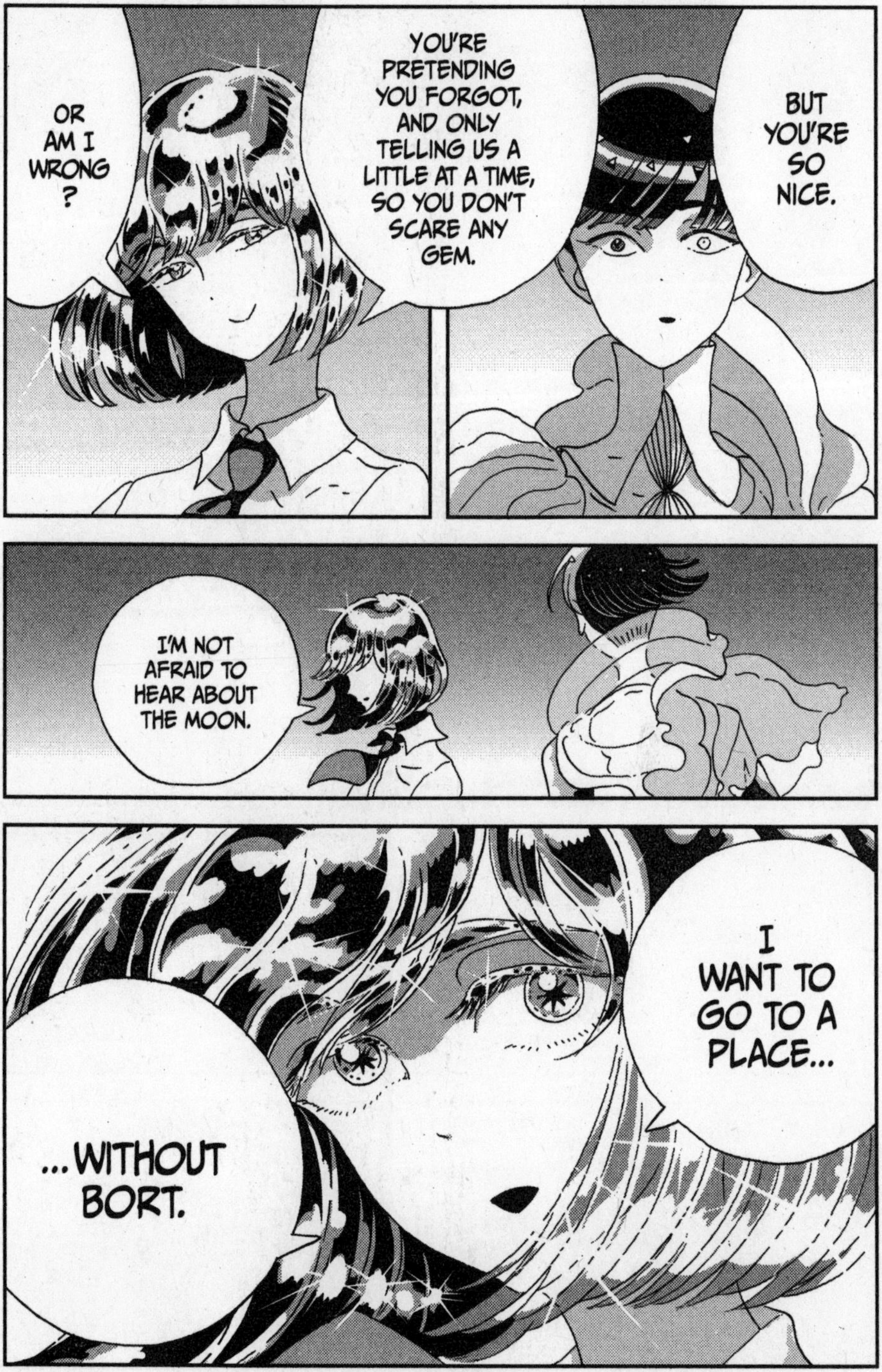
BUT YOU'RE SO NICE.
YOU'RE PRETENDING YOU FORGOT, AND ONLY TELLING US A LITTLE AT A TIME, SO YOU DON'T SCARE ANY GEM.
OR AM I WRONG?
I'M NOT AFRAID TO HEAR ABOUT THE MOON.
I WANT TO GO TO A PLACE...
...WITHOUT BORT.

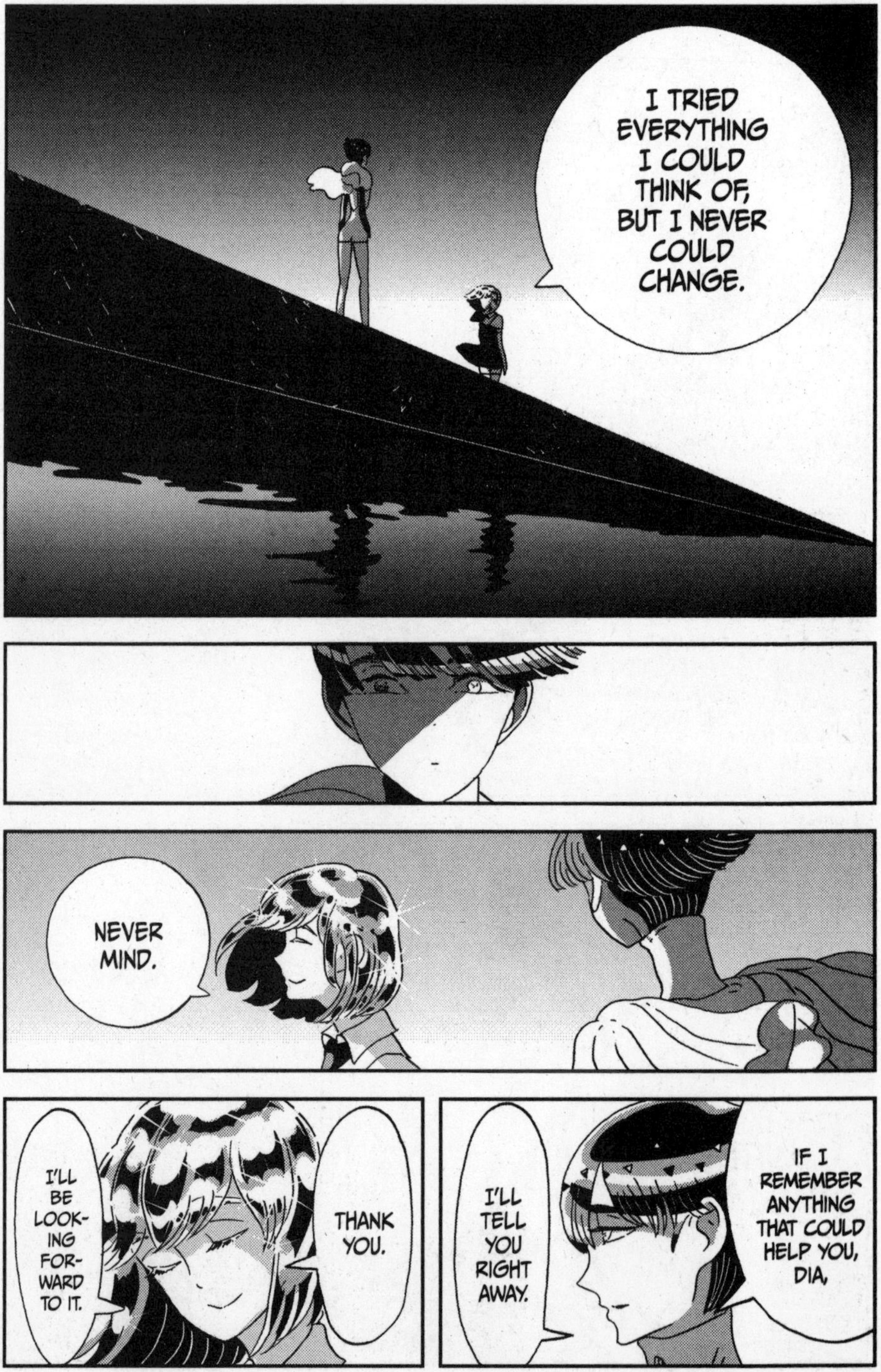
I TRIED EVERYTHING I COULD THINK OF, BUT I NEVER COULD CHANGE.
NEVER MIND.
IF I REMEMBER ANYTHING THAT COULD HELP YOU, DIA,
I'LL TELL YOU RIGHT AWAY.
THANK YOU.
I'LL BE LOOKING FORWARD TO IT.

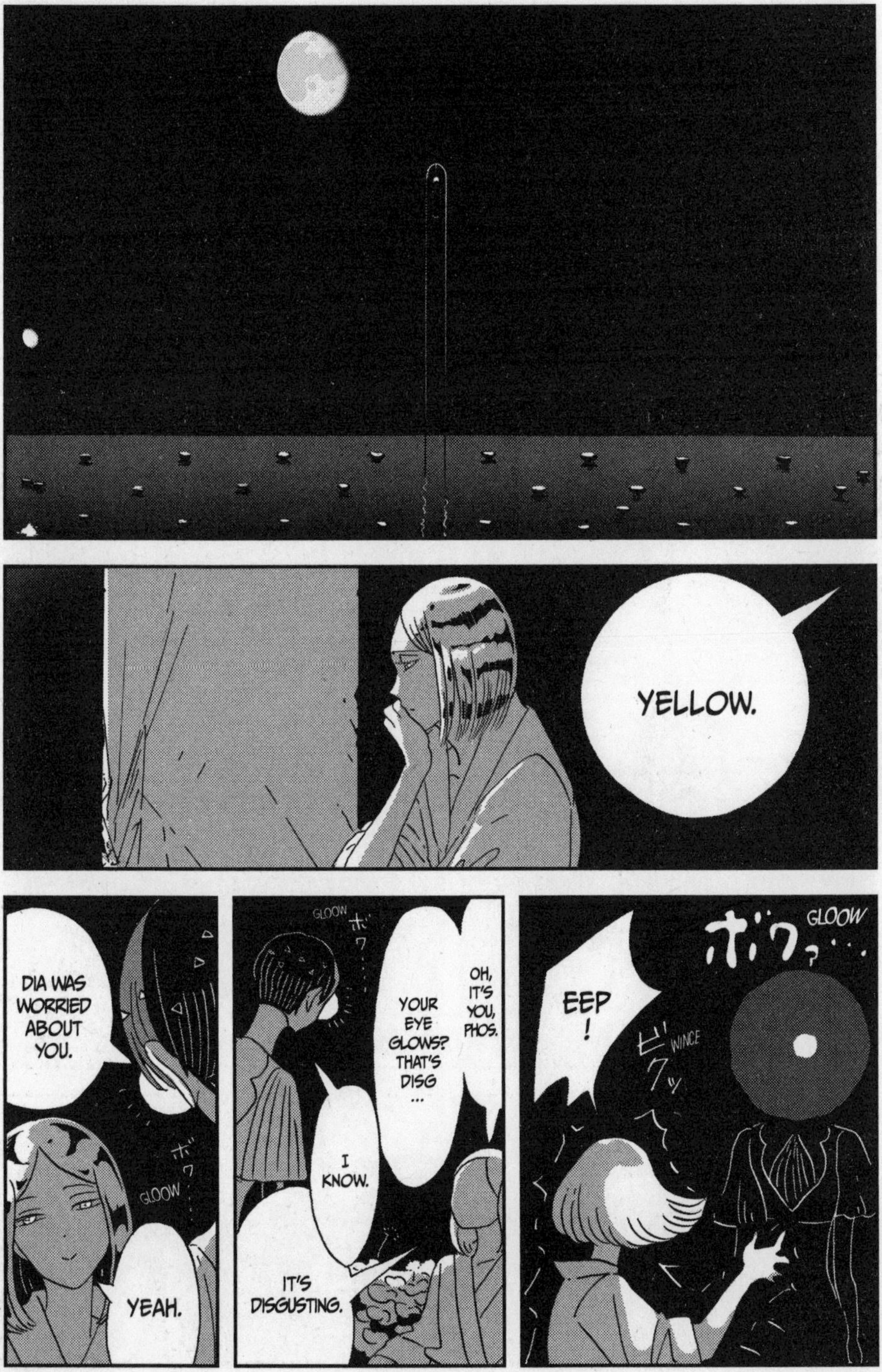
YELLOW.
ボワァ...
GLOOW
EEP!
ビクッ
WINCE
GLOOW
ボワ...
OH, IT'S YOU, PHOS.
YOUR EYE GLOWS? THAT'S DISG...
I KNOW.
IT'S DISGUSTING.
DIA WAS WORRIED ABOUT YOU.
ボワ...
GLOOW
YEAH.

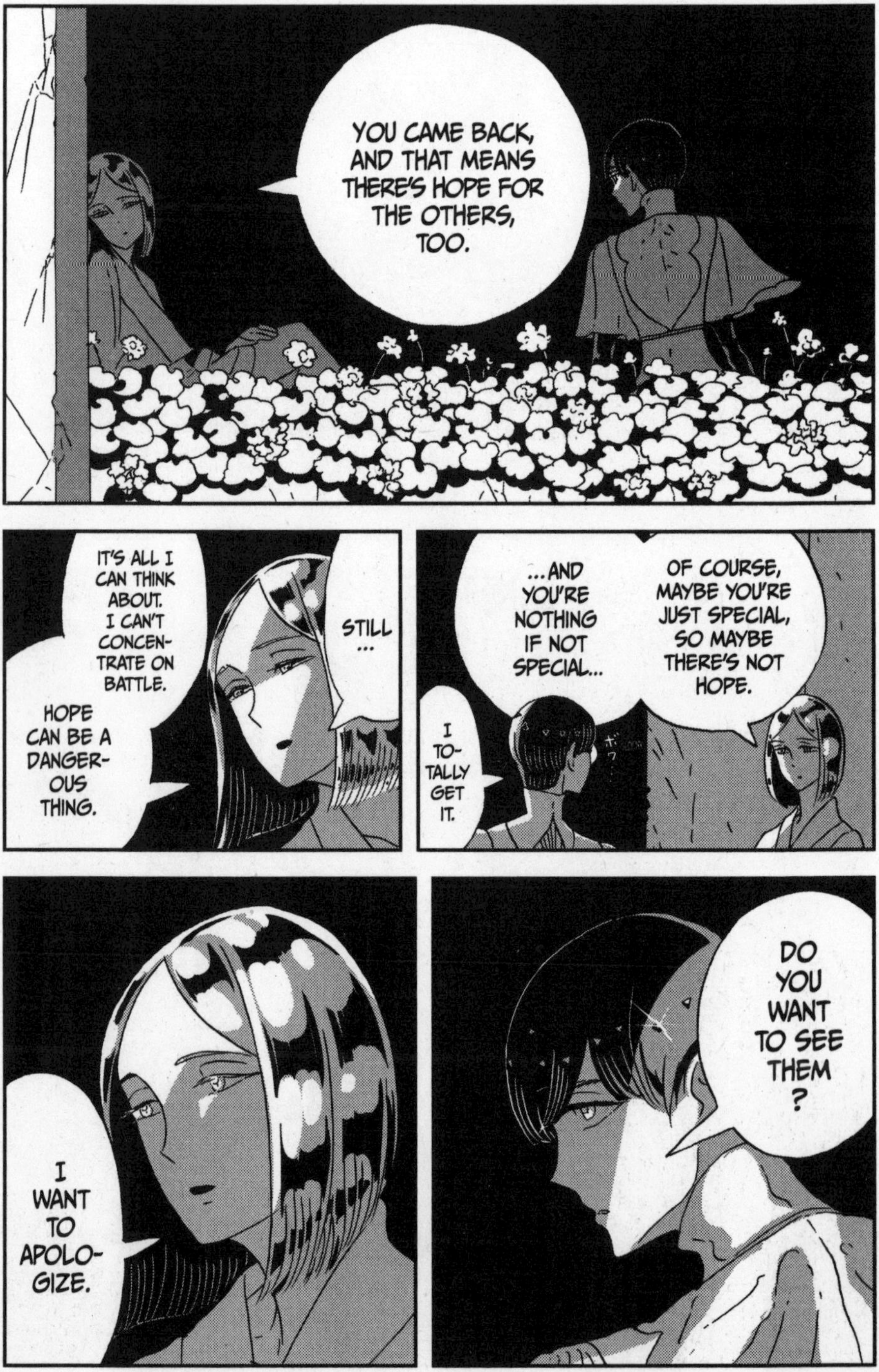
YOU CAME BACK, AND THAT MEANS THERE'S HOPE FOR THE OTHERS, TOO.
OF COURSE, MAYBE YOU'RE JUST SPECIAL, SO MAYBE THERE'S NOT HOPE.
...AND YOU'RE NOTHING IF NOT SPECIAL...
I TO-TALLY GET IT.
STILL ...
IT'S ALL I CAN THINK ABOUT. I CAN'T CONCEN-TRATE ON BATTLE.
HOPE CAN BE A DANGER-OUS THING.
DO YOU WANT TO SEE THEM ?
I WANT TO APOLO-GIZE.

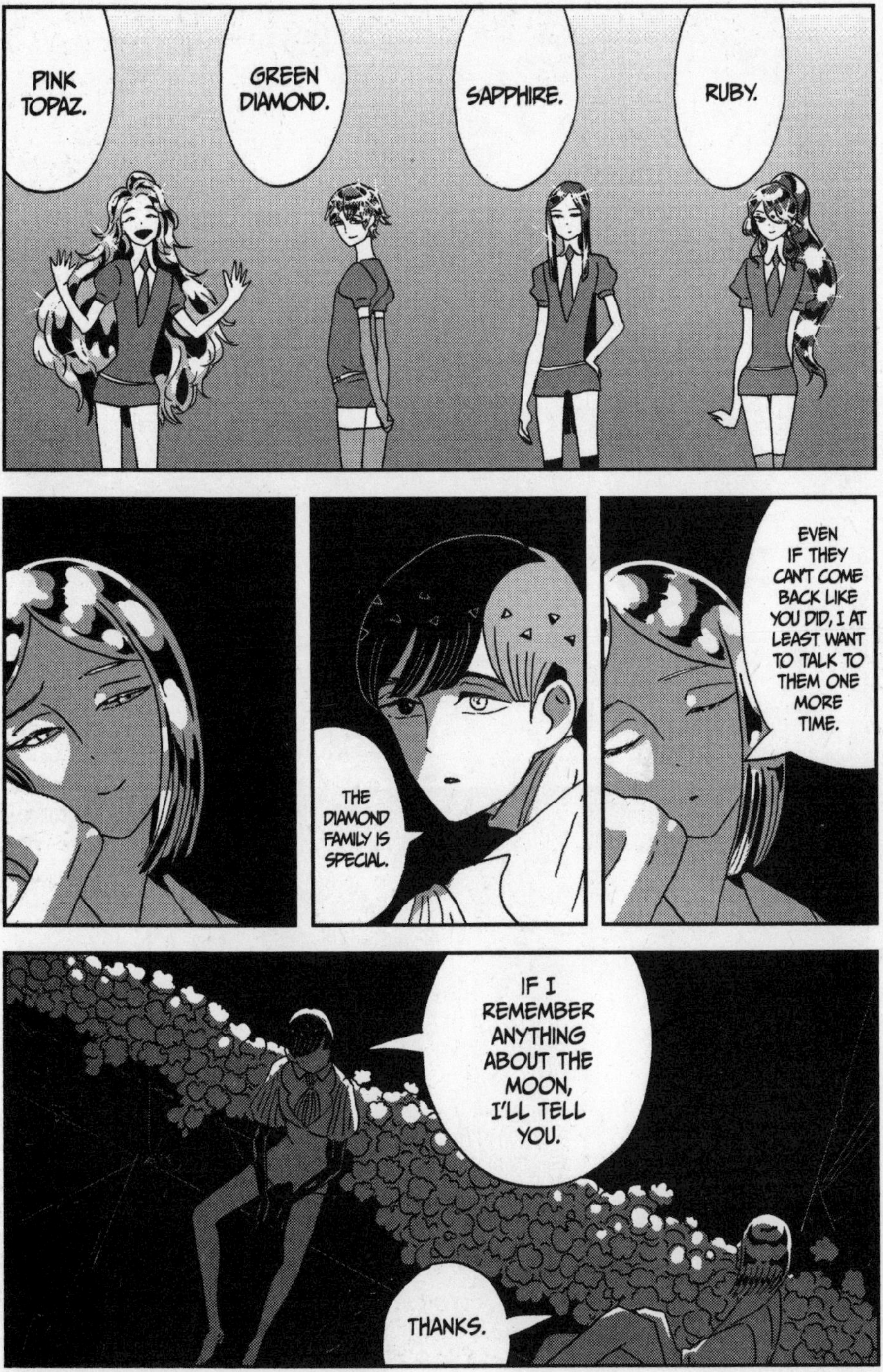
RUBY.
SAPPHIRE.
GREEN DIAMOND.
PINK TOPAZ.
EVEN IF THEY CAN'T COME BACK LIKE YOU DID, I AT LEAST WANT TO TALK TO THEM ONE MORE TIME.
THE DIAMOND FAMILY IS SPECIAL.
IF I REMEMBER ANYTHING ABOUT THE MOON, I'LL TELL YOU.
THANKS.

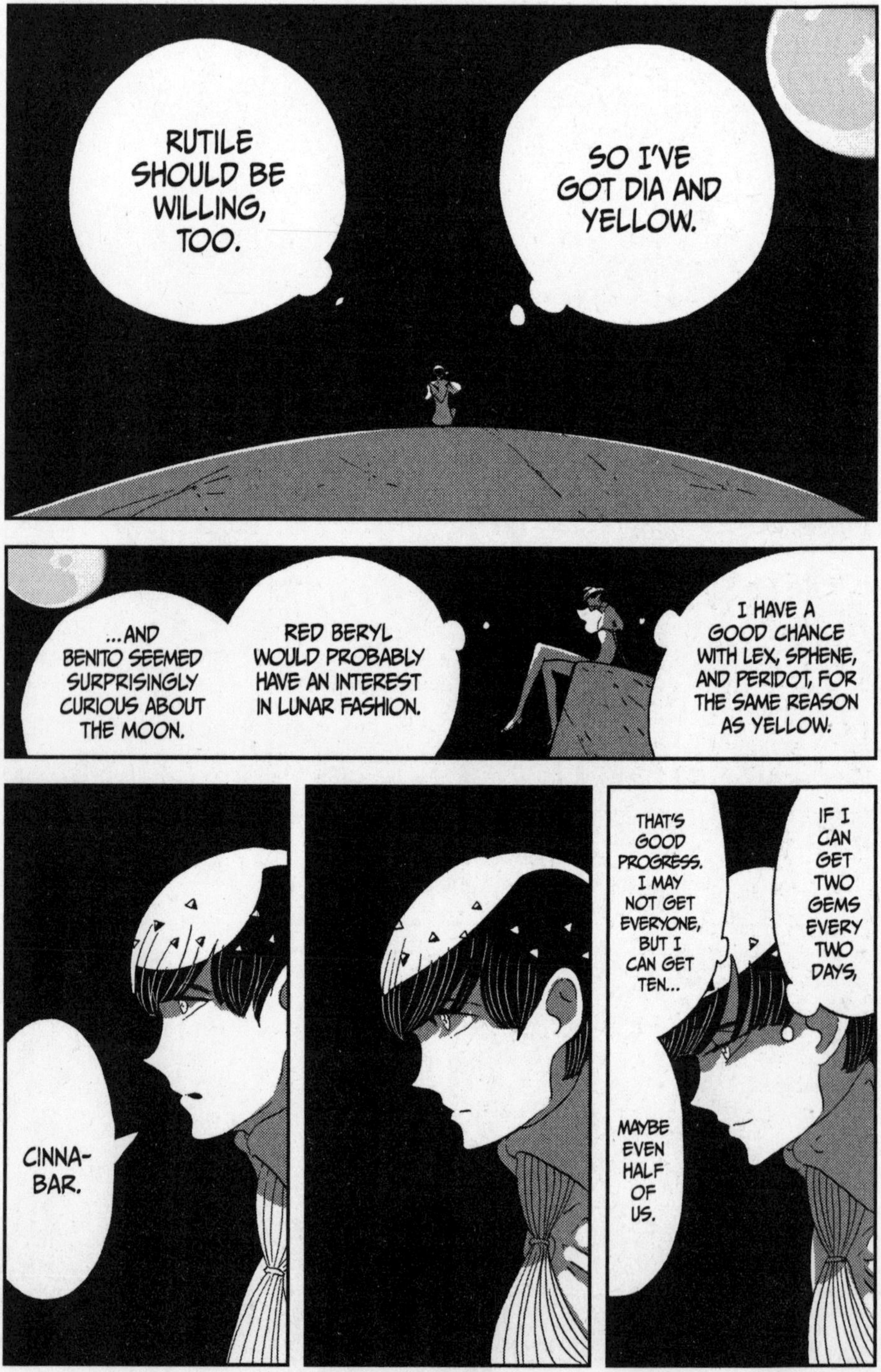
SO I'VE GOT DIA AND YELLOW.
RUTILE SHOULD BE WILLING, TOO.
I HAVE A GOOD CHANCE WITH LEX, SPHENE, AND PERIDOT, FOR THE SAME REASON AS YELLOW.
RED BERYL WOULD PROBABLY HAVE AN INTEREST IN LUNAR FASHION.
...AND BENITO SEEMED SURPRISINGLY CURIOUS ABOUT THE MOON.
IF I CAN GET TWO GEMS EVERY TWO DAYS,
THAT'S GOOD PROGRESS. I MAY NOT GET EVERYONE, BUT I CAN GET TEN...
MAYBE EVEN HALF OF US.
CINNA-BAR.

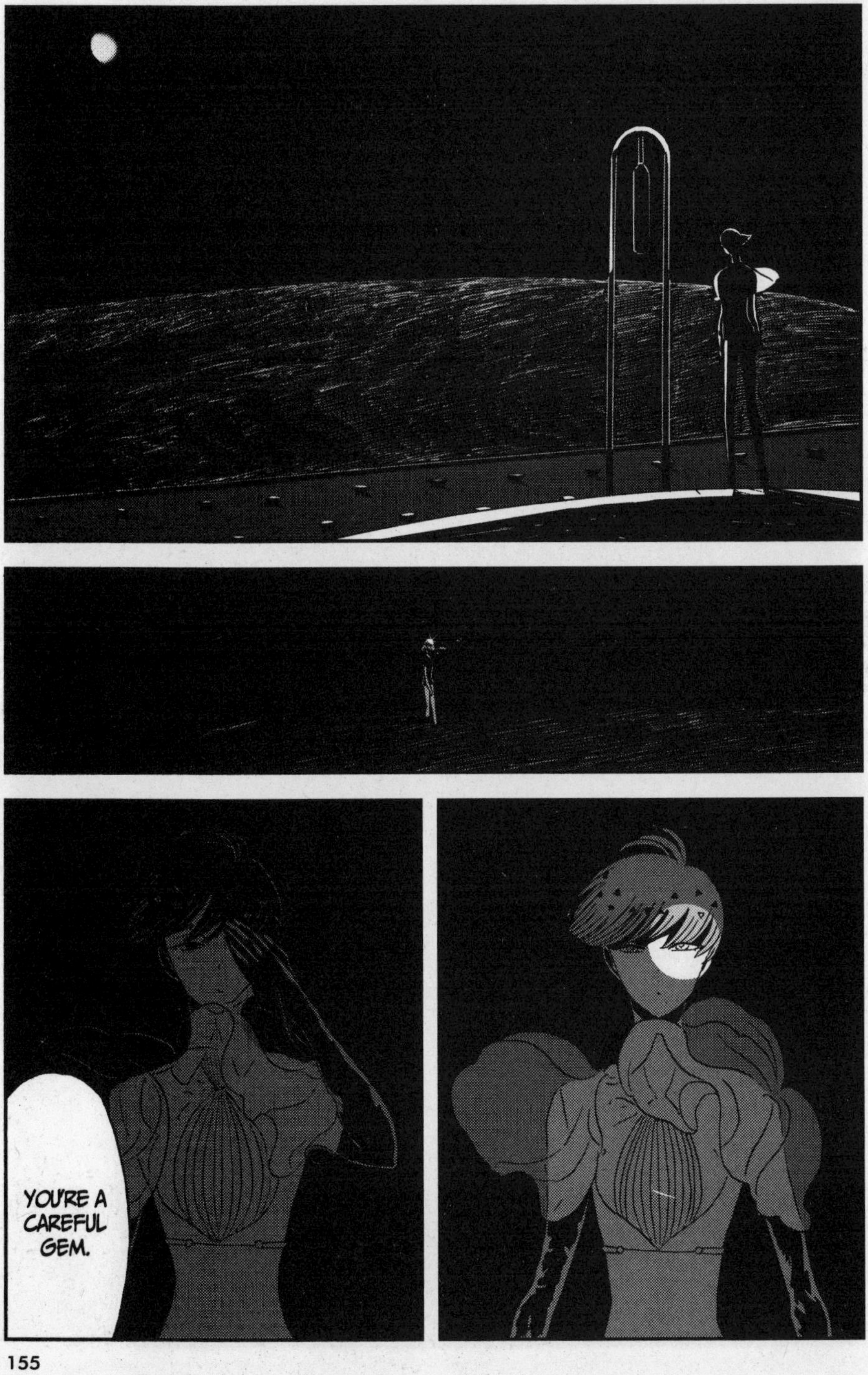
YOU'RE A CAREFUL GEM.

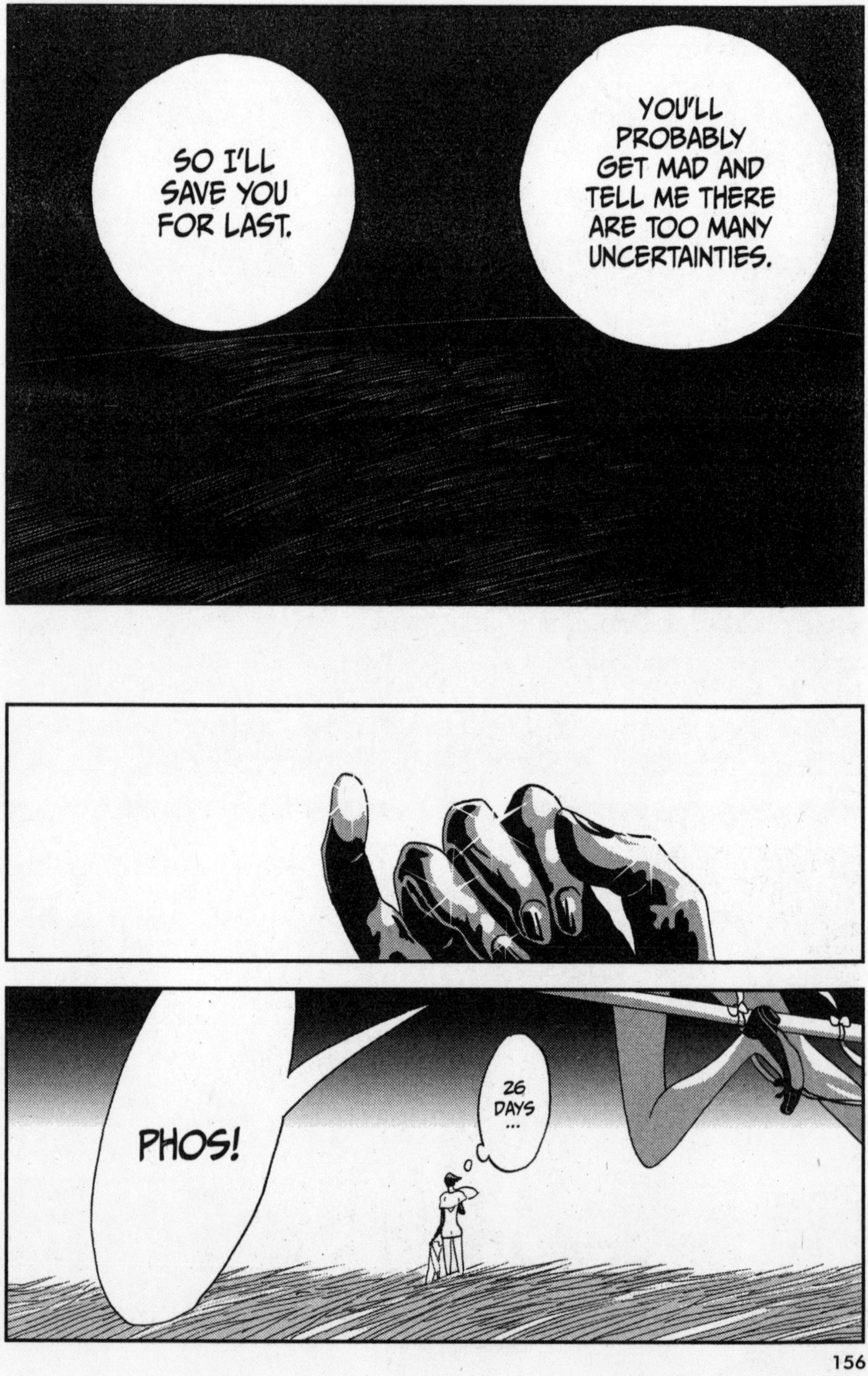
YOU'LL PROBABLY GET MAD AND TELL ME THERE ARE TOO MANY UNCERTAINTIES.
SO I'LL SAVE YOU FOR LAST.
26 DAYS ...
PHOS!

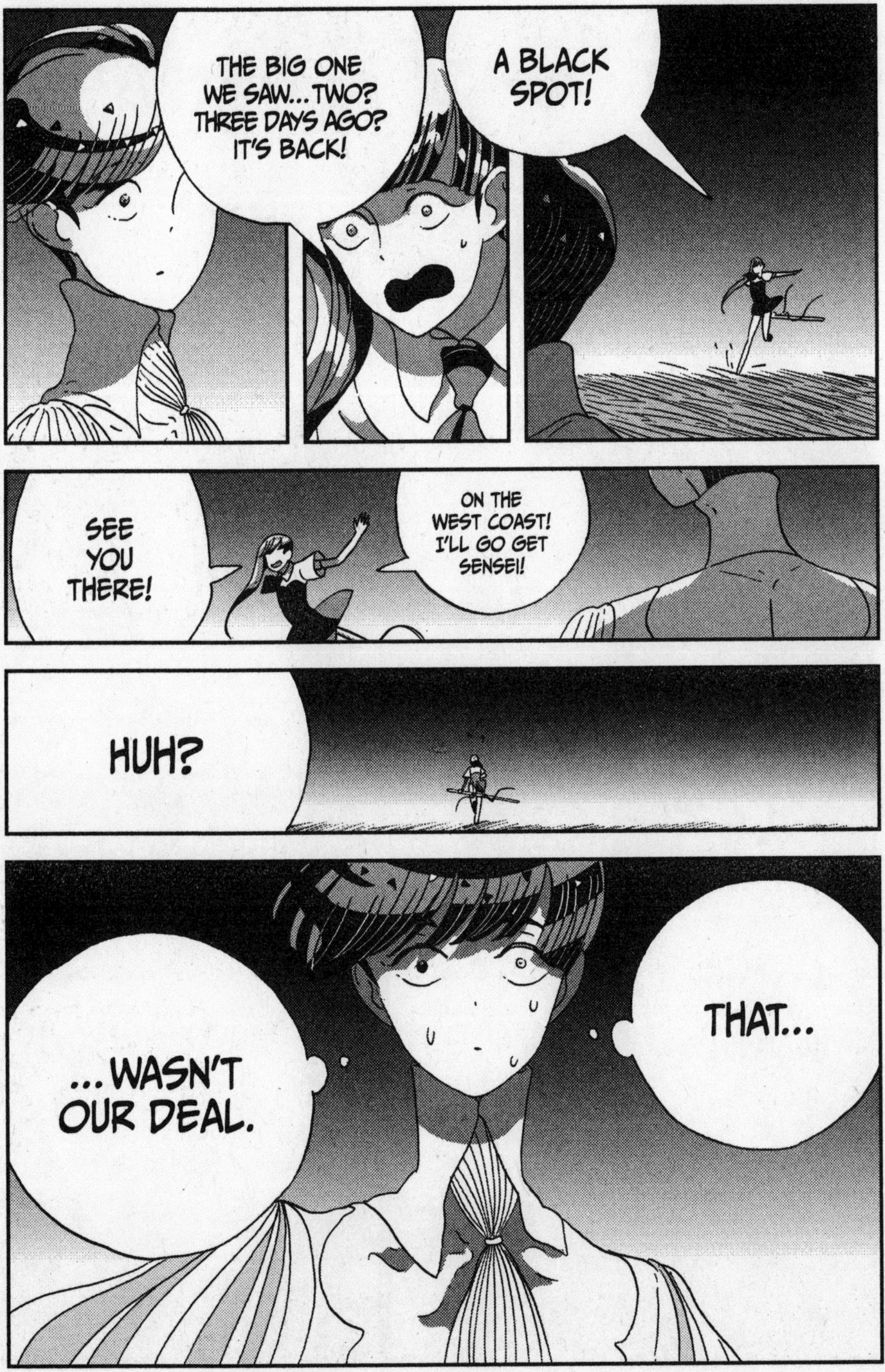
A BLACK SPOT!
THE BIG ONE WE SAW... TWO? THREE DAYS AGO? IT'S BACK!
ON THE WEST COAST! I'LL GO GET SENSEI!
SEE YOU THERE!
HUH?
THAT...
...WASN'T OUR DEAL.

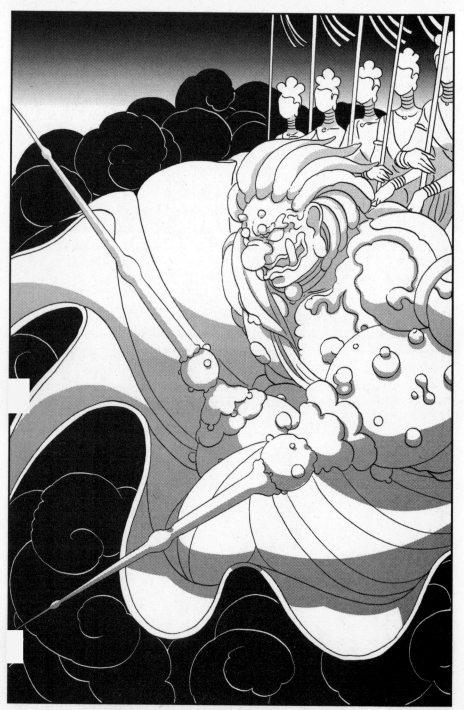

CHAPTER 60:

Suspicion

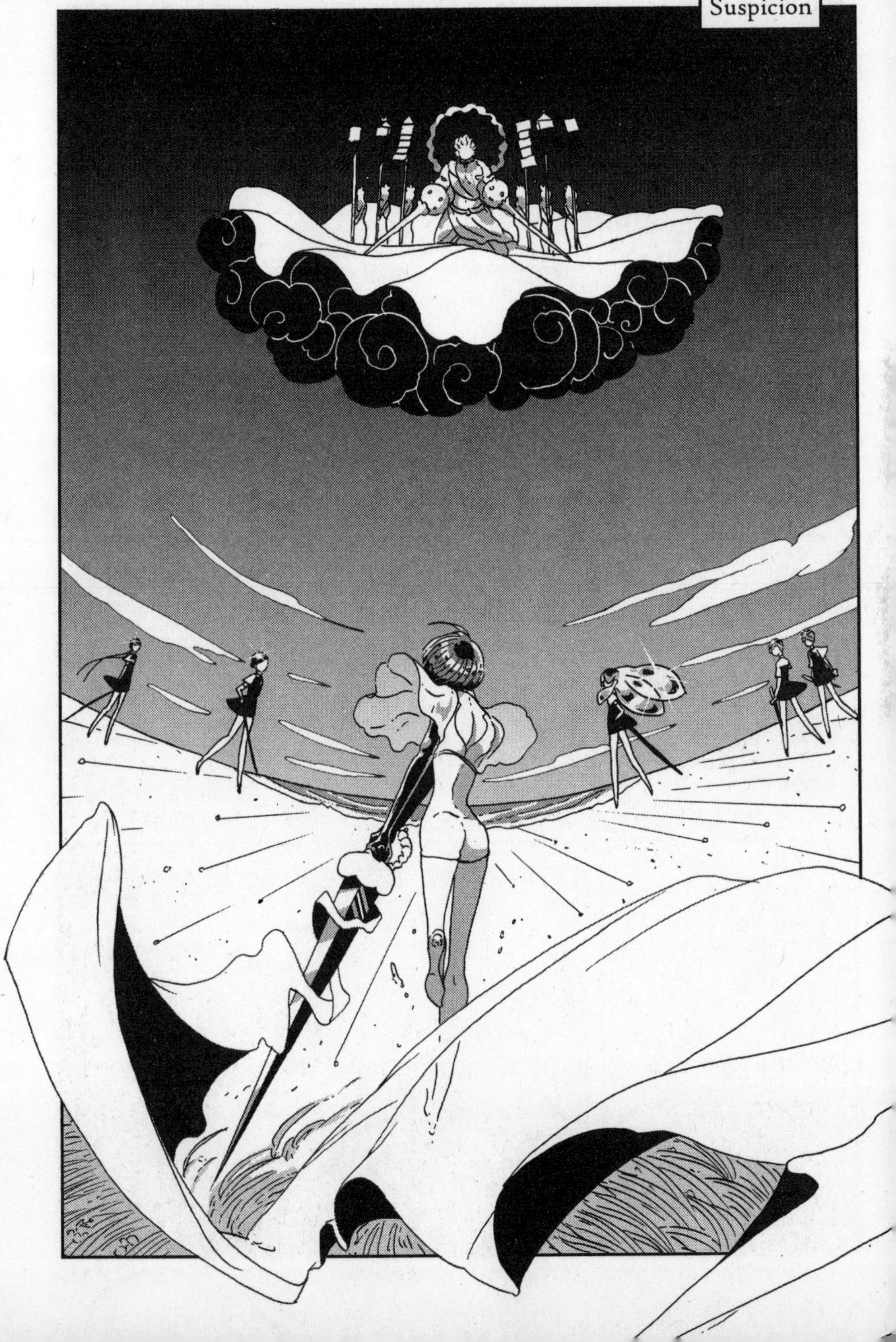

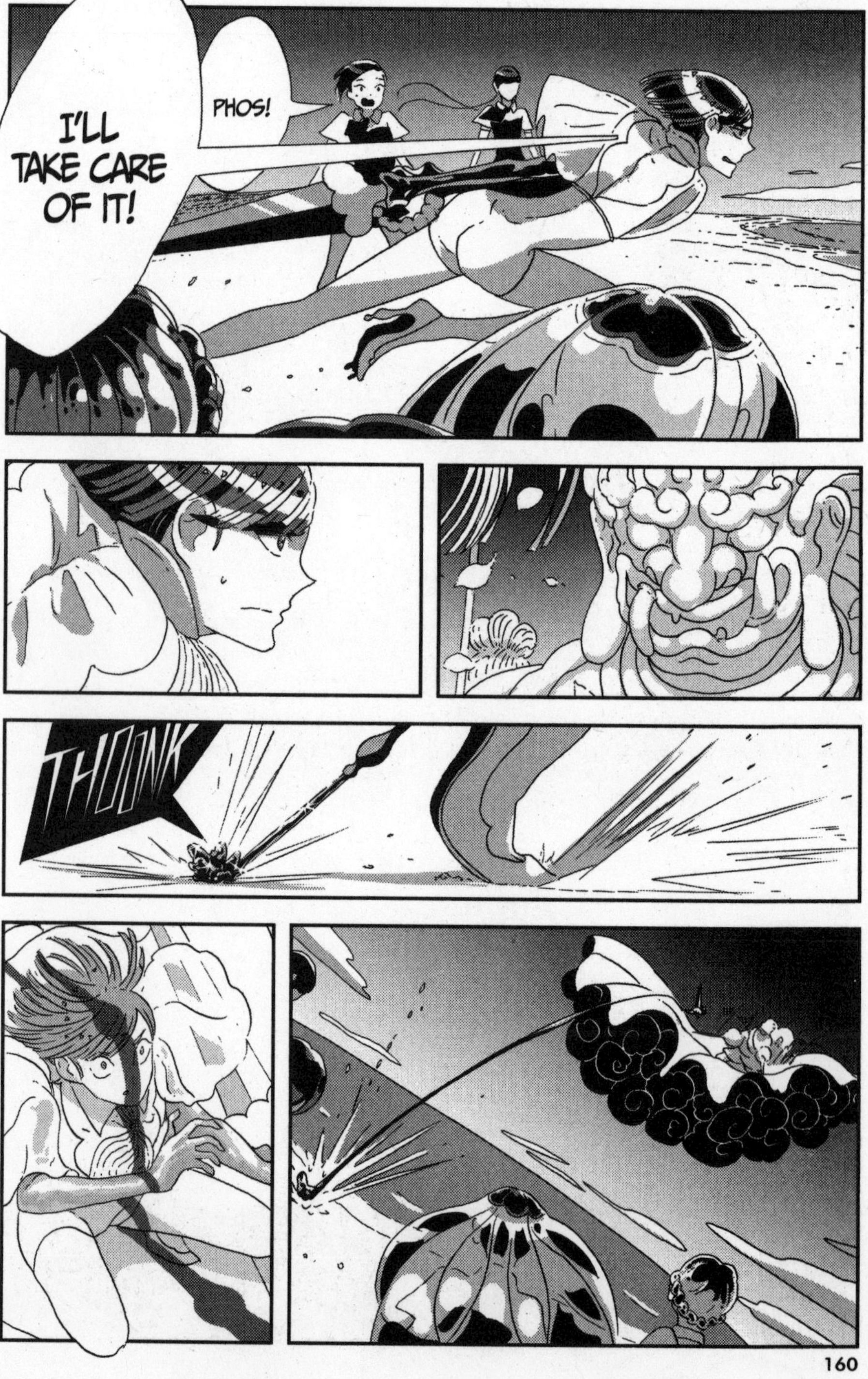
PHOS!
I'LL TAKE CARE OF IT!
THOONK

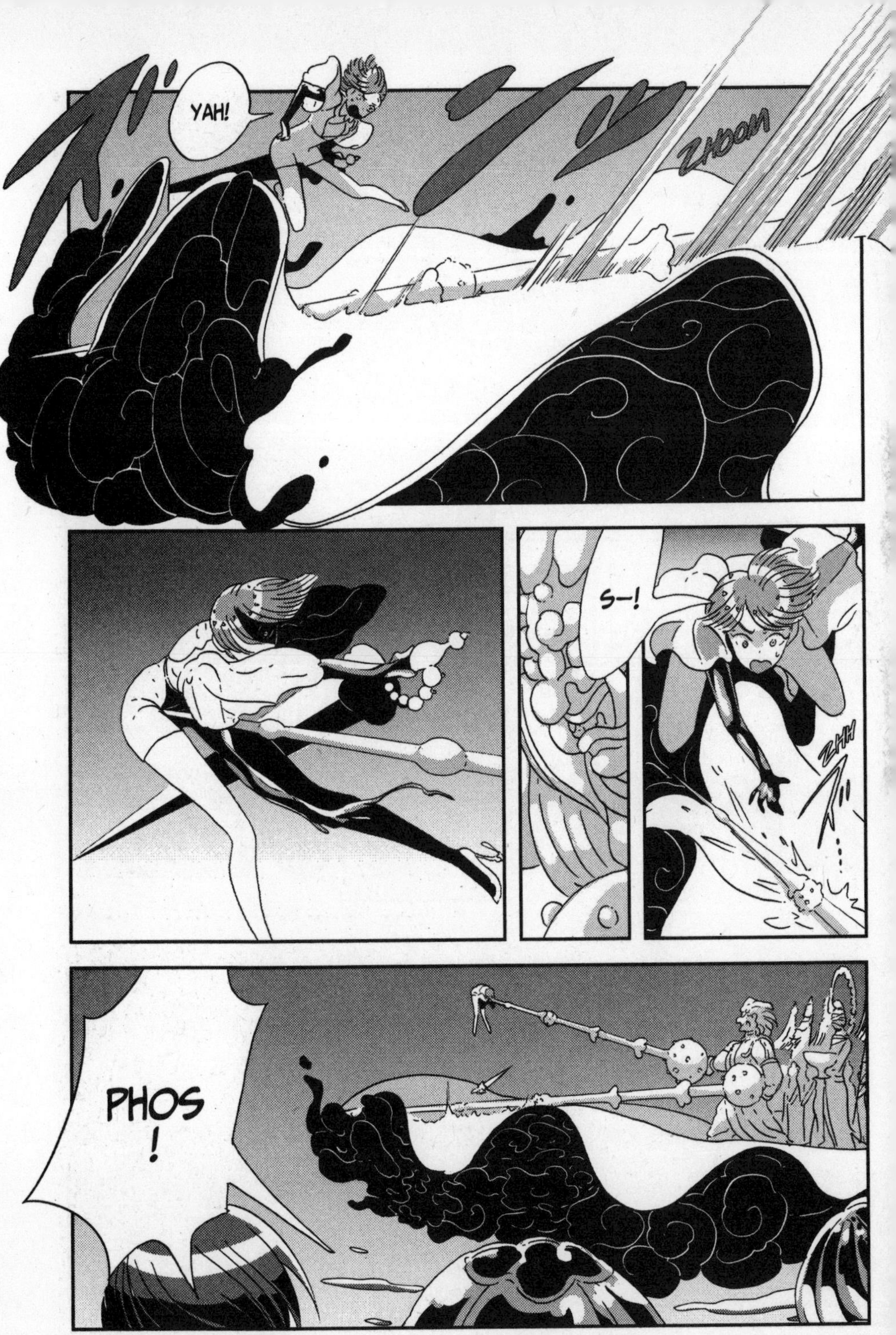
ZHOOM
YAH!
S–!
ZHH
PHOS
!

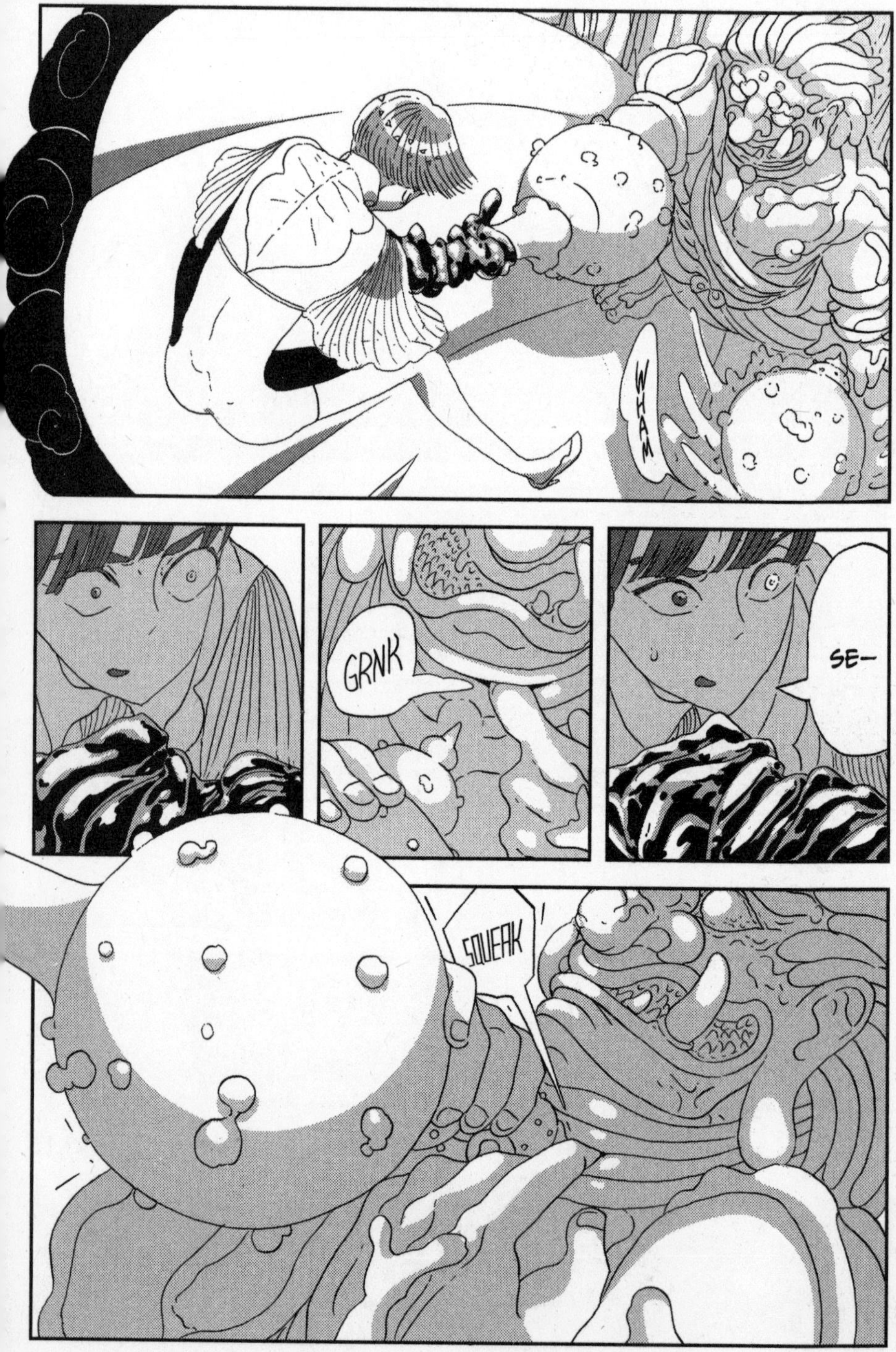
WHAM
SE—
GRNK
SQUEAK

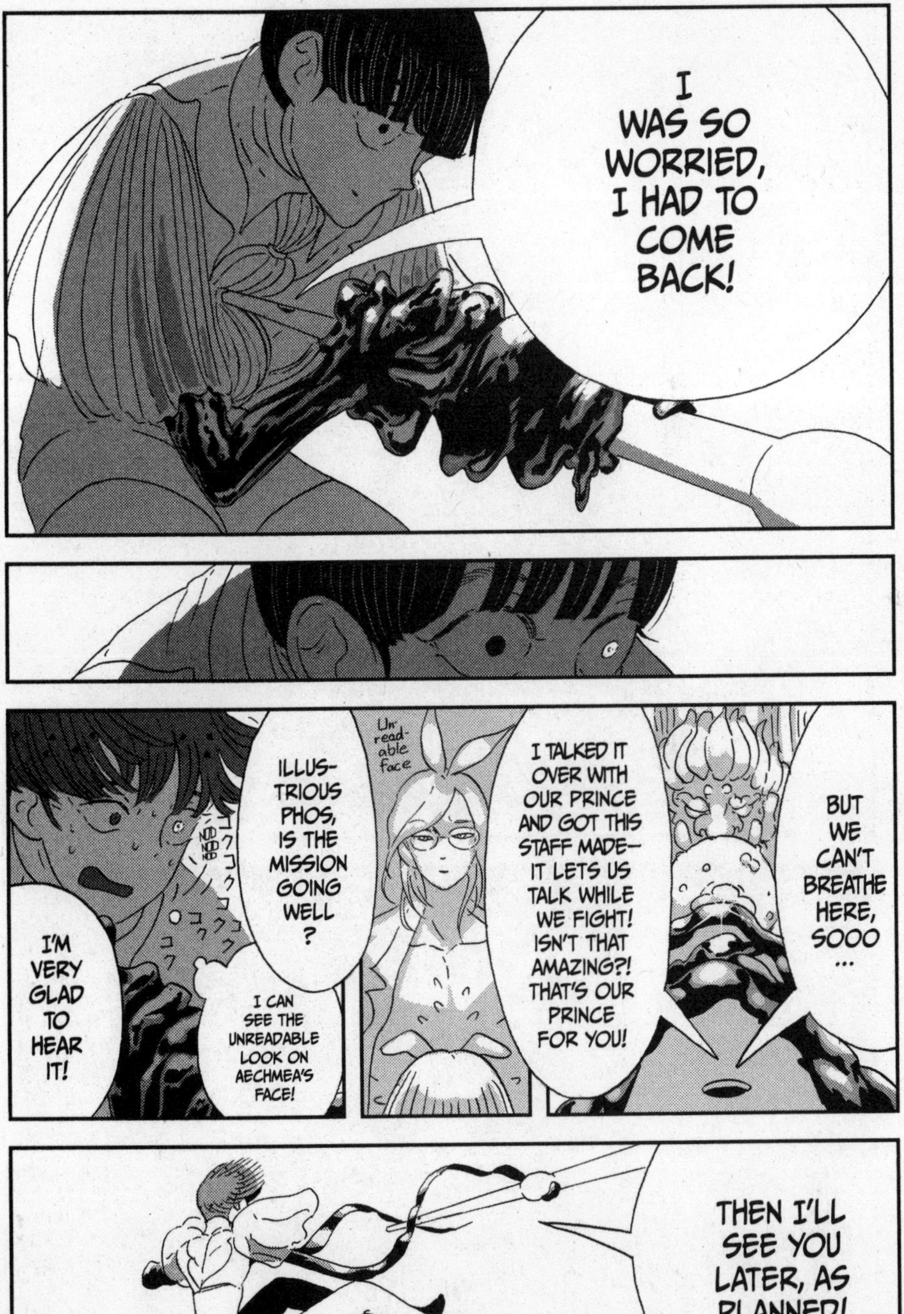
I WAS SO WORRIED, I HAD TO COME BACK!
BUT WE CAN'T BREATHE HERE, SOOO...
I TALKED IT OVER WITH OUR PRINCE AND GOT THIS STAFF MADE— IT LETS US TALK WHILE WE FIGHT! ISN'T THAT AMAZING?! THAT'S OUR PRINCE FOR YOU!
Un-readable face
ILLUS-TRIOUS PHOS, IS THE MISSION GOING WELL?
NOD NOD NOD
I CAN SEE THE UNREADABLE LOOK ON AECHMEA'S FACE!
I'M VERY GLAD TO HEAR IT!
THEN I'LL SEE YOU LATER, AS PLANNED!

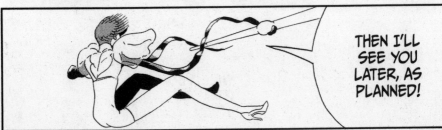

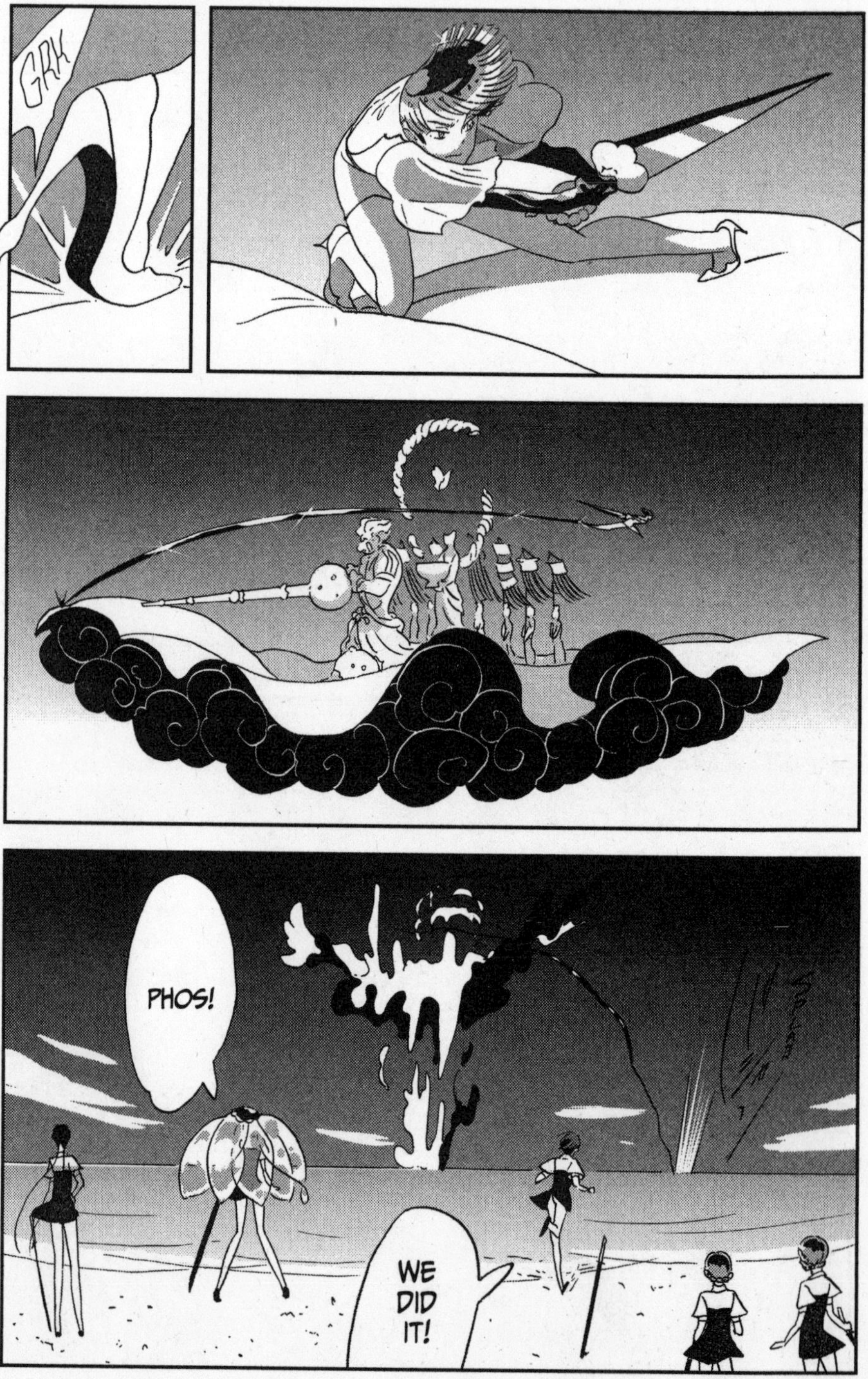
GRK
PHOS!
WE DID IT!

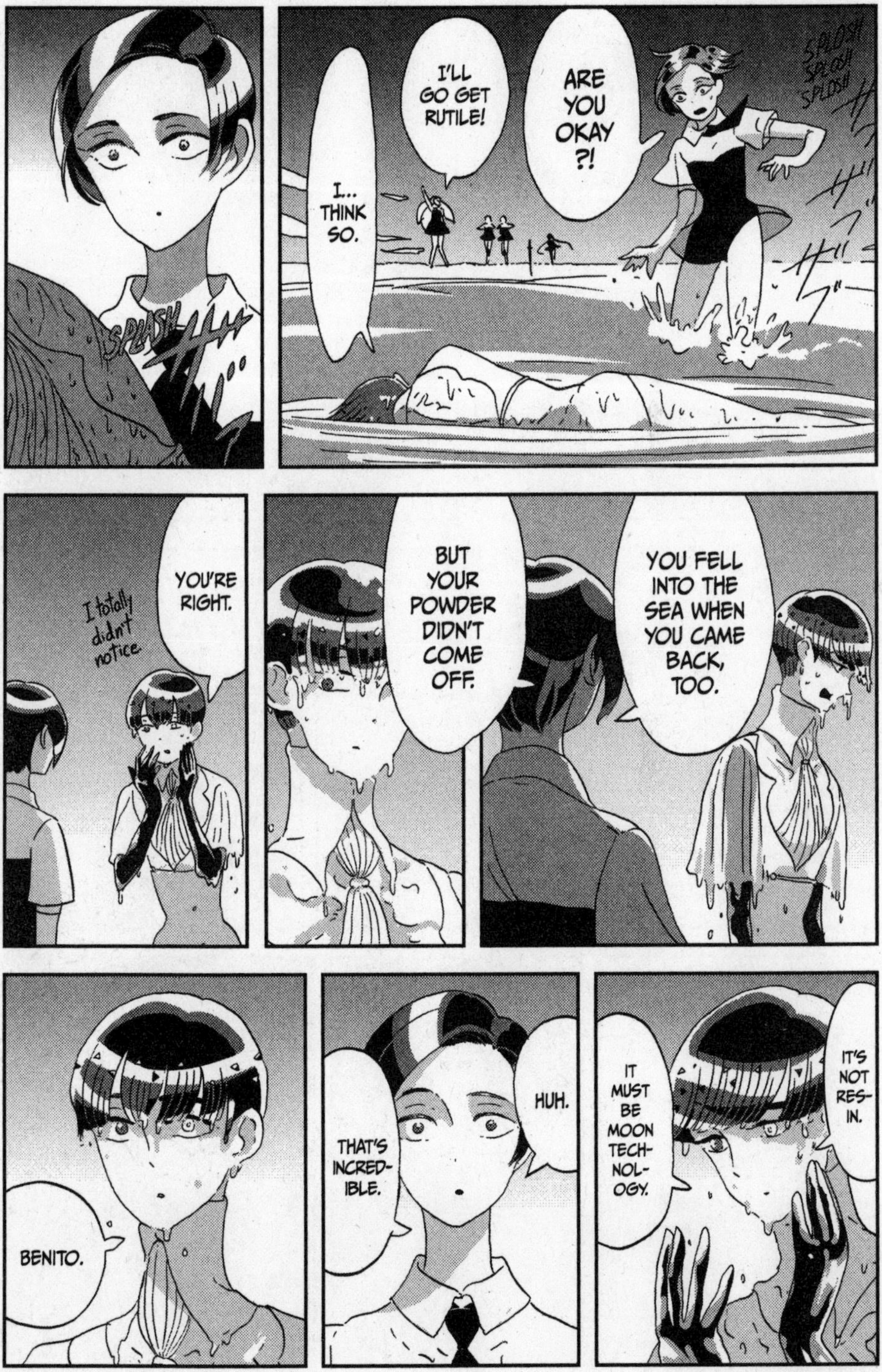
SPLOSH SPLOSH SPLOSH
ARE YOU OKAY ?!
I'LL GO GET RUTILE!
I... THINK SO.
SPLASH
YOU FELL INTO THE SEA WHEN YOU CAME BACK, TOO.
BUT YOUR POWDER DIDN'T COME OFF.
YOU'RE RIGHT.
I totally didn't notice.
IT'S NOT RES-IN.
IT MUST BE MOON TECHNOLOGY.
HUH.
THAT'S INCRED-IBLE.
BENITO.

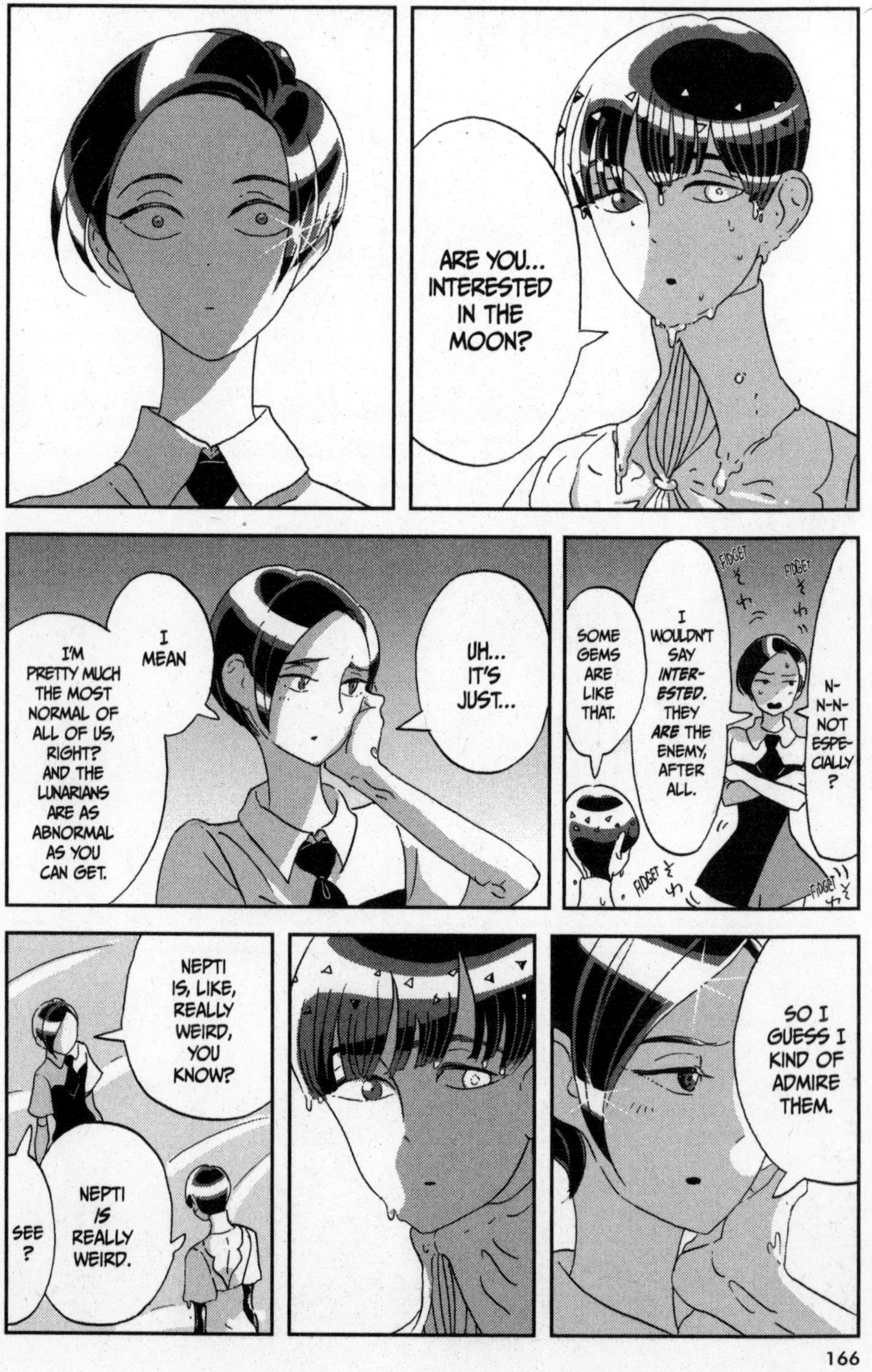
ARE YOU... INTERESTED IN THE MOON?
N-N-N-NOT ESPECIALLY?
FIDGET
FIDGET
I WOULDN'T SAY *INTERESTED*. THEY *ARE* THE ENEMY, AFTER ALL.
SOME GEMS ARE LIKE THAT.
FIDGET
FIDGET
UH... IT'S JUST...
I MEAN
I'M PRETTY MUCH THE MOST NORMAL OF ALL OF US, RIGHT? AND THE LUNARIANS ARE AS ABNORMAL AS YOU CAN GET.
SO I GUESS I KIND OF ADMIRE THEM.
NEPTI IS, LIKE, REALLY WEIRD, YOU KNOW?
NEPTI *IS* REALLY WEIRD.
SEE?

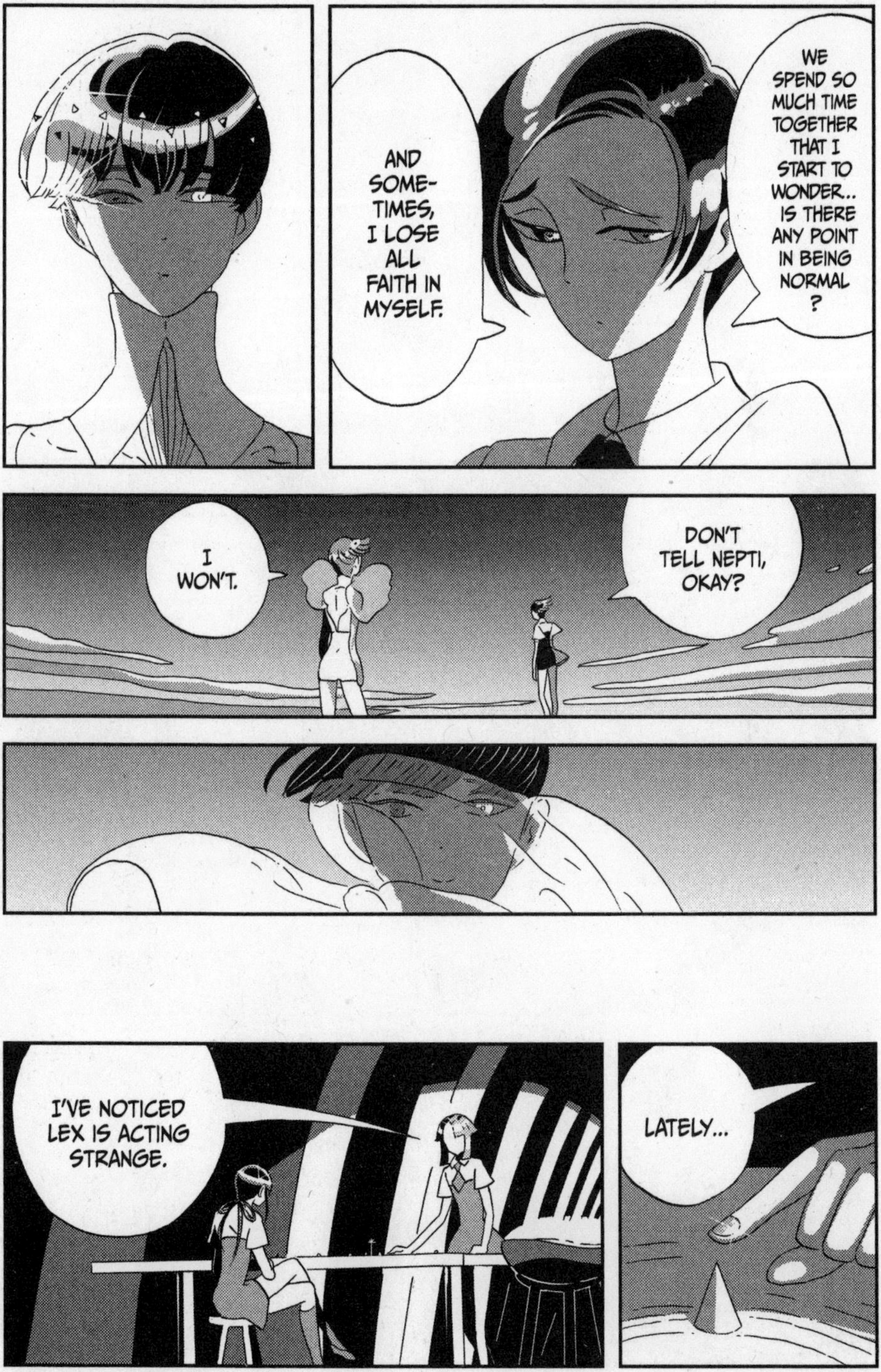
WE SPEND SO MUCH TIME TOGETHER THAT I START TO WONDER.. IS THERE ANY POINT IN BEING NORMAL ?
AND SOME-TIMES, I LOSE ALL FAITH IN MYSELF.
DON'T TELL NEPTI, OKAY?
I WON'T.
LATELY...
I'VE NOTICED LEX IS ACTING STRANGE.

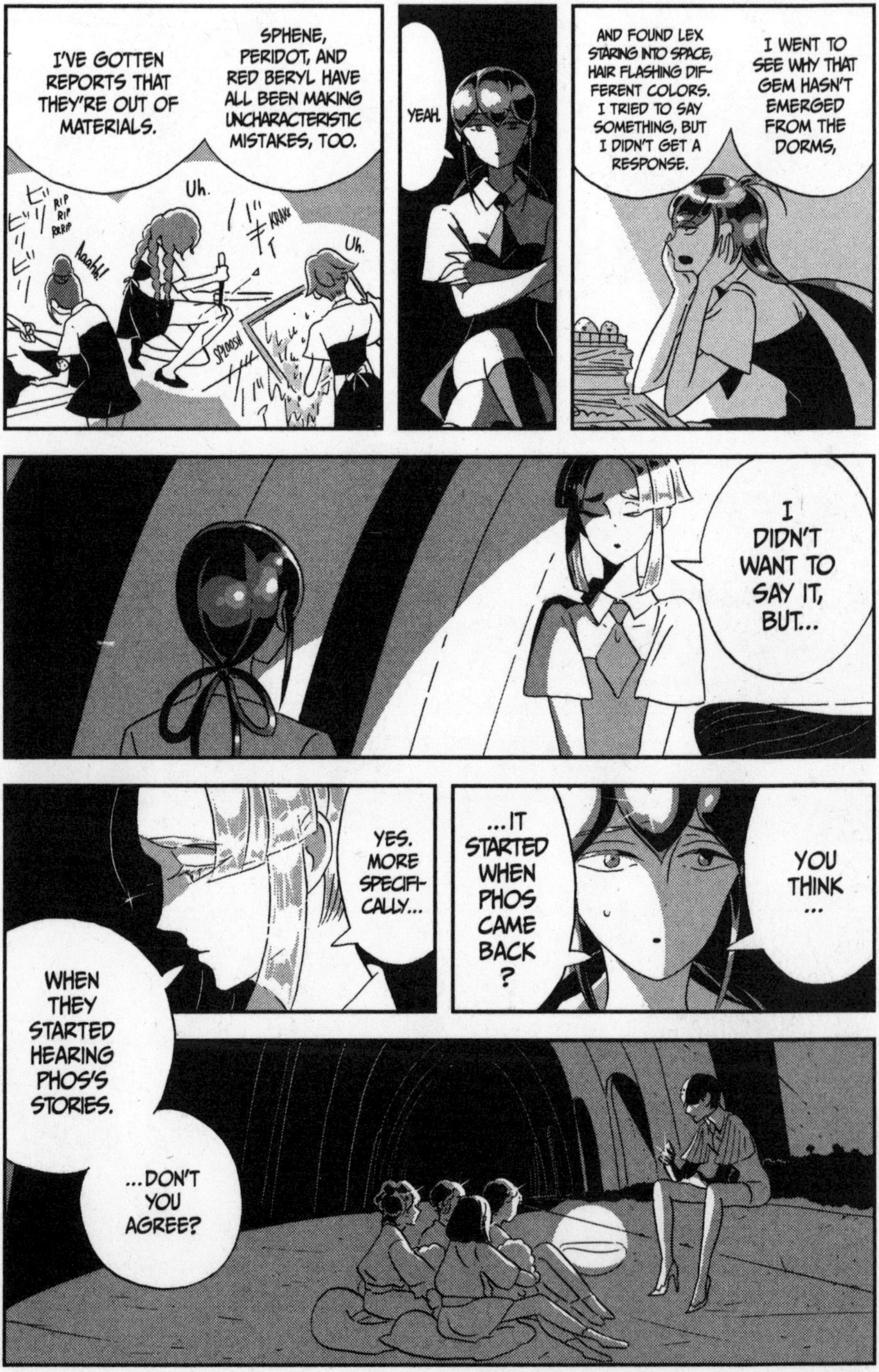
I WENT TO SEE WHY THAT GEM HASN'T EMERGED FROM THE DORMS,
AND FOUND LEX STARING INTO SPACE, HAIR FLASHING DIFFERENT COLORS. I TRIED TO SAY SOMETHING, BUT I DIDN'T GET A RESPONSE.
YEAH.
SPHENE, PERIDOT, AND RED BERYL HAVE ALL BEEN MAKING UNCHARACTERISTIC MISTAKES, TOO.
I'VE GOTTEN REPORTS THAT THEY'RE OUT OF MATERIALS.
Uh.
KRAKK
Uh.
RIP RIP RRRIP
Aaahh!
SPLOOSH
I DIDN'T WANT TO SAY IT, BUT...
YOU THINK ...
...IT STARTED WHEN PHOS CAME BACK?
YES. MORE SPECIFICALLY...
WHEN THEY STARTED HEARING PHOS'S STORIES.
...DON'T YOU AGREE?

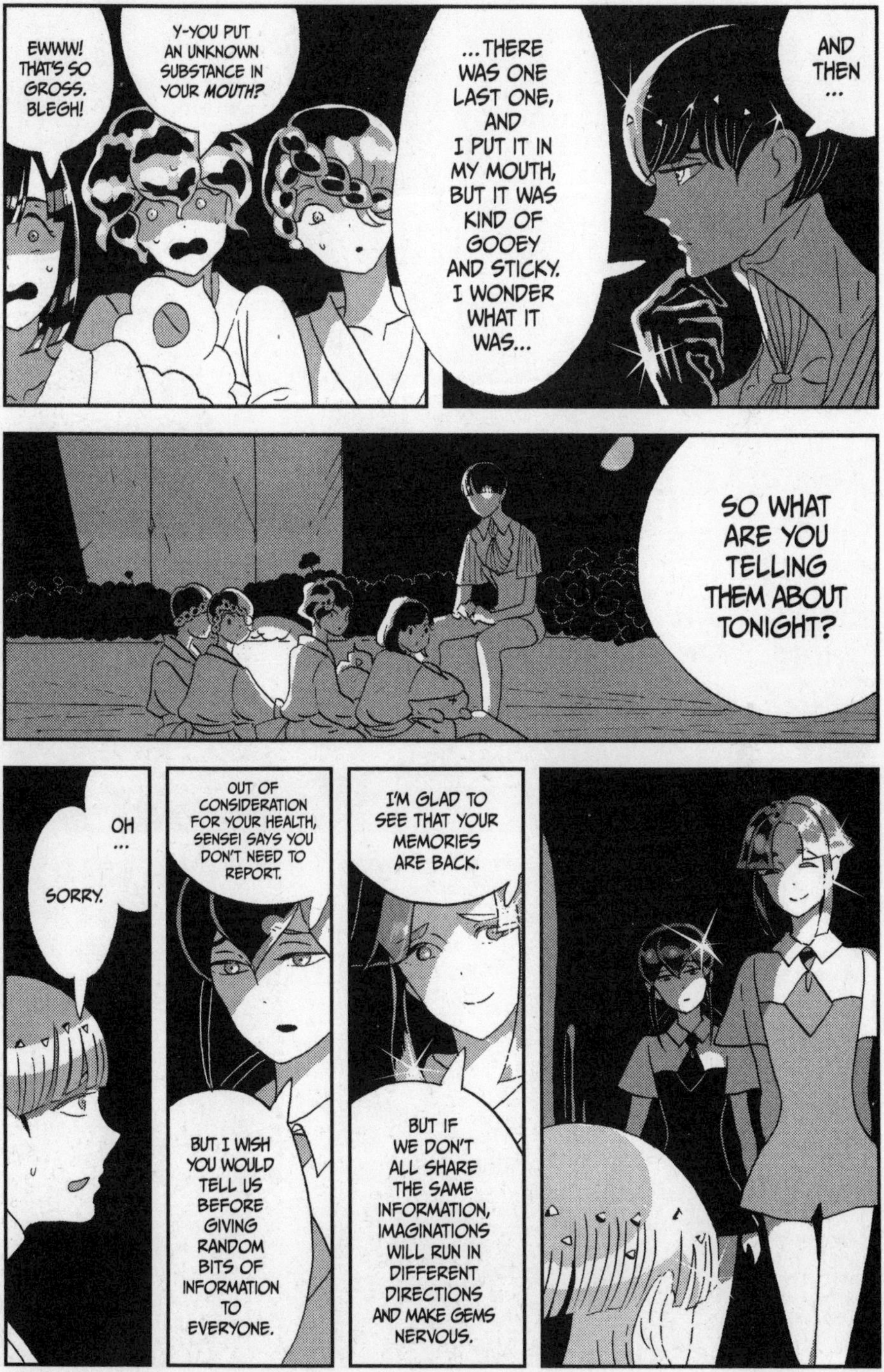
AND THEN ...
...THERE WAS ONE LAST ONE, AND I PUT IT IN MY MOUTH, BUT IT WAS KIND OF GOOEY AND STICKY. I WONDER WHAT IT WAS...
Y-YOU PUT AN UNKNOWN SUBSTANCE IN YOUR *MOUTH?*
EWWW! THAT'S SO GROSS. BLEGH!
SO WHAT ARE YOU TELLING THEM ABOUT TONIGHT?
I'M GLAD TO SEE THAT YOUR MEMORIES ARE BACK.
BUT IF WE DON'T ALL SHARE THE SAME INFORMATION, IMAGINATIONS WILL RUN IN DIFFERENT DIRECTIONS AND MAKE GEMS NERVOUS.
OUT OF CONSIDERATION FOR YOUR HEALTH, SENSEI SAYS YOU DON'T NEED TO REPORT.
BUT I WISH YOU WOULD TELL US BEFORE GIVING RANDOM BITS OF INFORMATION TO EVERYONE.
OH ...
SORRY.

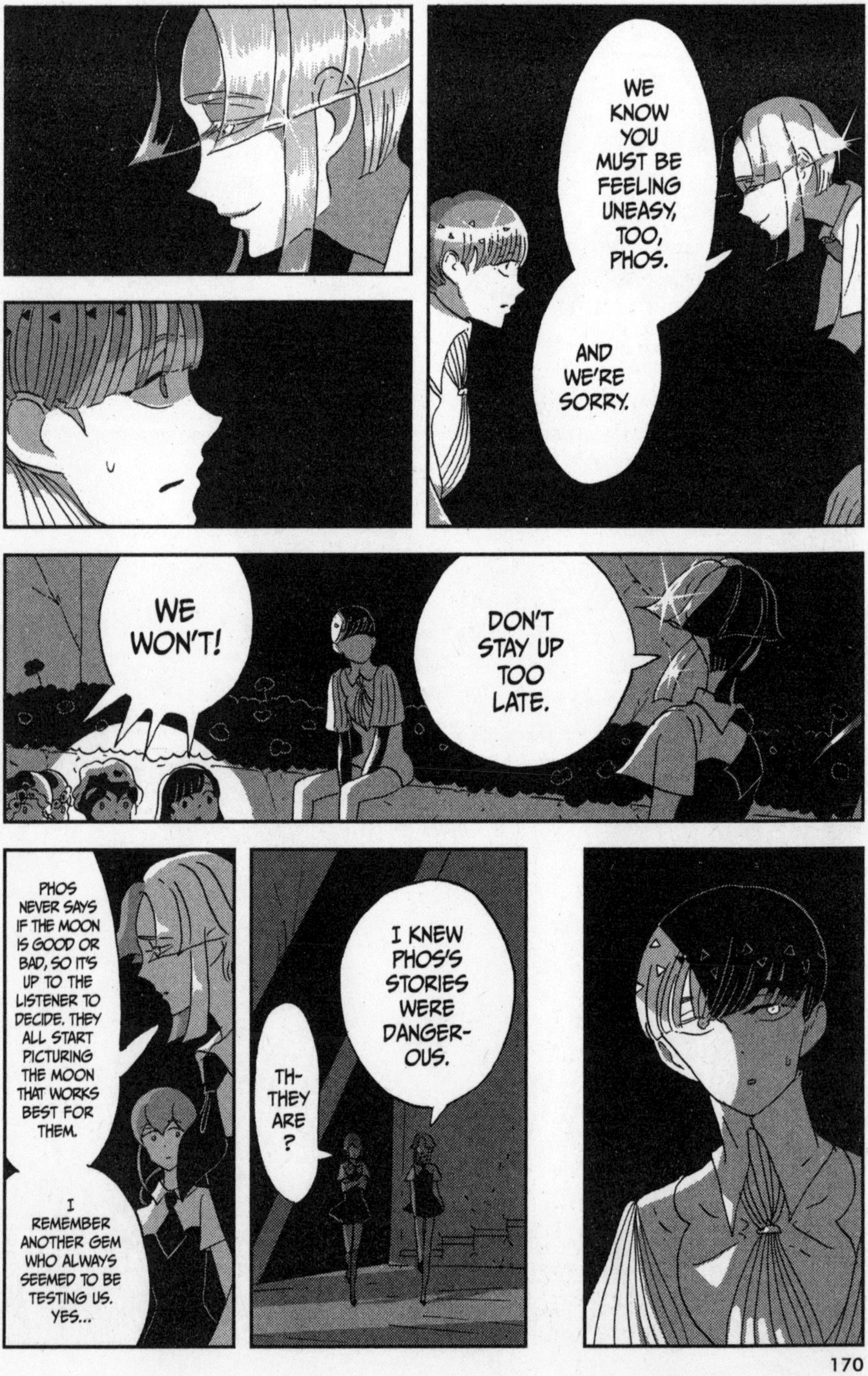
WE KNOW YOU MUST BE FEELING UNEASY, TOO, PHOS.
AND WE'RE SORRY.
DON'T STAY UP TOO LATE.
WE WON'T!
I KNEW PHOS'S STORIES WERE DANGER-OUS.
TH-THEY ARE?
PHOS NEVER SAYS IF THE MOON IS GOOD OR BAD, SO IT'S UP TO THE LISTENER TO DECIDE. THEY ALL START PICTURING THE MOON THAT WORKS BEST FOR THEM.
I REMEMBER ANOTHER GEM WHO ALWAYS SEEMED TO BE TESTING US. YES...

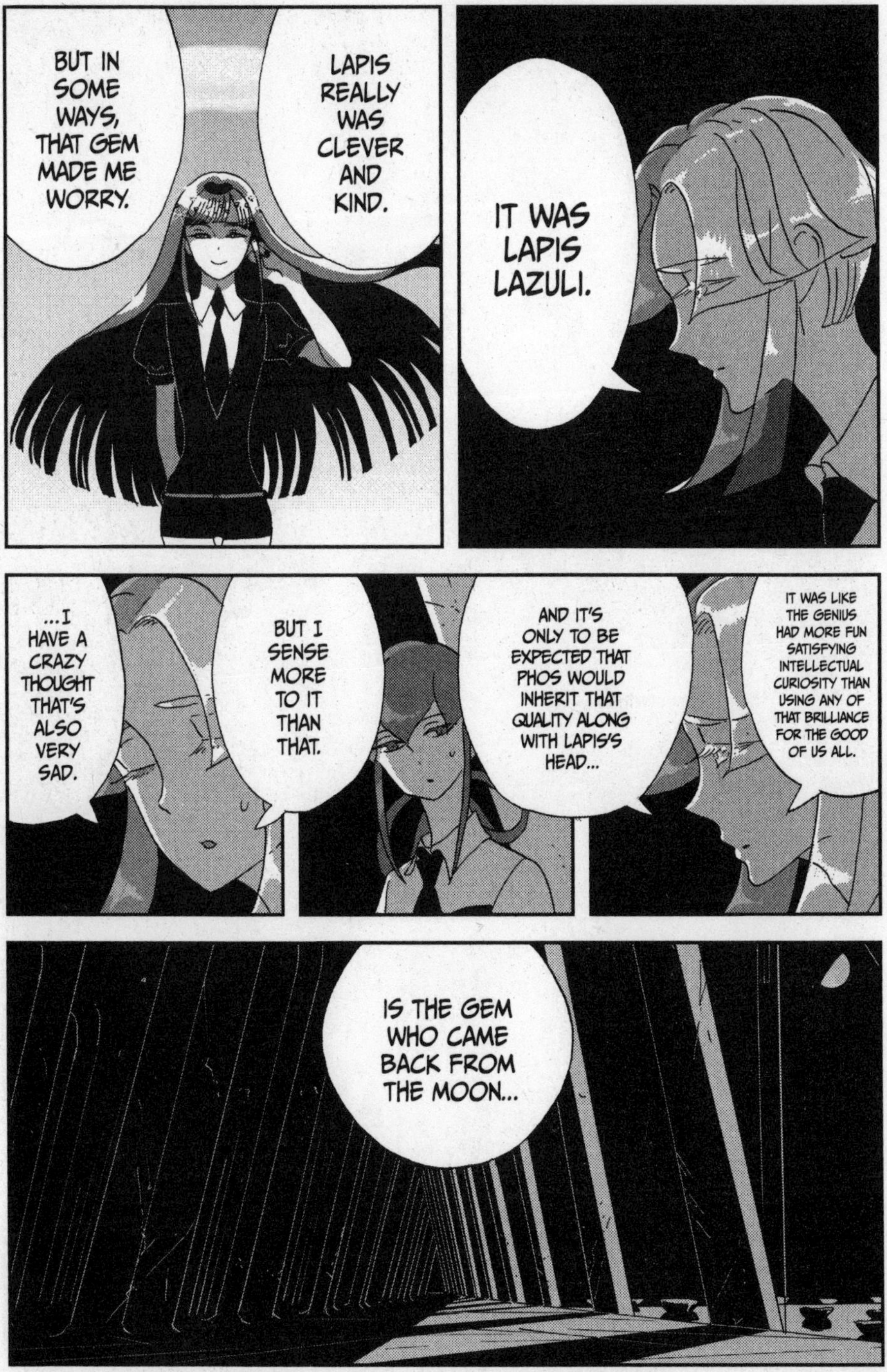
IT WAS LAPIS LAZULI.
LAPIS REALLY WAS CLEVER AND KIND.
BUT IN SOME WAYS, THAT GEM MADE ME WORRY.
IT WAS LIKE THE GENIUS HAD MORE FUN SATISFYING INTELLECTUAL CURIOSITY THAN USING ANY OF THAT BRILLIANCE FOR THE GOOD OF US ALL.
AND IT'S ONLY TO BE EXPECTED THAT PHOS WOULD INHERIT THAT QUALITY ALONG WITH LAPIS'S HEAD...
BUT I SENSE MORE TO IT THAN THAT.
...I HAVE A CRAZY THOUGHT THAT'S ALSO VERY SAD.
IS THE GEM WHO CAME BACK FROM THE MOON...

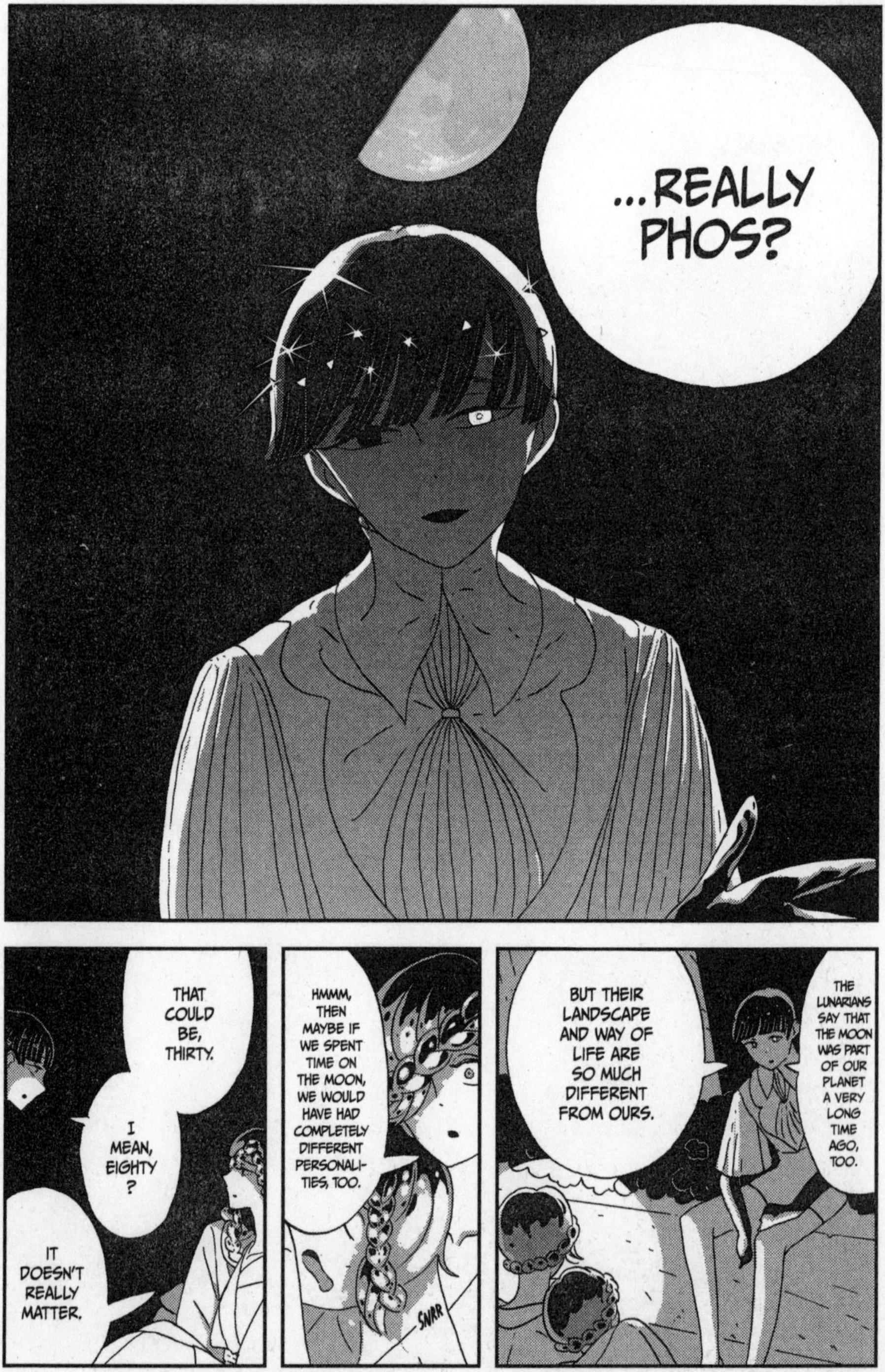
...REALLY PHOS?
THE LUNARIANS SAY THAT THE MOON WAS PART OF OUR PLANET A VERY LONG TIME AGO, TOO.
BUT THEIR LANDSCAPE AND WAY OF LIFE ARE SO MUCH DIFFERENT FROM OURS.
HMMM, THEN MAYBE IF WE SPENT TIME ON THE MOON, WE WOULD HAVE HAD COMPLETELY DIFFERENT PERSONALITIES, TOO.
SNRR
THAT COULD BE, THIRTY.
I MEAN, EIGHTY?
IT DOESN'T REALLY MATTER.

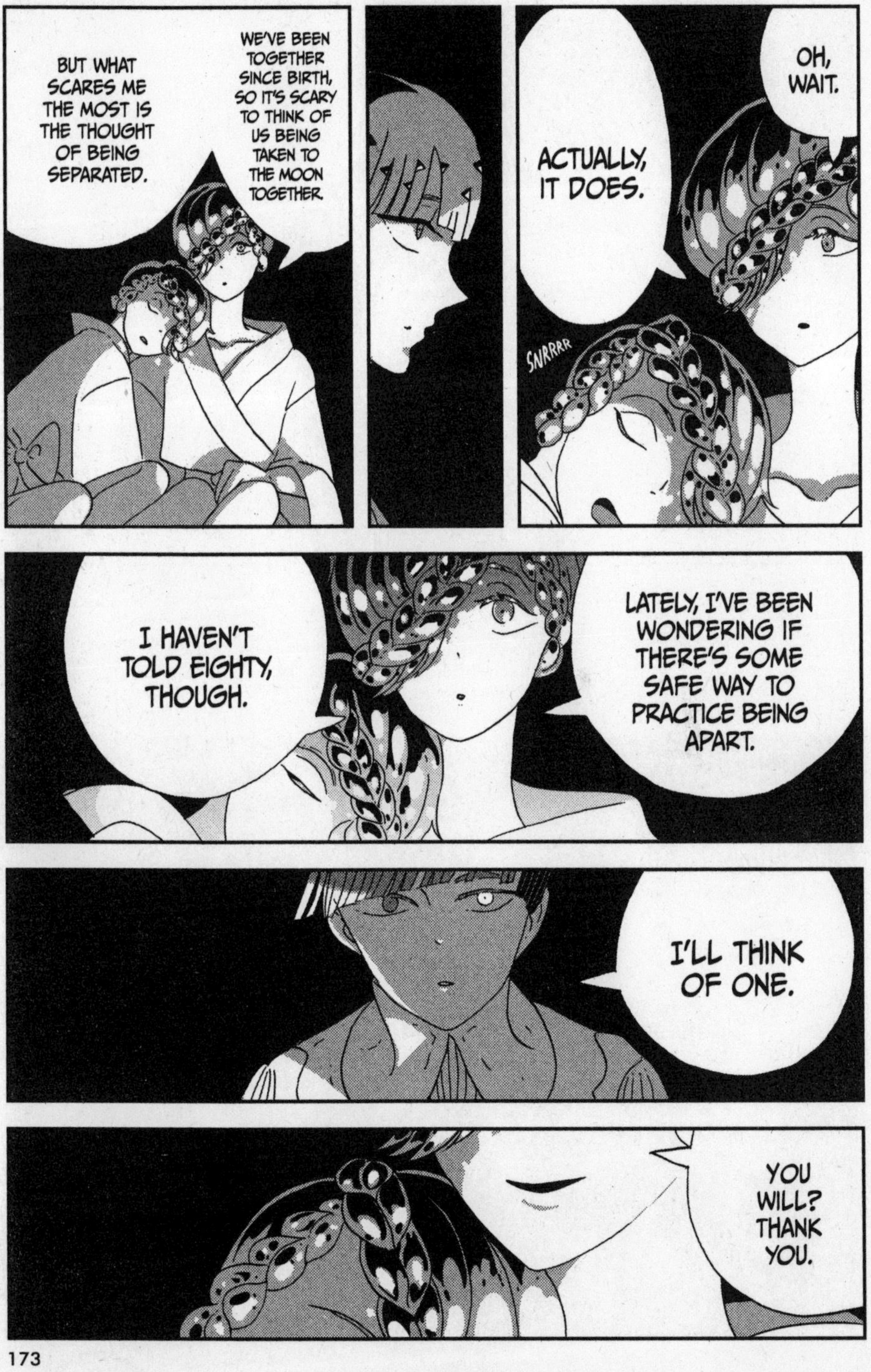
OH, WAIT.
ACTUALLY, IT DOES.
SNRRRR
WE'VE BEEN TOGETHER SINCE BIRTH, SO IT'S SCARY TO THINK OF US BEING TAKEN TO THE MOON TOGETHER.
BUT WHAT SCARES ME THE MOST IS THE THOUGHT OF BEING SEPARATED.
LATELY, I'VE BEEN WONDERING IF THERE'S SOME SAFE WAY TO PRACTICE BEING APART.
I HAVEN'T TOLD EIGHTY, THOUGH.
I'LL THINK OF ONE.
YOU WILL? THANK YOU.

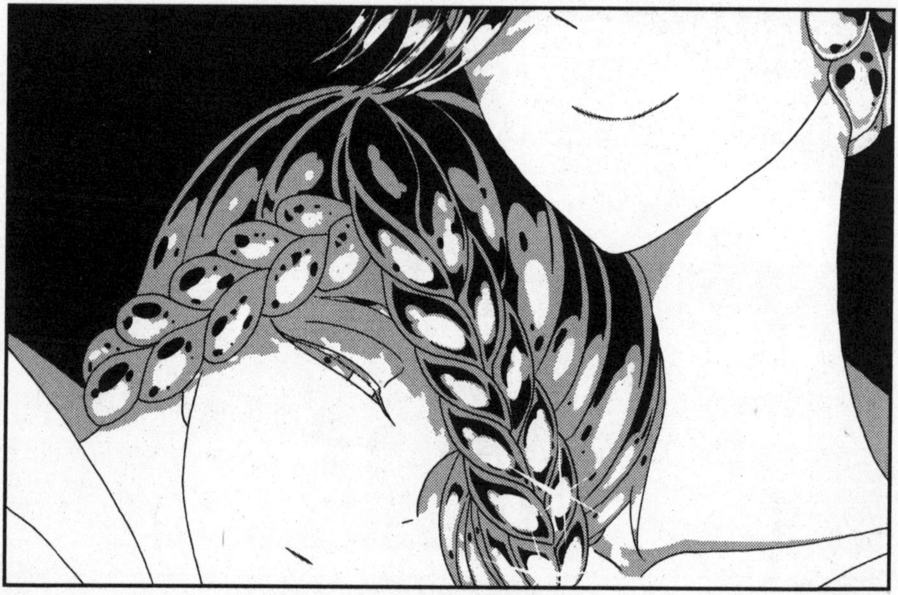

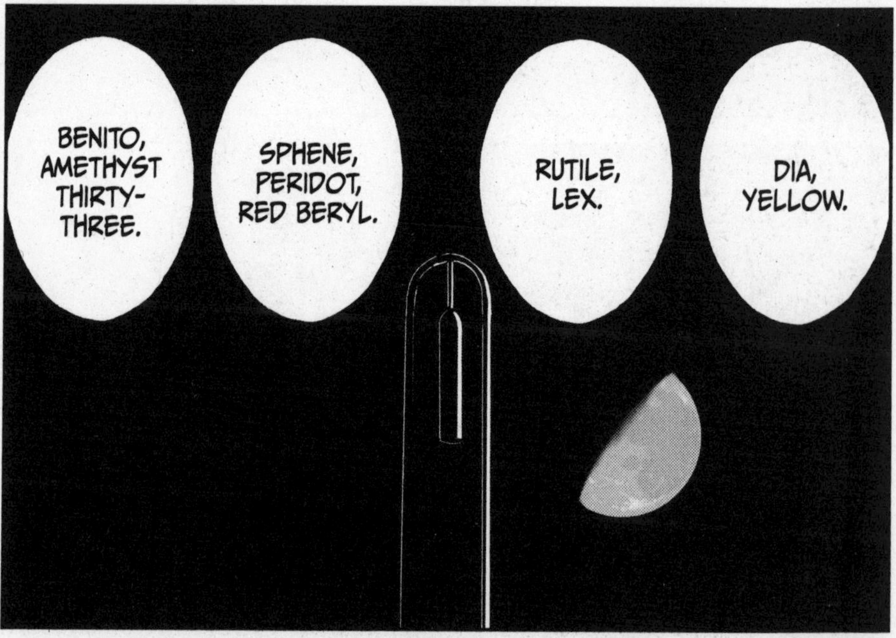
DIA, YELLOW.
RUTILE, LEX.
SPHENE, PERIDOT, RED BERYL.
BENITO, AMETHYST THIRTY-THREE.

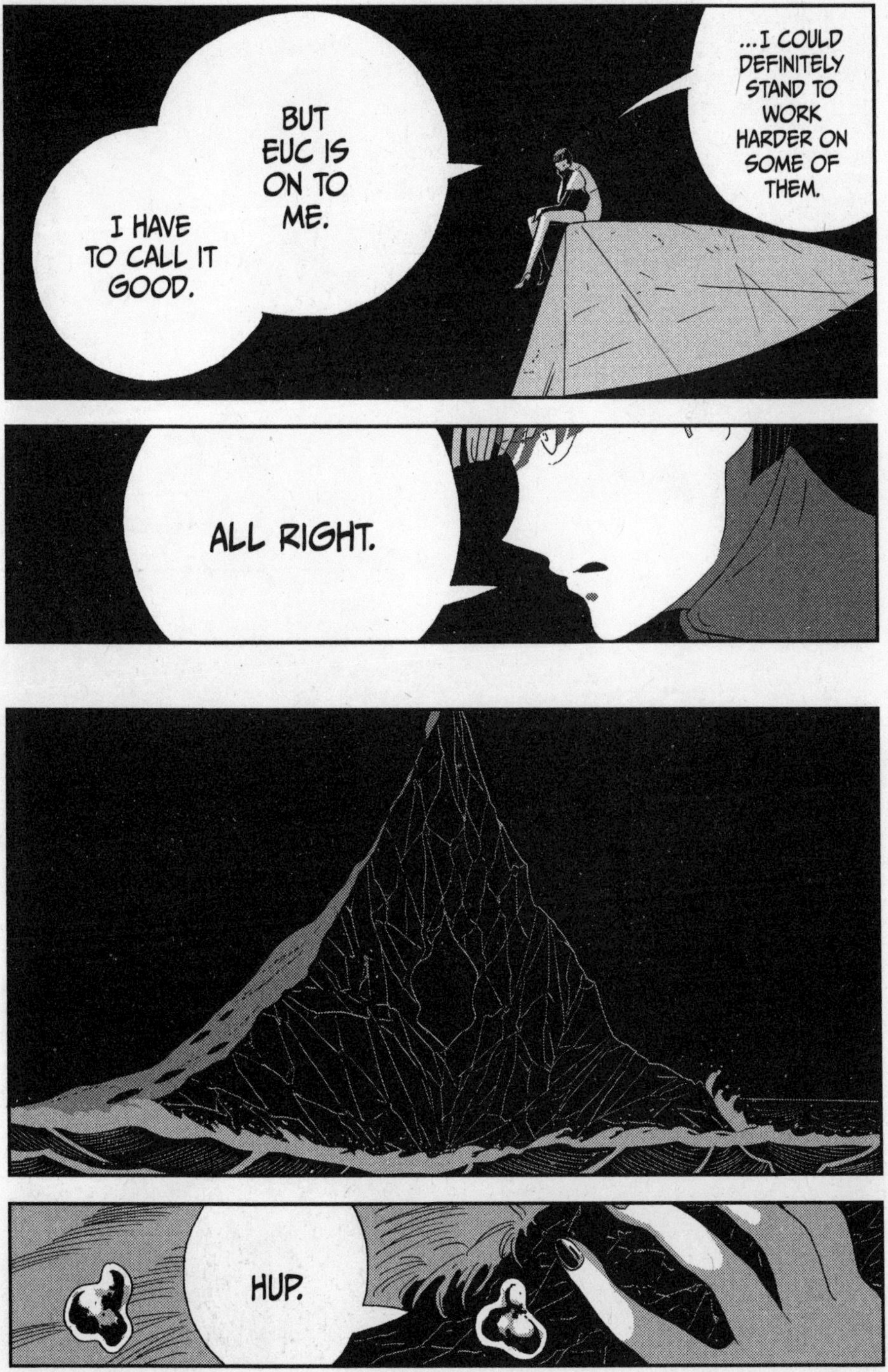
...I COULD DEFINITELY STAND TO WORK HARDER ON SOME OF THEM.
BUT EUC IS ON TO ME.
I HAVE TO CALL IT GOOD.
ALL RIGHT.
HUP.

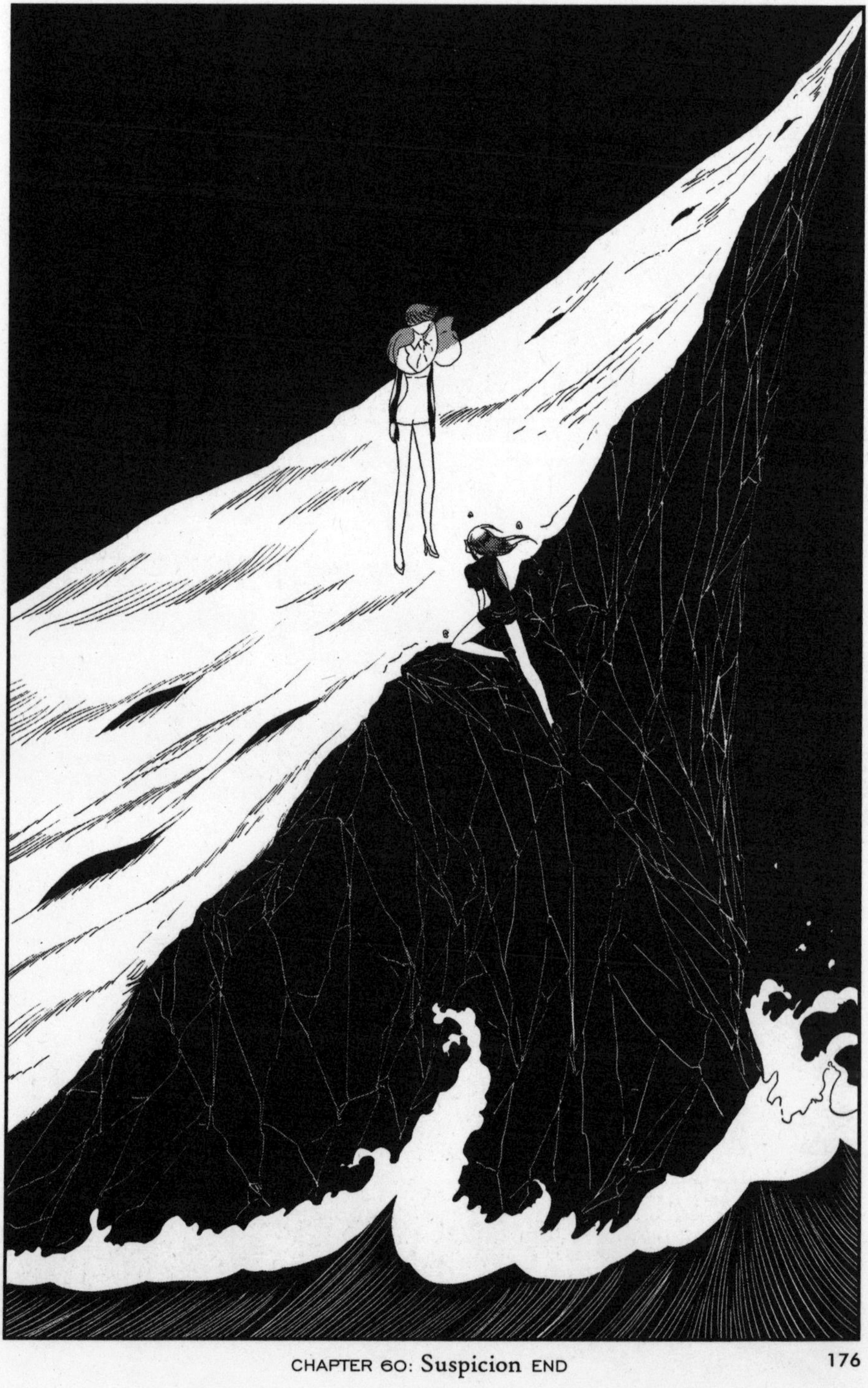

CHAPTER 60: Suspicion END

CHAPTER 61:

Parting

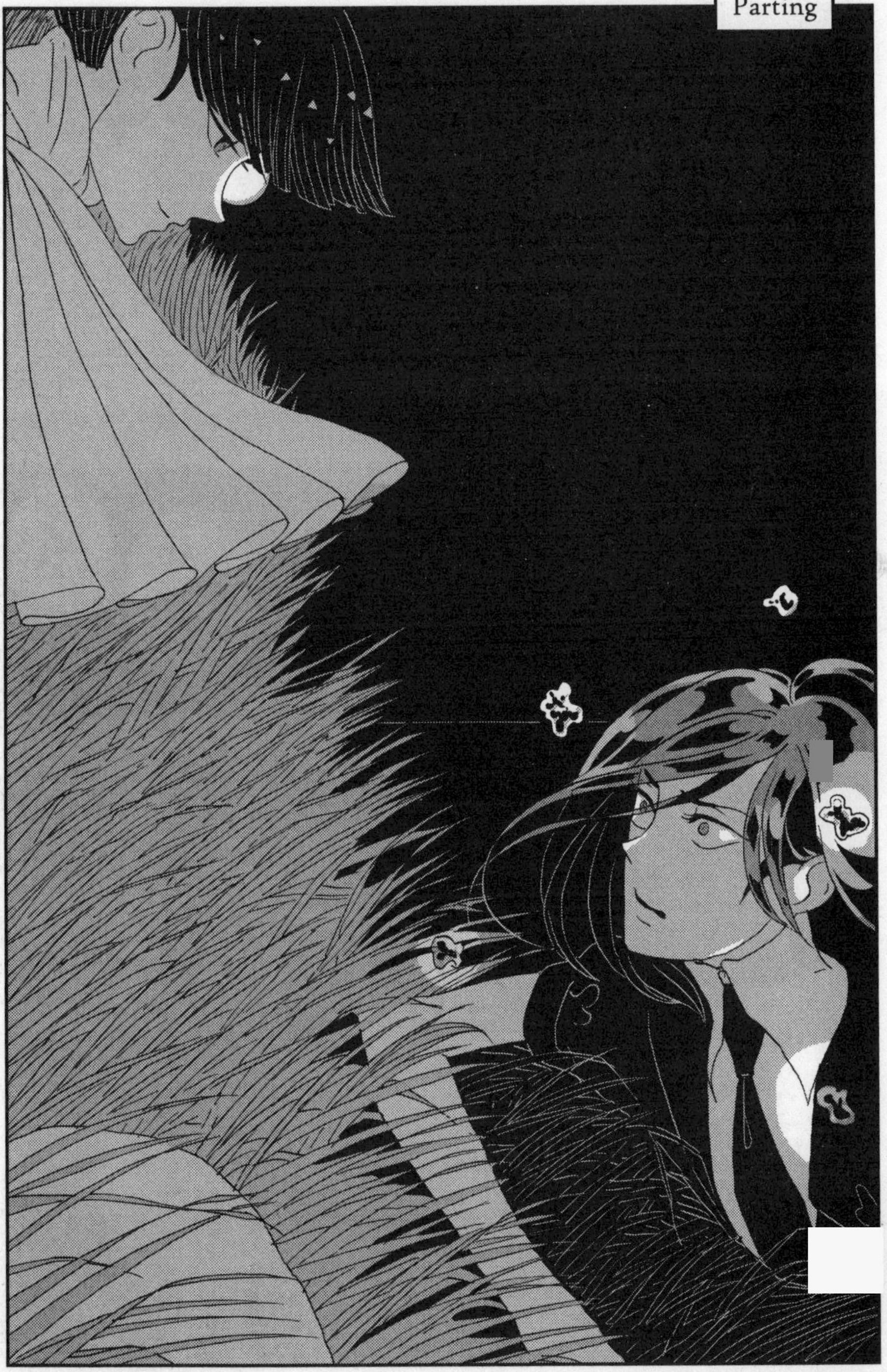

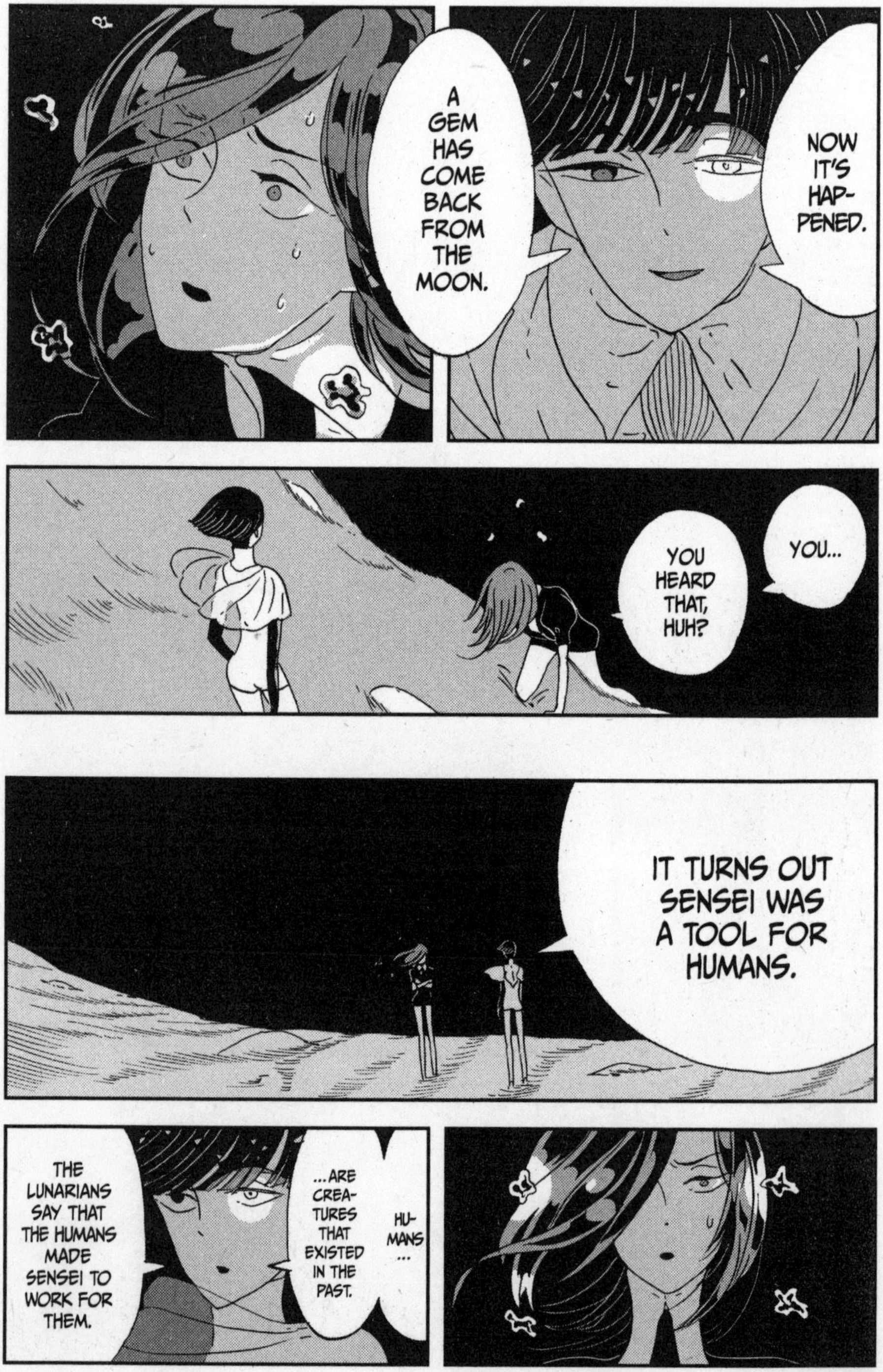
NOW IT'S HAP-PENED.
A GEM HAS COME BACK FROM THE MOON.
YOU...
YOU HEARD THAT, HUH?
IT TURNS OUT SENSEI WAS A TOOL FOR HUMANS.
HU-MANS...
...ARE CREA-TURES THAT EXISTED IN THE PAST.
THE LUNARIANS SAY THAT THE HUMANS MADE SENSEI TO WORK FOR THEM.

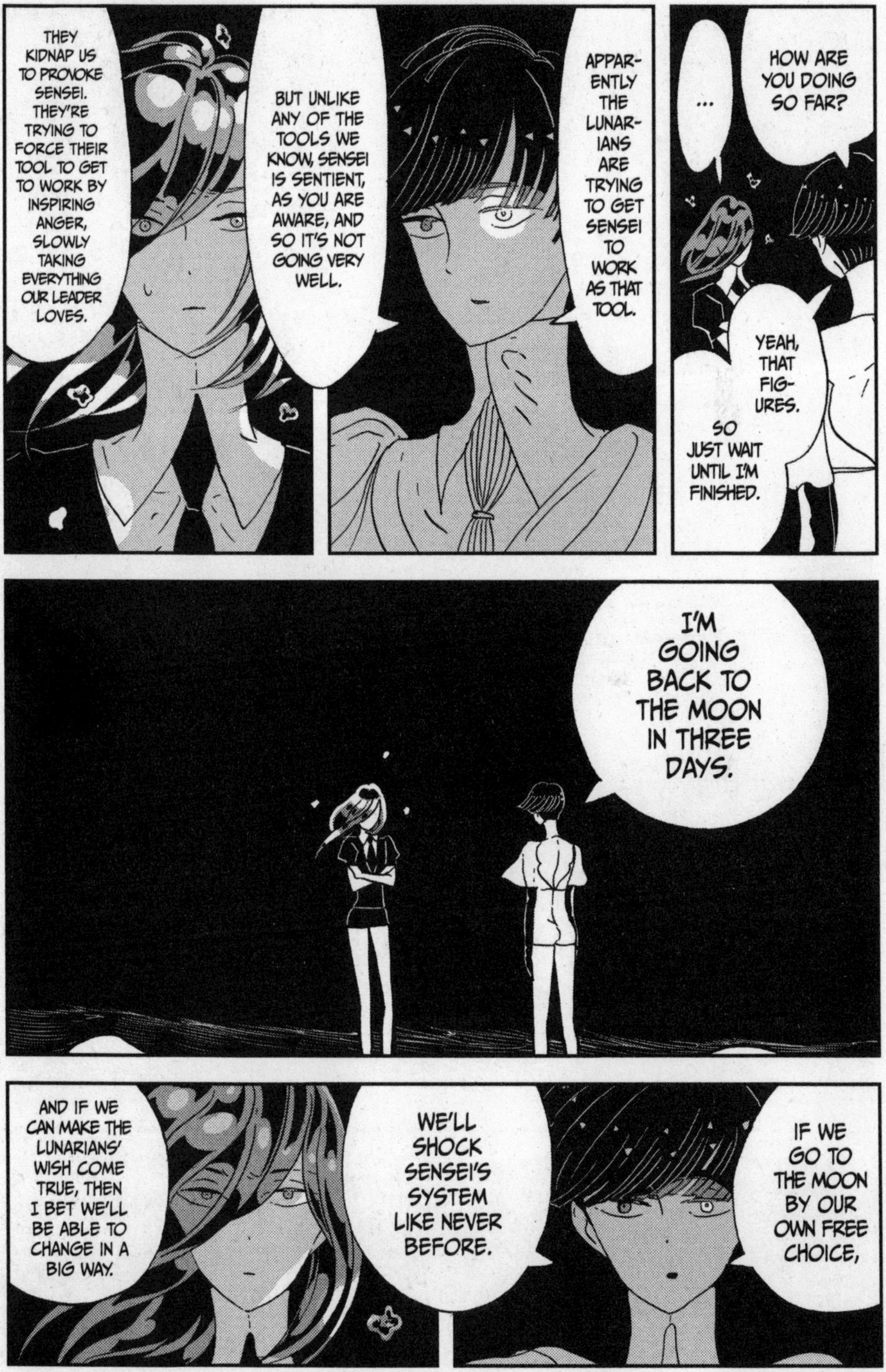
HOW ARE YOU DOING SO FAR?
...
YEAH, THAT FIGURES.
SO JUST WAIT UNTIL I'M FINISHED.
APPARENTLY THE LUNARIANS ARE TRYING TO GET SENSEI TO WORK AS THAT TOOL.
BUT UNLIKE ANY OF THE TOOLS WE KNOW, SENSEI IS SENTIENT, AS YOU ARE AWARE, AND SO IT'S NOT GOING VERY WELL.
THEY KIDNAP US TO PROVOKE SENSEI. THEY'RE TRYING TO FORCE THEIR TOOL TO GET TO WORK BY INSPIRING ANGER, SLOWLY TAKING EVERYTHING OUR LEADER LOVES.
I'M GOING BACK TO THE MOON IN THREE DAYS.
IF WE GO TO THE MOON BY OUR OWN FREE CHOICE,
WE'LL SHOCK SENSEI'S SYSTEM LIKE NEVER BEFORE.
AND IF WE CAN MAKE THE LUNARIANS' WISH COME TRUE, THEN I BET WE'LL BE ABLE TO CHANGE IN A BIG WAY.

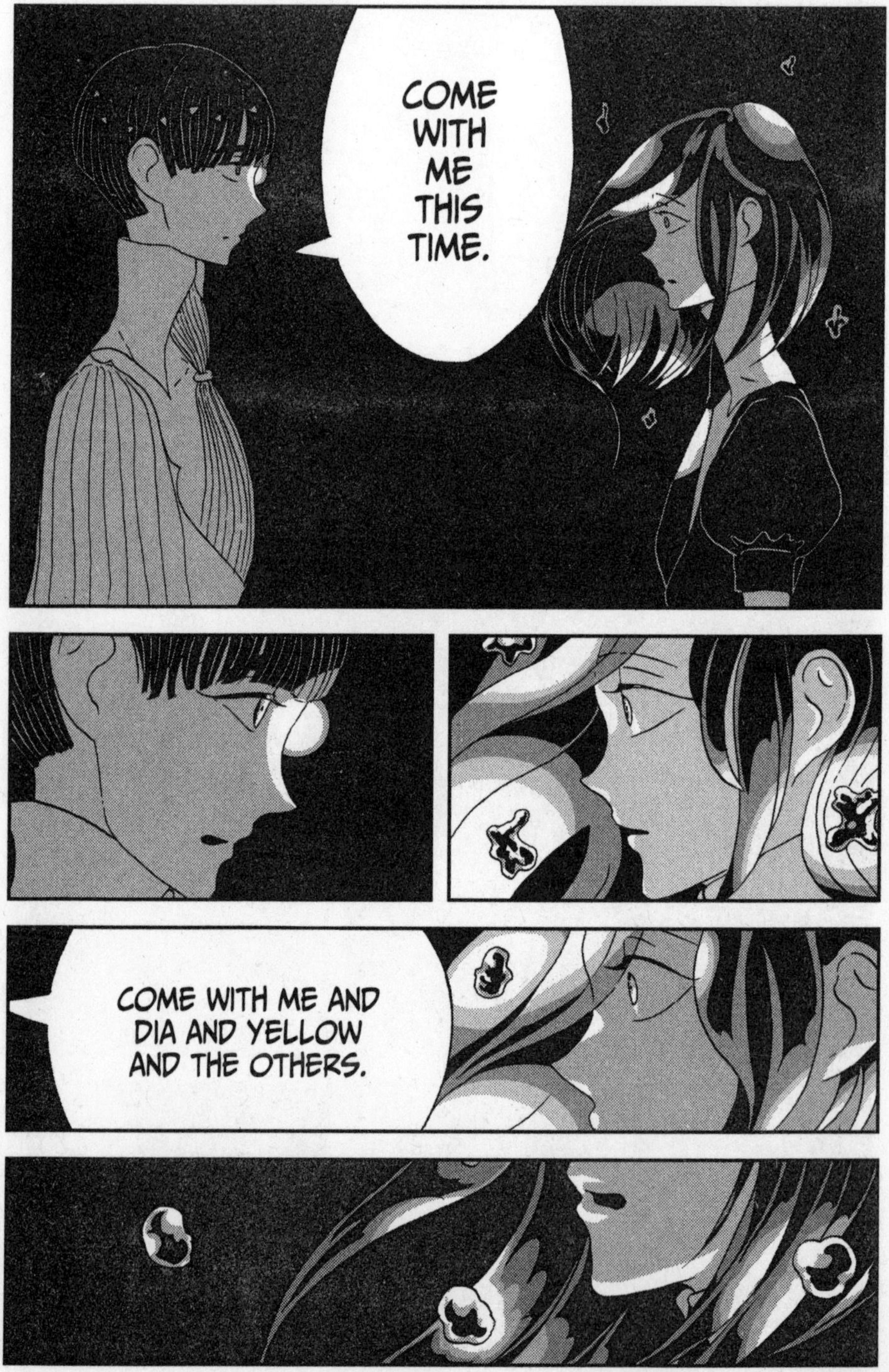
COME WITH ME THIS TIME.
COME WITH ME AND DIA AND YELLOW AND THE OTHERS.

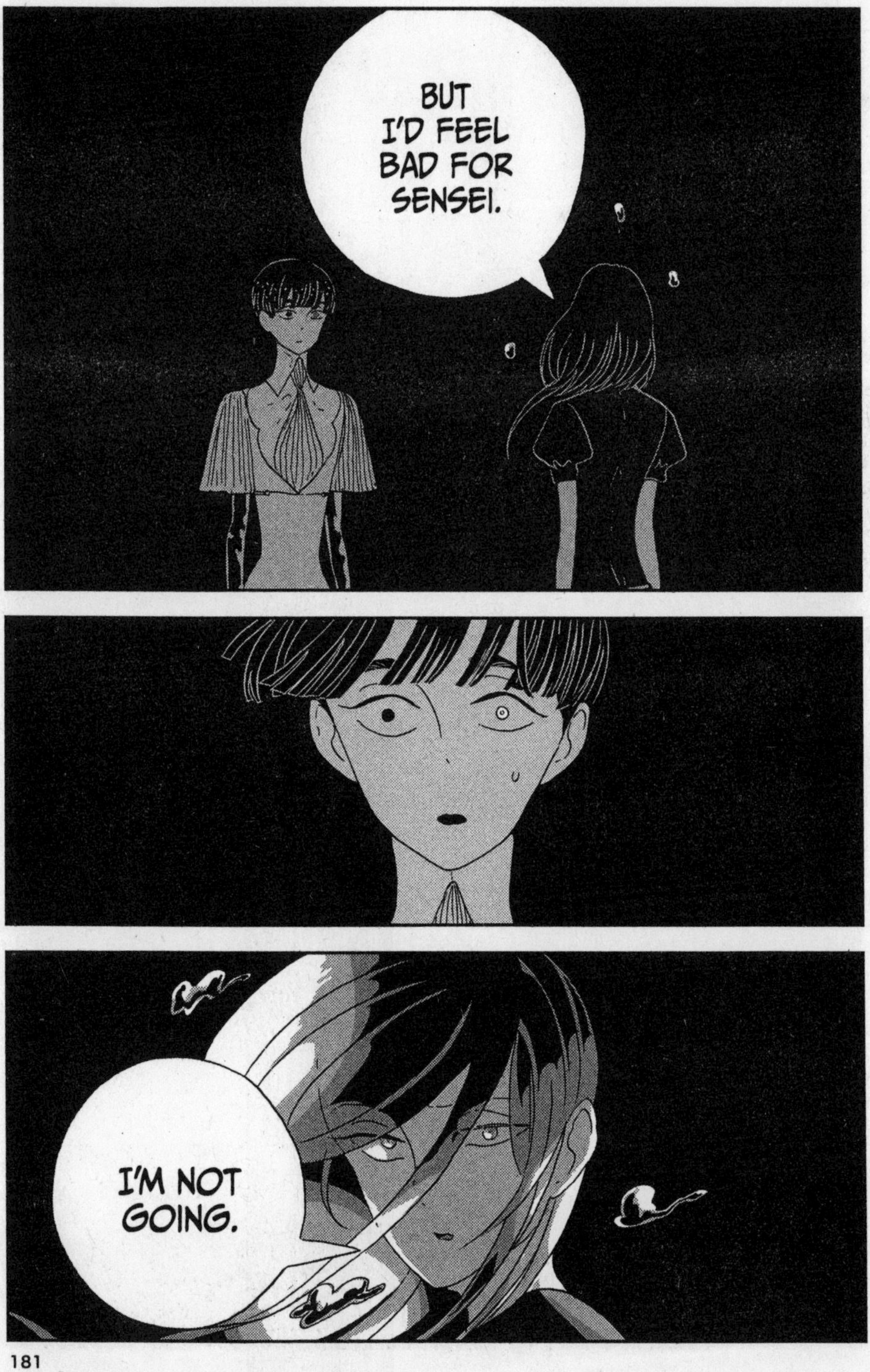
BUT I'D FEEL BAD FOR SENSEI.
I'M NOT GOING.

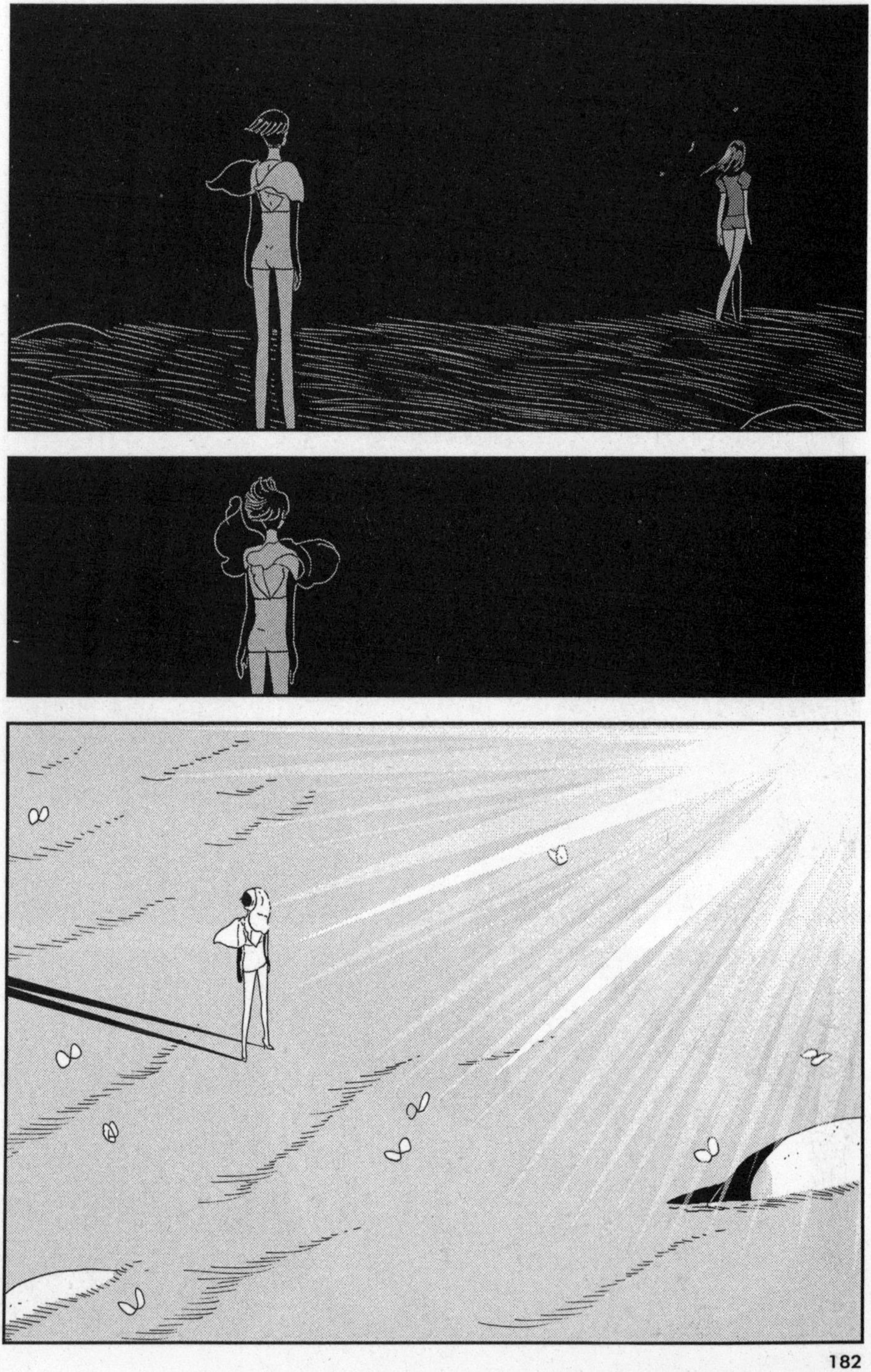

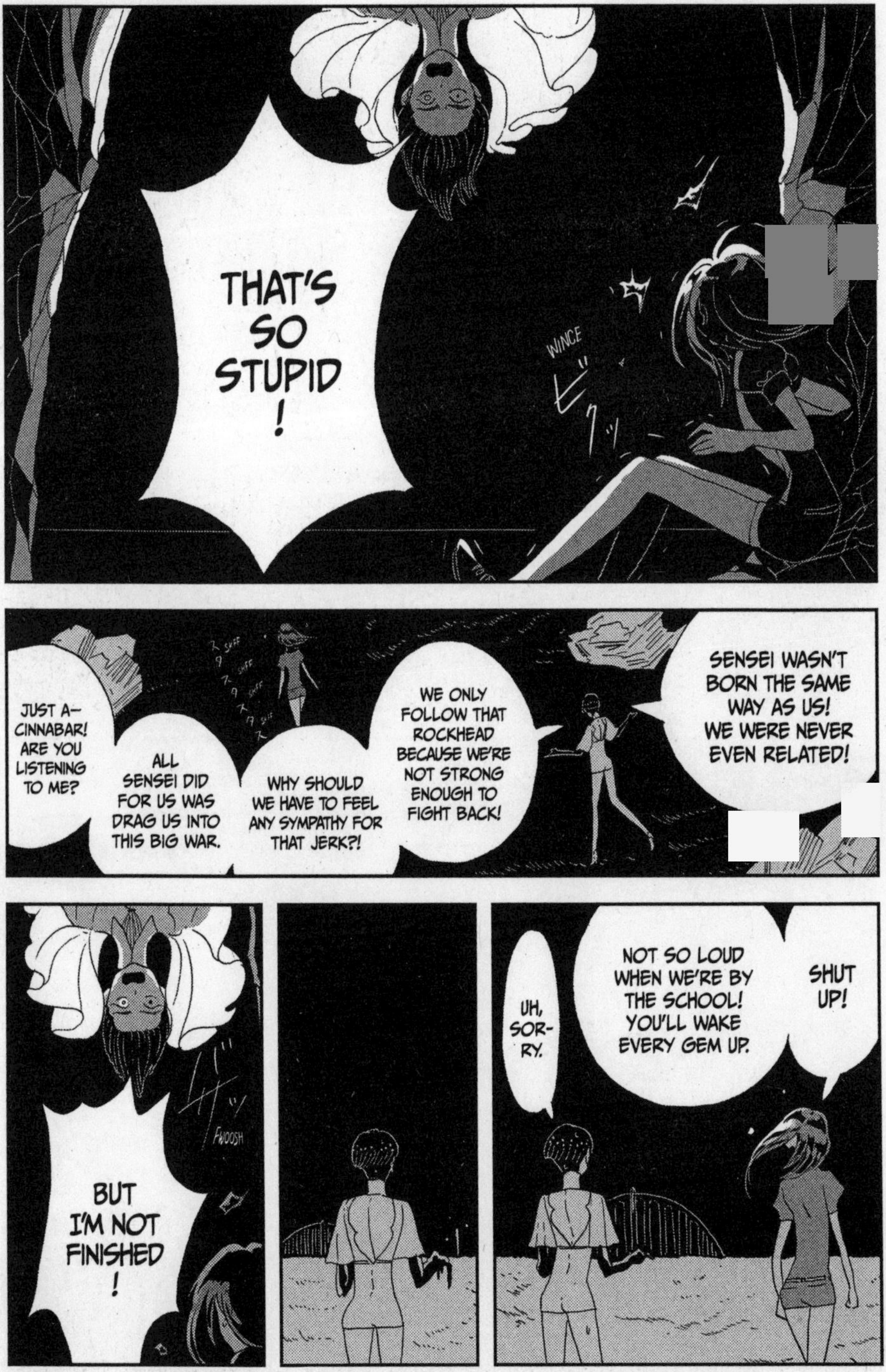
THAT'S SO STUPID!
WINCE
SENSEI WASN'T BORN THE SAME WAY AS US! WE WERE NEVER EVEN RELATED!
WE ONLY FOLLOW THAT ROCKHEAD BECAUSE WE'RE NOT STRONG ENOUGH TO FIGHT BACK!
WHY SHOULD WE HAVE TO FEEL ANY SYMPATHY FOR THAT JERK?!
ALL SENSEI DID FOR US WAS DRAG US INTO THIS BIG WAR.
SHFF SHFF SHFF SHFF
JUST A— CINNABAR! ARE YOU LISTENING TO ME?
SHUT UP!
NOT SO LOUD WHEN WE'RE BY THE SCHOOL! YOU'LL WAKE EVERY GEM UP.
UH, SOR-RY.
FWOOSH
BUT I'M NOT FINISHED!

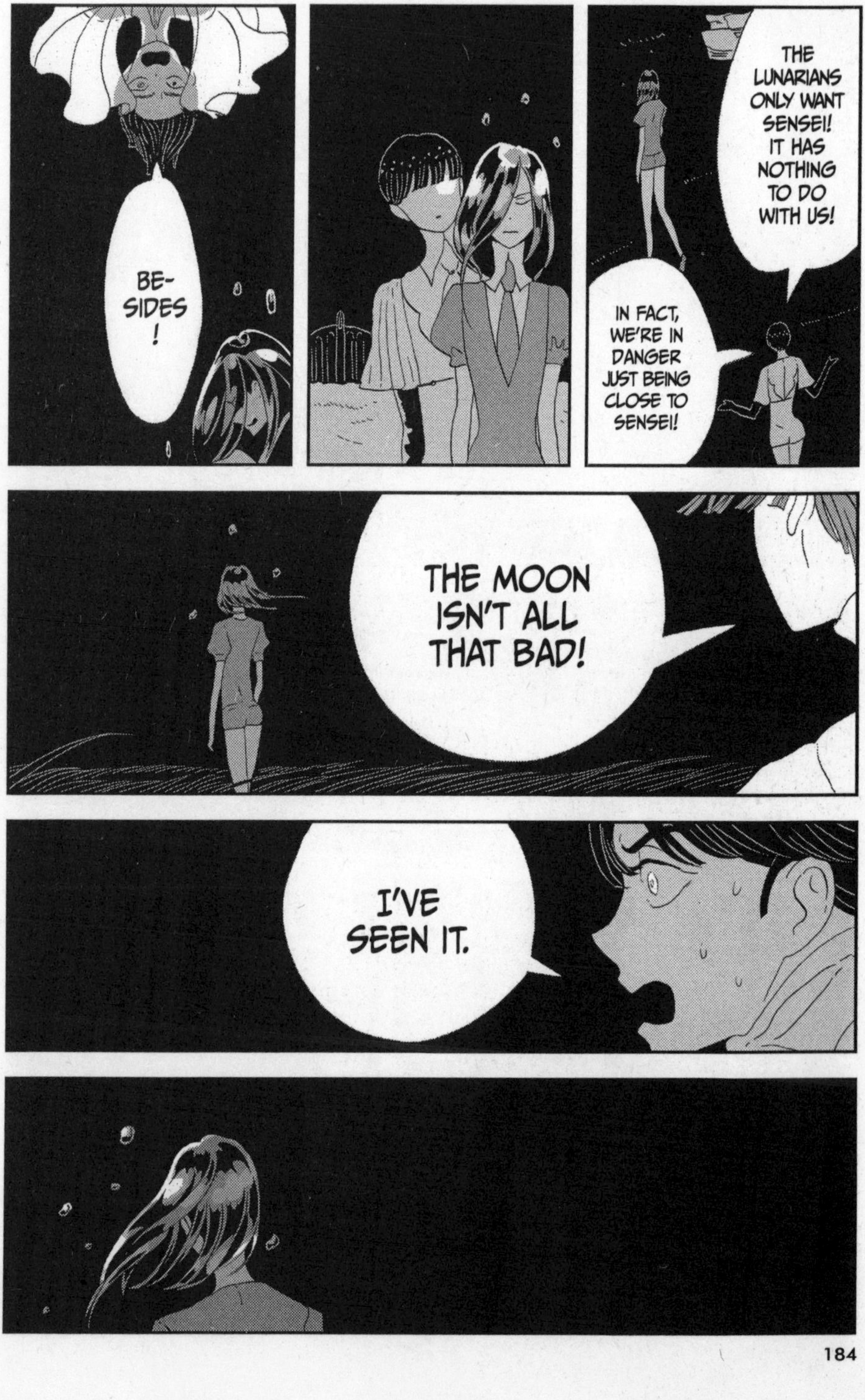
THE LUNARIANS ONLY WANT SENSEI! IT HAS NOTHING TO DO WITH US!
IN FACT, WE'RE IN DANGER JUST BEING CLOSE TO SENSEI!
BE-SIDES!
THE MOON ISN'T ALL THAT BAD!
I'VE SEEN IT.

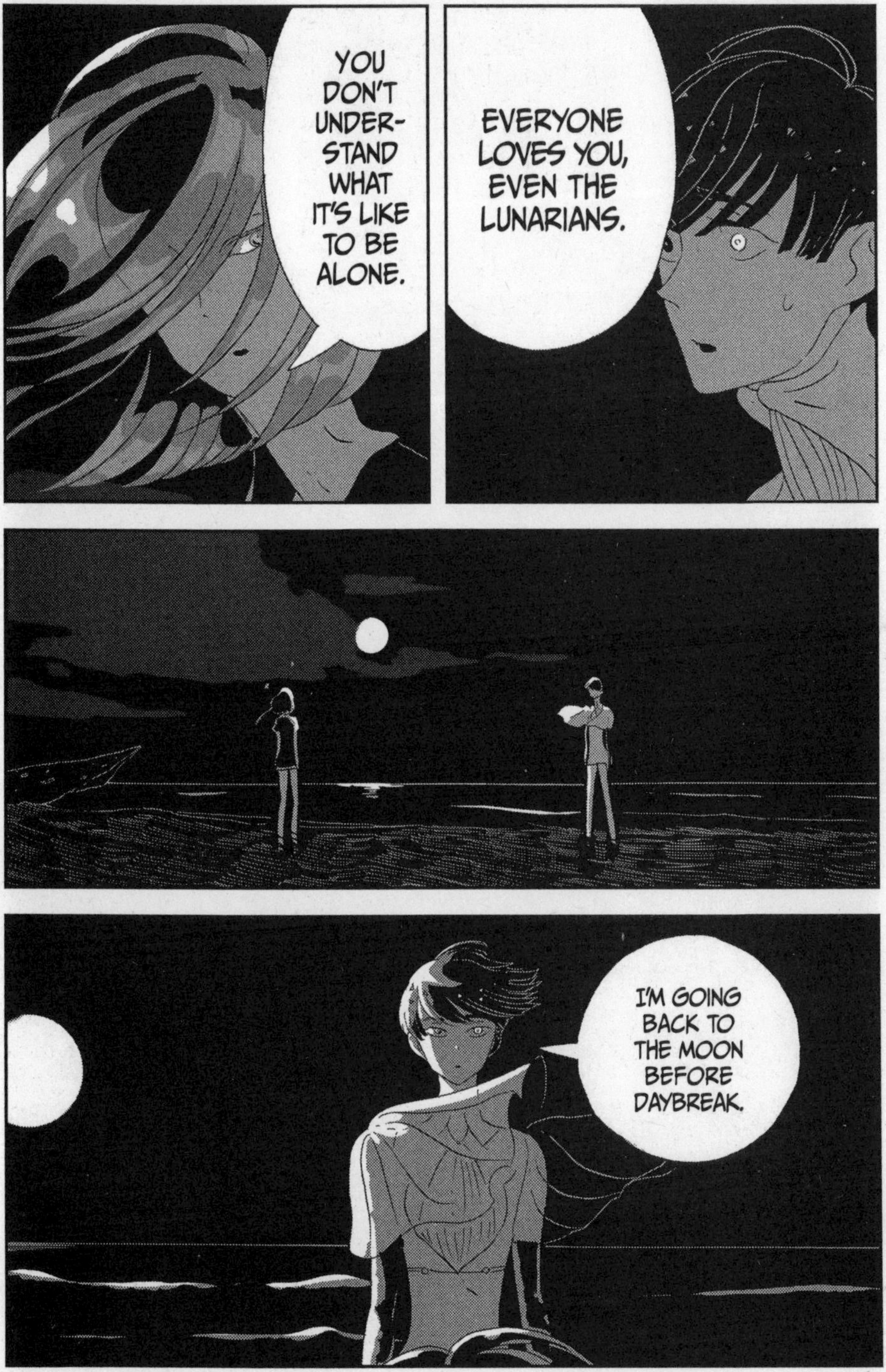
EVERYONE LOVES YOU, EVEN THE LUNARIANS.
YOU DON'T UNDER-STAND WHAT IT'S LIKE TO BE ALONE.
I'M GOING BACK TO THE MOON BEFORE DAYBREAK.

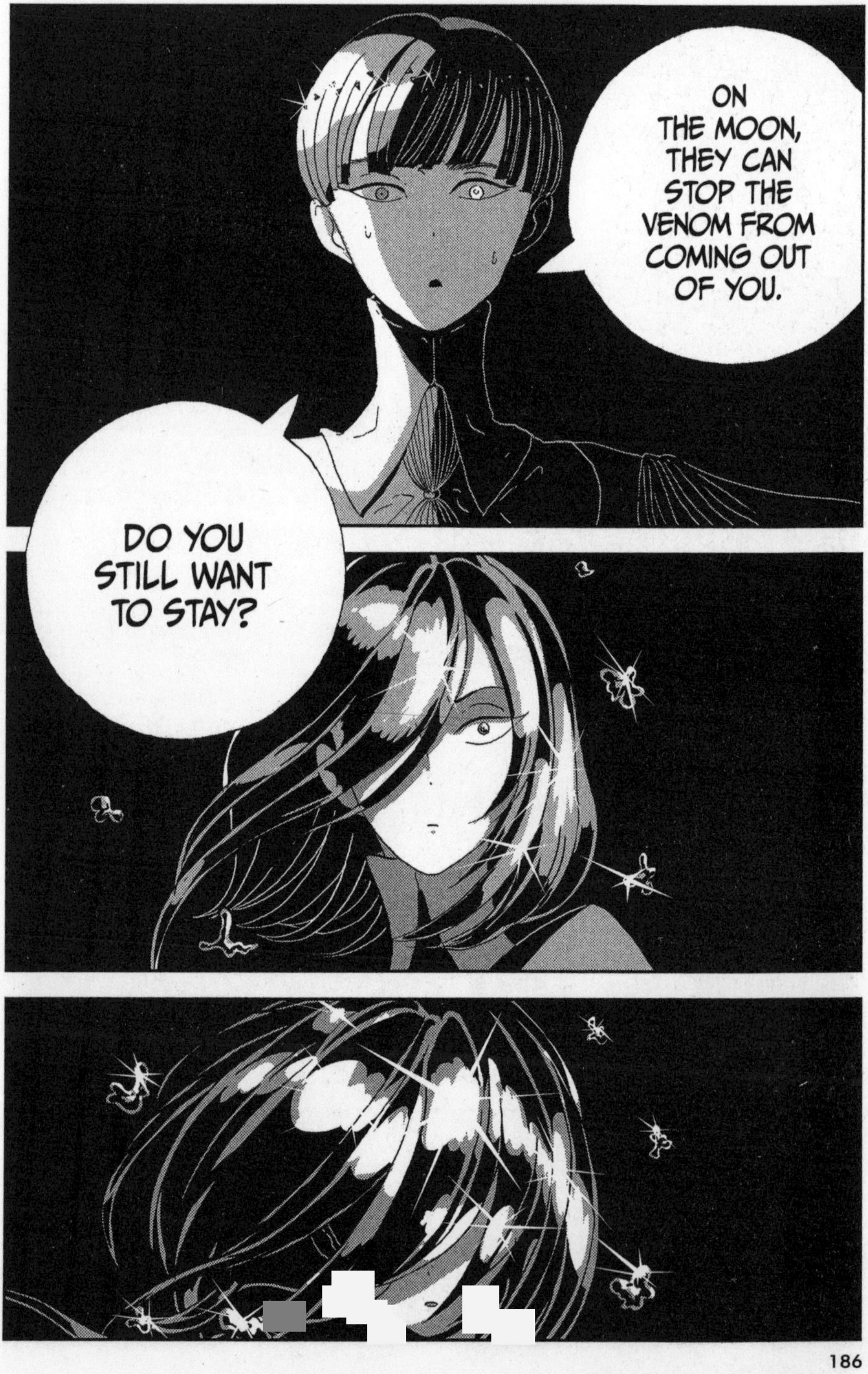
ON THE MOON, THEY CAN STOP THE VENOM FROM COMING OUT OF YOU.
DO YOU STILL WANT TO STAY?

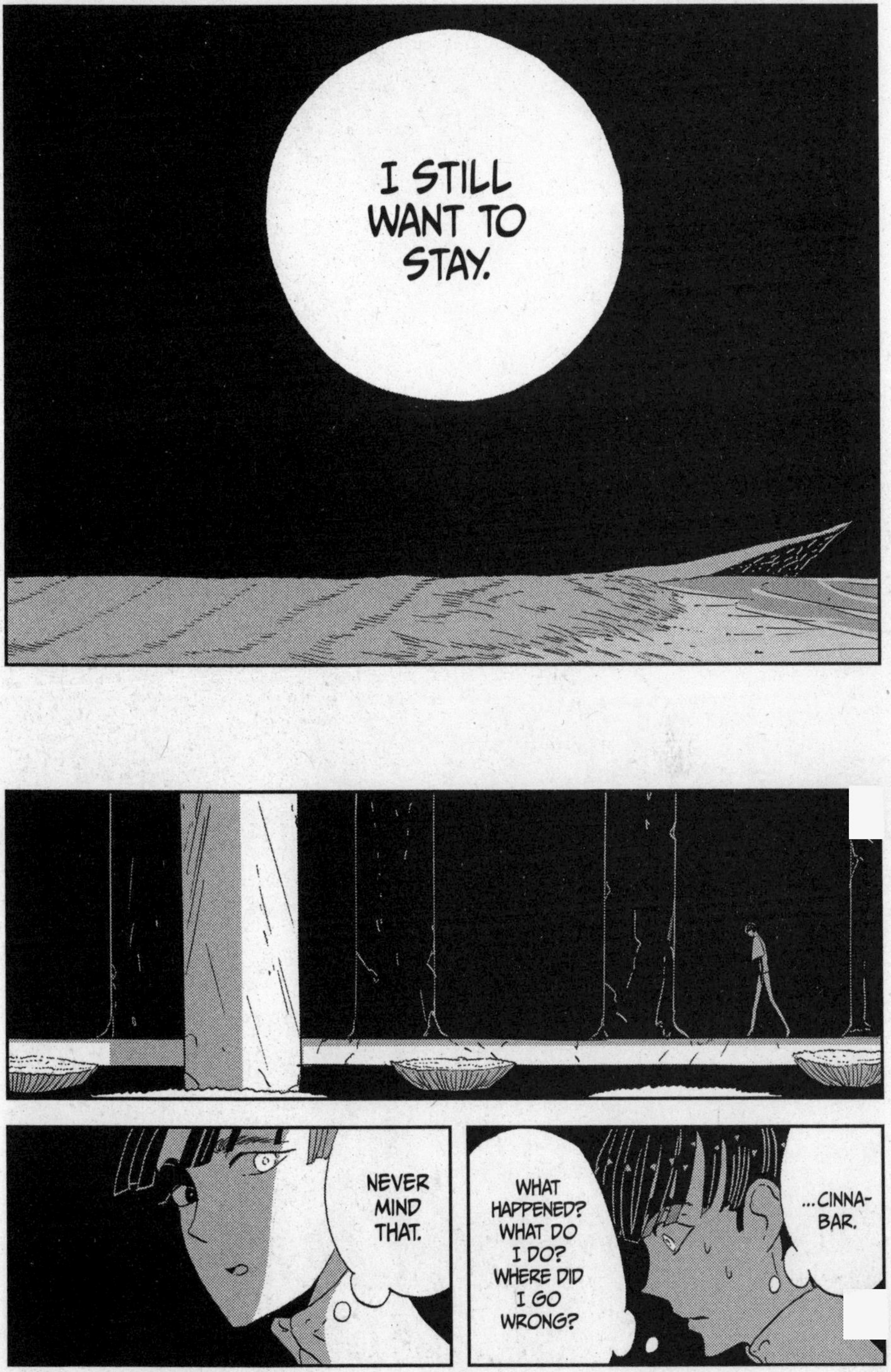
I STILL WANT TO STAY.
...CINNA-BAR.
WHAT HAPPENED? WHAT DO I DO? WHERE DID I GO WRONG?
NEVER MIND THAT.

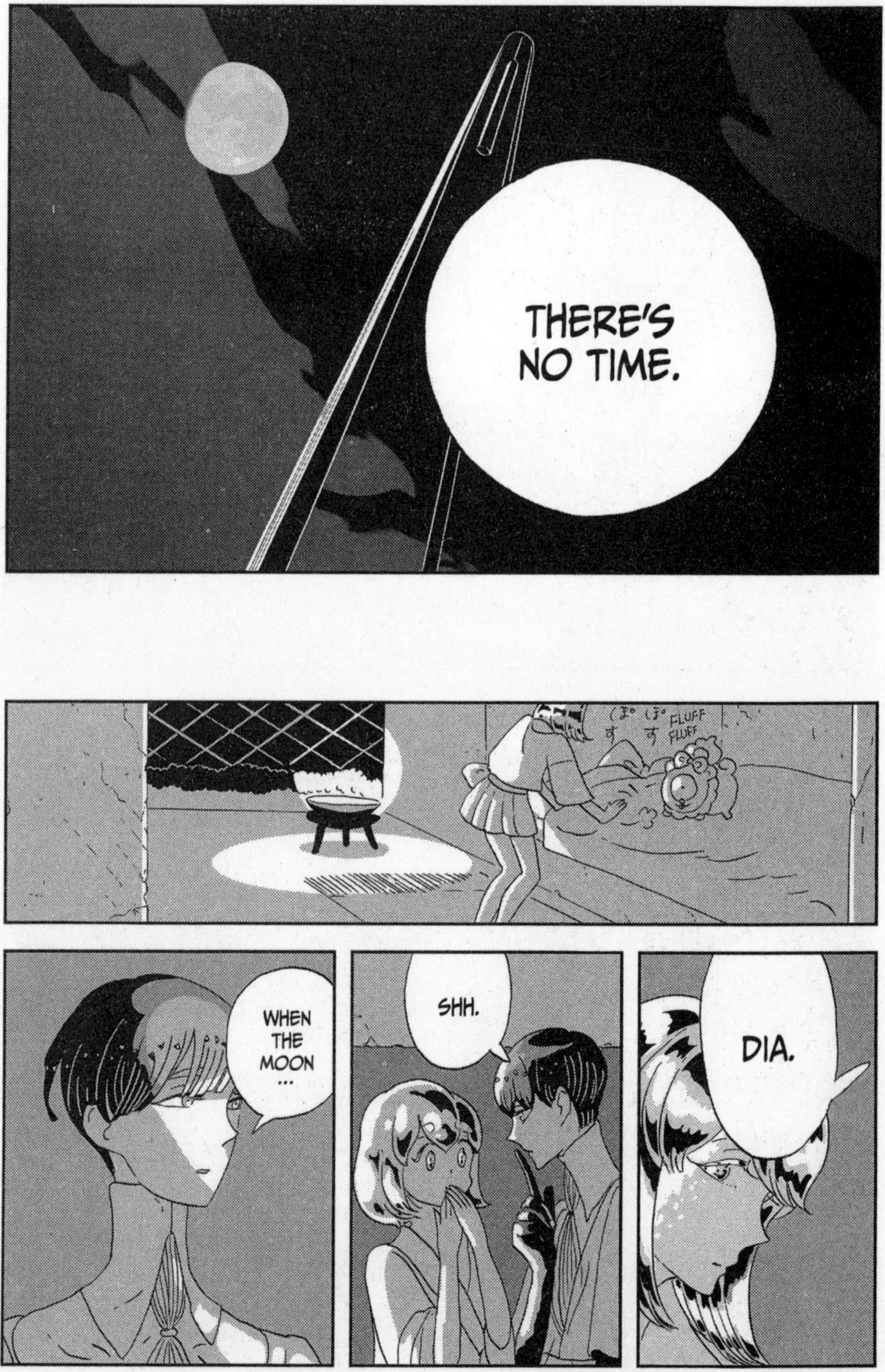
THERE'S NO TIME.
FLUFF FLUFF
DIA.
SHH.
WHEN THE MOON ...

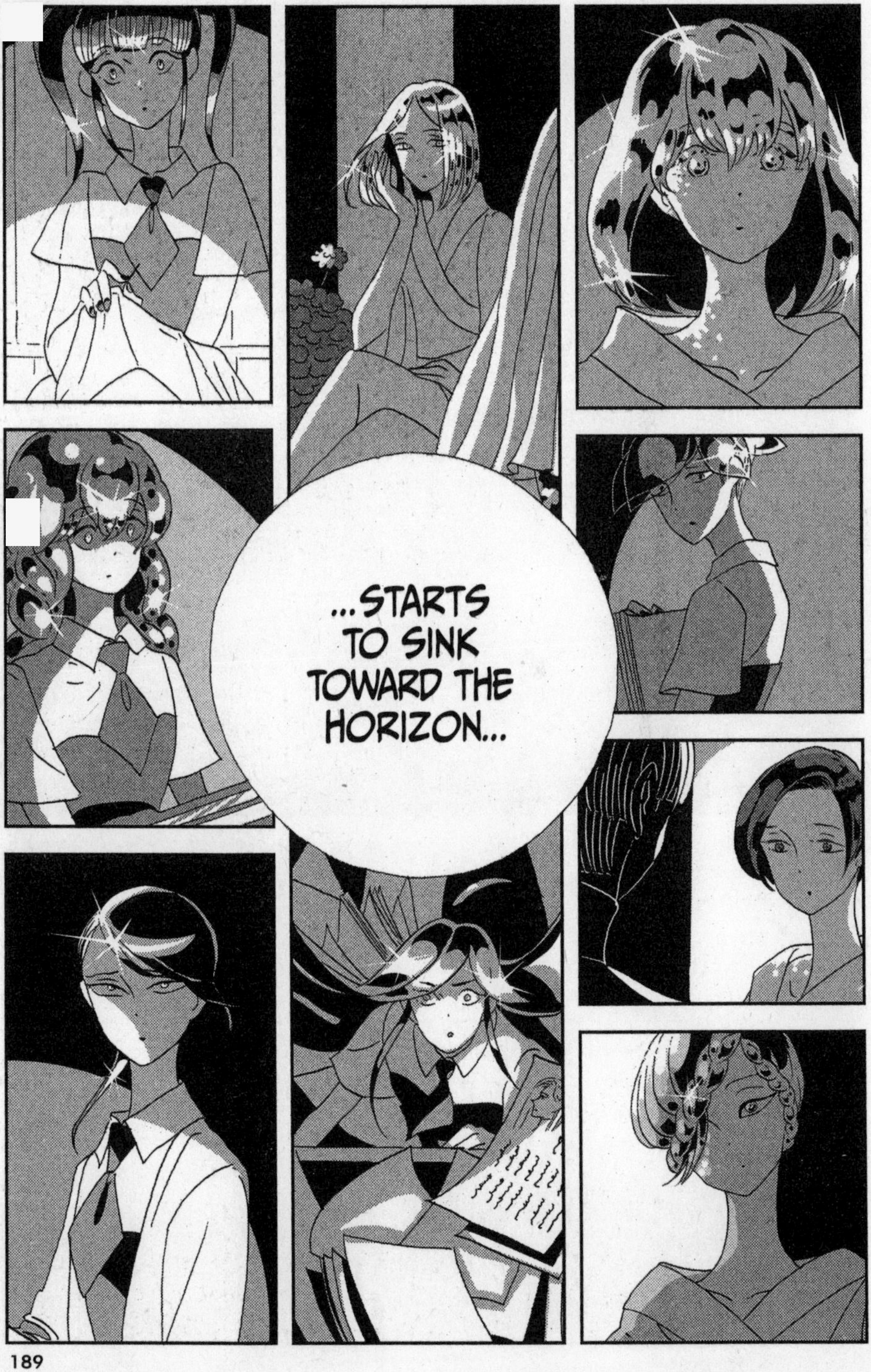
...STARTS TO SINK TOWARD THE HORIZON...

COME TO THE CAPE OF EMPTINESS.

NOW I JUST NEED...

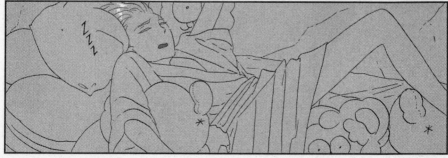

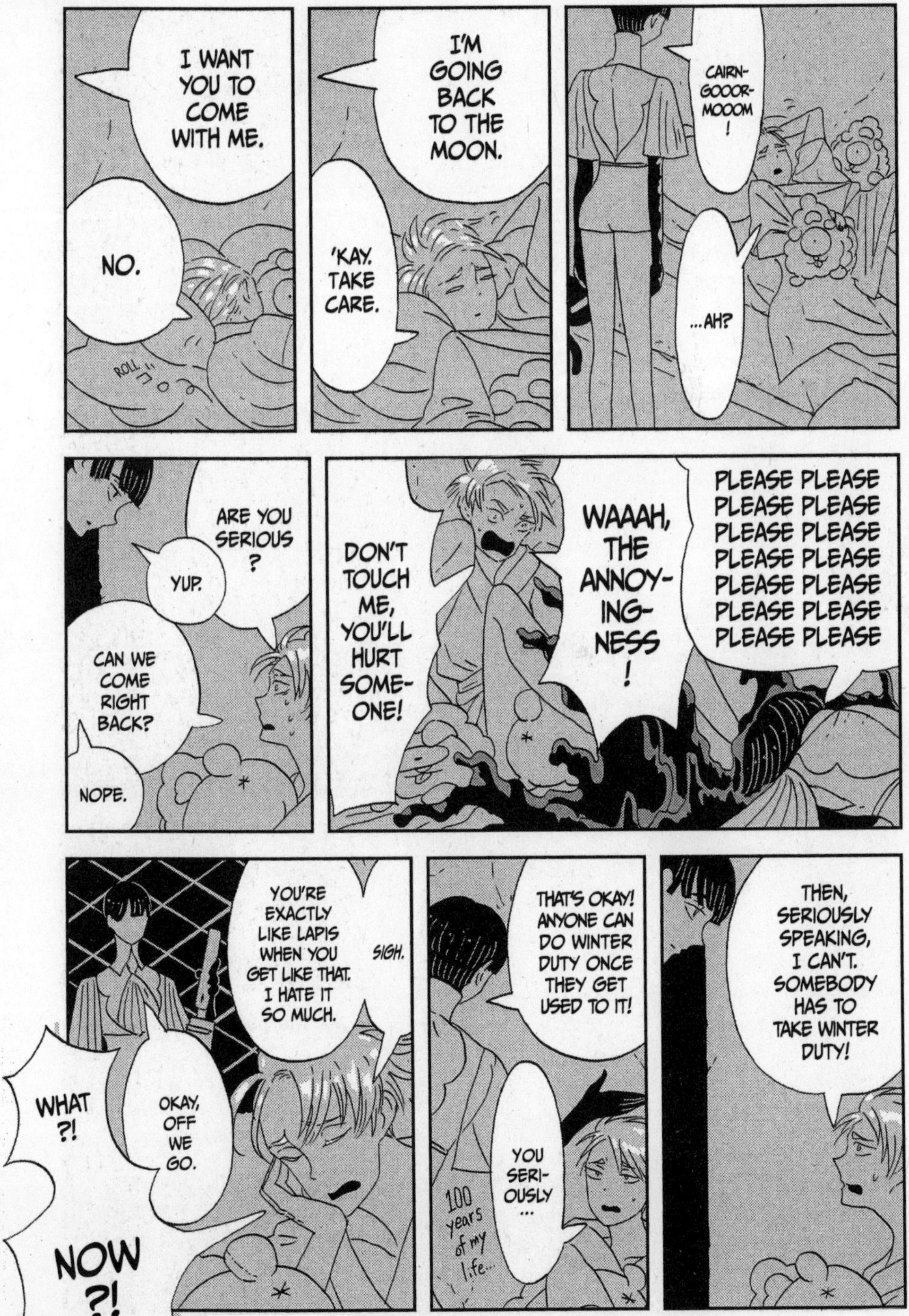
CAIRN-GOOOR-MOOOM!
...AH?
I'M GOING BACK TO THE MOON.
'KAY. TAKE CARE.
I WANT YOU TO COME WITH ME.
NO.
ROLL
PLEASE PLEASE PLEASE PLEASE PLEASE PLEASE PLEASE PLEASE PLEASE PLEASE PLEASE PLEASE PLEASE PLEASE
WAAAH, THE ANNOY-ING-NESS!
DON'T TOUCH ME, YOU'LL HURT SOME-ONE!
ARE YOU SERIOUS?
YUP.
CAN WE COME RIGHT BACK?
NOPE.
THEN, SERIOUSLY SPEAKING, I CAN'T. SOMEBODY HAS TO TAKE WINTER DUTY!
THAT'S OKAY! ANYONE CAN DO WINTER DUTY ONCE THEY GET USED TO IT!
YOU SERI-OUSLY...
100 years of my life...
YOU'RE EXACTLY LIKE LAPIS WHEN YOU GET LIKE THAT. I HATE IT SO MUCH.
SIGH.
OKAY, OFF WE GO.
WHAT?!
NOW?!

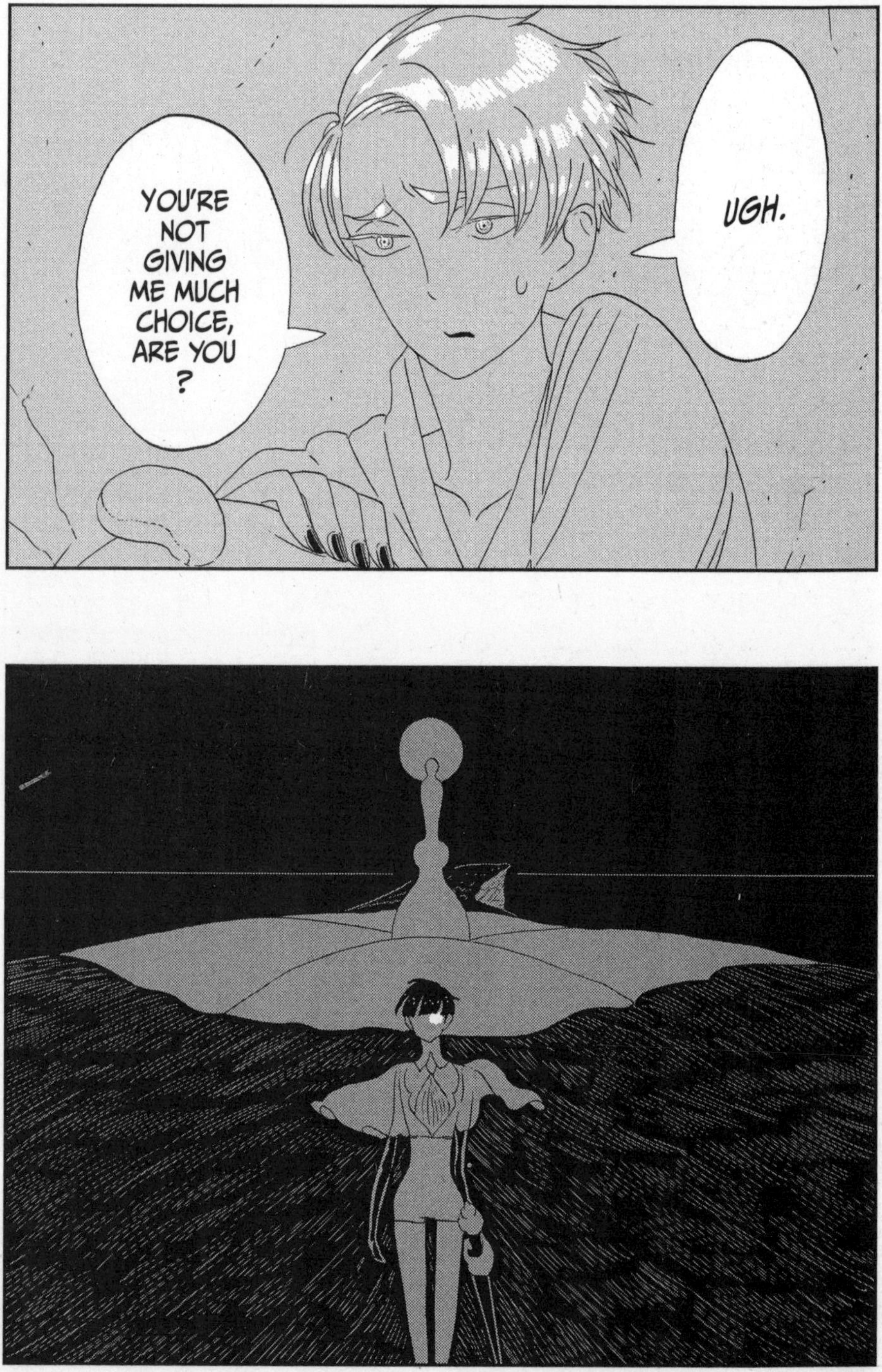
UGH.
YOU'RE NOT GIVING ME MUCH CHOICE, ARE YOU?

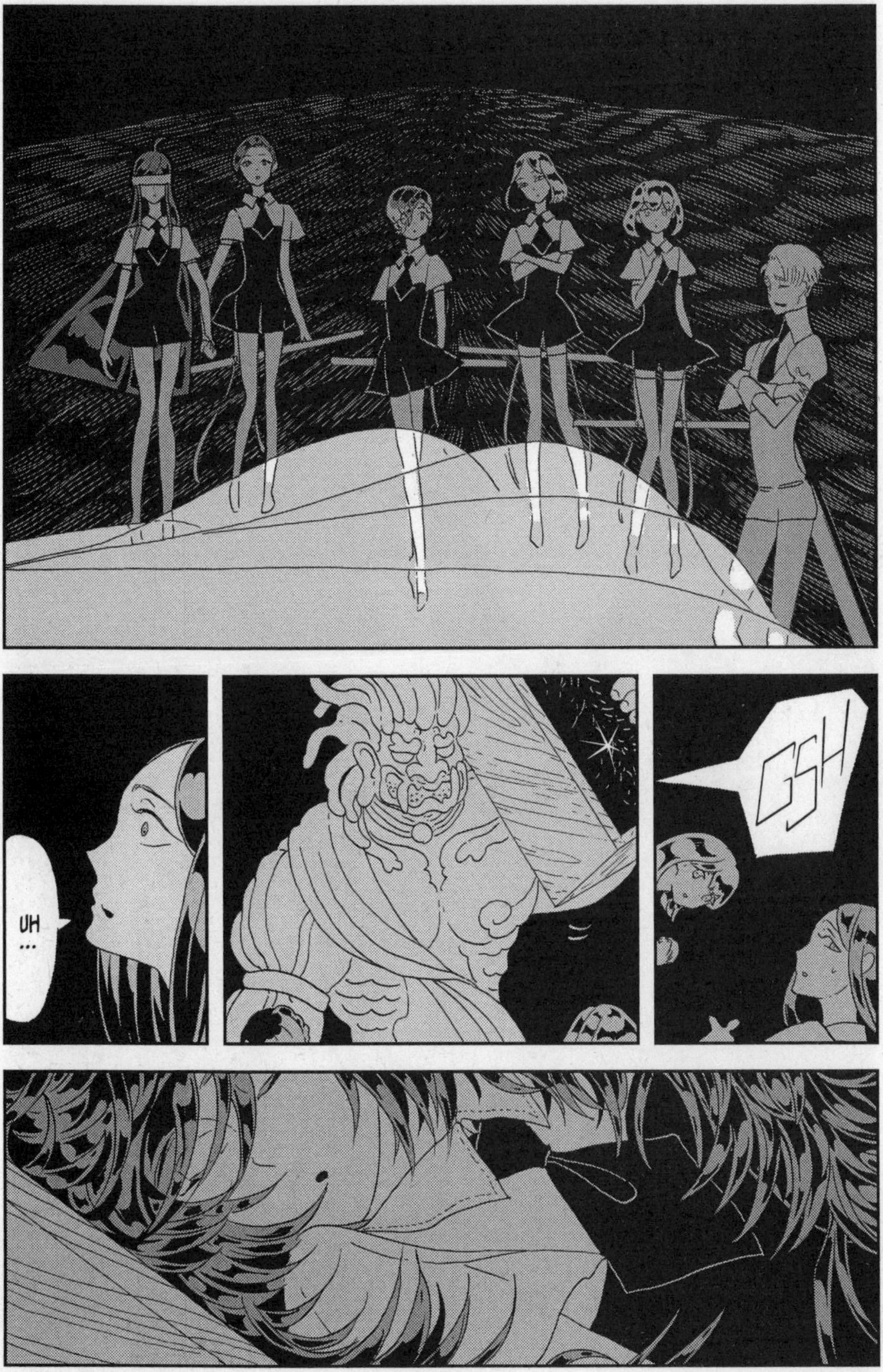
GSH
UH ...

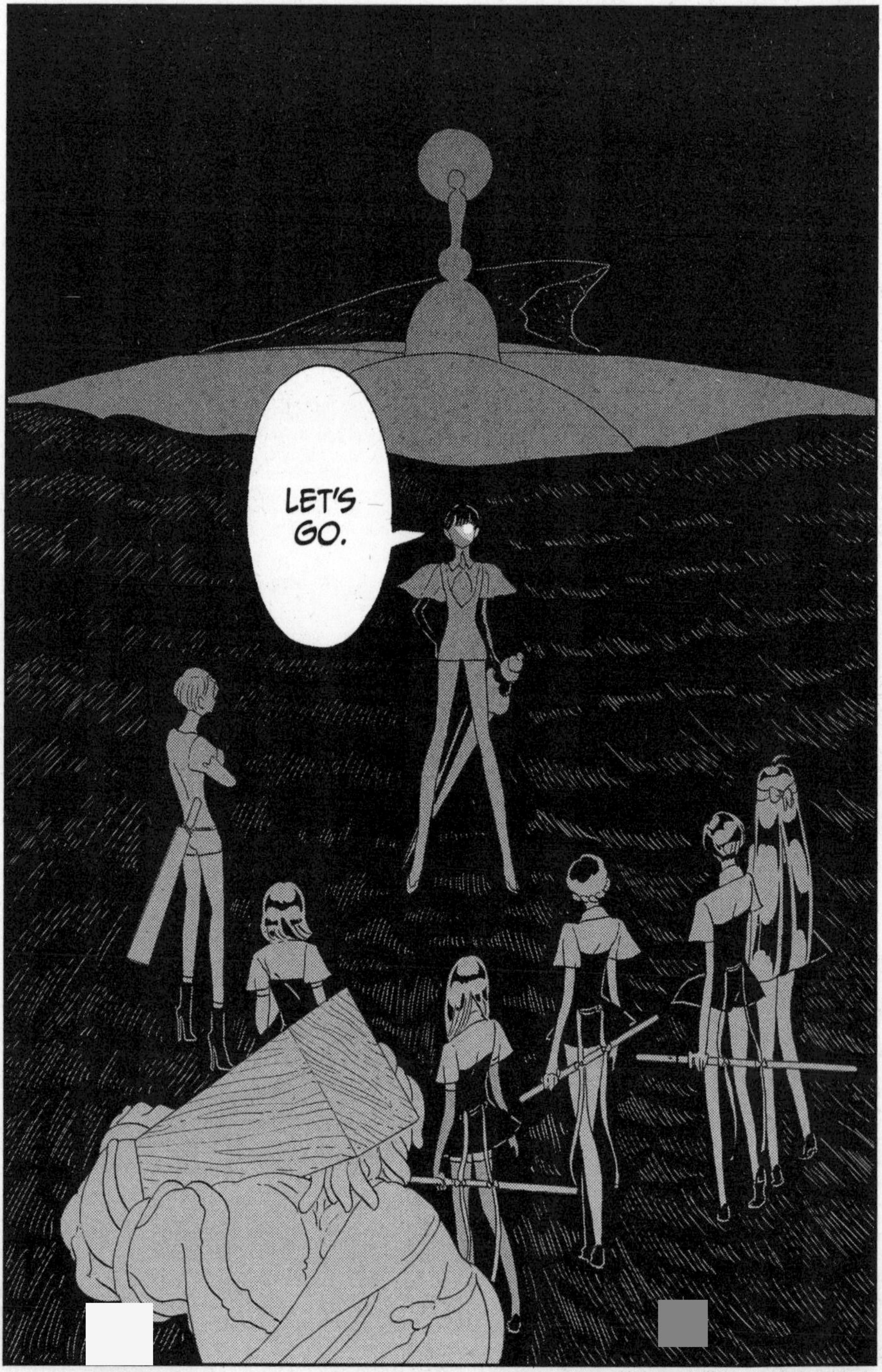
LET'S GO.

CHAPTER 61: Parting END

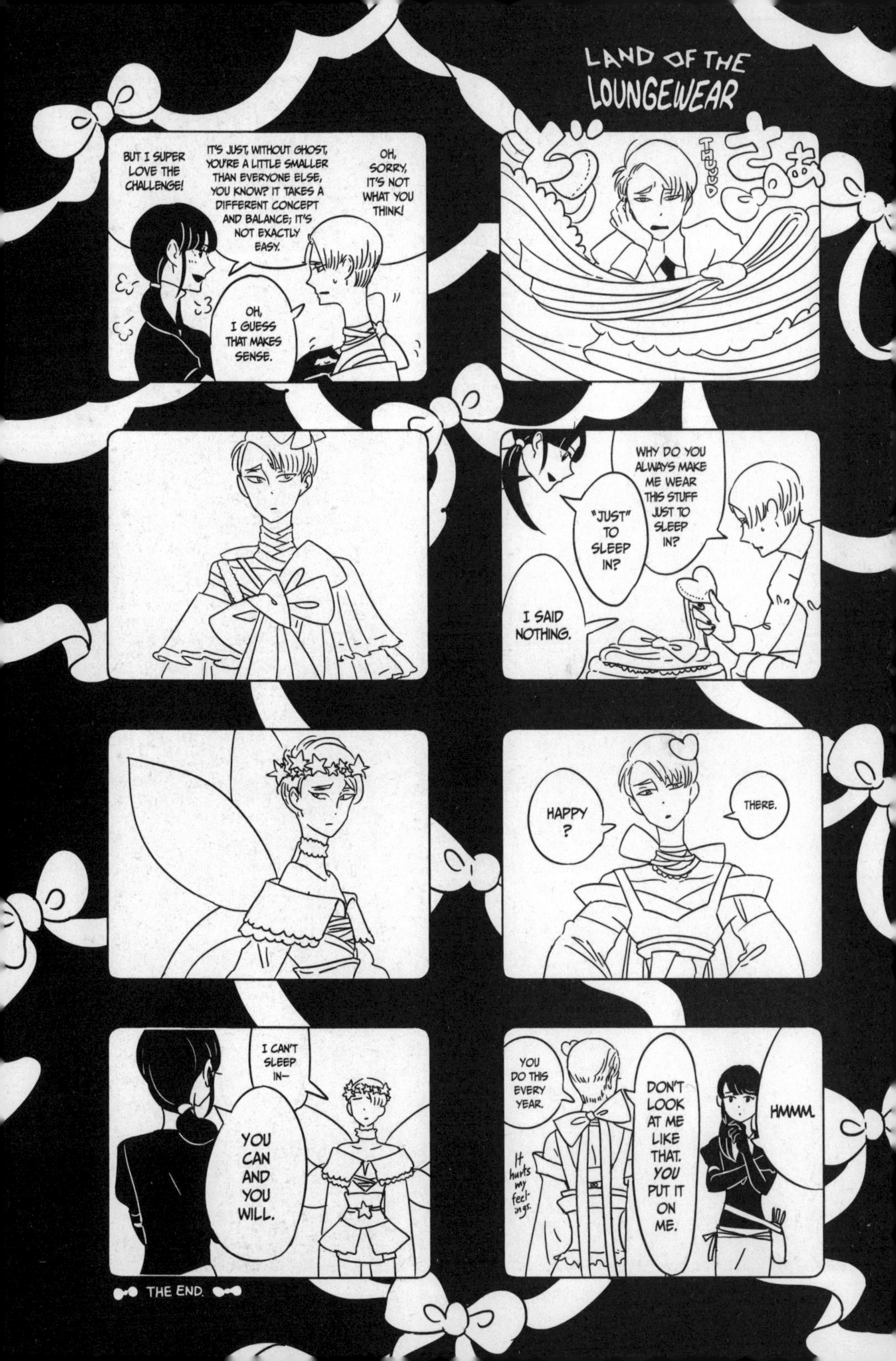
LAND OF THE LOUNGEWEAR
THUUUD
OH, SORRY, IT'S NOT WHAT YOU THINK!
IT'S JUST, WITHOUT GHOST, YOU'RE A LITTLE SMALLER THAN EVERYONE ELSE, YOU KNOW? IT TAKES A DIFFERENT CONCEPT AND BALANCE; IT'S NOT EXACTLY EASY.
BUT I SUPER LOVE THE CHALLENGE!
OH, I GUESS THAT MAKES SENSE.
WHY DO YOU ALWAYS MAKE ME WEAR THIS STUFF JUST TO SLEEP IN?
"JUST" TO SLEEP IN?
I SAID NOTHING.
THERE.
HAPPY?
HMMM.
DON'T LOOK AT ME LIKE THAT. *YOU* PUT IT ON ME.
YOU DO THIS EVERY YEAR.
It hurts my feelings.
I CAN'T SLEEP IN—
YOU CAN AND YOU WILL.
THE END.

TRANSLATION NOTES

CARE FOR A BITE? *page 51*

While the consequences of Phos's action here remain to be seen, myths and legends from all over the world have it that eating food from the land of the dead seals the diner's fate, preventing them from ever returning to the land of the living. In Japanese mythology, the practice is called *yomotsuhegui*, meaning "eating from the kitchen of Yomi." The most famous figure to have done this was Izanami, the mother of Japanese deities, who was unable to return with her husband and thence became the queen of Yomi, the underworld.

HEXAGONAL DIAMOND *page 56*

Hexagonal diamond, also known as lonsdaleite, is, as the name suggests, diamond with a hexagonal crystal structure (as opposed to regular diamonds, which are cubic). The gem was first discovered in meteorites, where the impact of hitting the earth from space created enough pressure to transform the graphite of the meteorite into diamond. Since this discovery, science has learned how to synthesize lonsdaleite in the lab, and while impurities will reduce the hardness of the mineral, pure hexagonal diamond has been tested to be significantly harder than regular diamonds.

SYNTHETIC GEMS VERSUS REAL ONES *page 58*

"Synthetic" is a fancy word meaning "not created by nature," and in the case of gemstones, the term has a reputation for referring to fakes. However, in reality, a synthesized gemstone created in a lab can be identical in appearance and chemical makeup to their naturally formed counterparts, and are therefore every bit as real. This would be why Kongō may have a difficult time telling the difference between moon-made clones and the real Lustrous.

LUNARIAN FASHION *page 59*

As a machine made for prayer, it is fitting that Kongō would be designed to look like a priest. Specifically, he dresses in the style of a Japanese Buddhist monk. Hence, when the Lunarians come to Earth, they take the forms of Buddhas and Bodhisattvas.

CICADA *page 75*

In China, cicadas represent rebirth, because of their life cycle. The young cicadas drop from tree branches to live underground until they emerge, sometimes years later, at which point they go high into the trees and shed their outer skin for one more time before they become adults. In Japan, because the life of the adult cicada is so short, the insect is a symbol of transience, and the impermanence of all things.

49 DAYS *page 96*

Some schools of Buddhism believe in an intermediate period between death and reincarnation that lasts seven weeks. Japanese Buddhism has it that the spirit spends this time wandering the afterlife before returning to the world of the living.

WAITING TO SEE IF I'LL SINK MYSELF *page 145*

When someone is suspected of wrongdoing, sometimes the strategy to catch them is to let them do their own thing until they get themselves into trouble, or lead investigators to enough evidence to convict them. The Japanese word for this is *oyogaseru*, which literally means "to let swim."

LUNARIAN RABBIT EARS *page 163*

The reader may have noticed that most of the Lunarians have what appear to be rabbit ears protruding from their hair. This may be because, according to Japanese tradition, the moon is home to rabbits. Specifically, the craters on the moon form an image that, from Earth, looks like a rabbit pounding mochi rice cakes.

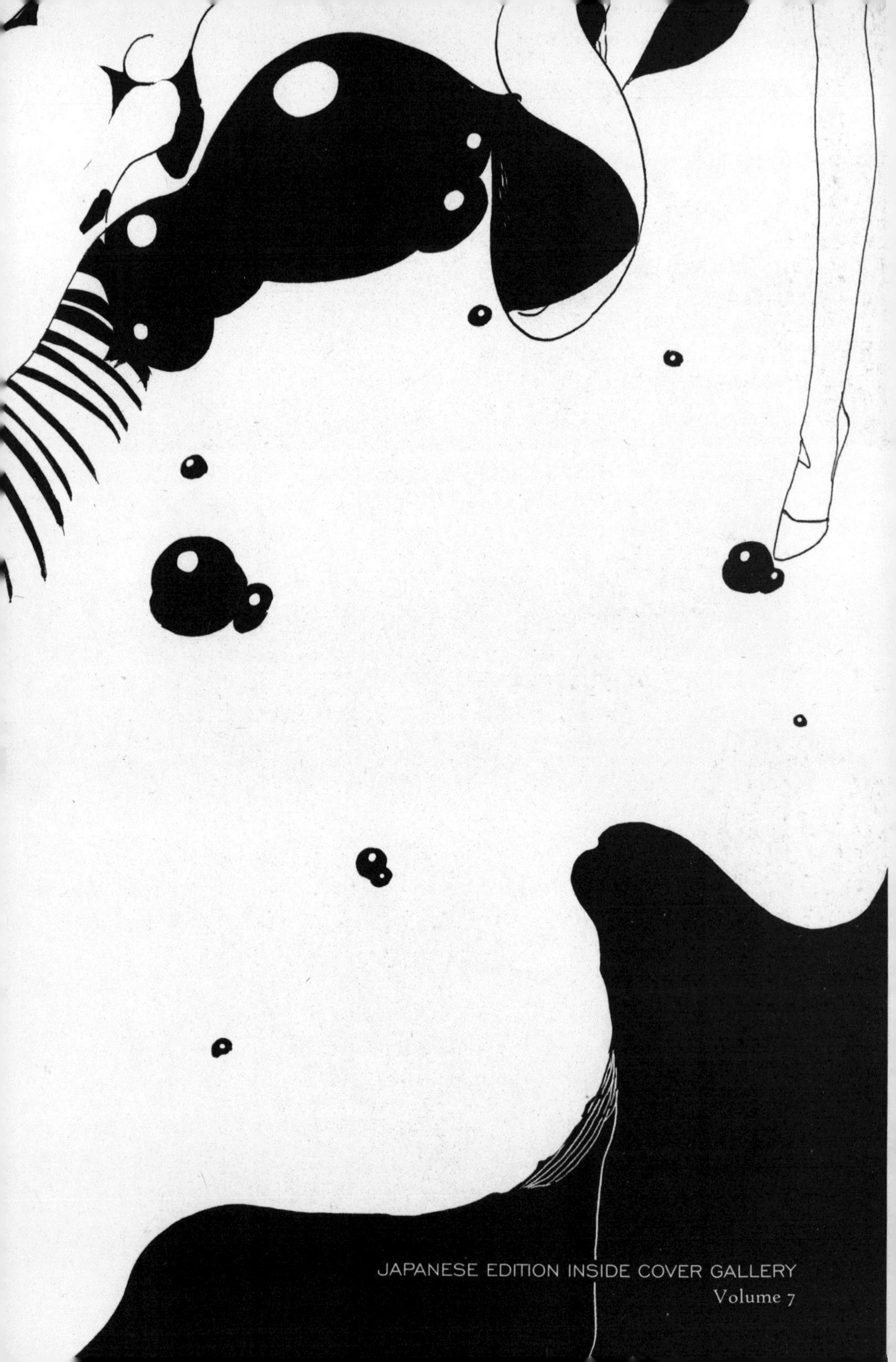

JAPANESE EDITION INSIDE COVER GALLERY
Volume 7

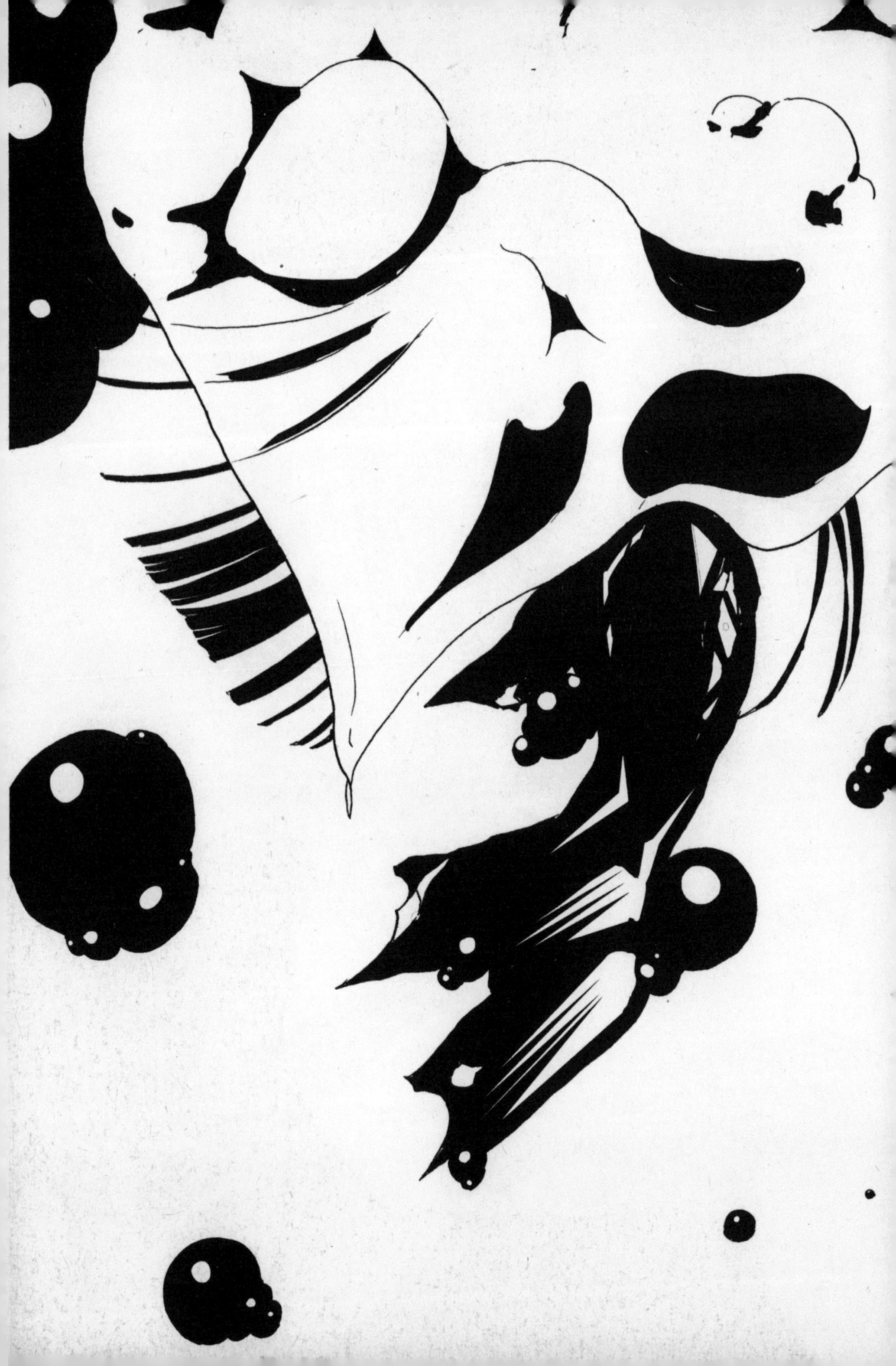

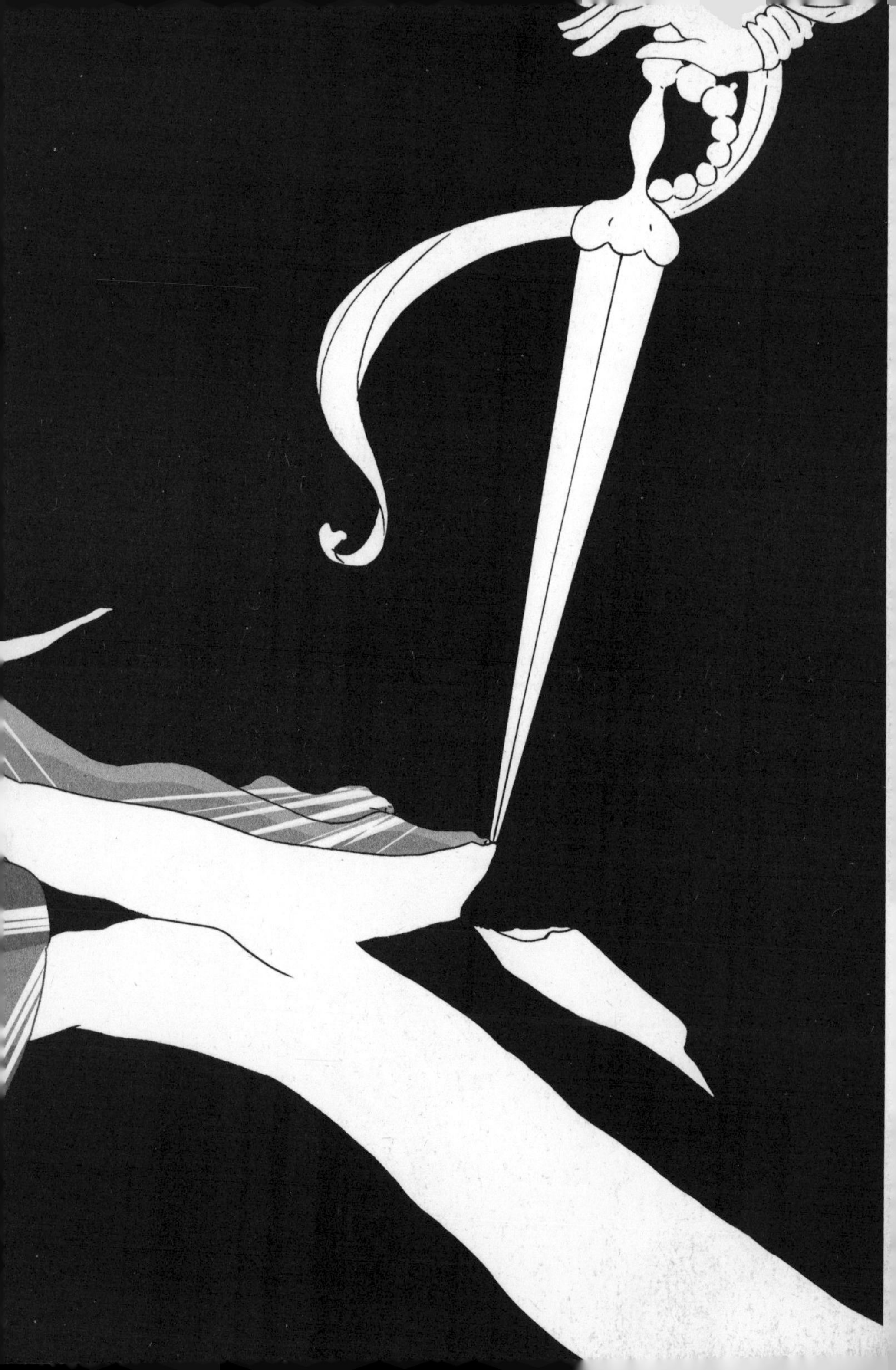

Volume 8

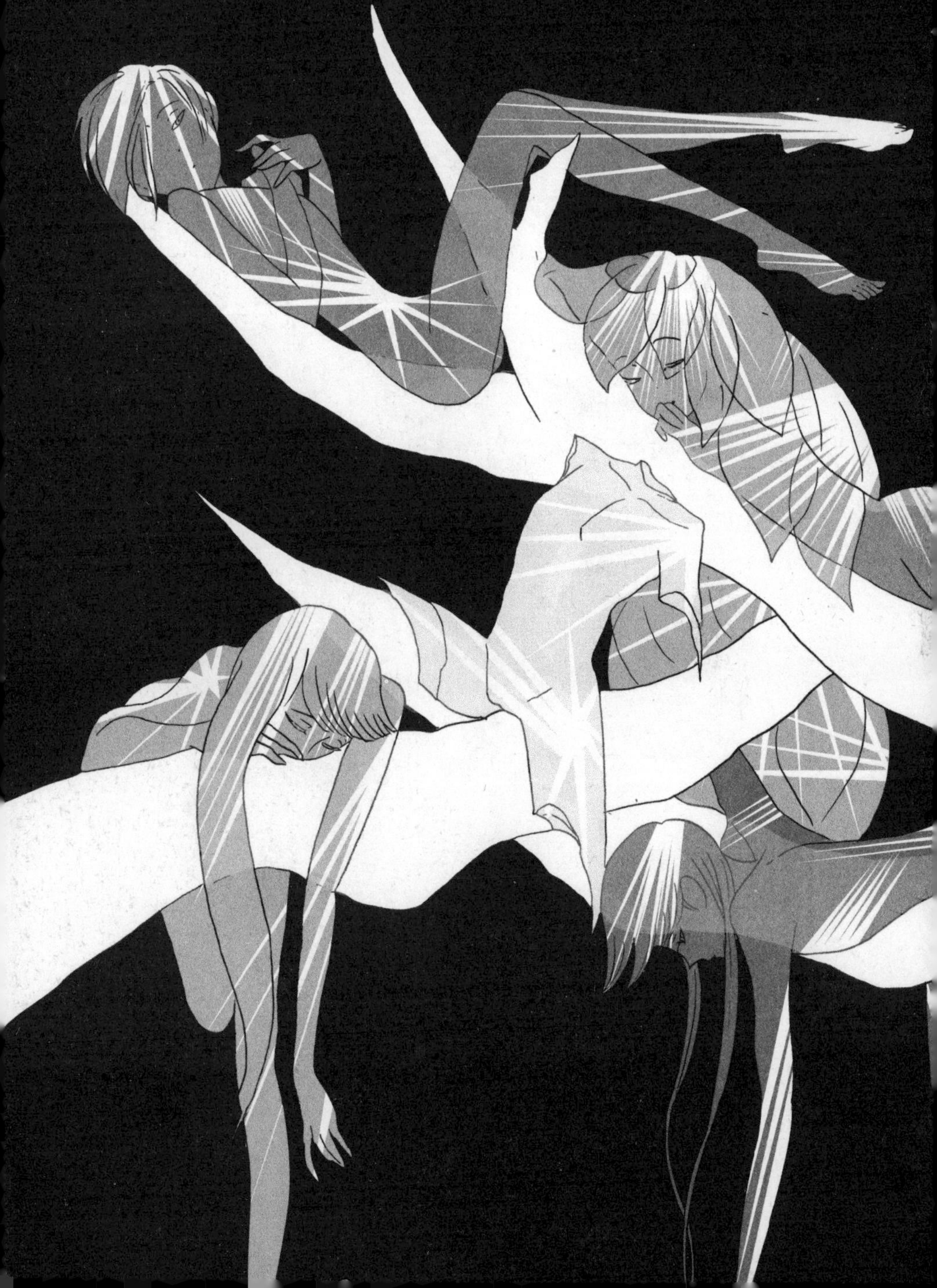

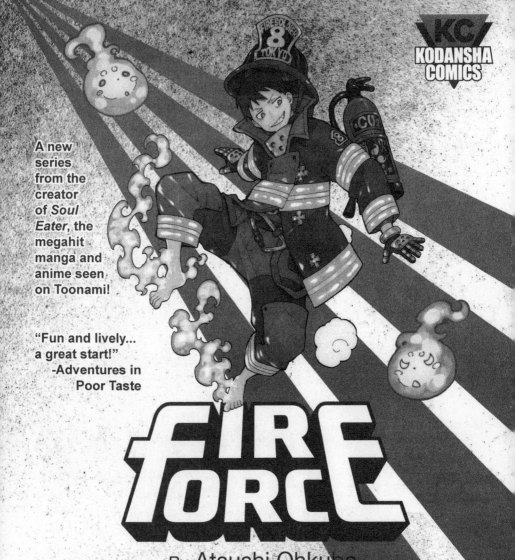

KC
KODANSHA
COMICS

A new series from the creator of *Soul Eater*, the megahit manga and anime seen on Toonami!

"Fun and lively... a great start!"
    -Adventures in Poor Taste

FIRE FORCE

By Atsushi Ohkubo

The city of Tokyo is plagued by a deadly phenomenon: spontaneous human combustion! Luckily, a special team is there to quench the inferno: The Fire Force! The fire soldiers at Special Fire Cathedral 8 are about to get a unique addition. Enter Shinra, a boy who possesses the power to run at the speed of a rocket, leaving behind the famous "devil's footprints" (and destroying his shoes in the process). Can Shinra and his colleagues discover the source of this strange epidemic before the city burns to ashes?

KODANSHA
COMICS

Japan's most powerful spirit medium delves into the ghost world's greatest mysteries!

Story by Kyo Shirodaira, famed author of mystery fiction and creator of *Spiral, Blast of Tempest,* and *The Record of a Fallen Vampire.*

Both touched by spirits called yôkai, Kotoko and Kurô have gained unique superhuman powers. But to gain her powers Kotoko has given up an eye and a leg, and Kurô's personal life is in shambles. So when Kotoko suggests they team up to deal with renegades from the spirit world, Kurô doesn't have many other choices, but Kotoko might just have a few ulterior motives...

IN/SPECTRE

STORY BY KYO SHIRODAIRA
ART BY CHASHIBA KATASE

KODANSHA COMICS

"I'm pleasantly surprised to find modern shojo using cross-dressing as a dramatic device to deliver social commentary... Recommended."

-Otaku USA Magazine

The prince in his dark days

By Hico Yamanaka

A drunkard for a father, a household of poverty... For 17-year-old Atsuko, misfortune is all she knows and believes in. Until one day, a chance encounter with Itaru-the wealthy heir of a huge corporation-changes everything. The two look identical, uncannily so. When Itaru curiously goes missing, Atsuko is roped into being his stand-in. There, in his shoes, Atsuko must parade like a prince in a palace. She encounters many new experiences, but at what cost...?

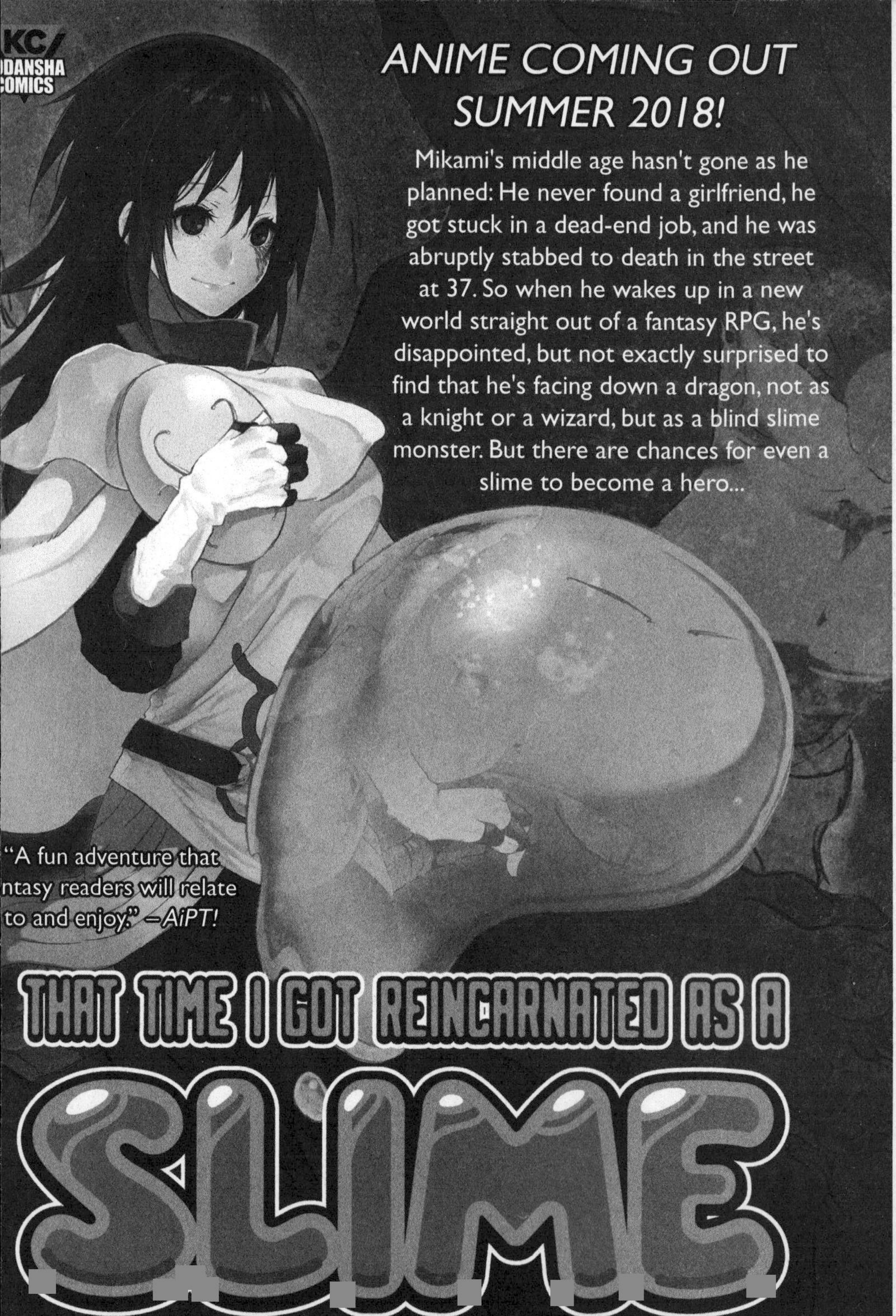
ANIME COMING OUT SUMMER 2018!
Mikami's middle age hasn't gone as he planned: He never found a girlfriend, he got stuck in a dead-end job, and he was abruptly stabbed to death in the street at 37. So when he wakes up in a new world straight out of a fantasy RPG, he's disappointed, but not exactly surprised to find that he's facing down a dragon, not as a knight or a wizard, but as a blind slime monster. But there are chances for even a slime to become a hero...
“A fun adventure that ntasy readers will relate to and enjoy.” —AiPT!
THAT TIME I GOT REINCARNATED AS A
SLIME

Based on the critically acclaimed classic horror manga

The first new *Parasyte* manga in over 20 years!

NEO PARASYTE f

BY ASUMIKO NAKAMURA, EMA TOYAMA, MIKI RINNO, LALAKO KOJIMA, KAORI YUKI, BANKO KUZE, YUUKI OBATA, KASHIO, YUI KUROE, ASIA WATANABE, MIKIMAKI, HIKARU SURUGA, HAJIME SHINJO, RENJURO KINDAICHI, AND YURI NARUSHIMA

A collection of chilling new *Parasyte* stories from Japan's top shojo artists!

Parasites: shape-shifting aliens whose only purpose is to assimilate with and consume the human race... but do these monsters have a different side? A parasite becomes a prince to save his romance-obsessed female host from a dangerous stalker. Another hosts a cooking show, in which the real monsters are revealed. These and 13 more stories, from some of the greatest shojo manga artists alive today, together make up a chilling, funny, and entertaining tribute to one of manga's horror classics!

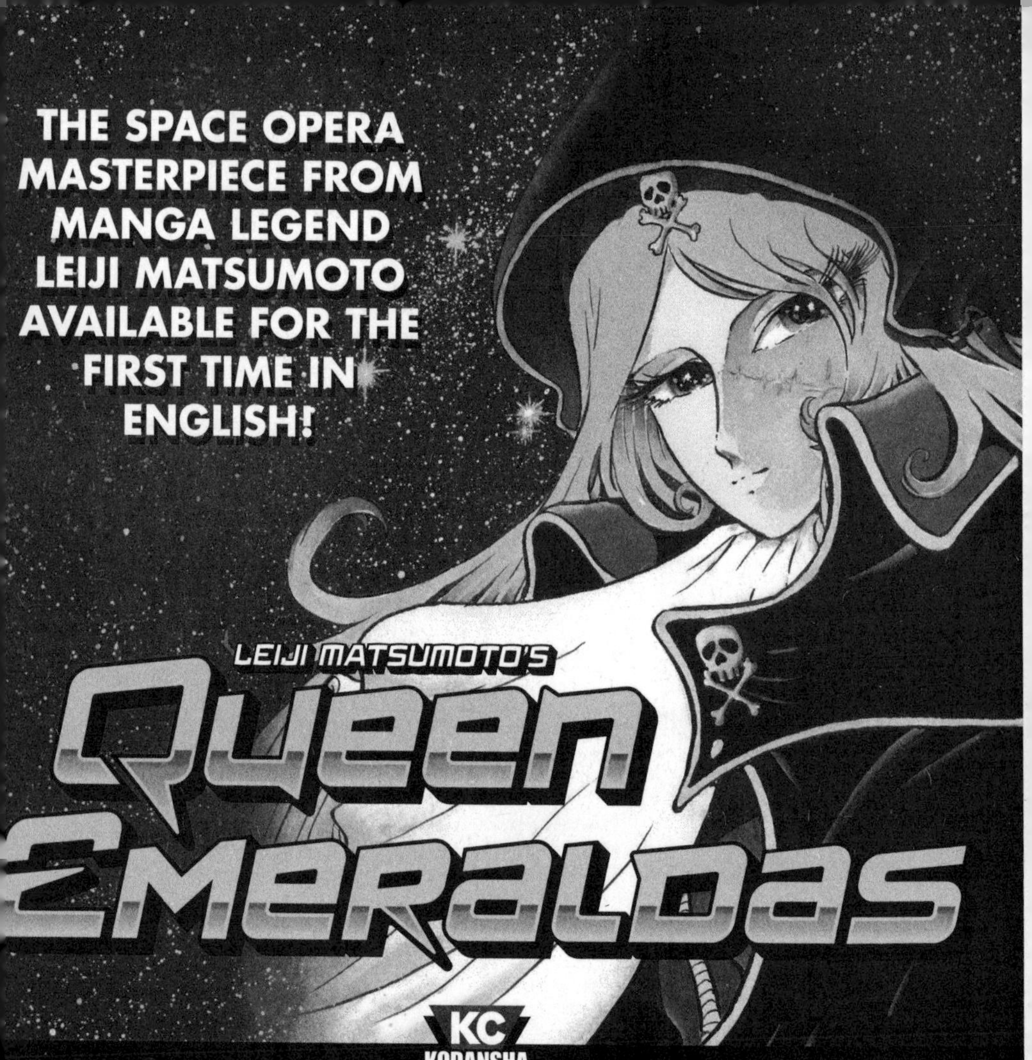
THE SPACE OPERA MASTERPIECE FROM MANGA LEGEND LEIJI MATSUMOTO AVAILABLE FOR THE FIRST TIME IN ENGLISH!
LEIJI MATSUMOTO'S
Queen Emeraldas
KC
KODANSHA COMICS

OTOMO

大友克洋

A GLOBAL TRIBUTE TO
THE MIND BEHIND AKIRA

A celebration of manga legend Katsuhiro Otomo from more than 80
world-renowned fine artists and comics legends
With contributions from:
- Stan Sakai
- Tomer and Asaf Hanuka
- Sara Pichelli
- Range Murata
- Aleksi Briclot
And more!
168 pages of stunning, full-color art

"An emotional and artistic tour de force! We see incredible triumph, and crushing defeat... each panel [is] a thrill!"
—Anitay

"A journey that's instantly compelling."
—Anime News Network

WELCOME TO THE BALLROOM

By Tomo Takeuchi

Feckless high school student Tatara Fujita wants to be good at something—anything. Unfortunately, he's about as average as a slouchy teen can be. The local bullies know this, and make it a habit to hit him up for cash, but all that changes when the debonair Kaname Sengoku sends them packing. Sengoku's not the neighborhood watch, though. He's a professional ballroom dancer. And once Tatara Fujita gets pulled into the world of ballroom, his life will never be the same.

KC
KODANSHA COMICS

KC KODANSHA COMICS

In love, there are no save points.

ヲタクに恋は難しい

NOW AN ANIME!

WOTAKOI:
LOVE IS HARD FOR OTAKU
by FUJITA

Narumi has had it rough: Every boyfriend she's had dumped her once they found out she was an otaku, so she's gone to great lengths to hide it. At her new job, she bumps into Hirotaka, her childhood friend and fellow otaku. When Hirotaka almost gets her secret outed at work, she comes up with a plan to keep him quiet. But he comes up with a counter-proposal: Why doesn't she just date him instead?

A Kodansha Comics Trade Paperback Original.

Land of the Lustrous volume 8 copyright © 2017 Haruko Ichikawa
English translation copyright © 2018 Haruko Ichikawa

Published in the United States by Kodansha Comics, an imprint of Kodansha USA Publishing, LLC, New York.

Publication rights for this English edition arranged through Kodansha Ltd., Tokyo.

First published in Japan in 2017 by Kodansha Ltd., Tokyo.

ISBN 978-1-63236-727-3

Printed in the United States of America.

www.kodanshacomics.com

9 8 7 6 5 4 3 2 1

Translator: Alethea Nibley & Athena Nibley
Lettering: Evan Hayden
Editing: Lauren Scanlan